THE AGE OF LIVESTREAMING

THE KUAISHOU WAY II

The Kuaishou Research Institute

Mc
Graw
Hill

NEW YORK CHICAGO SAN FRANCISCO ATHENS LONDON MADRID MEXICO CITY
MILAN NEW DELHI SINGAPORE SYDNEY TORONTO

1 2 3 4 5 6 7 8 9   LSI   26 25 24 23 22

ISBN   978-1-264-64080-5
MHID   1-264-64080-3

e-ISBN   978-1-264-64062-1
e-MHID   1-264-64062-5

McGraw Hill books are available at special quantity discounts to use as premiums and sales promotions or for use in corporate training programs. To contact a representative, please visit the Contact Us pages at www.mhprofessional.com.

McGraw Hill is committed to making our products accessible to all learners. To learn more about the available support and accommodations we offer, please contact us at accessibility@mheducation.com. We also participate in the Access Text Network (www.accesstext.org), and ATN members may submit requests through ATN.

Video expressions have smashed the threshold of textual expressions and the limits of culture, affording more people the opportunity to express themselves and be seen. The once-silent majority is no longer silent, the once-ordinary people are no longer ordinary, and the once-mundane things are no longer mundane.

———

– Su Hua, Co-founder and Chairman of Kuaishou Technology

From an emotional perspective, as powerful as algorithms are, I do not believe that everything in the future will be decided by algorithms— interpersonal feelings remain very powerful too. I very much believe that interpersonal trust and emotional connections are very valuable.

———

– Cheng Yixiao, Co-founder and CEO of Kuaishou Technology

7 KEY POINTS IN THIS BOOK

1. Video is a technological means that can greatly unleash forces of production, and a new infrastructure that drives inner and outer loops and consumption upgrading. It is currently changing everything. Livestreaming is not a means of extension and supplementation but instead an age in itself. Videos and livestreams will shorten time and space, bringing about a society with a greater sense of trust and warmth. Businesses will be restructured. An outbreak of new commercial species is on the horizon.

2. The "consumers→livestreamers→products" chain of livestream e-commerce is, so far, the shortest and most effective model that begins from consumers and connects with merchants.

3. Livestream e-commerce is rapidly evolving toward precision, personalization, and brandification worldwide. It is a large-scale upgrade of consumption.

4. Livestream e-commerce is remolding supply chains, scaling up C2Bs, redefining products according to demand, and reforming and energizing factories.

5. For local governments, livestream e-commerce is an opportunity not to be ignored. It can embed local resources into a larger market.

6. For enterprises and industries, livestreaming is not just a temporary act but rather a norm of the future. It thus must be taken seriously.

7. Livestream e-commerce is a good means of poverty alleviation and rural rejuvenation. It is an endogenous driving force and a long-term mechanism.

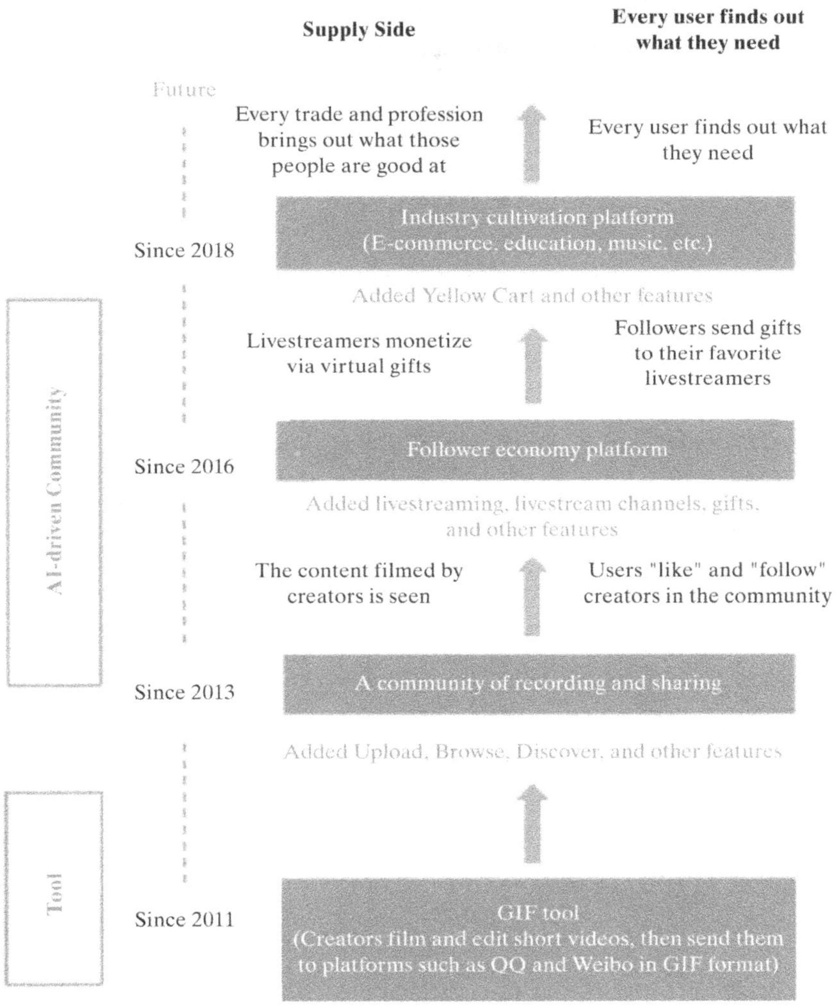
Supply Side
Every user finds out what they need
Future
Every trade and profession brings out what those people are good at
Every user finds out what they need
Since 2018
Industry cultivation platform (E-commerce, education, music, etc.)
Added Yellow Cart and other features
Livestreamers monetize via virtual gifts
Followers send gifts to their favorite livestreamers
Since 2016
Follower economy platform
Added livestreaming, livestream channels, gifts, and other features
The content filmed by creators is seen
Users "like" and "follow" creators in the community
Since 2013
A community of recording and sharing
AI-driven Community
Added Upload, Browse, Discover, and other features
Tool
Since 2011
GIF tool (Creators film and edit short videos, then send them to platforms such as QQ and Weibo in GIF format)

Figure 0.0 The Evolution of Kuaishou's Community

In the first half of 2020, 20 million people earned an income on Kuaishou, with many of them coming from remote areas of China.

CONTENTS

This book was published just in time for Kuaishou's tenth anniversary and listing. The preface was written by the two founders of Kuaishou. The first piece is Su Hua's speech during the listing ceremony, and the second piece is a preface specially written by Yixiao for this book.

ENABLING EVERY PERSON TO FIND OUT WHAT THEY NEED AND BRING OUT WHAT THEY ARE GOOD AT

—Su Hua
Co-founder and Chairman of Kuaishou Technology
(This text is Su Hua's speech during Kuaishou's listing ceremony on February 5, 2021)

Hello friends and colleagues!

I am very happy to be witnessing this moment with everyone. When Kuaishou was still at a very early stage, I had already imagined how its listing would be. This moment is somewhat similar yet somewhat different to what I had imagined. In my imagination, it was Kuaishou's loyal users who rang the bell, while Yixiao and I were still at work writing code.

Today, we have with us six community users from all over the globe to represent our hundreds of millions of creators and users. It is our users who have accompanied the growth of Kuaishou the whole way, and in return, Kuaishou has also stood by them faithfully. In a while, we will be inviting these six users to ring the bell.

In 2011, Kuaishou kickstarted the age of short video. Over 10 years of unremitting hard work, we have enabled video expressions to be accepted and liked by more people. This has smashed the threshold of textual expressions and the limits of culture, affording more people the opportunity to express themselves and be seen. The once-silent majority are no longer silent, the once-ordinary people are no longer ordinary, and the once-mundane things are no longer mundane.

When countless people are interconnected with content, a diverse yet authentic society would gradually emerge. The interactions among them serve to build an ecosystem with great vitality and strong evolutionary capabilities. In this ecosystem, new business models continually arise to restructure business systems and industrial structures. This was how our business in livestreaming and video e-commerce gradually developed. Through this process, our creators have gained respect, understanding, and trust, not to mention material rewards, thereby encouraging them to create even more. Meanwhile, our users have gained more consumption choices of a spiritual and material nature, as well as greater emotional resonance and warm companionship, thereby boosting their identification with the community.

Over the past year, we have produced over 13 billion videos, becoming a powerful testimony of social development and the populace's sense of gain. These videos were consumed (watched) for a total duration of nearly 9.6 trillion minutes, which is equivalent to 18 million years in the history of mankind. More than 20 million users have earned an income on our platform, consisting of individuals, groups, organizations, and industries from first-tier cities and rural regions alike. They have generated a combined GMV of over 300 billion yuan and made it possible to "shop enjoyably, choose products assuredly, and purchase products trustingly" in the community's diverse ecosystem. So far, we have helped many people improve their lives using technology, and we will continue to help more people survive and develop in the digital age.

Underlying all this is a belief that Yixiao and I have held since we first started out: respect for people, and respect for labor and creation. We help people find out what they need and bring out what they are good at, so that those with perseverance can gain property and those with property can gain perseverance. In doing so, we hope to build a community with the utmost warmth and trustworthiness. We have chosen 1024 as our stock symbol—as the tenth power of two, the number 1024 represents line after line of programming code, the power of technology, and leading-edge production capabilities. We hope to use the power of technology to amplify the energy released by labor and creation, enabling value creators to receive better rewards. Ultimately, we will keep on creating long-term value for our users and society.

Our public listing is a new starting point for us to be tested by the public and more so to receive greater opportunities and challenges. We will continue to forge ahead in driving social betterment and increasing individual happiness.

Lastly, I would like to take this opportunity to thank every one of Kuaishou's users, every partner who has striven together with us, every past and future investor, and every one of my supportive friends. I am also thankful to the village and town I was born and raised in, to 1024, and to this age that is filled with opportunities and challenges.

Thank you, everyone!

BUILDING AN ONLINE COMMUNITY WITH THE UTMOST WARMTH AND TRUSTWORTHINESS

—CHENG YIXIAO
Co-founder and CEO of Kuaishou Technology

Kuaishou was founded 10 years ago as a GIF tool, but it gradually became a nationwide short video and livestreaming platform. During this time, we have always persisted in creating value for our users and society and thought about how to create even more social value in the future. This is because only by creating social value would we be of value ourselves.

The social value that we have created is mainly reflected in improvements to efficiency. All the short videos and livestreams that we have produced and distributed are intended to match supply sides with demand sides in a better and more efficient way. This serves not only to improve the efficiency of information exchange but also to fulfill our mission: to help people find out what they need and bring out what they are good at, and to keep increasing every person's unique sense of happiness.

Bringing out people's strong suit is more central to our mission. This is because there are many producers in this world who have excellent products but do not know how to sell and promote these products or how to set up an online shop on an e-commerce platform. Kuaishou exists as a superior platform of choice for such people.

In carrying out our mission, what is the state of affairs or big picture that we want to achieve ultimately? In other words, what is our goal or vision? I believe that it is to "build an online community with the utmost warmth and trustworthiness."

Why do I use the words "warmth" and "trustworthiness"? With the continuous development of society, many things are changing. In particular, the pandemic in 2020 caused interpersonal relations to grow distant. Opportunities to dine or hang out with friends have decreased greatly, causing human feelings to weaken and turn cold. Humans are, after all, social creatures with a strong craving for warmth, which should not be compromised by the development of society. Therefore, I feel that a large community really ought to provide people with a sense of warmth.

Regarding trust, my personal experience is that when negotiating a collaboration with others, I would have inner misgivings and proceed cautiously prior to establishing trust, and slightly increase the level of collaboration after confirming that the other party is not cheating me. If I trust them, our collaboration may then deepen. I feel that trust is the most important thing in business and society—it can reduce our transaction costs and is an extremely important factor in determining whether many things can be successfully pushed forward.

More than just an entertainment community, our platform is becoming more deeply involved in trade and gradually influencing the daily lives of the masses, be it in the buying and selling of things or in local life services. I often wonder whether our users trust our livestreamers. If they do, our trading cycle and our future would be highly optimistic. But if they don't, our trust costs would be extremely high, affecting the entire trading cycle. Therefore, we hope to build a highly trustworthy community on our platform. In this way, we would be able to do all kinds of things very smoothly, enabling our future to be highly optimistic and creating greater value for society.

Two Especially Important Points in Time

Over the past 10 years, we have fortunately adapted to the development trends of video, continually added new technical features and community content, and developed from a community for recording and sharing to a "follower economy platform" to today's "industry cultivation platform." In particular, I want to bring up two important points in time from the past five years.

The first is in 2016, when we began doing livestreaming and developed our own business model. Previously, everyone was worried that we could not survive, but we have now proven that this business model is sound. Before 2016, most people hosted livestreams on PCs. Back then, mobile livestreaming was still rather choppy and faced many technical issues, and so everyone remained unsure about it. This was Dingjia's (Kuaishou's first CTO, Chen Dingjia) first project when he joined Kuaishou, and he very successfully handled it.

The second is in 2018, when livestream e-commerce began. It enabled us to provide services to a wider group of people, to provide better sales methods to producers, and to greatly reduce the cost of sales. This was an extremely positive thing to me.

At first, the supply chains of livestream e-commerce were still at an initial state. This was especially so in 2017–2018, when consumers had just experienced the era of WeChat Business and thought not quite highly of it. Thus, when we started doing livestream e-commerce, they wondered whether the things we were selling could create true value for consumers. Back then, there was a significant internal debate over whether we should do livestream e-commerce. We later did some deep thinking and realized that it is very difficult to satisfy consumers by selling "standard products" on-stream, whereas our users' satisfaction would be much higher if we sold "non-standard products" instead.

What was most shocking to me was the matter of selling jade. Once, I asked a colleague in the e-commerce department what the markup rate of jade in shopping malls is. He told me that it was 10 times. I said that there is something wrong with this industry because everything ought to have a reasonable markup rate. Why would anyone go to a shopping mall to buy something that is sold at 10 times the ex-factory price? I felt that this industry could be changed. Today, thanks to our efforts, the profit margin of jade has become quite reasonable.

In the past, we more often tried to change the entire supply chain. A change that is especially huge or good for Kuaishou today is the increasing price-per- customer, while users would only purchase cheap things as a way of testing if your products actually worked first. This implies that users' trust toward merchants is increasing and that users are more and more willing to buy expensive things on our platform.

In 2020, our e-commerce business made a breakthrough. I feel that the aspect we got most right in e-commerce was to develop a seller service rating system, a post-purchase rating index, and a user satisfaction index. Be it in our transactional business or elsewhere, the most important thing for us to think about is to greatly increase user satisfaction. In other words, deepening the trust between us and our users via transactions actually represents our big opportunity for the future.

Our e-commerce business is moving from the industry level to the content level. I believe that e-commerce should become a part of the content level; it is a business that has a "content" attribute or an exceptionally strong "shopping" attribute. Although e-commerce has not been able to produce a very powerful feeling of "shopping" yet, I firmly believe that this can definitely be done. This is also a huge expectation; I expect that within the next half a year, e-commerce business will establish a strong foothold at the content level.

Restructuring the Consumption Decision-Making of One Billion Users

Although we have done some work in integrating e-commerce with other industries, I believe that the age of livestreaming still has a lot of untapped potentials and that we are still at a very early stage.

I believe that if we get our "videos + algorithms + economy" right, we would be completely able to reconstruct our users' consumption decision-making and promote further innovation of the trust mechanism. Building an online community with the utmost warmth and trustworthiness is actually a rare and huge opportunity that the age of livestreaming has afforded us.

Looking back on the changes to the entire age of commerce, it all began with the age of small goods. When I was young, a few vegetable growers would come up to our doorstep to sell vegetables. Because they were always the same few people, my mother largely believed their goods to be reliable. Then, in the '90s, we gradually entered the age of products. I remember that branded products such as Coca-Cola emerged at that time. I was willing to buy it simply because it was a brand, such was my trust in brands.

The subsequent age was the age of malls and supermarkets. Around the year 2000, malls and supermarkets such as Walmart and 7-Eleven began appearing in my life. They sold many things that I had never seen before, including branded products and unpackaged items. Given their sizes, I believed that they were unlikely to sell counterfeit and low-quality things.

During the age of platforms such as Taobao, trust relations were built via user reviews. When I see that a Taobao store has a 5-star rating, I would feel that it is rather reliable.

From the "age of small goods" to the "age of products" to the "age of malls and supermarkets" to the "age of platforms," each change in consumption decision- making represented a tremendously large business, with huge companies emerging in every age. I believe that the age of livestreaming can restructure trust—this is also the beginning of a tremendous age.

At first, an ordinary user might join Kuaishou because it is refreshing, but what leads them to stay on long-term is, in my opinion, trust and warmth. Building an online community with the utmost warmth and trustworthiness and restructuring the consumption decision-making of 1 billion users is not only our dream but also a path with great social value and significance.

On Public and Private Domains

In the face of the opportunities afforded by this age, we want to build an online community with the utmost warmth and trustworthiness. This encompasses many challenges and uncertainties, albeit there are also several certainties that we must work hard to get right. One of them is to bring out the power of private domains and to integrate public and private domains well.

I highly believe that we would "gain the world" if we get the producers on our side. We should stand ever more firmly on the side of users and producers. After all, platforms do not generate content themselves, while producers are the cornerstone of the entire content industry. If we want to stand together with producers, then we would have to integrate private and public domains.

Everyone will certainly question why we want to work on private domains at a time when algorithms are so efficient and in an age when platforms have such powerful distribution capabilities. From an emotional perspective, as powerful as algorithms are, I do not believe that everything in the future will be decided by algorithms—interpersonal feelings remain very powerful too. I very much believe that interpersonal trust and emotional connections are very valuable. Of course, in working on private domains, we are not giving up on public domains; instead, we want to integrate public and private domains.

Private domains have many different aspects that move me greatly. I follow a livestreamer who talks with a Beijing accent and seems to be from Tongzhou District in Beijing. Every day when he begins livestreaming, there are only around 100 viewers, and most of them are from Beijing or nearby. During the Dragon Boat Festival one year, he said that he wanted to repay his ardent viewers with dumplings. He said, "I will go around Beijing on my trishaw and deliver the dumplings to you guys." I was extremely moved back then. His way of repaying his viewers is quite different from that of other livestreamers, who would offer red envelopes up for grabs instead. After steaming 50 to 60 sets of dumplings, he rode around Beijing on his trishaw and delivered them. His viewers commended him for his trustworthiness; although a kilogram of dumplings only costs around 20 yuan, he nevertheless gave his viewers a very good feeling. I feel that such a feeling can only be offered by private domains.

This particular livestreamer has a very strong basis of trust regardless of what he sells. I know what he is like as a person—he would not deceive the 100-odd viewers on his channel, otherwise, he would certainly not make any money from livestreaming. I feel that when there are more and more people like him, another huge era will arrive and it will restructure the entire trust system based on the follower economy. Although I see a few signs of its arrival, it can only be achieved through everyone's collective efforts.

In terms of management complexity, public domains are certainly much easier to manage. The reason is that whoever is capable would draw viewers, while whoever is incapable would not. Instead, private domains have a very complex problem, that is, when a livestreamer has their own industry in a private domain, it is very difficult to decide whether and how to manage it.

A relatively common verdict among ourselves is that we have helped those with property gain perseverance, but have not yet helped those with perseverance gain property. We must continue to exercise good management and cannot allow livestreamers and video uploaders to do things that harm users—instead, we must guide them to develop perseverance.

I firmly believe that managing private domains properly is the right thing to do. To give an example, not long ago, I brought Su Hua and a few colleagues to visit my hometown, where we watched a song-and-dance duet. Nowadays, such duets are performed only in theaters and no longer in outdoor squares. The theater's environment was very luxurious and classy, and the tickets were not cheap—a seat close to the front cost around 200 yuan, as compared to movie tickets, which only cost 20 to 30 yuan each. This implied that song-and-dance duets had become a highly elegant form of culture and entertainment in my hometown, whereas they never quite left the same impression in the past. It thus seems that these producers can still be changed or can be improved as long as the opportunity arises.

I believe that by doing and managing private domains well and enabling more producers to "blossom," we can increase the warmth and trust in society.

Upholding the Principle of Prioritizing User Interests

To achieve our vision, there is no doubt that we must uphold our users' interests as our priority. Using our e-commerce business for example, it is called experiential e-commerce and is better at satisfying user needs than "shelves-of-goods e-commerce." This involves a few conflicts of interest between our users and the company.

I personally feel that user interests always come first because our company's interests can only be satisfied after satisfying user interests. I have constantly emphasized this matter within the company; quite often, my colleagues have neglected user interests while paying attention to the company's interests because they are unable to balance the two well.

In addition, conflicts may arise among different departments because they consider different aspects of user interests. For example, the video team would consider user interests in video consumption, the livestreaming team would consider user interests in livestreaming services, while the e-commerce team would consider user interests in e-commerce services. I feel that these varying perspectives have to be balanced to maximize user interests.

Regarding how to look upon the prioritizing of user interests, I once shared two case examples with my colleagues.

The first example is when a livestreamer sold poor-quality wine onstream, eventually causing dissatisfaction among the buyers. When replaying the livestream, we discovered that our team had failed to control product quality well and provide reliable products for our users. Furthermore, our team did not punish the pertinent livestreamer hard enough. This is not in line with our value of prioritizing user interests.

The second example is when a livestreamer rode a trishaw from Sichuan to Tibet via the Sichuan-Tibet highway and showed how grueling the journey was. In doing so, he received the attention and support of his followers. One day, a passerby uploaded an exposé video on Weibo—it turned out that the livestreamer did not ride the trishaw himself but instead rode in a car in front. In fact, he traveled for most of his journey in a car after filming a short video of himself proceeding with the trishaw. Regarding this case, I pointed out to our team that this amounted to deceiving the feelings of our users. Although it is not easy to find out the truth in such cases, we must deal with them strictly—possibly by suspending the account—once they are found because deceiving the feelings of our users is no joking matter. I believe that preventing damage to our users' interests is our top priority, while the company's interests are our second priority.

Non-Standard Products Are More Suitable for Kuaishou

We are often asked about the differences between Kuaishou E-commerce and other e-commerce platforms. In the end, we should do things that are suitable for us to do—"non-standard products" are more suitable for Kuaishou because they are a better fit for on-stream display and may not sell well on other e-commerce platforms. Therefore, rather than stealing business from other people, we are instead creating a new business model whereby purchasing behaviors come about due to the mutual trust between livestreamers and their followers.

"Non-standard products" is a large category and a market with an annual trade volume worth several trillion yuan. Clothing is definitely its biggest sub-category, followed by jewelry. These types of non-standard products are more suitable for on-stream display and sale on Kuaishou.

The jewelry market might be a better example. This is more clearly an incremental market; previously, people did not have so much trust in shopping malls when it comes to buying jewelry, but after the emergence of livestreaming platforms such as Kuaishou, people have shown much greater trust when buying jewelry, to the extent that they are now "playing cards with an open hand." What the platforms have done is essentially to provide "credit endorsement" for jewelry.

When interacting with other e-commerce platforms, we have also "played cards with an open hand" and revealed our thoughts. Firstly, we are very certain that we are not doing "shelves-of-goods e-commerce." For standard products, we are willing to collaborate more with partners such as JD and Taobao. The market for non-standard products is very big and we will definitely work on it. Although there is certainly some competition between us and other e-commerce platforms in this market, I believe that "may the best platform win"—whoever can satisfy users best—would emerge victoriously.

The most important difference between us and other e-commerce platforms is our focus on non-standard products. For standard products, we do not have a particular advantage and would have to enter into "shelves-of-goods e-commerce," which is the strength of other e-commerce platforms.

Non-standard products are not brandless but instead have their own brands as well; "branded versus non-branded" is a level below "standard versus non- standard." We eagerly hope that more clothing brands will enter this market.

We have an open and welcoming attitude toward brand enterprises, such as in the clothing and jewelry categories. We have seen, for example, that the livestreamers who are better able to sell down jackets on Kuaishou are concentrated in a few top-tier domestic brands. A huge ongoing trend is the increasing number of such brands. We are also adopting measures to bring in brands from more categories.

In China, everyone is willing to talk about the two concepts of standard products and non-standard products. They are strongly linked to the flexible supply chains of China's factories. Without flexible supply chains, the "age of non- standard products" would not have arrived. This is also a change produced by the supply side. Because users certainly prefer personalized things, the market for non- standard products will grow ever bigger. Moreover, technological improvements in the factory side and the flexible supply chain side will probably keep on increasing the degree of "non-standardness."

Focusing on Our Mission

Finally, it's time to sum things up in a few sentences. This book is titled *The Age of Livestreaming*; livestreaming has increased the efficiency of information transmission, generated a considerable amount of productivity, and created social value, marking the progress of the times.

From the perspective of real-timeness and interactivity, livestreaming implies that the entire mode of information transmission has developed to its zenith. This will be a long-term process. In the future, technologies such as VR and AR may improve greatly and be integrated into livestreaming.

Various opportunities and temptations will arise during this long-term process. We are situated in the important segment that is distribution—all kinds of new things have use for a platform such as ours, and there seem to be many things that we can do. However, a company does not have to seize every opportunity out there. We need to think about what things belong on Kuaishou and persist in seizing opportunities that are closer to us. We will focus our attention especially on opportunities to connect with our users, livestreamers, and producers.

As a platform, we must have the field of view and broad-mindedness of a platform. We must think clearly about who we are and what kind of value we should provide to our users and society. In the end, we should return to our vision and mission: to build an online community with the utmost warmth and worthiness, to help people discover what they need and bring out what they are good at, and to keep increasing every person's unique sense of happiness.

WHAT IS THE LIVESTREAM ECONOMY?

*The feelings and meanings conveyed by text are incomplete(…) Text is an
indirect form of speech and a rather imperfect tool. When the telephone
and radio came about, they had a huge impact on the place of letters and
notices in people's lives. And when fax technology developed, there arose
the issue of whether text should still be used.
Since face-to-face contact is a direct form of interaction, why should we use
text in place of this relatively more complete form of language?
In a "face-to-face community," even language itself becomes a tool that is
only used due to a lack of alternatives.*
—FEI XIAOTONG (*FROM THE SOIL*, 1947)

*The most important understanding we have derived over the past few years
comes down to a simple truth: video is the text of the new age.
Video is not an industry but rather a new kind of information carrier. The
animated images that video offers are more vivid than text.
All industries will be redefined because of video.*
—SU HUA (SPEECH AT 36KR'S ANNUAL CONFERENCE, 2016)

This book contains more than 20 interesting case examples that readers can learn from according to their needs. The mission of this
chapter is to present and explain our thought process regarding the

age of video in a fairly traditional way for the reference and evaluation of readers. As this chapter is quite theoretical in nature, readers can skip it on the first reading and come back whenever they have the time.

The term "livestream economy" is used in the title because the concept of livestreaming has gained more attention in recent times. We are actually talking about a broader concept, that is, how the age of video will change our society, economy, and life. Our definition of video encompasses Kuaishou, Zoom (a multi- user mobile cloud video conferencing software), and WeChat video calls, as well as livestreams being promoted by Pinduoduo, Bilibili, etc., and enterprise-provided livestream lessons such as VIPKid (an online English-language education brand for children). The case examples used in this book are mainly from Kuaishou.

However, because livestreaming is a two-way method of instant information exchange, an invention on par with the telephone, and a very important scenario for video, talking about the livestream economy is also not too different.

We will answer a few questions. Why is the age of video not just a passing fad but will instead change everything? Why is the shift from the age of text to the age of video an inevitable trend? What new characteristics does the age of video have? How will ecosystems in the age of video evolve? What are the characteristics of the new kinds of things in the age of video? And what is the place of the age of video in the construction of Digital Earth?

I

At the tail end of 2016, Su Hua proposed that video would be the text of the new age and that it would change everything. Looking back now four years later, his insight has proven to be prophetic.

The author of this text is He Huafeng, vice-president of Kuaishou Technology and head of The Kuaishou Research Institute.

Video is a kind of information carrier. The universalization of smartphones and 4G after 2015 has greatly lowered the threshold for accessing the Internet and has allowed entire societies to enter the age of video. The amount of data in the age of video has increased exponentially from what it was in the past, driving the development of AI technologies. Previously, text and images were the main information carriers, but after 2015, the infrastructure necessary for video has gradually matured.

Text is a human-invented code for information transmission and an indirect form of communication. To use it, people have to undergo literacy training. By comparison, video has clear advantages in information transmission: it is more vivid and lively and does not have a learning threshold.

Media is a human extension used to transmit information and energy. Different forms of media are mutually competing—for a form of media to prevail over other forms and be adopted by people, it must have unique advantages in the transmission of information and energy.

Today, our lives can no longer do without video. Kuaishou's number of daily active users has exceeded 300 million, while WeChat video calls are made every day. In the world to come, the amount of digital information will continuously see exponential growth, and most of it will be presented in the form of video.

The book that we published at the start of 2020, called *The Kuaishou Way: The Power of Being Seen*, could also have been called "The Power of Being Digitalized." The contribution of video to the digital world lies in its digitalization of everything on Earth that can be seen with the human eye—this capability separates it from all previous forms of media.

It is not hard to understand that video was able to replace text as the main form of daily remote communication because it is more natural. But how do we explain why video will change everything? And why is it that life, business, and all trades and professions will be transformed by the age of video?

This involves an understanding of the nature of the world. At the economic level, the world is made up of individual transactions, which are in turn made up of the two components of information and physical deliveries. When efficiency at the information level is greatly increased, the transaction costs would be greatly reduced, allowing transactions to take place within a larger range and improving the rewards. Naturally, all transactions would adopt the new information technology, thereby changing the entire world.

In reality, all organizations are tools for transporting information and material things (bits and atoms). When changes take place at the information level, changes would also take place in all organizations, giving birth to new kinds of things. Such events have happened time and again in history.

When the telephone was invented in 1876, remote yet direct communication between people became possible. In 1976, to commemorate the hundredth anniversary of the telephone's invention, Massachusetts Institute of Technology (MIT) held a symposium and published a collection of essays called *The Social Impact of the Telephone*. There are a few interesting bits of content within.

> *"The telephone invented by Bell ultimately transformed from a toy into a social tool for strengthening organizations and economic power.*

> *"The use of the telephone by some families, such as doctors and businessmen who worked from home, served to increase economic efficiency. On the other hand, the telephone was ultimately favorable to the economic efficiency of economic fields (such as commerce and industry) as well.*

> *"When telephones entered commerce, merchants could relocate to areas where the price of land was lower while keeping in touch with business partners. Many companies relocated outward or moved to the 10th or even 20th floor of a new building.*

> *"Another social change inspired by the invention of the telephone was the appearance of women in the office. In fact, they have overtaken the men in numbers today (….) Together, the telephone and the typewriter destroyed the obstacles for women to seek employment in the clerical field (….) Advertisements at the turn of the century depicted the work of typists and operators as highly prestigious,*

causing the close-fitting uniform intended for new-fashioned women who were ready to enter the business world to become a fashion craze."

Just like the telephone, the automobile, and the railroad, entire societies will be built around video in the age of video, forming a new techno-economic paradigm.

During the age of video, we will be able not only to do things that were previously possible in a better way, but also to do things that were previously impossible. For example, a colleague told me that whenever she found a piece of clothing that she liked while browsing an online clothing store during the age of text and images, she often did not know whether it fit her. Nowadays, she can instead tell the livestreamer to put it on for her to see, and she will then buy the clothes if she feels that they fit her. This is a "miracle" that was impossible during the age of text and images.

Therefore, after the pandemic is over, livestreaming will not become a passing fad. In fact, the age of livestreaming has only just begun.

II

The foundations of the digital economy are connection and computation (which are also the key elements that make up the core of the entire human network). The age of video has undergone fundamental changes in terms of both elements. In terms of the mode of connection, the change lies in the emergence of videos with stronger digital capabilities. And in terms of the mode of computation, the change lies in the emergence of AI.

AI and video are mutually complementary. On the Kuaishou platform, the accurate matching of the tens of millions of videos produced every day with hundreds of millions of people would be impossible without AI technologies. On the other hand, AI algorithms would be hard to iterate without having video as one of their scenarios.

What are the differences between the age of video and the age of text and images? The most intuitive difference is that communication in the age of video is face-to-face, allowing anyone on Earth to become neighbors—across a flat screen—with another person at any time.

Looking back, many commercial facilities such as wholesale markets and shopping malls were actually solving a spatial problem. In the age of video, spatial distance has been eliminated.

Information and physical deliveries make up all transactions on Earth. Changes to these two elements will bring about changes to the modes of transaction and cause consumption to enter a brand-new age. At the same time, they will correspondingly bring about production-side changes and various other changes, causing new "business species" to arise.

Compared to the age of text, the first characteristic of the age of video is that it is bigger, faster, and deeper.

Firstly, the market is much bigger in size. This is mainly because video has a low threshold and can connect with more people. By having more people on the same platform and using AI recommendation technologies to match them, transactions can take place within a larger range.

Secondly, the face-to-face nature of video communication makes transactions more direct and thus faster. This will also cause the speed of the entire production process to increase.

Lastly, "deeper" means that video enables more information to be seen and offers more scenarios that are finer in granularity. These scenarios, which did not have commercial possibilities at first, now do so because they can be connected.

For example, Chen Libao, a suona player from the China National Traditional Orchestra, now has 800,000 followers on Kuaishou. The suona is a highly niche instrument with only an estimated 1 in 1,000 people interested in it. In other words, only 1.4 million people throughout China enjoy listening to it. On the Kuaishou platform, these people have the chance to be connected and to have real-time communication with Chen. As for Chen, he is able to earn an income from selling lessons, suonas, and such like while providing his services every day.

Kuaishou emphasizes the principle of inclusivity. Every lawful video will be recommended, ensuring greater fairness and the universal sharing of traffic. This is also related to the fact that transactions can take place in a larger, faster, and deeper range. Transactions that were impossible in the past are now possible, while people who had no chance to be seen in the past can now be seen.

In *The Kuaishou Way: The Power of Being Seen*, we mentioned the case example of Jiang Jinchun, who sells local specialties on-stream from the mountainous area of Jiangxi Province. When students from the Cheung Kong Finance MBA program went to Kuaishou's headquarters to conduct an interview in September 2020, we invited Jiang to talk to them remotely. We were astonished by the speed of his growth over the past year—Jiang said that his sales figure for that year reached 5 million yuan and added that his target for the future was 20 million yuan. In the past, such an accomplishment would have been impossible in the mountainous area of Jiangxi Province.

III

Based on our survey and research, the second characteristic of the age of video is the emergence of C2Bs (consumer-to-business) on a large scale. First proposed by Alibaba, C2B was touted as a new economic trend. It generally means that the development of the Internet has given consumers a greater voice in guiding the products sold by businesses.

Internet celebrities who gained popularity on Weibo's and Alibaba's ecosystems are good examples of this. They interact with their followers on Weibo and sell their goods on Taobao.

On Kuaishou, every livestreamer is a representative of the consumers. Livestreamers communicate seamlessly with users via video; in particular, they interact with users for a few hours every day via livestreaming, during which time the users are online in real time. Everyone interacts continually and can fully express whatever opinions they have to the livestreamer. Subsequently, the livestreamer communicates with the back end supply chains and factories in order to choose the products.

Therefore, the entire process consists of the livestreamers and users being online in real time, the livestreamers's selection of products, and the research and development of products, not to mention the competition among countless livestreamers on the platform and the transparentization of platform data by data companies. This process provides goods and services with a closed loop of real-time feedback, which has a much faster feedback speed than what was possible in any preceding age.

From the perspectives of connection and computation, the two elements have become much faster than ever before, thereby greatly increasing the evolution speed of the entire ecosystem.

Take Xu Xiaomi, a livestreamer from Linyi, for example. She is able to sell tens of thousands of SKUs in one year. As of December 2020, the average number of real-time viewers on her livestreams—which last for six hours each—was 44,000. To put things in perspective, the clothing brand Zara also only has tens of thousands of SKUs in one year. The speed of things in the age of video is much faster than before.

During their livestreams, livestreamers would find out what the users' latest preferences are. These preferences have become extremely valuable business information. Nowadays, prior to manufacturing products, many factories would consult livestreamers on questions such as the tastes of users.

Therefore, the age of video has served as fertile soil for C2B, allowing it to truly attain scale. Driven by consumers, more high-accuracy and excellent products have sprouted.

Looking back on history, C2B has actually always been around. Every product is an extension of humans, except that the speed of information exchange was not as fast in the past and thus the response speed of production was also not as fast.

We can also see the progress made by C2B each time the speed of information exchange is increased. For example, after the invention of the telephone, people began selling insurance over the phone. In the past, many companies would register their telephone number in the yellow pages to establish contact with consumers. During the age of text and images, many examples of C2B appeared on Taobao. Today, C2Bs are much bigger and faster than before, satisfying many subset scenarios and needs that could not be satisfied previously.

IV

The third characteristic of the age of video is service orientation and non-standardization. When livestreaming, livestreamers have face-to-face communication with users in real time, enabling users' needs to be better satisfied. There is a clear trend toward the service orientation and non-standardization of goods.

Non-standardization is made possible by the finer granularity of scenarios. In the case of Kuaishou livestreamer "Matcha Sweet," the founder of the account, Du Qishuai, said: "At first, all of the clothing we designed was intended for tall women. However, comments from our followers made us realize that many of them were short women—approximately 60 percent of them were in the 148–162 cm range. Subsequently, we mainly served this group of women and taught them how to match clothing and conceal their imperfections."

From this example, we can see that businesses in the past could only provide commercial services for scenarios that were relatively mainstream and coarse in granularity—these scenarios made up only a small portion of all possible scenarios. Today, consumers at a finer-grained level are able to be seen and to state their demands. At the same time, the finer-grained scenarios have gained commercial value because they can be interconnected within a larger range and can interact in real time with producers.

For example, Matcha Sweet now focuses on producing clothing for women in the 148–162 cm height range. Previously, it was difficult to find these people accurately, but now that they can be directly contacted on the Kuaishou platform, commercialization can be done.

From a past perspective, this is what non-standardization is about.

In the standardization of old, because users and producers could not communicate directly, the producers' initiative to produce better products was undermined. For example, rice produced using green methods cannot be distinguished by the appearance from that produced using non-green methods, and so the price for both types of rice was the same. Producers were thus inclined to produce the lower-cost products. But with livestreaming nowadays, users can pay a higher price for "green" rice, thereby encouraging producers to produce better quality rice.

At the same time, consumers have learned how to consume better quality rice by watching videos. This is what "service deepening" is about.

Today's goods are developing a service style like that of Traditional Chinese Medicine (TCM) doctors in medical halls. The doctor would first diagnose a patient by "looking, listening, questioning, and feeling the pulse," which is the service provided. Subsequently, the doctor would write and dispense a prescription, which is the goods provided. This is a service-oriented and non-standardized process.

When discussing the characteristics of a network society in his book *Out of Control*, Kevin Kelly mentioned that whereas shoes were produced in the past, we now produce things that fit our legs and continually iterate on them.

From this perspective, goods are an extension of service and are iterated on endlessly.

V

We mentioned earlier that entire societies and economies will be reconstructed around video. What will this process of reconstruction be like? Or, in other words, how will ecosystems in the age of video evolve?

This process is mainly about market forces at work. At first, a few individuals will stumble upon new tools for using information and receive tremendous rewards. This is actually what *The Power of Being Seen* mainly talks about. Next, more organizations enter the field and receive even greater rewards by making use of the new information tools. Subsequently, market signals lead the entire change. In *Technological Revolutions and Financial Capital*, Carlota Perez said:

> The appearance of a new techno-economic paradigm affects
> behaviors related to innovation and investment in a way that could
> be compared to a gold rush or the discovery of a vast new territory. It
> is the opening of a wide design, product, and profit space that rapidly

fires the imagination of engineers, entrepreneurs, and investors, who, in their trial and error experiments applying the new wealth-creating potential, generate the successful practices and behaviors that gradually define the new best-practice frontier.

Video is a new phase in the development of the Internet and a process of building the age of video. It is not an extension but instead a subversion of text and images. This process is akin to the displacement of the PC Internet by the mobile Internet.

For instance, the invention of the automobile expanded humans' field of activity and changed cities. Walmart and Ikea are "business species" from the age of automobiles. Meanwhile, the age of carriages was gone forever.

Livestream e-commerce is the epitome of the age of video. The new business species in the age of video have seven characteristics.

From our research on Linyi (see Chapter 3 Linyi: City of Kuaishou), we can derive the following four characteristics:

First, face-to-face communication between livestreamers and users, which has eliminated spatial distance and greatly reduced marketing costs. Commerce has reverted to face-to-face communication and transaction.

Second, co-creation and scaling up of C2Bs with users. By interacting a lot with users, obtaining user feedback in real time, and by continuously iterating on their products, livestreamers can satisfy users' individual demands more accurately and earn a higher premium.

Third, limitless expansion of market reach, causing regional consumption to no longer be a thing. When put up for sale, a product would become available to the whole of China or even the world. Many regional products would thus earn global rewards.

Fourth, the "consumer–livestreamer–product" model. Its business channel is shorter and more efficient as compared to any other business model in history, such as department stores, large marketplaces, and traditional e-commerce businesses.

In summary, the four characteristics are: short chain, high efficiency, higher accuracy, and greater personalization.

New business species have three other characteristics. We can derive two of them from the case example of Chen Libao.

> *Fifth, the community effect. Videos and recommendation technologies have brought about a stronger "like seeks like" effect. More than just having buyer-seller relations, consumers and livestreamers make up a community of mutual emotional support. Specialist livestreamers have emerged and created new brands.*
>
> *Sixth, a full-knowledge economy. Aside from the products themselves, their production process and all related information are also displayed. A full-knowledge economy is a new type of trust economy.*

Allow me to briefly mention the last one.

> *Seventh, a "grand liberation" of unused resources. Because they are now seen, many unused resources that were originally immobile have been liberated to take part in trade. They include the beautiful scenery, specialty products, and folk culture of ethnic minority regions.*

VI

We have come up with seven characteristics for new business species in the age of video, and all of them seem like a breath of fresh air. However, if we look at them in the context of informatization and the development of the Internet, there really is nothing new under the sun.

We have two viewpoints:

> *First, all new species bred by informatization have these seven characteristics and are similar in essence.*
>
> *Second, informatization is a process of continual evolution. Due to differences in informatization capabilities at different stages, new species present themselves in different appearances and forms.*

Every age has its own new species of informatization. In McLuhan's famous work, *Understanding Media*, we can see that the invention of the telephone greatly increased the freedom of many industries and caused them to become business species with higher degrees of informatization.

Take the ambulance and the fire engine for instance. Before the invention of the telephone, they were but ordinary vehicles. But when people could call 120 or 119, the ambulance and the fire engine became new species of informatization.

Today, with the availability of an even more powerful tool of informatization that is the mobile Internet, taxis have upgraded to "DiDi taxis."

Therefore, informatization is no mystery. It is simply the fact that due to the invention of the Internet, informatization has suddenly sped up and become ever greater in capability over the past few decades, causing new species to be continuously bred at an ever-faster rate.

When new species are bred, where do the old ones go? If they still exist, they become artwork. For instance, several decades from now, landline telephones might only be found in antique markets. Today, banknotes are used with decreasing frequency due to the emergence of payment platforms such as WeChat Pay and Alipay, which might in turn be replaced by the digital currency that the central bank of China is issuing as part of a pilot program.

What are the similarities and differences between the new business species in the age of video and those in the age of traditional e-commerce?

Professor Zeng Ming, who was previously Chief of Staff at Alibaba, derived the C2B model from Taobao's model. We believe that the new species he derived are essentially the same as those seen on Kuaishou—both are new species of the Internet age, or in other words, they are both new species bred by informatization.

However, they also have differences. New species in the age of traditional e-commerce were individualized and unique, whereas those in the age of video are universal and more powerful. In terms of sales volume, a few top livestreamers in the age of livestreaming have greatly surpassed the Internet celebrities in the age of text and images.

VII

Earlier on, we said that all new species are essentially the same; they are the products of digitalization and informatization and possess similar characteristics, albeit they differ in breadth and depth. The next question is: Why does informatization breed new species?

As we had discussed earlier, what we call commercial organizations (or business species) are just organizations that transport information and material things (bits and atoms).

Digitalization and informatization are processes in which commercial organizations' capabilities of information transmission continuously improve. The increase in information eliminates uncertainty and correspondingly enables consumers to get goods and services that are more accurate and personalized.

When the capabilities of transporting bits are greatly improved, commercial organizations naturally take on a new look.

The Internet, which can eliminate time and space, is evolving in the direction of ever-larger amounts of information, ever-greater accuracy and personalization, and dematerialization. For instance, in the past, we needed an alarm clock to wake us up. Today, however, physical alarm clocks have become less common; they have been replaced by a piece of code on a phone.

We have discovered three patterns:

1. *When improvements are made to the capabilities of inputting, storing, handling, controlling, and outputting a certain type of data, business efficiency would increase and new business species would be born. For example, Linyi's livestreamers have better capabilities of information transmission than Linyi's Huafeng Wholesale Market.*

2. *When a new type of data is utilized on a large scale, it would produce new business species. For example, after GPS location data became widely used, "DiDi taxis" and bike-sharing came about.*

3. *Given that the efficiency of information transmission is equal, industries with relatively higher degrees of informatization would be the first to be reformed.*

From the history of the Internet, we can see that there is an order to this kind of reformation: from news to entertainment (games) to e-commerce. Industries with high degrees of informatization would be first to be reformed, while industries with low degrees of informatization would be reformed later. Table 0.1 shows the representative products of different stages of the development of the Internet.

Table 0.1 The Representative Products of Different Stages of the Development of the Internet

Stage of Internet development		Representative Internet products from this stage
Narrowband, text		Sina, NetEase, Sohu, QQ (an instant messagingsoftware), Baidu
Broadband, text		Shanda, Taobao
Mobile, broadband		WeChat, Taobao Mobile
Mobile, broadband	GPS	DiDi, Mobike
	Voice	Dedao, Himalaya
Mobile, broadband, video, AI		Kuaishou

The process of informatization has gone through many stages, such as the shift of narrowband and broadband Internet from PC to mobile. Today, we are in the age of video and AI.

Information systems have five basic functions: input, storage, handling, control, and output. The development of the Internet, or the process of informatization, is a process of continuously expanding the aforementioned functions.

Today, the age of video and AI is a new stage. Compared to the past, the capabilities of informatization and digitalization have increased by an order of magnitude.

VIII

Because industries with high degrees of informatization are the first to be reformed, we can find complete reference cases from history when investigating the new species in the age of video.

A widely known example is banknotes. Today, they have been all but dematerialized. The People's Bank of China is already using digital currency in an internal pilot program, while most people in China use WeChat Pay and Alipay to make payments in their daily lives, greatly reducing the usage of banknotes.

I would hereby like to go into detail about the book-sharing (or knowledge-sharing) industry, which provides a very good reference. We can use Dedao as an example.

Dedao is the successor of Luogic Knowledge, which was founded by Luo Zhenyu at the tail end of 2012. Back then, he would upload a 60-second audio clip on a WeChat official account every day. In 2012, WeChat launched a voice feature—this was an important moment. From the perspective of information retrieval and transmission, voice is a direct form of interaction that is high in efficiency and low in threshold. During the age of voice, a bunch of products such as Qingting FM and Himalaya emerged.

At that time, many people did not know about Luo's upcoming business model. Around the end of 2014, I heard him saying that his business model was very clear-cut and that he had "become" the largest bookstore in China. Whenever he recommended a book to everyone in his audio clips, tens of thousands or even hundreds of thousands of copies of the book would be sold at once. He was essentially a goods-promoting livestreamer and Internet celebrity.

During the age of text, books were information carriers that consisted of the two components of information and material. The material component was revolutionized early on by Amazon in the form of the Kindle (a reading device developed and sold by Amazon), which could deliver books into your hands. As for the information component, Luo has transmitted the knowledge found in books more accurately to readers by helping people read books.

Today, the knowledge-sharing industry is all the rage. This contrasts with brick-and-mortar bookstores. At the start of June 2020, Eslite's Dunnan branch (the first Eslite bookstore in Taiwan, China) ended operations.

The events that took place in the knowledge-sharing field will be repeated in many industries during the age of video, which has greater capabilities of informatization. We predict that the transformation of Linyi's wholesale markets and the rise of "the city of Kuaishou" would serve as the epitome of the age.

In fact, a closer look at the case of Dedao would reveal that the path of its rise is being repeated time and again in different industries in today's age of livestreaming. I have tentatively sorted this path into four steps:

The first step is Luogic Knowledge's recommendation of selected books, which is akin to brand promotion and is done to promote awareness among its followers. The second step is Luo's coverage of out-of-print yet exceptionally good books, which is akin to finding high-quality source goods and can serve to increase his profit margin. The third step is the creation of selected courses that are tailored to consumers. After all, books are just one of the various carriers of knowledge, and many questions that consumers are concerned about do not have books that deal with them. Luo has sought the best knowledge experts to help him produce knowledge, which is akin to the C2B production of knowledge. Many critics in society have claimed that Luo is "selling anxiety." In fact, he is simply finding people's pain points and providing products that are more accurate and that did not exist in the past. The fourth step is the renaming of Luogic Knowledge to Dedao due to its successful platformization. According to Growth Enterprise Market's prospectus published in September 2020, Dedao is valued at 4.15 billion yuan.

We can see many examples of these four steps—promoting goods for others, covering high-quality supply chains and providing them to consumers directly, performing C2B customization according to consumers' needs, and gradually transforming from a personal brand into an organizational brand—being followed in today's age of livestreaming.

IX

The aforementioned case of Dedao took place in the knowledge-sharing industry, where the proportion of information (bits) is higher. How, then, will industries with a higher proportion of material (atoms) be reformed by informatization and "videonization?" And what will the outcome be like?

In Beijing's Xi'erqi area where Kuaishou's headquarters is located, there is a KFC restaurant and a Bianlifeng convenient store. Perhaps we can glean something about the future from them.

In traditional KFC restaurants, everyone orders their meal at the counter, while the back kitchen performs on-site processing and production. KFC has done fairly well in the standardization and informatization of production. There is a screen in front of every employee's workbench, which shows that there is already a considerable foundation for the intelligentization of production.

Nowadays, KFC has a WeChat applet for customers to order their meals on. There are no longer order-taking staff members in their restaurants; instead, everyone scans a QR code to order their meal.

We can see KFC's changes from here:

1. *The number of order-taking roles in brick-and-mortar stores has been greatly reduced. In fact, the roles that interact with customers have been removed. Brick-and-mortar stores have become centers of production and distribution.*

2. *Placing an order used to require queuing up, but it can now be done concurrently.*

3. *The customers whom KFC serves come simultaneously from a real-world space and a network space.*

KFC has become a smart enterprise that is concurrently open for business in Xi'erqi and in a network space. It is now a C2B enterprise with digitalized and intelligentized production processes. This is actually the same model adopted by Hema Fresh.

Next to KFC, Bianlifeng is a similar enterprise. All of its goods have been digitalized and are "commanded" via their connection with the "brain" in the company's headquarters. The SKUs in each store are different and are iterated on every week. The company has many algorithm engineers who perform modeling and efficiency optimization according to data.

These stores have become "multi-habitat creatures;" the best service point can be found on multiple platforms, while efficiency optimization can be simultaneously performed on multiple platforms.

To my understanding, a platform like Kuaishou actually serves as the soil for enterprises to grow in. The Kuaishou platform is an ecosystem with all kinds of AI technologies that make the platform ever-more intelligent. It maximizes the convenience for all kinds of enterprises to join. In such an ecosystem where they are together with various other roles, these enterprises can provide the best services to customers.

For a relatively complex industry such as clothing, the intelligentization of backend supply chains and factories is driven by the intelligentization of users. This will continue until all enterprises and industries have been intelligently reformed.

This is the process by which AI continuously reforms each and every industry.

X

To recap, the history of mankind is a history of informatization, networkization, and intelligentization. Two of its variables are connection and computation. In the path toward a smart economy and a smart society, the age of video is currently the newest stage. In terms of connection and computation, significant improvements have taken place, causing an extension of human capabilities and forming a society of face-to-face communication.

Technological improvements will change societies, economies, and life, forming a new techno-economic paradigm and bringing about new business species.

Another aspect of technology that we have not mentioned is its neutrality. For new technologies to truly benefit mankind, a governance framework that corresponds to the new techno-economic paradigm is yet required.

We emphasize that algorithms have values. If new technologies are misused, they would have a negative effect on society. Therefore, we have to coordinate every aspect of society, find an appropriate governance framework, and make AI technologies benefit mankind.

CASE STUDIES FROM
DIFFERENT PLACES

HANGZHOU:
THE LIVESTREAMING CAPITAL

- Jiubao was originally situated on the outskirts of Hangzhou. How did it become the birthplace of Hangzhou's livestream ecosystem, draw in so many livestream organizations, and subsequently become the information bridgehead of China?

- How has livestream e-commerce changed each phase of commerce?

- How will AI and big data change the clothing industry?

"It was difficult for me to even find a conversation partner in Linyi. But after coming to Hangzhou, I found this city to be a bridgehead of information." One night in the summer of 2020, Wu Meng— husband of Kuaishou livestreamer Taozi—attended back-to-back gatherings and only finally drove back to his hotel at three in the morning.

Taozi is one of the top livestreamers from Linyi, Shandong Province. Her Kuaishou account is called Taozi's. As of January 2021, she had more than 8 million followers on Kuaishou. Today, Linyi is called the "City of Kuaishou" because it has many livestreamers with a million followers or more. But in the summer of 2020, many of Linyi's livestreamers came to Hangzhou to conduct livestreams, including Wu Meng and Taozi, who spent a month there. They held promotional livestreams from supply chain bases in Hangzhou and nearby, covering goods such as clothing, shoes, household appliances, and home textiles.

Hangzhou's supply chain advantages in clothing and "daily chemicals" within the Yangtze Delta have given it great weight in the livestream ecosystem of China. At the same time, Wu Meng values Hangzhou for its talented people and rapid flow of information. This is a place where livestreamers, MCNs (Internet celebrity management agencies that incubate and serve livestreamers), supply chain bases, service providers, and all kinds of people can exchange livestreaming expertise and experiences.

Equipped with the intention of turning Hangzhou into the "capital of livestreaming," the local government has also introduced many supportive policies related to the livestreaming industry. On September 9 2020, the Hangzhou Municipal Bureau of Commerce released "Several Opinions on Speeding up the Development of Hangzhou's Livestreaming E-commerce Economy" (henceforth referred to as "Opinions"), providing support and rewards to livestream e-commerce enterprises, livestream e-commerce parks, and livestreamers.

The goals proposed in "Opinions" were for Hangzhou to achieve, by 2022, a turnover of 1 trillion yuan and an annual consumption growth rate of 20 percent in livestream e-commerce; to nurture and bring in 100 top livestream e-commerce MCNs, to build 100 livestream e-commerce parks (or bases), to unearth 1,000 livestream e-commerce brands (or check-in locations), to encourage 100 top livestreamers to relocate to Hangzhou, and to groom 10,000 livestreaming talents.

There is a saying within the livestreaming circle that in Hangzhou, "Jiubao is near to the goods, Binjiang has many Internet celebrities, while Yuhang has many Internet talents." Although the livestreaming business is constantly evolving, the livestream layout in Hangzhou has already developed distinctive characteristics and a clear division of functions.

THE RISE OF JIUBAO (PART 1): THE GROWTH OF THE "UNIVERSAL CENTER OF LIVESTREAMING"

Key Points

- Supply chain bases of various sizes are densely distributed within three kilometers of Xinhe Lianchuang Park.

- The location advantages of Jiubao are: proximity to clothing wholesale markets, factories, and industry belts, convenient transportation, accessibility to talented people, and so on.

- The supply chain bases of Jiubao have attracted livestreamers from across China to visit in droves.

Xinhe Lianchuang Is Weiya's "Maiden Home"

To understand Hangzhou's livestreaming ecosystem, we must begin with Jiubao, where it all started. Jiubao is regarded by elderly Hangzhouers to be a desakota area in the northeast corner of the city. According to media reports, nearly 600 Internet celebrity incubation and marketing platforms have sprouted in Jiubao's entrepreneurial parks and office buildings within a mere few years, consisting of more than 10,000 e-commerce livestreamers and hundreds of brand agencies and supply chain enterprises.

The beginnings of Jiubao's livestream ecosystem are closely related to "Xinhe Lianchuang." Xinhe Lianchuang Park is located at No. 1 Jiuhua Lu, Jianggan District, Hangzhou. Before 2019, it was often referred to as the "maiden home" of Weiya, a top livestreamer on Taobao. But since 2019, due to the large concentration of supply-chain livestream bases in the area, it has gradually become known in the media as the "universal center of livestreaming."

The author of this chapter is Yang Rui, a researcher at Kuaishou Research Institute.

It is hard to imagine that the "universal center of livestreaming" was initially the production workshop of a factory. To date, a brick-red tablet continues to stand by the roadside of Xinhe Lianchuang. On it, the four large golden Chinese characters that read "Nova Photoelectric" have turned a little mottled, conveying a sense of the passage of time.

Founded in 1978, Nova Photoelectric mainly produces home appliance components. Its chairman, Ji Shian, had built up the company in Yueqing County, Wenzhou, before relocating it to Jiubao in 2003.

According to Ji's recollections, Jiubao was surrounded by farmland back then. In addition to Nova Photoelectric, several other enterprises such as Xizi Elevator Factory have also witnessed the urbanization of Jianggan District the entire time. And when the Internet age arrived, the destiny of these enterprises caught yet another wave, and so their stories continued to be brilliant.

When Hangzhou promoted the outward relocation of manufacturing and processing enterprises in 2015, Nova Photoelectric started to relocate its factory as well. Consequently, the issue of what to do with the emptied factory space of 180,000 square meters became a problem.

In late 2015, Ji Jianxing, the son of Ji Shian, renovated the 11 old industrial buildings of Nova Photoelectric and added two more business complexes, then renamed the place "Xinhe Lianchuang Park." "Xin" is the first Chinese character in the name "Nova Photoelectric," and "he" is the radical of the surname Ji. Together, "Xinhe" also refers to an upcoming entrepreneur or a budding enterprise. Besides this, in 2015, the idea of "mass entrepreneurship and widespread innovation" was promoted throughout China—it was on this basis that Xinhe Lianchuang (which means co-entrepreneurship and co-innovation) came into being.

When trying to attract tenants, Xinhe Lianchuang determined three directions: a hardware processing base, a cultural and creative center, and an Internet industry base.

Back then, however, only a few clothing-related e-commerce enterprises had decided to establish themselves in Xinhe Lianchuang. One of them was the Taobao brand "MG Elephant," which focuses on fashion for young women. The stories of these e-commerce enterprises are more or less the same—initially, they depended on Alibaba's 1688 platform and the nearby Sijiqing Women's Clothing Wholesale Market for the procurement of goods, before slowly linking up with factories and becoming involved in design and production themselves.

In the first half of 2017, Weiya—a first-generation "Taobao girl"—and her team relocated from Guangzhou to Xinhe Lianchuang Park, becoming the first livestream e-commerce company to join.

After she gained fame, the park became commonly referred to as Weiya's "maiden home." At first, she only rented an office that was a few dozen square meters in area. One day in October 2017, she livestreamed for five hours and sold 70 million yuan worth of goods for a fur shop in Haining, thereby gaining overnight fame for herself. It was also the first time that e-commerce livestreaming drew public attention.

Subsequently, many suppliers went to Xinhe Lianchuang from all over China to discuss a collaboration with Weiya. However, Weiya was often only able to talk to them in the wee hours of the morning after she had ended her livestream for the day. Because there was a foot spa in the same building as Weiya's company, the suppliers would often be found massaging their own feet and exchanging information with each other while waiting for Weiya. This laid the groundwork for the story to come.

As clothing-related livestream e-commerce inadvertently took center stage, No. 1 Jiuhua Lu got a new name in July 2018—Xinhe Lianchuang Digital Fashion Industry Park. Subsequently, after two years of development in 2018 and 2019, the park became a significantly representative livestreaming e-commerce park in Jiubao District and was poised to break out in 2020.

Why Jiubao?

"Why Jiubao? Because of its natural 'genes.' Jiubao is close to clothing wholesale markets, factories, and industry belts. Livestream e-commerce started with clothing, and collecting goods from the markets is more convenient in Jiubao." This is the analysis offered by Huang Yihang, head of tenant attraction at Xinhe Lianchuang Digital Fashion Industry Park.

Huang believes that the livestream ecosystem in the Jiubao area started with the clothing industry. The area enjoys location advantages, as many aspects of clothing were already concentrated in the area originally. Shoes and clothing markets such as Sijiqing, Yifa, and Huamao, as well as the defunct Dongtaimen, were formerly Taobao stores and the places where WeChat merchants procured their goods.

Founded in 1989, Sijiqing Clothing Group is one of the biggest first-tier clothing wholesale markets in China. Within 30 years, it achieved the outstanding feat of having "an average of one piece of clothing per capita coming from Sijiqing" nationwide. In Hangzhou, the clothing wholesale industry, comprised of markets such as Sijiqing, Zhongzhou, and Yifa, is gathered on the same street.

From a production point of view, nearby places such as Linping Town and Qiaosi Street in the eastern suburbs of Hangzhou consist of many small-scale clothing processing enterprises, logistics companies, and industrial workers, and thus have relatively comprehensive industry chains for clothing processing. For instance, there are clothing manufacturers in every one of the nine villages under the jurisdiction of Qiaosi Street, with Chaoyang Village having the greatest density of manufacturers.

Further away, there are many well-known specialty products in the clothing industry belts around Hangzhou, such as the down jackets of Pinghu County, Jiaxing, the business suits of Changshu County, Suzhou, the socks of Zhuji County, Shaoxing, and the leatherwear of Haining County, Jiaxing. Jiubao is only a one- or two-hour drive away from these industry belts. Figure 1.1 shows the location advantages of Jiubao.

"There are many clothing industry workers here—tailors, designers, and e-commerce operators, you name it," said Huang.

The "new residents of Jiubao" who are engaged in livestream e-commerce often mention the comprehensive living facilities there. For example, in Xinhe Lianchuang Park, there is a fully occupied youth apartment with 200 rooms, each of which can accommodate up to two people. Opposite the park is Vanke's residential area, which is just a five-minute walk away. And on one floor of the commercial complex, there is a diverse offering of cuisine.

In addition, Jiubao also has other location advantages. For example, in terms of transportation, it is close to Hangzhou East Railway Station and Xiaoshan Airport. It is also close to Xiasha University Town—upon

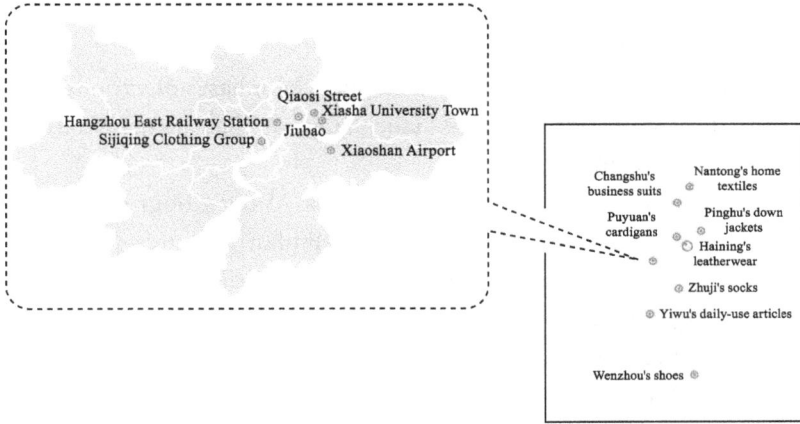

Figure 1.1 Jiubao's Location Advantages

graduation, many university students would come straight to Jiubao with their luggage to seek employment.

Becoming a Hub of Supply Chain Bases After Gaining Widespread Popularity

Standing at the forefront of its kind, Weiya's company rapidly expanded. Their office space grew from dozens of square meters at first to nearly 1,000 square meters eventually. In 2019, Weiya proposed a need for 10,000 square meters of space—the company's sample products required a two-story warehouse to be used. However, Xinhe Lianchuang was unable to satisfy these space demands. Thus, in October 2019, Weiya relocated her company headquarters to Ali Center in Binjiang District, where the company occupies a 10-story building with an office space of more than 30,000 square meters.

To integrate with their supply chains or to expand in scale, other organizations have also moved out of Xinhe Lianchuang after financing. However, stories continue to take place here despite the departure of such organizations. After the departure of Weiya and her brilliance, Xinhe Lianchuang entered the spotlight on its own and gradually gained the title of "the universal center of livestreaming," attracting many supply chain bases to take root here.

There is a dense distribution of supply chain bases of various sizes within three kilometers of Xinhe Lianchuang—Aichaoshang Livestream Base is one of them.

After more than 10 years of hard work, Wang Congrong has set up his own clothing factories in Shishi, Fujian Province (where he hails from), Wuhan, Hubei Province, and Zhongshan and Dongguan, Guangdong Province. He has also become the main supplier of a certain popular fast fashion brand.

In 2018, to create his own women's clothing brand in Hangzhou, Wang rented a floor in Bodi Center of Xiaoshan District. However, be it from a management or a supply chain perspective, Xiaoshan was a little out of the way. Thus, in early 2019, he relocated 20 kilometers to Jiubao and entered Xinhe Lianchuang—the third floor of the building next to his new office is Weiya's former stomping ground.

By the time he moved in, Xinhe Lianchuang had already fostered a very strong livestreaming atmosphere. In 2019, he also began to try out Taobao Live and was able to achieve sales worth 100 to 200 thousand yuan per livestream. Though lacking in experience and only conducting livestreams with the products he had on hand, he was nevertheless astounded by the power of livestreaming. He had six brick-and-mortar stores in Hangzhou, each of which had a monthly turnover of 300 to 400 thousand yuan; in comparison, he was able to make half that figure per day of livestreaming.

Shanghai-born Wen Di built her fortune in traditional e-commerce. In 2019, like other supply chain merchants from all over China, she visited Xinhe Lianchuang to discuss collaborating with Weiya. During a dinner one day, she hit it off instantly with Wang Congrong, and the two of them decided to collaborate to enter the livestreaming industry together. Hence, they rented a floor in Xinhe Lianchuang and spent two months fixing it up, thereupon establishing Aichaoshang Livestream Base.

In 2020, livestreamers on Kuaishou and other short video platforms became the darlings of livestream base scheduling. In August that year, Kuaishou livestreamer Taozi conducted a special livestream at Aichaoshang, garnering more than 60,000 orders and a GMV of over 5 million yuan.

"We have dealt with livestreamers from many different platforms and cooperated with entertainment livestreamers from Kuaishou. However, Taozi's livestream turned our understanding of Kuaishou's 'vertical livestreamers' upside down. This woman is way too good at selling goods—she can generate 60,000 orders in one night of livestreaming! On top of that, she doesn't act any different on or off camera—she's the kind of person who always shows her true nature," said Wen Di.

There are many bases like Aichaoshang in Jiubao. The reason they are gathered there is simple: there are many "outdoors livestreamers" in this industry. Originally, livestreamers did not know how to stock goods on their own and often went to market stalls to procure goods, but this was very troublesome. Then, someone discovered a business opportunity in helping these livestreamers stock and mix and match their goods. Operation teams would set up and prepare the livestream studio, so the livestreamer simply had to focus on livestreaming and marketing their products. Over time, supply chain bases took shape.

"The number of supply chain bases in Jiubao has grown from 10 to 100 to 1,000. Today, an industry belt has come into being. Livestreamers can simply stay here and livestream about whatever they want—be it affordable luxury goods, sports, food products, shoes, home furnishing, jewelry, or male fashion," explained Di.

Supply chain bases have solved a pain point of traditional brands, that is, a relative lack of SKUs. Take women's clothing for instance, new products are introduced once or twice per month and at most three or four times per season. However, supply chain bases are different; they can prepare 100 different models for each livestreamer every time, ensuring that there is no clash between the livestreamers.

The sales figures of a livestreamer in a supply chain base are often called their "battle report"—this is also the best advertisement for the base itself. "Just like the 'siphon effect,' publicizing good sales figures would always attract other livestreamers to come," said the head of a livestream base in Jiubao.

TIP

Supply-chain Livestream Bases

A supply-chain livestream base refers to an offline venue that has its own inventory (such as clothes and shoes), livestream operators, and at least two livestream studios. Here, livestreamers can simply select the goods they want and begin livestreaming immediately after.

Supply chain bases have to mix and match goods on behalf of the livestreamers, and this is a science unto itself. The goods promoted by a livestreamer during a livestream are collectively called "a plate of goods." The assortment of goods is generally the same for every livestream: 30 percent are high-volume products, 20 percent are parityproducts, 10 percent are unique-style products (that is, high price-per-customer products), 20 percent are tie-in products (such as the matching of interior and exterior decorations), 10 percent are in-demand products (which refer to the goods most likely to sell out on the night), and the final 10 percent are clearance products.

In addition to mixing and matching goods, most supply chain bases would also place emphasis on their own operational capabilities in "central control" and "scene control". If we were to liken a livestream session to an episode of a variety show, then "scene control" would be akin to directing. The tempo of the entire livestream session must be paced well. The scene controller must "see all and hear all," such as the tempo of introducing each product and the tempo of flash sales. Besides this, they often have totake part in duet collaborations with the livestreamer and explain the features of each product. For some supply chain bases, the boss would personally take charge of scene control because their familiarity with the goods is the greatest. The central controller is instead the backstage operator, as they have to modify the inventory and shelve or unshelve goods in a timely manner.

Livestreamers are often quite reliant on the scene controller. This is because they come into contact with many different products on a daily basis and may not be too familiar with specific products. If the scene controller and the livestreamer can collaborate well, they would be able to generate high yield, and consequently, the livestreamer would be willing to keep coming back for schedules. Conversely, if a base lacks a good scene controller, the livestreamer would not generate a high GMV and may not be willing to come back in the future. Figure 1.2 shows the services that supply chain bases can provide for livestreamers.

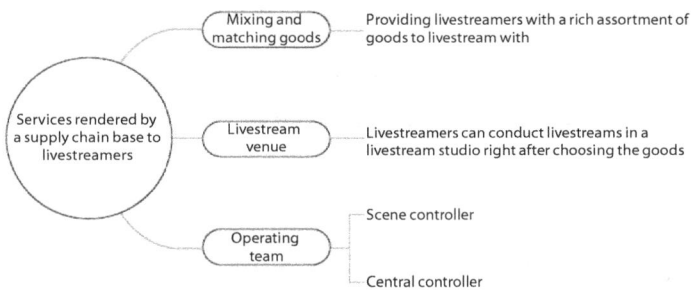

Figure 1.2 Services Rendered by a Supply Chain Base to Livestreamers

Stories of Creating Wealth with No Regard for the Time of Day

Just across the road from Xinhe Lianchuang is another cluster of livestream supply chain bases—Xizi Huanqiu. "Five, four, three, two, one…" is what one often hears as one approaches it. Needless to say, this is the voice of a livestreamer counting down while changing prices, publishing links, and getting followers to pit their luck against one another.

Although Xizi Huanqiu's livestream ecosystem came about later than Xinhe Lianchuang's, the two parks share similar stories. As mentioned earlier, Xizi Elevator Factory was one of the other enterprises—aside from Nova Photoelectric—that witnessed the development of Jianggan District. At first, Xizi Huanqiu was its office, but the company eventually relocated due to business expansion, leaving the park vacant.

Following the rise of livestream e-commerce, this place gradually became one of the livestream centers in the Jiubao area. While Xinhe Lianchuang has a lot of communal space, it has a relative lack of floors. In comparison, Xizi Huanqiu is more compact.

"We started out with clothing enterprises, then shifted to livestream e-commerce after the era of Internet celebrities came about. While there were probably more Taobao livestreams at first, Kuaishou and other platforms took off in the second half of 2019," explains Huang Jiancheng, head of real estate operations at Xizi Huanqiu.

It was in 2013 that the Internet celebrity economy caught on. There was an MCN that rented two floors in one of Xizi Huanqiu's buildings for a period of time, and much of the rented space was used to store their clothing. Since 2015, livestreams have emerged one after another. By 2018, livestream-related enterprises made up approximately 50 percent of the enterprises at Xizi Huanqiu. And after the second-phase construction of Xizi Huanqiu was completed in 2019, the two newly built high-rise buildings were just in time for the livestreaming craze, attracting hundreds of enterprises to join. According to Huang, there were more than 150 enterprises in Xizi Huanqiu as of September 2020, and 95 percent of them were enterprises or MCNs within the livestream e-commerce supply chain.

One afternoon, Huang was receiving wave after wave of guests in his office when he received a phone call from a man who spoke in a Guangdong accent. The man inquired whether Xizi Huanqiu had a vacant lot of approximately 700 to 1,000 square meters. When Huang answered in the negative, the man persisted, "Perhaps something a little smaller? Or could you help me find out if there's anything nearby?"

"We had developed so quickly that we didn't have the space he asked for. With that sort of demand, he would probably be a big client elsewhere. It's a pity that we couldn't offer him that kind of space," said Huang with some regret. In Xizi Huanqiu, some livestream bases had expanded so quickly that they ran out of space and thus had to convert their offices into livestream studios.

In the era of the Internet celebrity economy (around 2013), the rental price of Xizi Huanqiu's real estate was 1.1 yuan/m2. This slowly increased to 1.8 yuan/m2 in 2018–2019. By 2020, this had risen to more than 2 yuan/m2 depending on the floor location.

Today, there are nearly 40 companies on the waiting list to enter Xizi Huanqiu. In 2020, the strategic goal of Xizi Huanqiu was "brandification," so it demanded all incoming enterprises to develop their own brands and contribute toward a park of "branded livestreaming."

Every night, all of the lights in Xizi Huanqiu's buildings would be turned on. Livestreams would often go on until two or three in the morning. The tightly drawn curtains ensure that the livestreamers and operating teams are continually able to produce wealth creation stories regardless of the time of day.

These supply chain bases in Jiubao have attracted livestreamers from all across China. In the summer, influential livestreamers from Linyi would flock to Hangzhou to conduct special livestreams. Then in September, livestreamers from Guangzhou would start coming to Hangzhou for studio sessions. Guangzhou is better for summer and spring wear, but in the winter, livestreamers there have fewer goods to promote and would thus go to Hangzhou. Besides goods, what attracts them there is Hangzhou's rapid circulation of information.

THE RISE OF JIUBAO (PART 2): HOW HAS LIVESTREAM E-COMMERCE CHANGED EACH PHASE OF COMMERCE?

Key Points

- Sijiqing transformed from a wholesale market that was purely for goods procurement into a weathervane of fashion trends.

- There is a methodology behind how livestream e-commerce accurately identifies followers' s needs.

The author of this chapter is Yang Rui, a researcher at Kuaishou Research Institute.

- Livestream "flash sales" are spurring changes to the backend methods of production. Many "quick-response" factories have emerged, greatly reducing the production cycle time for clothing.

If Part 1 is said to have investigated how Jiubao gradually became the "universal center of livestreaming" from a historical perspective, then in Part 2 we are going to look at the characteristics exhibited by livestream e-commerce today and how livestreaming changed business from the perspective of the present or even the future.

For example, let's take the clothing market Sijiqing, which is located on the periphery of the Jiubao area. In the livestream e-commerce ecosystem, it has transformed from a place for "procuring goods" into a place for "viewing goods," becoming an offline "shop window" for livestream e-commerce. It is positioned more as a weathervane of fashion and not as a first-tier wholesale market. After identifying the goods they want from Sijiqing, the purchasing teams deployed by the supply chain bases would contact the original manufacturers directly.

In addition, livestream e-commerce can use various methods to measure and gather followers's consumption demands, and then spur changes to the backend methods of production. Many "quick-response" factories have emerged, greatly reducing the production cycle time for clothing.

We have also discovered that the founders of supply chain bases in Hangzhou, where there is a high density of information, are beginning to develop a sense of crisis. They are paying close attention to the ongoing changes to livestream formats and thinking about how to become super supply chains on livestream e-commerce platforms.

Sijiqing Market: From Wholesale to "Shop Window"

A'zhen is a purchaser for Aichaoshang Livestream Base. Aichaoshang's purchasing team consists of five to seven people in total and is distributed between Guangzhou and Hangzhou. Their usual work is to go shopping.

The first time I met A'zhen, she had just returned from Sijiqing Market with a huge black plastic bag. It was packed full with her yield for the afternoon, including a few trendy hats and fashionable accessories, which were mainly for the livestreamer to match and use while livestreaming. If followers inquire about the prices of these items during the livestream, more can be procured from the market and sold to them.

Sijiqing Market is a 40-minute drive away from Jiubao. A'zhen is highly familiar with the ins and outs of this place. It does not have the capacity of a building but rather that of a street. There is a dense distribution of markets here, such as Yifa, Zhongzhou, and Changqing. Each market has a different positioning and style; they also differ in their sources of goods, prices, and traits.

Every floor of these buildings is crammed with clothing stalls. Zhongzhou Building offers a few goods from Korea, Thailand, and Guangzhou, so the prices there are relatively high. Yifa Building mainly sells Hangzhou-style women's clothing and is volume-focused; most of its stalls are opened by women's clothing factories in Hangzhou, while the third floor also provides goods to Internet celebrities. Changqing Building is mainly focused on low-price women's clothing.

We arrived in Sijiqing Market using the directions A'zhen provided. There, we saw many trolleys shuttling back and forth among the cramped stalls—able-bodied men were delivering bags of clothes they had brought from the factories to each stall, then taking the to-be-shipped clothes from each stall to the express delivery point. An advertisement poster seeking beautiful women to serve as fashion models is pasted on the wall of every stall. In the bigger stalls, fashion models can be seen in sample clothes, providing the visiting wholesale merchants with an idea of how the clothes look when worn.

Pointing at an overcoat, the female owner of a stall tells a visiting non-local merchant, "This overcoat sold very well here last year, and it will definitely sell tremendously well in your city this year. Here, we are always ahead of the trend." Whereas traditional wholesale markets often lag behind in time and information, "first- tier" markets enjoy the fastest circulation of information and are thus natural places for data aggregation.

A'zhen believes that Sijiqing Market is highly responsive. The stalls have a very high "update" frequency; new clothing designs are added two or three times per week. If there is a "response" in the market to a particular design, it would continue to be offered for sale. Otherwise, it would be delisted and replaced by newer designs.

In reality, "response" refers to the demands and preferences of consumers. As one of the biggest "first-tier" clothing markets in East China alongside Shanghai's Qipu Lu and Guangzhou's Baiyun Market, Sijiqing is a favorite haunt of wholesale merchants from all over China for goods procurement, and that is why it has nationwide "response" data. "This is the place with the fastest circulation of clothing- related information. Merchants from all over China come here to procure goods; supplementary orders mean that there is a response. The market quickly reveals which designs are popular—this is the pace of fast fashion," said A'zhen.

Yifa Building also has stalls that specialize in a single product, such as an overcoat or a one-piece dress. "When a single product is done to perfection, it is very likely to become popular. There are a few stalls that focus on a single product; they would purchase a prototype and conduct their own research and development on it. The more research that they do, the more certain that the product would sell well," says A'zhen.

For livestream bases such as Aichaoshang, markets play the role of a weathervane. Nowadays, purchasers visit markets to find out about the popular designs and trends rather than to procure goods as they traditionally did. When they see a design they like, they would contact the original manufacturer directly. For example, when Aichaoshang takes a fancy to a silk dress from a certain stall and wants to add it to a livestreamer's collection, they would contact the manufacturer to negotiate a "livestream supply price."

Aside from wholesale markets, purchasing teams would also visit shopping malls to look at big-brand women's clothing, paying attention to color schemes, combinations, displays, product types, popular products, and fashion trends. They do so mainly to get a better feel of things, whereas visiting wholesale markets allows them to see specific hot-selling designs. In addition, purchasing teams would go on Diction Net to find out news about fashion shows and use Instagram (a social networking app for sharing photos and videos) to check out fashion trends. Nowadays, Aichaoshang often uses "AI data" from Zhiyi Tech (an AI company) to obtain real- time data on hot-selling designs from the entire Internet.

Frontend: Accurate Identification of Consumer Demands

It is often said in the livestreaming circle that Taobao only has one "Singles' Day" every year, whereas every day is "Singles' Day" for livestreaming. In reality, hot- selling designs serve as a concentrated reflection of market demand and are assessed differently by each supply chain base.

Situated within Xizi Huanqiu, Changlaiwang Livestream Base only does livestreams for a down jacket brand called "Snow Flying." Compared to women's clothing, which demands a large number of SKUs and fast addition of new designs, down jackets have relatively longer production and sales cycles and thus are usually purchased off the shelf.

September is the month designated as the test period for new down jacket models by Zhao Liwei, head of Changlaiwang Livestream Base. It is only after a product has received genuine feedback from the market that further research and design can be done when selecting products during the peak season.

Zhao's test method is to arrange a strategic cooperation with an influential livestreamer. The livestreamer would conduct a livestream exclusively on down jackets and introduce 100 pre-selected designs. The emphasis is on introducing each design quickly rather than explaining them in detail. Due to the influencer's large follower base, one livestream is enough to get some rough figures. The subsequent livestreams—up to 10 of them—would be conducted with greater focus until all the necessary sales figures have been collected.

On September 13, 2020, Kuaishou livestreamer "Master Yuda" conducted a special livestream for "Snow Flying," achieving a GMV of over 10 million yuan. Zhao's first "plate of goods" consisted significantly of basic men's clothing, which was why he decided to seek a cooperation with "Master Yuda."

A winning practice is to assess the products carefully prior to the peak season for down jackets. In a supply chain base, nobody can tell for sure which of the 100 designs would sell well. Because every person has different experiences and preferences, there would certainly be opinion differences among a team, and so data is needed to back up any assessment.

For livestreamers, the possibility of a "flop" when promoting goods on-stream is very real if there is a lack of solid data and the products are not chosen well. "The structure of the goods is very important for the livestreamer to succeed. A down jacket priced at 99 yuan is a 'fighter plane' as far as benefits are concerned. It is just like a bomb—throw it and it will explode. But it is intended as a fallback and should only be used as a last resort," said Zhao.

The structure of the goods must be clearly arranged during a livestream—which goods to introduce at the start, which goods to introduce halfway through, which goods are for emergency purposes, and which goods are for ensuring a certain GMV. The main products to be introduced usually begin from the fourth product. Using "Snow Flying" for example, the fourth product is always a "label product"—the intention is for people to know that this product comes from "Snow Flying" whenever it is mentioned. The fifth product is a product that has high price-performance. The entire livestream session must string these products together at a certain tempo.

For a livestream base, orders can be confidently placed after the likely hot-selling designs have been determined, thereby preventing overstocking. Zhao explains that they would order 10,000 pieces of each down jacket design for the first round of assessment, while during the peak season, they might order up to 800,000 pieces of the likely hot-selling designs. "If we hadn't assessed the likely sales performance of a product so accurately, we certainly wouldn't dare to place such a large order." During the peak season, overstocking would affect product turnover, dealing a fatal blow to the supply chain.

After performing assessments, Zhao and his team would choose approximately 40 out of the 100 designs. "Nowadays, these 100 designs are produced together. In time, half or more would be discontinued, leaving only the better ones. To obtain the most accurate 'plate of goods,' we would select the designs based on the product structure—such as short, hooded, low-necked, or fur-necked—and match them with sweatshirts or trousers."

When they have built up enough confidence to place an order for 800,000 pieces, they would gain bargaining power with the manufacturer.

"There's a price for 100,000 pieces and a different price for 800,000 pieces. Costs can be cut at every phase—be it labor costs, procurement costs, or assembly line production time."

Attention must be paid to the methods of assessment. When selecting designs to order, positioning must be done to determine the number of assessment pieces to order. If a design is positioned as a "basic design," 10,000 assessment pieces might not be enough because they still have to be divided according to color and size.

Pre-orders can be taken for a design even if it is in stock. If the pre-order duration is 30 days and yet there are consumers placing pre-orders, it would mean that this design has the potential to be hot-selling. "For such products, I would have no qualms about placing an order for 1 million pieces. Moreover, a schedule must be arranged immediately," Zhao said.

Backend: The Miraculous Speed of Quick-response Factories

On a livestream channel, goods are often sold out within a few seconds or minutes. Aichaoshang Supply Base used to provide goods for a top livestreamer on Kuaishou. More than 80,000 pieces of three different short-sleeve T-shirt designs were sold within three minutes, generating a GMV of 3.8 million yuan.

This kind of flash sale has greatly shortened the sales cycle, thereby straining the supply chain.

For a clothing business, inventory is the greatest pain point of all. If they accidentally overstock and thus incur a high goods-return rate or are unable to sell off the goods, they might bring about their own demise—such lessons can be found everywhere within the industry. Yet, if they understock but receive an excessive number of orders on the livestream channel, they might be unable to ship the goods, causing the livestreamer's rating to drop and the livestream base's reputation to plummet.

Frontend hot-selling designs are also spurring changes to backend production.

Take Aichaoshang's cooperation with the aforementioned livestreamer for example, Wen Di explains that there were only seven days from designing the t-shirts to the livestreamer receiving the prototypes and conducting the livestream. During these seven days, the livestreamer's team even visited the factory and asked Wen Di where the goods were, to which Wen Di pointed at a heap of cloth and said, "The goods are right there."

"We actually hadn't begun production at all. However, the livestreamer's team said that we had signed a contract and had to ship the goods within 48 hours of the time that the livestreamer ended the livestream, otherwise we would have to pay huge damages.

"I told them not to worry because our factory could produce most of the goods within three days. In the end, we shipped all the 80,000-plus orders within 48 hours of the end of the livestream.

"In fact, we had prepared to produce 130,000 t-shirts, but the figures showed that the livestreamer had sold 80,000 pieces during the livestream. Production was ongoing in the factory at that time. Based on the figures we saw, we realized we had not produced much of certain sizes. In the end, we produced around 85,000 t-shirts. Compared to the traditional mode of ordering, this mode greatly reduced inventory pressure," explained Wen Di.

Inventory overstocking is the greatest fear in the clothing industry. Whenever leftover stock has to be cleared out, the business may not even be able to recoup the costs. However, in the e-commerce industry and especially in livestream e-commerce, which has a huge "burst effect," inventory can be effectively kept at a minimum by using the capabilities of quick response to organize production after finding out the sales figures.

For example, women's clothing is high in technological complexity; given the process from the preparation of materials such as fabrics and accessories to manual labor to backend manufacturing, the production cycle is relatively long. The concept of "quick response" is about reducing the production time of a piece of clothing—such as from 15 days to 7 days—by making use of a fast production line after the necessary fabrics and accessories have been fully prepared.

Among different clothing categories, quick response is easier to achieve for casual and fashionable wear such as sweatshirts and T-shirts. After the patterns have been confirmed, plain pieces of such clothing can be produced. The colors and designs can subsequently be added within a very short period of time according to the buyers' s choices. In this way, the clothing can be produced within two to three days and delivered within four days.

Let's take hoodies for example. Fifty thousand plain hoodies can be produced in advance, while the exclusive designs of the invited livestreamer can be added at a later time. This is a typical example of "quick response"—plain pieces of clothing are prepared in advance, and then given designs according to the numbers sold during the promotional livestream.

In reality, "quick response" is about turning non-standard products into standard products in a certain sense. For standard products such as self-heating hotpots, mooncakes, and pastries, one simply must negotiate a price with the manufacturer and list the samples. That is not the case for frequently-purchased non-standard products such as women's clothing. Although women's clothing has a high price-per- customer and can stimulate GMV, being a non-standard product, it has a certain rate of product return.

Wen Di believes that although the "plate of goods" for women's clothing cannot be entirely turned into standard products, a supply chain for making standard products is nevertheless necessary to build up volume.

Behind the Speed and Fervor of Livestream Studios

The Jiubao area in Hangzhou has a loosely organized circle of supply chain bases and is not administered by a unified organization or association. However, information never stops circulating within this circle; when a certain livestreamer conducts a livestream in a certain base, news about the matter, including the sales results and ROI, would quickly spread throughout the area. This has to do with the unique methods of information exchange within the area.

In the livestream studios, livestreamers can often be heard shouting, "Five, four, three, two, one... link added!" While reveling in the action, their GMVs hit new heights time and time again. Supply chain bases usually have an isolated office that is undisturbed by the hubbub in the studios. The boss of the base would be found sitting at the tea table, boiling water, making tea, and pouring tea, while his guests would be seated on the two sides of the table. Information is exchanged over the course of pouring and drinking tea—even among people who had not been acquainted with each other.

One night, the manager of a livestreamer came to Aichaoshang Livestream Base for tea. "I have a 'plate of goods' to debut at the end of the month. Do you want to conduct its premiere?" "Okay, leave this exclusively to me." It was almost as if this place had become the Wall Street of the livestream e-commerce world.

Taking a seat in the restaurant in Xinhe Lianchuang at eight or nine in the evening, one can eavesdrop on the conversations going on at neighboring tables. Words such as "livestreamer," "brand," and "supply chain" are commonly heard. To the people working in Xinhe Lianchuang, the dining table is never simply a place for eating, but also a place for exchanging information such as business expertise and experiences.

According to media reports, a new F&B brand called Pengpeng Beef Hotpot was slated to open in Xinhe Lianchuang Industrial Park in July 2020. Today, the 60 m2 shop has a monthly turnover of more than 400,000 yuan and a daily table turnover rate of five.

Information is circulating rapidly, and so is the replacement of industry workers. In 2019, a large number of supply chain bases in the Jiubao area collapsed. According to Xizi Huanqiu's statistics, although they had 100 percent occupancy, they also had an occupant turnover rate of 30 percent. In Xinhe Lianchuang, large enterprises with 1 to 2,000 square meters of space tend to have strong risk resistance, whereas small and medium-sized supply chain enterprises or fledgling brands are often replaced very quickly. After the pandemic, 40 percent of the small and micro-sized livestream enterprises in Xinhe Lianchuang were replaced.

This group of people has the greatest sense of crisis.

One of the distinct changes in 2020 was a shift towards brands among all of the livestream e-commerce parks in Jiubao. Some parks even proposed that this was the "first year of brand strategy" and demanded all incoming supply chain bases to have their own brands. Prior to this, the model of mixing-and-matching goods, by procuring goods from the market, had gradually lost its advantage.

Some supply chain bases have also realized that what works this year might not work the following year; the replacement rate in this industry is too fast and intense. Wen Di recently conceived that there are ultimately only two ways of doing Kuaishou livestreams.

"The first way is to work on brands. However, supply chain bases would forever remain as middlemen if they do not have their own brands; they would sell goods for one brand today and for another brand tomorrow. To follow up on this matter, they need to have a lineup of livestreamers and exert control over their livestreamers." In the second half of 2020, Aichaoshang Livestream Base began incubating their own livestreamers and placed focus on goods that have a medium to high price-per-customer.

Wen Di believes that if all of their incubated livestreamers sell brands or goods that have a medium to high price-per-customer, they would virtually have nailed down the 20 percent (referring to Kuaishou's "whales") as described in the Pareto principle. Even if the GMV is not high, they would at least have this share of the market.

"The other way is to create another SHEIN (an international brand of women's clothing) on Kuaishou." Wang Congrong's factory, which provides goods to SHEIN, is able to produce 10,000 to 20,000 pieces of clothing per day. Wen Di plans to make use of Wang's involvement in SHEIN's setup to form partnerships with SHEIN's suppliers and subsequently with their designers to achieve "quick response" for small orders.

A self-contained clothing supply chain certainly cannot do without R&D, design, prototyping, production, and placing supplementary orders according to the overall figures. Products with poor figures will be discontinued immediately, whereas hot-selling products will get repeat orders. "Such a process will go on without end."

Wen Di cites an example—for SHEIN's clothing, at least 100 pieces of each design are produced each time. However, the factory would not be profitable and might even incur losses if it only produced 100 pieces; expenses such as labor costs and accessory costs would be spread across this quantity of clothing. Instead, the factory is banking on subsequent orders—large numbers of supplementary orders would be placed if a design is hot-selling. As long as there are two hot-selling designs among 10 different designs, the factory would be able to break even or make a profit. This is the only reason that it is willing to accept the remaining eight designs; it would otherwise be very difficult to actuate.

Wen Di believes that SHEIN has tested and educated their suppliers on everything they needed to. She hopes to collaborate with three or four high-quality suppliers to produce 50 to 100 designs every day. These designs would be distributed on all platforms and disseminated to all livestreamers. When a hot-selling design emerges, the factories would continue to produce it.

"Being a super supply chain is actually about catering to the 80 percent (referring to the majority of users) rather than the 20 percent on Kuaishou. I hope to be able to disseminate all goods that have a low to medium price-per-customer and open up the entire supply chain, allowing livestreamers to place orders conveniently. Even if I earn only one or 2 yuan per piece, it would be fine as long as the volume is big enough," said Di.

TIP

The Supply Chain Innovation of SHEIN

SHEIN is a cross-border B2C (business-to-consumer) e-commerce platform focused on the R&D, production, and sales of fast fashion for women. Its primary markets outside China are the European, American, Australian, and Middle Eastern markets.

According to SHEIN's official website, as of April 2020, its sales covered more than 200 countries and regions worldwide. In 2019, SHEIN launched hundreds of new products per day on average. Supported by an excellent and agile supply chain system, its highest shipment volume in one day exceeded three million.

When recruiting suppliers, SHEIN would lay out four conditions. Firstly, the supply model must integrate production, R&D, and sales into one. Secondly, goods must be shipped on time—in-stock goods must be shipped within 40 hours, while pre-ordered goods must be shipped within five days.

Thirdly, the source of goods must be stable, as reflected by an ample inventory, quality assurance, and a preference for industry leadersin each product category. Fourthly, the supplier must have independent R&D and designcapabilities, such that it can create more than 30 new products per month.

According to media reports, SHEIN launched 150,000 new products in 2019, which works out to an average of more than 10,000 new products per month. In justone or two months, it launched as many new products as Zara did for the entire year. Moreover, its speed of product creation is still increasing. In July 2020, it launched an average of 2,000 new products per day in the women's clothing category alone (including accessories and old designs).

SHEIN's official website mentions that the company has gradually become an industry leader in cross-border fashion e-commerce through deep cultivation of its supply chain management and continuous improvement of its operational capabilities. A business plan in 2018 revealed that SHEIN's hot-selling product rate was 50 percent, while the unsalable product rate was around 10 percent. By figuring out the hot-selling designs and making supplementary orders, the cost per piece can be greatly reduced.

CHAPTER TWO

GUANGZHOU: A TRADITIONAL COMMERCIAL CENTER ENTERS THE AGE OF VIDEO

- Guangzhou is a traditional commercial center and a main source of goods for livestream e-commerce. In this chapter, we have chosen to study two of its industries: clothing and cosmetics.

- For the clothing industry, we shall find out the perspectives and strategies of Sister Zhen and Sister Mi, who have each been doing e-commerce for 10 years.

- For the cosmetics industry, we have chosen two relatively well-known enterprises: Uniasia and Hanhoo. We shall find out how they think and how they act.

Guangzhou is a national commercial port where first-tier wholesale markets and support supply chains are gathered. As an important source of goods, Guangzhou has long supplied goods for China's wholesale and retail system, as well as for global exports.
Following the rise of Taobao and other e-commerce platforms, Guangzhou drew on its advantage as an important source of goods to attract a bunch of Taobao merchants from across China.
With the arrival of the age of video and the rise of livestream e-commerce, what opportunities and challenges lie in store for Guangzhou? And what

*kind of influence will they have on various roles within Guangzhou's com-
mercial ecosystem, such as first-tier wholesale markets and brand enterprises? These are questions everyone is paying close attention to.*

E-COMMERCE VETERAN SISTER ZHEN: PERSONA AND BRAND ARE THE KEY TO KUAISHOU E-COMMERCE

Key Points

- Having done traditional e-commerce for many years and residing in the major source of goods that is Guangzhou, Sister Zhen had a very huge impact on other livestreamers when her team entered Kuaishou with a novel style and way of thinking.

- Sister Zhen believes that persona- and brand-building are the most important things for livestreaming on Kuaishou. She says that she is on a path of brandification and is highly approved of by her followers.

- In the future, Sister Zhen will stratify her brand to create a fair-priced brand and a high-end brand. She will intersperse a few high-end designs during her daily livestreams so as to slowly change the perception of her followers.

Sister Zhen and Sun Pengtao are a couple who have been exploring the field of e-commerce for 10 years, achieving a mix of successes and failures. During the age of picture and text, they once "gained overnight fame," becoming big names in Taobao e-commerce. Yet, during the age of livestream e-commerce, they missed out on the first wave of rewards because of their habitual thinking.

The author of this chapter is Li Zhao, a senior researcher at Kuaishou Research Institute.

In October 2018, they studied each of the major e-commerce platforms and eventually decided—on Sister Zhen's birthday—to do e-commerce on Kuaishou. Having built up many years of e-commerce experience, they can be considered professional players. After joining Kuaishou, they made it on to the Trending page on the first day and amassed 700,000 followers within a week.

At present, they have their own factories and brands and are constantly innovating their business model. They certainly have many experiences to share.

◎ *The following is an account by Sister Zhen and her husband.*

. . .

From Starting a Business as a College Student to Owning 34 Tmall Stores

We are from Shandong Province and were schoolmates in Qingdao Agricultural University. Back in university, we already started a Taobao store. While I graduated in 2013, Pengtao—who is one year my senior—dropped out in order to manage our business.

It was in 2010 when we first tried selling things on Taobao. Back then, opening a Taobao store had a low barrier to entry and did not require much startup capital or fees. Our small business achieved decent results. We started out as a "Taobao C Store" (an ordinary store) and only upgraded to a Tmall store after building up sufficient funds. In 2010, Tmall was still called Taobao Mall and required only 10,000 yuan to join. This increased to 160,000 yuan the following year, keeping out many merchants.

On Singles' Day in 2011, we had an event hot-seller and sold several thousand pieces of the product. However, Qingdao could not ship enough pieces. Pengtao went on the Internet and found a few factories in Guangzhou that offered the same design. He quickly booked a plane ticket to Guangzhou, hoping to bring back some pieces of the product. As a hub of first-tier wholesale markets, Guangzhou offers an immense number of goods. After arriving in Guangzhou at the end of November, he decided to take root there straight away.

In the past, we mainly procured goods from Jimo, a second-tier wholesale market in Qingdao. It charged a unit price that is 5–10 yuan higher than what is charged in Guangzhou. However, we came to Guangzhou to procure goods for a more important reason: design. Women's clothing is very sensitive to design. Guangzhou has many new and better-looking designs as compared to Jimo's relatively old designs. If you have watched our livestreams on Kuaishou, you would discover that our designs are very new and can be considered to be at the forefront of fashion.

In 2013, we upgraded to Tmall mainly so that we could conduct events on "Juhuasuan." Between 2013 and 2016, group purchases were all the rage. A Tmall store had a greater chance of gaining approval for Juhuasuan events as compared to a C store. To gain approval for many of our events, we had 34 Tmall stores to our names at some point in time. On average, we sold 50,000 pieces of our products every day and had a price per customer of more than 80 yuan. Back then, we were one of the core partners in Alibaba's section for women's clothing. E-commerce has truly helped fulfill the business dreams of a few ordinary people who slowly built up their sales volumes. For us, however, our growth was explosive in nature, increasing from several thousand to tens of thousands in only a short period of time, albeit this has stabilized in recent years. Instead of spending our revenue frivolously, we would use it to open new stores, investing 200,000 yuan in each of them. In this way, we accumulated 34 Tmall stores.

Two Failures: The Internet Celebrity Model and the Offline-and-Online Store Model

After "Juhuasuan," we opened a store similar to Xueli's Internet celebrity store in 2016, whereby the celebrities would bring their own traffic with them. At that time, Weibo-guided traffic was the trend. Many Taobao stores turned in this direction and focused on private domain traffic and on becoming a "style shop."

We crossed over to run an Internet celebrity store, in which the celebrities—who brought their own followers with them—would attract external traffic to our Taobao store to generate orders. However, this project ultimately failed because Internet celebrity stores were subjected to many uncontrollable factors. We engaged five or six Internet celebrities in succession; some of them could not endure the hardship of e-commerce after working for a period of time, some did not take photos that our followers approved of, while some wanted to do photoshoots overseas and were thus very costly. We ended the project after approximately half a year—it could be considered a failed attempt. Back then, livestream e-commerce was not huge in volume and there were not many viewers. Unimpressed by it, we wanted to focus our energy on running an Internet celebrity store that was paired with our blog on Weibo; our mindset was still fixated on a picture-and-text format. In the second half of 2017, feeling that a Taobao C Store was no longer suitable for us, we prepared to run offline-and-online stores, that is, a chain of stores as was recommended at that time. Purchases could be made online, while the shopping experience of a women's clothing store was offered offline. This was a daring attempt. The first plan we executed was to open stalls in Guangzhou's wholesale markets, including Wanjia, Nancheng, and Shisanhang—it cost us approximately 20 million yuan in investment. Hoping to attract outstanding agencies from all over China to invest and partner with us, we told them during our meetings that they could set up stores in their own cities. For example, the brick-and-mortar store of a certain brand could conduct community marketing via our app.

However, we gave up on this after just one year. The first reason it failed was that we did not have enough experience in managing the clothing designs for brick-and-mortar stores. We had always been focused on online sales, the designs of which were different from those for offline sales. The second reason was that the rent for stalls in Guangzhou's wholesale markets was steep. The rent in Nancheng was two million yuan a year; we bought a five-year lease in Wanjia at a slightly cheaper price than that. The most expensive among the three markets was Shisanhang, where the rent per stall was 280,000 yuan a month. However, the profits there were slightly higher as well. Merchants who procured goods from Shisanhang were more accomplished and owned many stores, and so they made larger orders on average. I feel that such a business model will be a trend, albeit nobody has truly done it before. How can this kind of experience be realized in the future? I believe that brick-and-mortar stores can be regarded as sub-warehouses that radiate 10 to 20 kilometers into their surroundings. Consumers can access an app to check the designs that are available in a store and place orders directly. The goods will then be shipped from the warehouse and delivered within two hours. Consumers can also visit the store to choose the designs they want. I believe that this model is not only feasible but also combinable with livestreaming, such as by placing greater emphasis on Kuaishou's "Same City" feature—this is what I might do in the future.

Making It on to the "Trending" Page Regularly Right After Joining Kuaishou

It was in October 2018 when I truly understood what Kuaishou was about. Back then, my chain of offline-and-online stores failed, and I realized that livestreaming would definitely be the trend in the future. We thus began to analyze every livestreaming platform.

We observed the livestreamers on Kuaishou, especially the clothing livestreamers from Linyi, Shandong Province. One of them was "Taozi's," whose impressive sales volume convinced me that livestreaming was feasible. We spent a week thinking about it and eventually decided on my birthday to do e-commerce on Kuaishou.

Because we were residing in the major source of goods that was Guangzhou and were equipped with "e-commerce thinking," our introduction to Kuaishou livestreaming had a huge impact on several livestreamers from Linyi. They had started out as merchants in second-tier markets and had indeed driven the first wave of Kuaishou E-commerce livestreaming. However, we came in with a novel style and way of thinking and thus captivated followers.

Our videos were distinct from theirs and kept making it on to the Trending page. Within a week, we amassed 700,000 followers. Our way of doing things was akin to fusing the elements of traditional e-commerce together. This seemed very novel at that time; many Kuaishou livestreamers who had started out as "second-tier" merchants were curious about what we were doing, why we were so successful, and how we gained followers so quickly. Hence, they began to study our way of publishing videos. Many people would DM me, asking, "What software did you use for this photo? I will pay you if you teach me how to publish such videos."

This was the impact of "first-tiers" on "second-tiers." As a first-tier, we had run our own stall and established our own production since our Tmall days. Besides, our mindset on e-commerce operations posed a challenge to them. In the future, it will definitely be the latecomer that prevails—we have not done well enough so far, and many e-commerce heavyweights have not yet entered the field.

Sister Zhen Design: Taking a Path of Brandification

We are now on a path of brandification. We were actually the first on Kuaishou to brand ourselves. In 2019, we began to put our own trademark—"Sister Zhen Design"—on every piece of clothing. At times, our designs would draw inspiration from hot-selling designs of the day, but production was entirely done by ourselves.

In reality, producing and selling our own goods does not reduce our costs by much. This is because we put the saved costs into our fabrics. For example, the wholesale unit price of a skirt is 50 yuan in markets such as Jinma and Wanjia, whereas the price of my self-produced skirt could be 53 yuan, albeit its quality is two grades higher. Self-production is not only for the sake of reducing costs. If the products I manufacture are the same as those in the markets, then I would earn a little more profit at most. Instead, by placing more emphasis on quality, what I am considering is our branding.

Nowadays, our followers highly approve of Sister Zhen Design. I have done a test by selling other brands on my livestream channel—few orders were placed. After all, my followers come to my livestream channel for the purpose of buying my "homemade" clothing; they can no longer accept the quality of goods on the market.

The core of branding is design. Capabilities in design and innovation are of utmost importance. We mainly employ a "purchasers + designers" model, with our purchasers spread across different markets in Guangzhou. We have our own homegrown designers, but they are still in the break-in period. Our purchasing team consists of six people who have followed me for many years and have a solid grasp of clothing designs.

We are actually very certain about Kuaishou's future trends. Unlike what many people believe, it is actually not just about selling goods. I believe that the two most important points about Kuaishou livestreaming are persona creation and brand building, which naturally complement each other. This is because Kuaishou is a people-centered platform, and so persona creation is the top priority. Branding also depends on the person—followers must feel that the livestreamer is trustworthy and dependable.

I feel that brands in the age of livestreaming are completely different in concept from brands in the traditional sense, which are dissociated from specific people. Traditional brands can become household names—for example, mention "ONLY" (a big brand in China) and everyone will think that the product must be high in quality and grade. What we hope to build is a brand that belongs to our livestream channel on Kuaishou; when followers buy Sister Zhen's clothing and find it good yet inexpensive, they would approve of Sister Zhen's brand and feel at ease buying more.

It has become very difficult—and in my opinion, pointless—to build a pan-Internet brand. This is because it is not possible for anyone to attract followers from all over the Internet to their livestream channel. It would suffice for Sister Zhen's followers to acknowledge her brand, which can be deemed a "fast brand."

Pain Point: Getting Out of the Vicious Circle of Low Pricing

We have a pain point, and that is an inability to match good quality with its due price. Although we have a brand that is highly approved of by our followers, we cannot increase the price of our products. This is despite the fact that Kuaishou followers are willing to pay for expensive things.

I believe that followers would rather buy things with high price-performance than things that are cheap. Therefore, after we have built up our brand, we would be able to raise prices appropriately.

We are currently selling clothing manufactured in our own factories. The goods we sell in Wanjia Market are all top-quality, while those sold in Shisanhang are also not bad. Even though my goods are made with expensive materials and high processing fees, I do not dare to sell them at a high price—this would lead people to counterfeit my products in small workshops using substitute fabrics, thus reducing the costs greatly. Once produced, the counterfeit goods would be sold at a much lower price than ours, bringing us nothing but agony.

I have a number of "sticky" followers who watch my livestreams regularly and know that my goods are of a different quality. However, newer followers who have never bought my things before would simply get the first impression that my things are more expensive than elsewhere. This is why I dare not sell my things at too high a price. I hope to attract and convert new followers, and thus I must keep prices low—even though this causes my operational costs to become a considerable burden.

However, through our efforts in self-production and brandification, we will soon escape the vicious cycle of low pricing. This is because we are selling things that others do not have. Furthermore, the followers who have approved of our brand will not look for low prices alone; instead, they will feel that it is reasonable for us to charge a few yuan more.

We Will Stratify Our Brand in the Future

Our future direction is brand stratification. We will first have a main brand that is sold at a fair price, and subsequently a slightly higher-end brand that is also sold on our livestream channel. We will intersperse a few designs every day and slowly increase the price per customer on our livestream channel.

We are currently focused on getting our main account in good order. We will soon see whether our model of "packaging livestreamers" (including collaborations with the entertainment circle and participation in local television programs) can work. Through our packaging plan, we will build the image of our livestreamers among followers and expand our renown, ultimately allowing us to increase our prices.

We also want to perform a supply chain integration that is aimed at the Kuaishou ecosystem. In other words, we want to export our existing factory resources, teams, designs, etc., and supply goods to livestreamers. In doing so, we will solve the pain point of livestreamers who lack a proper source of goods. This will be different from Kuaishou Alliance's "distribution library," which allows anyone to sell the goods and earn a commission. What we hope to build is a deep kind of cooperation. Everyone would negotiate a framework agreement together. For example, I would stock a certain clothing design for livestreamers at 5–10 percent below their selling price. They would not have to face any inventory pressures and can simply focus on selling goods, but they must sell a certain number of my designs every month.

In this way, we would bear responsibility for inventory risks, albeit we would do our best to control such risks. If sales are good, I would increase the stock by 60–70 percent, open the entire supply chain, and allow all livestreamers to sell my goods. Why are so few people able to create a product that is extremely high in price-performance these days? This is either because their goods are OEM products or they lack development capabilities and production knowledge. Conversely, we understand the entire system very well and have a superior control on costs, and our team-building has been honed for many years.

Kuaishou's development has been very fast. In my opinion, the era of Kuaishou e-commerce only truly arrived in the second half of 2019—it was a significant turning point that proved that Kuaishou recognized e-commerce and was determined to get it done well. The pandemic in 2020 sped up this development. I believe that many merchants will be weeded out within a year of development, leaving only those who can survive by 2021.

My Experience Running a Factory in Guangzhou

Our factory in Guangzhou has been around for five years already, and it employs approximately 60 people. Production also requires a system, and it can only be smoothed out after a long time of operation. It encompasses way too many phases. Firstly, fitting. Producing a piece of clothing requires going through various processes, including sampling, fabric selection, testing, modification, cost calculation, fabric and accessory procurement, delivery time confirmation, tailoring, and manufacturing. The tailoring process must be monitored to prevent wastage, while manufacturing will be performed by workers after tailoring is done. Subsequently, the goods can only be shipped after order handling and quality inspection have been completed.

The bigger one's clothing business on Kuaishou gets, the smaller the proportion of one's own factories becomes. The purpose of livestreamers having their own factories is mainly to increase their speed of response to unexpected "emergencies." For example, when a certain design experiences a surge in demand, those with their own factories would be able to handle the demand with greater flexibility and prioritize the production of this design. However, when one's sales volume reaches a certain level, one's own factories would be unable to satisfy demand. If you want both speed and flexible response, then coordinating with a small-sized factory of 30–40 workers would be better for scheduling and matching purposes. For example, if I have 50 designs today, then arrangements cannot be made and scheduling would have to be done. Big factories need to have a production plan and need to make arrangements at least one week in advance. For livestreamers, however, pre-sales usually last only seven days—so how can production analysis be done?

Source factories are usually OEMs that cannot build their own brands, and so they are at the very bottom of the food chain and earn little profits. The owner of a source factory earns two to three yuan per piece of clothing sold, which is a tiny profit on top of the production costs.

Due to the pandemic in 2020, many factories were left without work. We thus adjusted our strategy and sought long-term cooperation with 10 to 20 factories in Nancun Town, Panyu District, Guangzhou. We had not manufactured many of our products in Panyu previously because the factories there used to manufacture branded goods that were high in quality but also high in labor costs. Factories in Nancun are more standardized; there is usually little overtime or rushed production. We used to have greater cooperation with factories in Kangle Village, Haizhu District, but their products were only up to standard for Wanjia Square and not Shisanhang.

Were it not for the pandemic, the factories in Nancun would get a large number of orders from foreign brands. For example, if their production capacity is 5,000 pieces per day, they might break even at 3,000 pieces sold and make a profit on the remaining 2,000 pieces. These days, however, they cannot even get orders of 3,000 pieces. Their owners have thus had to reduce their own profits, such as from two yuan to one yuan per piece of clothing sold. They do so to preserve their production capacities and keep their workers. Furthermore, they still must pay fixed expenses such as tailors' salaries, packing costs, and factory rent.

A bona fide source factory would not do its own sales; all factories that do their own sales produce very expensive products. Factories in Guangzhou are very diverse in business format. In the clothing industry, there is a type of factory that has its own clothing designers and creates 100 designs every season. The factory earns a profit of at least 15 percent on every order, and so the costs to the livestreamer are fairly high. However, there are very few of such factories today—most factories do not have their own development capabilities.

There are also a small number of factories that employ nearly a thousand workers each—all of them have basically been contracted by the big brands of joint ventures or foreign enterprises. Because of a need to stock up in advance, the big brands would provide production schedule plans after entering into contracts with these factories. When we were producing summer wear, the factories of these brands were already producing autumn and winter wear. Factories of this scale have very high costs, such that they might not make a profit for the month if they go even one day without work. Therefore, their owners must ensure sufficient sales volumes, otherwise, it would be folly to maintain factories of this scale.

KUAISHOU DARK HORSE SISTER MI: HOW I BUILT A BRAND, DEVELOPED BASIC SKILLS, AND PLANNED FOR THE FUTURE

Key Points

- Sister Mi sold more than two million yuan worth of goods during her first livestream on Kuaishou. Many people call her a dark horse, but the truth is that she has 10 years of e-commerce experience and did not come out of nowhere.

- Sister Mi has her own clothing factory in Guangzhou that employs thousands of workers. This is very rare for a Kuaishou livestreamer. Why did she open her own factory instead of adopting the same OEM model as most people?

- Sister Mi basically sells the "Mi Rui" brand. She says that she is happy to incur some losses on her factory if it means that people in third- and fourth-tier cities are able to wear the same fashionable clothing as people in first- and second-tier cities.

It was in April 2019 when Sister Mi began livestreaming on Kuaishou. Back then, she had 120,000 followers, but this grew to 5,000,000 followers by June 2020. On June 6, 2020, she hosted a 40-minute livestream that generated sales of more than 10 million yuan; more than 1,000,000 orders were received that day, totaling 81 million yuan in sales. By the start of January 2021, she had more than nine million followers.

In August 2020, Sister Mi shared how she became a "dark horse" on Kuaishou.

The author of this chapter is Li Zhao, a senior researcher at Kuaishou Research Institute.

◎ *The following is an account by Wang Chen, husband of Sister Mi and founder of the "Sister Mi" team.*

. . .

When Sister Mi made her livestream debut on Kuaishou on April 28, 2019, we only had 120,000 followers. That day, we received more than 10,000 orders and achieved a GMV of more than two million yuan— our first taste of the "sweetness" of Kuaishou E-commerce. We originally intended to livestream once a week, but later changed this to once every other day. In July 2019, we began livestreaming every day. For the following two months, we were awarded the first prize for "rising influencers."

During the Kuaishou shopping carnival in November 2019, Sister Mi received more than 800,000 orders over two days, clinching second place for Kuaishou's clothing category and fourth place in the overall rankings. We had around 1.5 million followers at that time, yet we fared better than many top livestreamers who had tens of millions of followers. On June 16, 2020, Kuaishou held the "616 Quality Shopping Festival." That day, Sister Mi hosted a 40-minute livestream that generated sales of more than 10 million yuan; more than 1,000,000 orders were received that day, totaling 81 million yuan in sales. And in November 2020, Sister Mi's livestreams generated a total of 156 million yuan in sales.

We attribute Sister Mi's rapid rise to the following reasons:

The first is that, because of our 10 years of experience in e-commerce operation, we have complete teams for livestreaming, operations, after-sales, and customer service, and also have our own warehouse, logistics center, supply chain, and such.

The second is that we have an excellent source of goods. We have our own clothing factory—which employs thousands of workers—in Guangzhou, one of China's most important sources of clothing.

The third is that our products are very "close to life" and not the exaggerated sort. They are targeted at our follower base on Kuaishou and are superior in quality and price.

Before Becoming a "Dark Horse:" 10 Years of E-commerce Experience

Many people call us a dark horse on Kuaishou. The truth is that we have nearly 10 years of e-commerce experience and did not just come out of nowhere.

I came to Guangzhou in 2004 when I was 16 years old. It was my first time leaving Sichuan to seek work. I later returned to Wenjiang District in Chengdu to run a ladies' accessories business for two years. Subsequently, I went to Guangzhou again and started doing e-commerce on Taobao—that was in 2010 when I was 23 years old. Our business on Taobao has always been good. In 2012, we received around 5,000 orders per day, which should be among the highest on Taobao.

Why did I choose Guangzhou? Guangzhou's core advantage is its products. Hangzhou has Alibaba and focuses on Internet celebrities and business operations. Instead, Guangzhou has been the fashion capital of China for a century and is close to Shenzhen and Hong Kong. It is a very fashionable place—many brands were built up in Guangzhou. Labor costs can be very cheap here and are approximately 8–10 yuan cheaper than in Hangzhou. Nevertheless, workers are still able to make a living.

Our main-line products consist of three types: casual wear, fast fashion, and "temperament and style." We do not target a singular category of people, otherwise, we would lack variety. With the increase in the number of Taobao sellers, many product-oriented merchants like us have fallen on hard times. This is why we have crossed over to goods provision, 1688, and so on.

In 2013, we began transforming our business into a wholesale business. We set up our own stalls in Wanjia Clothing Wholesale Market in Guangzhou's Shahe Commercial District and Daying Clothing Wholesale Market in Humen Town, Dongguan, and mainly supplied goods to Taobao stores.

Later, we ran a wholesale business on Alibaba's 1688 platform for approximately five years. We were constantly ranked among the top and were the leader in women's clothing. The platform was initially only for product display, but transactions officially became possible about seven years ago.

> ## TIP
>
> ### Sister Mi's Entrepreneurship Path
>
> *In 2004, I went to Guangzhou to work, but later returned to Chengdu to run a brick-and-mortar store called "Aiyaya."*
>
> *In 2010, I began doing e-commerce on Taobao.*
>
> *By 2012, my business received around 5,000 orders a day, which was among thehighest on Taobao.*
>
> *In 2013, I transformed my business into a wholesale business. I opened stalls in Guangzhou's wholesale markets and mainly supplied goods to Taobao stores.*
>
> *In 2018, I began doing Alibaba 1688 Live.*
>
> *In 2019, I began doing Kuaishou E-commerce.*
>
> *In 2020, my sales for the year exceeded 1 billion yuan.*

Because we have the blood of e-commerce in our veins, we have a certain ability to operate an e-commerce business. Having come over from Taobao, things have been very convenient for us. Within a year or so, our output exceeded 100 million yuan. On Alibaba, we started out with a wholesale business and later did "Taohuoyuan". Alibaba has a few horizontal markets: the first is Taohuoyuan, which supplies goods to small sellers on Taobao; the second is Caiyuanbao, which supplies goods to WeChat merchants, and the third is Alibaba 1688 Live.

We started doing Alibaba 1688 Live in 2018. 1688 Live is different from Taobao Live; the two have completely different platform traffic. Taobao is targeted at consumers, whereas 1688 is targeted at merchants. We were highly popular on 1688 Live and amassed more than 20,000 viewers in total, while Sister Mi's livestream channel drew up to 3,000 concurrent viewers. By the same token, every one of our livestream sessions generated 10,000 orders or more. Sister Mi was the "First Sister" of 1688 Live at that time.

It was also around then that Kuaishou began doing e-commerce. However, we were a little reluctant to leave the 1688 platform and thus we decided to wait and see. I had begun paying attention to Kuaishou earlier on—this was around 2015 when Kuaishou had not offered livestreaming yet. I felt that Kuaishou was very "close to life" and found its clips very funny and unpretentious. Nowadays, people prefer to watch livestreamers rather than celebrities because they are closer to our lives.

I began posting videos on Kuaishou in 2018. They mainly consisted of Sister Mi's videos. After we started doing 1688 Live, many of our clients would ask us to film a few videos when collecting their goods. Sister Mi is akin to a model; videos of her can be found on every major platform. Before we started using Kuaishou, many agents were already reposting Sister Mi's videos on Kuaishou, and these videos often made it on to the Trending page. Hence, we later decided that we might as well post our videos on Kuaishou ourselves.

Seeing that the top livestreamers on Kuaishou could generate so many sales per day, we felt that we could probably do just as well as them. We figured that if we went on Kuaishou and challenged ourselves, we would have a chance to make 200 million yuan or even one billion yuan within a year. Therefore, on April 28, 2019, Sister Mi made her livestream e-commerce debut on Kuaishou.

Because we had nearly 10 years of e-commerce experience, we had complete teams for livestreaming, operations, after-sales, and customer service, and our own warehouse, logistics center, supply chain, and such. In our e-commerce team, there is a new media company that is responsible for managing all of the company's livestreamers. Aside from Sister Mi, we have also trained five livestreamers from scratch—each of them now has up to one million followers and can generate approximately 10,000 orders a day.

We Have Stocked Warehouses and Supplementary Factories

Nowadays on Kuaishou, some livestreamers have traffic but no goods, while some have goods but no experience in selling them. Business operation is very important; having high-quality goods does not necessarily mean that one would be able to sell well. Of course, astute operation is pointless without having any goods. Fortunately for us, we have all the necessary conditions—our warehouses contain goods that are high in quantity, quality, and diversity.

We currently have 1.5 million pieces of clothing in our warehouse, and they are all summer wear. I do not clear out my stock when everyone else is doing so; instead, I would continue to launch new products because I feel that this is viable in July, August, and times of seasonal change. I am unafraid of this risk because we have held deep inventories all these years and have no need to worry about inventory pressures. Our warehouse in Guangzhou is more than 10,000 square meters in area, and based on our storage and logistics capabilities, we can ship 200,000 orders per day.

More importantly, we have a supplementary clothing factory. When the pandemic struck in 2020, many clothing factories in the Pearl River Delta closed, causing many workers to lose their jobs. Instead, our clothing factory expanded and had more than 1,000 workers at one point in time.

This factory is wholly owned by us and is not under a partnership model. At the end of 2019, we opened a factory that specialized in fashionable clothing in Panyu District, Guangzhou. From site selection to construction to furnishment to production commencement, Kuaishou has witnessed every step of our growth.

Guangzhou is the source of clothing wholesale markets throughout China, and its clothing manufacturers are mostly concentrated in Panyu District. The source factories in Panyu produce branded goods and have mainly followed offline sales channels. When many of them closed due to the 2020 pandemic, some of their workers came over to our clothing factory. This was how we quickly expanded to more than 1,000 workers, exceeding our expectations.

In reality, a factory with 1,000-plus workers is still only able to produce 20,000-odd pieces of clothing per day. Yet, we get orders for 80,000 to 90,000 pieces of clothing in total per day on average. Back when we were still on Taobao or doing 1688 Live, the orders we received were already large enough, but they were not as large as what we get on Kuaishou Live.

Many clothing livestreamers prefer the model of OEM cooperation. However, we prefer opening our own factories. What is the difference, you ask? For example, if you engage an OEM, you would have to multiply the unit cost of a design by at least 2.5. In other words, for a unit cost of 10 yuan, you would have to pay 25 yuan, of which 10 yuan would go toward the workers' wages. And of the remaining 15 yuan, 10 yuan would cover the factory's costs, while five yuan would go to the owner. However, by opening our own factory, we only need to multiply the unit cost by 1.5. In other words, for a unit cost of 10 yuan, I would have to pay only 15 yuan, of which 10 yuan would go toward the workers' wages and five yuan toward covering the factory's costs—I can save on the five yuan for the factory owner.

This is why we have a price advantage on Kuaishou Live and can sell higher volumes than others. Although our factory incurs a loss, it does not matter as long as the company makes a profit overall.

Why am I willing to lose money in order to have my own factory? By producing my own goods, I can maximize their quality. Instead, if I were to engage an OEM, the quality might not be as consistent and there would be many uncontrollable elements.

On Kuaishou nowadays, there are "market livestreamers" who must procure goods from wholesale markets. Not only do the stalls need to make profits, but because such livestreamers do not have intellectual property rights, competition is cutthroat and they constantly seek to undercut one another. They are essentially market porters—if a market has 100 porters, consumers would seemingly have a lot of options but would be unable to discern the good stalls from the bad.

When pricing our clothing, we only look at the production costs of our factory and not at our competitors' prices. Because consumers approve of our brand, they naturally approve of our prices as well.

Building the "Mi Rui" Brand, Developing Basic Skills, and Planning for the Future

Opening one's own clothing factory is a very "heavy" business model. Perhaps this decision was not the wisest—generally speaking, the bigger one's business gets, the lighter one should become so as to make money faster. Why, then, did we choose to be so "heavy?" The reason is that I want to show my followers that we are not into making fast money and taking advantage of them financially. Instead, we want to do things better and closer to perfection, and so our strategy is more long-term and focused on the future.

I hope that we will eventually reach a point when consumers can obtain high- quality clothing for just dozens of yuan. All the clothing that we sell today belongs to the "Mi Rui" brand.

Based on my understanding, there are still not many clothing livestreamers on Kuaishou who truly have their own brands. The reason we have this advantage is that we were already building our own brand and owned a chain of dozens of brick-and-mortar stores prior to joining Kuaishou Live. Today, Mi Rui's quality is gradually improving, and it is also getting better in terms of style and fashion. We want every consumer to know that there is a clothing livestreamer called Sister Mi on Kuaishou and that she is a very professional seller, such that they can purchase high-quality factory goods on Kuaishou as well.

We do not only have our eyes on our existing loyal followers on Kuaishou. Instead, we are striving to increase the stylishness of our clothing gradually. While enabling users in first- and second-tier cities to purchase fashionable clothing on Kuaishou, we also hope that, in time, people in third- and fourth-tier cities would be able to wear clothing that is just as fashionable as what is worn by people in first- and second-tier cities.

Clothing aside, we have also developed a few branded skincare products that have their own registered trademark. We have engaged a first-tier brand processing factory to manufacture them.

What I pay attention to is whether our followers truly like Sister Mi and whether we get repeat customers, not how many new customers we get each month. We want consumers to understand us and not just Sister Mi. More importantly, we want them to understand the "Mi Rui" brand.

Livestreamers certainly play an important role. Many outstanding livestreamers such as "Sister Rui of Shijiazhuang" and Xu Xiaomi are typical examples of highly capable livestreamers. However, we believe that the better our strategy in terms of brand-building, source factories, and backend strength, the more successful we will become. What we are developing right now are the basic skills—it will be some time before we see who has the most staying power.

CHAPTER **THREE**

LINYI: CITY OF KUAISHOU

- The first batch of Kuaishou E-commerce livestreamers originated from the wholesale markets of Linyi. Today, Linyi is also one of the cities in China with the highest concentration of Kuaishou E-commerce livestreamers. Why Linyi of all places? And why its wholesale markets?

- Xu Xiaomi is a top livestreamer and rising star from Linyi. It took her only half a year to go from setting a record of tens of millions of yuan in daily sales to hitting hundreds of millions of yuan in daily sales. What is her recipe for success? And how did she surpass her peers?

CHAPTER CONTENTS

There are 136 specialized wholesale markets in Linyi, Shandong Province. Among them, Huafeng International Clothing City is a nationally-renowned clothing wholesale market and Linyi's first specialized wholesale market.

The author of this text is He Huafeng, vice-president of Kuaishou Technology and head of Kuaishou Research Institute.

It was the clothing wholesale markets of Linyi that gave birth to the first batch of Kuaishou E-commerce livestreamers nationwide. Today, Linyi is also one of the cities in China with the highest concentration of Kuaishou E-commerce livestreamers. Within a mere few years, tens of thousands of livestreamers have sprung up in Linyi, among whom are thousands of active livestreamers who are highly influential nationwide, including Taozi's, Damengzi, Super Dan, and Xu Xiaomi.

The locals proudly acclaim that "Kuaishou is the place for livestream e-commerce; Linyi is the place for Kuaishou E-commerce." Linyi has become "the city of Kuaishou" in both name and fact.

Linyi's livestream e-commerce has gone through the three phases of "rising from the grassroots," "enterprise operation," and "incorporation of brick-and-mortar heavyweights." Today, its top livestreamers are upgrading, iterating, exploring new business models, and developing their own brands.

Other cities would do well to learn from Linyi's exploration in the age of livestreaming.

LINYI: THE HISTORY AND INSPIRATION OF TRANSFORMING FROM A CITY OF WHOLESALE MARKETS INTO THE CITY OF KUAISHOU

Key Points

- Many female stall owners in Linyi have transformed into popular Internet celebrities overnight; their sales revenue per livestream session ranges from millions to hundreds of millions of yuan. How did they transform from husband-and-wife duos into livestream enterprises?

- After a certain livestreamer generated a greater sales revenue than several local enterprises combined, Linyi's marketplace magnates experienced a mix of doubt and fear and quickly entered livestream e-commerce. Could they be successful?

- Livestreamers connect good source products with consumers directly. As one of the biggest market clusters in China, how did Linyi's 136 wholesale markets make the transformation?

"At 11:02 p.m., Xu Xiaomi's promotional livestream exceeded 10 million yuan in sales!"

On April 28, 2020, the founder of Shandong Ricearth Network Technology Co., Ltd. (hereafter referred to as Ricearth Network), Song Jian, and two of Linyi's clothing marketplace magnates, Liu Yilin and Du Bin, were gathered on a rooftop in Linyi's Shunhe Livestream E-commerce Technology Industrial Park together with a few suppliers. All of them had their heads lowered to watch the livestream of Xu Xiaomi, a livestreamer from Ricearth Network, on Kuaishou. In the meantime, an employee was on standby to inform them of the backend figures for sales on that night.

When the sales revenue exceeded 10 million yuan, everyone toasted in celebration of this new record. That night, Xu Xiaomi livestreamed for more than six hours and generated more than 280,000 orders, with sales revenue exceeding 12 million yuan. Just half a year later, on November 2nd, Xu Xiaomi hit more than 100 million yuan in daily sales.

As a Kuaishou livestreamer, Xu Xiaomi is a rising star. Linyi's earliest well-known livestreamers include Taozi's, Damengzi, Super Dan, and Sister Bei, who are together called the "Four Golden Flowers."

Linyi is a hotbed for nationally renowned Kuaishou livestreamers. Most of them had crossed over from being merchants in traditional wholesale markets.

Rising from the Grassroots: "Second-Tier Young People" Became the First Batch of Livestreamers

Linyi has 136 specialized wholesale markets, which together comprise more than 80,000 merchants and more than 300,000 workers. Among the various wholesale markets, Huafeng International Clothing City (henceforth referred to as Huafeng) is the most famous and the first large-scale specialized wholesale market throughout Linyi and even the entire Shandong Province.

During the decade preceding 2018, Linyi's wholesale markets enjoyed extremely good business, such that Huafeng enjoyed a glorious period of history.

Among Linyi's first batch of Kuaishou livestreamers, Taozi's and Damengzi were previously top merchants in Huafeng. Taozi's mainly sold women's clothing while Damengzi mainly sold men's clothing, with both enjoying annual turnovers of tens of millions of yuan. Although their brick-and-mortar stores were doing very well back then, they nevertheless faced two problems.

The first problem was that clothing wholesale businesses had a limited geographical reach, which was confined to southern Shandong and northern Jiangsu. Huafeng is a "second-tier" that needs to procure goods from "first-tiers" throughout China, such as Guangzhou's Wanjia Square and Shisanhang. Goods are then sold via Huafeng to counties in Linyi as well as some parts of southern Shandong and northern Jiangsu.

The second problem was that the trading mechanism between clothing wholesalers and retail marketplaces often led to arrears and excess inventory stocks. Wholesalers are not immediately paid for the goods they supply to marketplaces; instead, settlement is only made after the marketplaces have sold the goods, posing difficulties for wholesalers' cashflow turnover. In addition, the goods that marketplaces are unable to sell must be returned, causing the biggest pain point of all "second-tiers"— high inventory levels.

Furthermore, marketplaces can bypass wholesale markets entirely and procure goods from first-tiers directly. Or they can even procure goods directly from source factories and brands.

Due to a mix of multiple factors, doing business in Huafeng became increasingly difficult. It was just then when "second-tier young people" such as Taozi's and Damengzi discovered a new sales channel in Kuaishou.

Taozi's started using Kuaishou as early as 2017. She discovered that Kuaishou was not just an entertainment tool but also contained a lot of trading information and could be used to sell goods.

In the summer of 2018, Taozi's began focusing her energy on promotional livestreaming, with her main goal initially being to sell her own inventory. She discovered that the results were great—she would get several hundred orders a day, which was more than her sales in Huafeng. Hence, her focus gradually shifted from wholesale to promotional livestreaming, and she eventually gave up her wholesale business completely to specialize in livestream e-commerce. During the "Singles' Day" event in 2019, she received more than 400,000 orders over two days, with a total turnover of 20 million yuan—back then, she was the "First Sister of Linyi" in livestream e-commerce.

"I remember most clearly that I made 100 yuan on my first day on Kuaishou. There were only five viewers on my channel, but this quickly increased after several days of livestreaming." It was around the end of May 2018 when Damengzi sold goods via Kuaishou for the first time. Because she had worked for 10 years in Huafeng, she was very professional when it comes to clothing and had ready sources of goods. As a result, her sales on Kuaishou quickly boomed. She said, "Things were great back then. I sold out several thousand pieces of clothing in a flash. At first, I received orders via WeChat and had dozens of customer service officers working the backend, which was a spectacular sight indeed. Later on, my order-receiving capabilities improved when I switched to a Kuaishou Store. On June 18, 2019, I received 100,000 orders that amounted to a turnover of several million yuan, shocking many of my peers."

By using Kuaishou Live, "second-tier young people" such as Taozi's and Damengzi have, on the one hand, solved the problems of high inventory levels and arrears owed by retail marketplaces, and on the other hand, broken through the old geographical limitations—which was confined to southern Shandong and northern Jiangsu—to sell their products throughout China.

"I remember most clearly that I felt a strange and novel feeling when my loyal followers from Gansu and Inner Mongolia bought my clothing. This was because I could only sell goods to nearby counties back when I was doing wholesale, so I suddenly discovered a bright and warm feeling on Kuaishou," said Damengzi.

By livestreaming, Taozi's, Damengzi, and others have connected high-quality source goods directly with the mass consumers and transformed from "second-tier young people" into Kuaishou livestreamers.

The confined space in each and every wholesale market stall is no longer suitable for the new business model. In 2018, Taozi's was the first to close its brick-and-mortar store in Huafeng and open its own livestream studio, thus switching its focus completely to livestream e-commerce.

Her approach was copied by many "second-tier young people" such as Damengzi and Sister Bei. In this way, Huafeng became a breeding ground of livestream e-commerce and a source of e-commerce livestreamers.

"Because the few of us did well on Kuaishou, thousands of merchants from Linyi's wholesale markets, especially Huafeng, began to do livestreaming as well," said Taozi's.

Enterprise Operation: Xu Xiaomi Came from Behind to Take the Lead

Unlike Taozi's and Damengzi, who started out as "second-tier young people," Xu Xiaomi previously ran a WeChat business that employed 20,000 people at its peak. However, the team racked up huge debts when business declined. Influenced by Damengzi, Xu decided in September 2018 to do e-commerce on Kuaishou. Figure 3.1 shows Xu's homepage on Kuaishou.

"It was by chance that I saw Damengzi doing very impressively on Kuaishou. I then told my boss, Song Jian, about it. At first, he did not believe it and felt that it was a scam," said Xu. Under her persistence, however, Song allowed her to give it a try—she made 1,400 yuan on the first day. Realizing that Xu was a good salesperson and that Kuaishou E-commerce was developing steadily upward, Song decided to go all-out on it and told Xu to run livestreaming as an enterprise rather than a business.

Linyi's early livestreamers, including the "Four Golden Flowers," mostly started out as husband-and-wife duos. When they crossed over to livestreaming, the wife became the livestreamer while the husband took charge of operations, and so everything was managed by one person. Instead, from their very first day on Kuaishou, Ricearth Network—the company that Xu works for— ran livestreaming in a formal, corporate manner. The livestreamer was only responsible for

Figure 3.1 Xu Xiaomi's Homepage on Kuaishou

the final stage of product selection and the on-stream promotion of goods, while everything else was handled by the company's relevant department. Therefore, Ricearth Network remained in a loss-making state for the first six months of livestreaming—Song calls it a "strategic loss."

However, Xu's sales grew steadily and doubled by June 2019, becoming profit-making. During the Spring Festival of 2020, Ricearth Network's figures showed that they generated 120 million yuan in sales for the year of 2019, surpassing those of the "Four Golden Flowers."

On April 28, 2020, Xu Xiaomi's promotional livestream generated 12 million yuan in sales, ranking first among clothing e-commerce livestreams nationwide. This became noted in Linyi's e-commerce circle, drawing the attention and thought of other livestreamers from Linyi.

"Song Jian's enterprise framework is very sound. Xu Xiaomi's emergence has provided livestreamers with a new way of thinking that husband-and-wife duos like us really ought to think about," said Super Dan.

Super Dan has more than nine million followers on Kuaishou (as of January 2021), making her one of the most followed livestreamers from Linyi and one of the top livestreamers in the shoe category nationwide. She believes that she has been fairly successful in terms of sales and follower accumulation but is rather slow to develop in various aspects related to the transformation from a husband- and-wife duo into an enterprise.

"Over the past few years of doing Kuaishou, we have been highly stretched and exhausted to the point of collapse and thus haven't had time to pause and think. People often say that we must look at today from the perspective of the future and make plans for tomorrow, but we haven't done so for a very long time," said Super Dan.

"Why is Xu Xiaomi successful? What in the future will affect her development? I have long been thinking about the issue of our enterprise's sustainable development and have come up with three points: livestreamers, products, and team," said Song Jian.

Ricearth Network currently employs 300 people and six livestreamers, among which Xu accounts for 80 percent of the total sales. As of April 29, 2020, 178 employees serve Xu alone. Song said, "From the start, we have done livestream e-commerce as a business and made plans for Ricearth Network as a company. Therefore, our system is more standardized and our division of work is more meticulous."

For the sake of Ricearth Network's long-term development, Song engaged a human resource company in Shanghai to assist him in refining the corporate culture, sorting out the internal structure of the company, planning the overall processes of each department, and constructing a corporate system and its key processes, as well as analyzing the obstacles that the company will face down the road, such as what sales strategy to adopt after the sales performance of the livestreamers have doubled, whether the corporate structure will hold strong in that event, and what areas need to be improved to keep on doubling the sales performance of the livestreamers. Ricearth Network was the first livestream e-commerce company in China to engage the consulting services of this human resource company, which had served a few Global 500 companies before.

Several top livestreamers in Linyi are also conducting enterprise transformation. Taozi's said, "We already have an impeccable financial system and finance team today, including accountants, assistant accountants, and treasurers. Our personnel structure and team organization are highly complete and aligned with corporate development. Our reserves are also excellent and sufficient to support our development of n number of brands."

Incorporation of Brick-and-mortar Heavyweights: The Establishment of Linyi's Livestreaming Chamber of Commerce

The success of Xu Xiaomi directly led Linyi's first-tier clothing marketplace magnates to join Kuaishou Live. The more typical examples among them include Liu Yilin, Wu Jun, and Du Bin.

Liu Yilin, director at Shandong Baichenghui, has witnessed the development history of Linyi's clothing markets. He is also the founder of Linyi's clothing retail marketplace model. He began working as a clothing street vendor at the age of 18 and subsequently worked as a wholesale merchant in Huafeng for eight years. In 2003, he opened Linyi's first clothing retail mall in Yinan County.

"Back then, many small stalls in southern Shandong and northern Jiangsu procured their goods from Linyi's wholesale markets. I was the first wholesale merchant to open a large marketplace," said Liu. Today, Baichenghui has nearly 100 malls to its name, with many of them having tens of thousands of square meters in area. In total, these malls employ up to 2,500 people and generate an annual revenue in excess of 1 billion yuan.

While Liu was the first person from Linyi to open a marketplace in a county seat, Wu Jun, chairman of Guihe Commerce and Trade, was the first person from Linyi to open a marketplace in a town. In 2004, he opened a clothing mall that covered several hundred square meters in area in Yitang Town, Linyi.

"We earned a profit of 20,000 yuan on our first day of business, and 50,000 to 60,000 yuan on the second day. From then on, I knew that the chain store model with centralized procurement and chain development was definitely feasible," Wu said.

"Liu Yilin and Wu Jun 'made money lying down' back then. In the past, if I was looking to buy a pair of trousers but a shop did not offer it, I would have had to visit a different shop. Then, if I wanted to buy a pair of shoes, I would have had to find yet another shop. But suddenly, someone opened a large marketplace that sold shirts, trousers, and shoes for men, women, and even children. As soon as this one-stop marketplace model emerged, Linyi's brick-and-mortar stores boomed," said Damengzi. During the phase when small stalls and vendors transformed into large-scale supermarkets and malls, Liu and Wu controlled the points of sale while Taozi's of Huafeng Market served as a supplier. "That was the golden age of not only Liu Yilin's and Wu Jun's marketplaces but also wholesale merchants like us and more so Huafeng Market."

"Liu Yilin was also considered an industry pioneer during the age of traditional commerce. From a spatial perspective, his malls were well-positioned and high in traffic. He was thus the 'Xu Xiaomi' of that age," said Song. "However, because the age of livestreaming is despatialized, the location advantages of brick-and-mortar stores have greatly declined. The large marketplace business model is past its golden age. As the commercial revolution entered its next phase, Taozi's, Damengzi, and Super Dan became the industry pioneers in the age of livestream e-commerce."

The successes of Taozi's, Damengzi, and others have not only impelled many wholesale merchants to cross over to do e-commerce on Kuaishou but also attracted the attention of marketplace magnates such as Liu and Wu, leading them to set up Kuaishou accounts. Unlike "second-tier" merchants, they did not manage livestream operations themselves but instead assigned their subordinate departments to give it a try. However, because they as the top leaders did not pay much attention to livestreaming, their employees often gave up halfway.

Du Bin, chairman of Shandong Lidu Clothing and Accessories, has more than 50 malls and clothing stores to his name. At first, he did not look favorably on livestream e-commerce, instead spending much of his energy on high-end customization and on founding Woiwoga, a first-tier brand in China. That was until one day when Xu Xiaomi claimed that she alone could outsell Liu, Wu, and him combined. It was only then that Du truly realized the power of livestream e-commerce.

"Around September 2019, Xu Xiaomi warned the three of us that she would surpass us the following year. Back then, we didn't believe her and found her words funny. Liu even told her that she was too arrogant. But when we saw the figures on Kuaishou, we felt that what she said was actually possible. It was then that we panicked a little and began to think about what we should do next. True to her prediction, the value that she alone created in 2020 surpassed the combined value created by the three of us and our 4,000 to 5,000 employees," said Du.

As Liu, Du, Wu, and others became more and more impressed by Xu, they began to take Kuaishou seriously once again.

"We were one step behind the competition, so our advantage turned into a disadvantage. Today, we can only 'catch the last bus.' We thought highly of ourselves when we were doing marketplaces, but we now feel like absolute beginners and must learn from Xu Xiaomi and Damengzi," Liu said. He has already decided to go all-in on livestreaming and treat it as a top-level project in his company.

During the 2020 pandemic when Linyi's clothing stores were forced to close, Du mobilized the employees from his 50-odd malls to do Kuaishou. He said, "While others chose to stay home and avoid risks during the pandemic, I instead chose to go against the flow and work on filming Kuaishou videos. Several of my clips made it on to Trending page and increased my followers. I not only sold out my inventory but also explored models for doing livestream e-commerce."

"In September 2019, I made the decision to terminate our Kuaishou account. I now regret that immensely," said Wu Jun. Together with Taozi's, Damengzi, and Super Dan, he was originally part of the first batch of people from Linyi to do Kuaishou, but he—like Liu Yilin—did not take it seriously. Worried that livestreaming would affect sales in his brick-and-mortar stores, he terminated the company's Kuaishou account. "That was my biggest strategic error. I now have no choice but to restart the plan. I have specially established a livestream e-commerce company and built a livestream studio and warehouse. Like Song Jun and Xu Xiaomi, I will implement standardized operations and go all-out in doing Kuaishou E-commerce."

In November 2019, Liu, Du, and several other clothing magnates from Linyi jointly established the Maibo Group, with Du serving as the chairman and CEO of this livestream e-commerce enterprise.

On August 24, 2020, the Linyi Federation of Industry and Commerce's Short Video and Livestreaming Chamber of Commerce was formally established. Its founders included Yilin, Bin, Jun, and other representatives from clothing enterprises, as well as Xu Xiaomi, Damengzi, Super Dan, and other livestreamers. Yilin was elected as its president while Du was elected as its executive president.

"Many of our partners in the brick-and-mortar economy are eager to sell their products via livestreaming so that they won't lose out on the future. Our vision in establishing a livestreaming chamber of commerce is to carry out commercial reform together with everyone." On August 24, Du Bin spoke at the founding conference of the Linyi Federation of Industry and Commerce's Short Video and Livestreaming Chamber of Commerce. "All of us started from scratch. The field of livestreaming is full of dangers and business opportunities. There are no experts in this field—it is only through application and perseverance that everyone can find a place for themselves."

Livestream Bases: Wholesale Markets Seek a Transformation

When people like Taozi's began doing Kuaishou in 2018, they were supported by Huafeng. However, Huafeng changed its attitude toward them upon seeing the impact of livestream e-commerce's price advantages over brick- and-mortar stores.

"When we decided to start selling goods on Kuaishou, we never imagined there would come a day when we would discontinue our brick-and-mortar stores. However, we had no choice but to do so after we were prohibited from livestreaming in markets—we were forced out," said Taozi's.

In 2018, Taozi's was the first to give up on her brick-and-mortar store in Huafeng and set up her own livestream studio. The studio was based in a rented apartment with an area of 100-odd square meters at first, but was subsequently moved to a studio with an area of 2,000 square meters. Today, Taozi's livestream operations center is located in Lingu E-commerce Sci. & Tech Innovation Incubation Park. This four-story office building and a warehouse in Machanghu Industrial Park together provide more than 20,000 square meters in area.

When people like Taozi's were forced out of Huafeng, others instead spotted an opportunity—they established specialized livestream e-commerce bases or parks and invited livestreamers to join them.

Lingu—where Taozi's company is located—is an iconic e-commerce livestream base in Linyi. Because it was previously a traditional wholesale market for textiles and foodstuffs under the Lanhua Group, it contains more than 20 abandoned factories that were built two decades ago. In 2019, seizing the opportunities afforded by the emergence of many livestreamers in Linyi, the Lanhua Group rebuilt these factories into livestreaming buildings.

On October 18, 2019, Lingu's first-phase buildings were officially opened, with Taozi's and Super Dan among the first batch of livestreamers to move in. Today, following the addition of the second-phase construction on the west side, the park has more than 30 livestreaming buildings and accommodates dozens of livestreamers.

"The original 'textile and foodstuff city' collected an annual rent of nearly 9 million yuan in total. But after it was rebuilt into Lingu Livestream Base, the annual rent collected by the first-phase buildings alone is more than 24 million yuan," said Nie Wenchang, director of the Linyi E-commerce Public Service Center and founder of Xingu Digital Technology. As the first manager of Lingu E-commerce Sci. & Tech Innovation Incubation Park, he was one of the first people in Linyi to realize the value of livestream e-commerce bases and parks.

After the rise of Kuaishou's livestream e-commerce, the Shunhe Group, a traditional business logistics enterprise in Linyi, decided to build a new type of livestream e-commerce park. In December 2018, the Shunhe Group rebuilt Shunhe Home Furnishing City Building No. 5 into Shunhe Livestream E-commerce Town, the first livestream e-commerce base in Linyi.

The transformation of Shunhe Home Furnishing City is a micro-cosm of the transformation of Linyi's wholesale markets. In 2014, this building made plans to become a wholesale market for home furnishing materials in collaboration with Red Star Macalline. In 2015, an Internet company from Hangzhou moved in and built a Taobao eco-city. In 2016, the building reached a collaboration with the Qingdao Fuerma Group to become an eco-city for home furnishings, but the plans never material-ized. In 2017, the Shunhe Group decided to manage the building itself and transformed it into a wholesale market for home furnishing mate-rials, but business was poor. Finally, in December 2018, Shunhe Home Furnishing Building No. 5 was rebuilt into Shunhe Livestream E-commerce Town. At the same time, just across the street, a second livestream e-commerce base was built in Shunhe Maternal and Child Supplies City, another building owned by the Shunhe Group.

In 2019, Zhao Guoqiang, son of the Shunhe Group's founder Zhao Yuxi, became the chairman of Shunhe Home Furnishing City and Shunhe Maternal and Child Supplies City. He decided to merge the two buildings into Shunhe E-commerce Livestream Technology Industrial Park, with the 100,000 m2 Shunhe Home Furnishing City serving as the park's first-phase building, and the 50,000 m2 Shunhe Maternal and Child Supplies City serving as the park's second-phase building.

"Linyi has 136 specialized wholesale markets, and so competition in that business is very cutthroat. Traditional markets are no longer lucrative for merchants. Many vacant malls are thus seeking trans-formation. Shunhe Home Furnishing City is part of the first batch of buildings in Linyi to transform into a livestream e-commerce base. It has been fairly successful and has the highest occupancy rate in Linyi," said Zhao.

Today, Linyi has more than 10 livestream bases and parks. All of them were converted from wholesale markets, industrial parks, or tradi-tional malls. Among them, Shunhe E-commerce Livestream Technology Industrial Park and Lingu E-commerce Sci. & Tech Innovation Incuba-tion Park are the more representative ones.

Linyi's livestream bases provide livestreamers with a place for livestreaming and operating, warehousing and logistical services, and data and operation services, as well as supply chain and other services. Zhao said that after two years of finding its way about, Shunhe Livestream Industrial Park is now undergoing upgrade and iteration and has mainly done the following things: The first is the construction of a 60,000 m2 smart cloud warehouse that is equipped with automatic sorting equipment and automatic storage. After it is built, up to 200,000 orders can be shipped per day.

The second is the creation of an optimal supply chain. Because the Shunhe Group is one of Linyi's six largest business logistics groups and has supply chains and smart cloud warehouses throughout China, it can provide livestreamers with cheap yet excellent products.

The third is the provision of 5G (fifth-generation mobile communications technology) shared livestreaming services to livestreamers. By making use of 5G Internet to deliver product status information from smart cloud warehouses throughout China to livestreamers's livestream studios in real time, it has enabled livestreamers to select products from all over China without stepping out of Linyi. "Operating a livestreaming park is not something that can be done once and for all or only by looking at the present. Livestreaming parks and bases must constantly provide merchants with more services not just in physical space but also in extending to related industries. Iteration, innovation, and upgrade must be continuously done for livestream e-commerce and its extended industries," said Nie. He is currently devising an upgraded livestreaming park in Linyi—China Xingu Livestreaming HQ, which takes up 560,000 m2 in land area. For this new project, he plans to build brands and bring in brands such as Nike and Adidas.

During the transformation of Linyi's wholesale markets and traditional malls, several organizations and enterprises from places such as Hangzhou and Guangzhou also played a part. Zhao explains, "Because Linyi has many livestreamers and is logistically well-developed, organizations from all over China are coming here. Mockuai has built a livestream base in Lanshan District, Yowant has built a brand mall in Hedong District, and Kmeila is also preparing to build a supply chain base in Linyi. Meanwhile, JD and SF Express are also looking for land here to build warehouses on."

Taozi's believes that Huafeng also had an opportunity to do livestream e-commerce initially—its fourth floor, fifth floor, and top floor were all vacant. Had it converted some of this space into livestream studios, it could have become a leader in Linyi's livestream e-commerce sector. Instead, this opportunity has been seized by Shunhe and Lingu.

Huafeng is now also undergoing transformation—30 percent of its wholesale business owners are already doing livestreaming on the side. An operations head in Huafeng has also visited Lingu to see how Taozi's does her livestreaming. Taozi's said that livestream e-commerce is a trend and a new retail format that cannot be ignored, and so even wholesale markets have to make the crossover.

TIP

Linyi's Main Livestream Bases

· *December 2018: Shunhe Livestream E-commerce Town (first phase of Shunhe Livestream E-commerce Technology Industrial Park), Shunhe Maternal and Child Supplies E-commerce Livestream Town (second phase of Shunhe Livestream E-commerce Technology Industrial Park)*

· *September 2019: Linyi Weiye Livestream Base*

· *October 2019: Lingu E-commerce Sci. & Tech Innovation Incubation Park*

· *June 2020: Yunzhigu Supply Chain Livestream Town*

· *November 2020: China Xingu Livestream HQ*

2021: Yowant Technology Linyi E-commerce Livestream Industry Base

---

Product Upgrading: Emphasize Product Quality and Incubate Brands

Having gone through a period of development, Linyi's merchants are now developing toward brandification.

Song Jian said, "Incubating our own brands is a very important strategy for Ricearth Network in 2020. We have an independent cosmetics trademark called 'Jiangnan Impression.' When Xu Xiaomi was promoting it, it sold better than a few big brands. We are now working on its third upgrade and preparing to build it into a 'fast brand.'"

Ricearth Network also has two clothing brands, namely "Jouiemee" and "Quansheng." "Jouiemee" is mainly focused on underwear and is manufactured by self-sourced factories. It is also preparing a few other brands that will cover categories such as home appliances, washing, food, and home furnishing.

"Having our own brands gives us the power to control their quality and set their prices. Brands are very important for our company's development. They are the core competencies of future livestreamers and also serve as barriers to competition. For Linyi's livestreamers to cross over, brandification is a path that must be taken. Brand incubation requires time, and this time difference represents one's competitive edge," said Song.

The Maibo Group also plans to incubate a few brands, such as "Huaguan" for cosmetics, "Three Fish" for washing, and "Good Family Life" for home furnishing. Liu Yilin said, "Creating brands will be the direction for the next step of our development. If we cannot keep up with things, we will definitely be eliminated by the competition."

Kuaishou livestreamer Xiye believes that she went through several phases during her crossover from a brick-and-mortar business to livestream e-commerce in 2018. The first was a transitional phase when she did livestream e-commerce while continuing to run her brick-and-mortar stores. The second was when she ascertained that livestream e-commerce was the trend of the times and thus devoted her full attention to it after closing all her brick-and-mortar stores. The third was a phase of brandification when she adopted the "super factory" model and launched co-branded products in collaboration with several famous brands such as Bonas, U.S. Polo, and Kangol.

"Because I did the designing myself, I would modify and redesign each piece of clothing according to my followers' demands," said Xiye. In April 2020, she took part in Guangzhou Fashion Week, greatly increasing her brand recognition among followers and enjoying the financial benefits brought about by brandification. During the "sales off-season" for other merchants, she instead received more sales than before, with a price per customer of approximately 240 yuan for clothing and more than 400 yuan for home textiles. She said, "We shifted toward brands to elevate ourselves to the height of fashion."

In Linyi, Taozi's and Damengzi have both begun to develop their own brands. Taozi's has her own factory in Guangzhou and a joint venture company in Hangzhou, and she is currently developing several all-category trademarks. Damengzi began paying attention to brand planning in the winter of 2019; all of her clothing is labeled with the "Damengzi" brand. In the future, she will have her own mid-range and high-end brands.

"We have always wanted to create our own brands, but we knew we had to get our quality right first—only then would our followers approve of our brands and livestreamers and thereby be willing to make repeat or expensive purchases," said Damengzi.

TIP

Notable Events Related to Livestream E-commerce in Linyi

· *October 1987: Linyi's first specialized wholesale market—Huafeng Wholesale Market—opened for business. Today, Linyi has 136 specialized wholesale markets.*

· *June 2018: Taozi's, a "second-tier" merchant, left Huafeng Wholesale Market to focus on Kuaishou E-commerce. Other "second-tier young people" followed suit. Top livestreamers including Taozi's, Damengzi, Super Dan, and Sister Bei became known asLinyi's "Four Golden Flowers."*

· *December 2018: Linyi's first livestream e-commerce base—Shunhe Livestream E-commerce Town—was established. Today, Linyi has more than 10 livestream bases and parks.*

· November 6, 2019: During Kuaishou's shopping carnival event, Taozi's received more than 400,000 orders over two days, generating a turnover of nearly 20 million yuan.

· Linyi Express Industry Association announced that Linyi's express order volume for 2018 was 850,000 orders per day. This rose sharply to two million orders per day in 2019.

· After the 2020 Spring Festival: A batch of enterprises from Linyi's brick-and- mortar economy entered the livestream e-commerce industry.

· April 28, 2020: Xu Xiaomi received 280,000 orders worth 12 million yuan in six hours, setting a new record among Linyi's livestream e-commerce businesses.

· August 24, 2020: The Linyi Federation of Industry and Commerce's Short Video and Livestreaming Chamber of Commerce was established.

· September 19, 2020: The inaugural China (Linyi) 919 Livestreaming Festival wassuccessfully held.

November 2, 2020: Xu Xiaomi's sales exceeded 100 million yuan.

THE MAKING OF XU XIAOMI, A TOP LIVESTREAMER ON KUAISHOU

Key Points

- Since Linyi has so many outstanding livestreamers, how did the latecomer Xu Xiaomi surpass them all?

- How did Xu create her persona, choose her products, and build her team?

- What does Xu's company, Ricearth Network, think of the competition going forward?

On September 26, 2018, Xu Xiaomi hosted her first livestream on Kuaishou, garnering 1,400 yuan in sales. This gave her the confidence that promoting goods on Kuaishou was indeed possible. On April 28, 2020, she generated sales worth 12 million yuan in one night, setting a record among Linyi's livestream e-commerce merchants. On November 2, 2020, she livestreamed for nearly nine hours, generating sales of more than 100 million yuan for the first time, while her followers increased to 6.5 million from over 1.5 million in April. Although Xu was not the first person from Linyi to do livestreaming, she has ultimately risen above the competition, surpassing the "Four Golden Flowers" and becoming the "First Sister" of Linyi's livestream e-commerce industry.

"Livestreaming has changed the destiny of a generation of people—I'm just one of them," said Xu. Regarding her own success, Xu believes that she has simply done something that suits her at the right time and in the right place. Her boss, Song Jian, has been crucial to the development of her and her team. Since April 2020, Song has shared his experiences and methods of crossing over from a WeChat business to livestream e-commerce on several occasions. He has also talked about how Xu transformed from a livestreaming "onlooker" into a top livestreamer who has generated sales of more than 100 million yuan in one day.

◎ *The following is an account by Song Jian, founder of Ricearth Network.*

. . .

How We Overtook Others in Doing Livestream E-commerce

Early on, I calculated that we lost 540,000 yuan in total in one day, yet I was very happy about it—a loss of just 540,000 yuan on a sales figure of 5 million yuan could be called a strategic loss. In June 2019, our sales performance doubled to 7 million yuan in monthly sales; this figure was the sum of the sales figures for the previous few months. From then on, we began to be profitable. The Kuaishou shopping carnival that started on November 6, 2019, produced momentous changes for us. Over this three-day event, Xu sold more than 6 million yuan worth of goods, adding up to more than 8 million yuan when combined with the figures for our other livestreamers.

During the 2020 Spring Festival, our statistics showed that our yearly sales amounted to 120 million yuan. This was a relatively happy year for me. The past five or six years had been full of ups and downs; whenever I thought I had finally achieved something, it would instead end in failure. This was also a year when Xu's sales figure surpassed that of other livestreamers in Linyi. One of our partners, Liu Yilin, constantly advised Xu to keep a low profile, but this became impossible after the fact. In Linyi, every livestreamer's sales figure is publicly disclosed.

Before doing livestream e-commerce, Xu lived by credit card—she would spend half of every month thinking about how to juggle her six or seven credit cards. In July 2020, when more than 10 media outlets came to interview our company, someone asked Xu what her "life happiness index" was currently. Xu replied that she had no time to spend money at the moment. She once told me in private that she felt like she had been in a dream all this time because life did not feel real. She is highly grateful to Kuaishou and believes that livestreaming has truly changed the destiny of a generation of people.

Why is Xu successful? What in the future will affect her development? I have long been thinking about the issue of our enterprise's sustainable development and have come up with three points: livestreamers, products, and team.

Three of Xu Xiaomi's Traits as a Livestreamer

It was purely by chance that Linyi's early livestreamers, including Xu Xiaomi, were able to succeed. In my opinion, prior to 2019, these people made money predominantly through luck, with ability playing only a small part.

Taozi's, Damengzi, and other livestreamers had inherent advantages; they previously did clothing wholesale businesses and thus already had channels for procuring goods. It would not have mattered if they failed to sell their goods on Kuaishou; they could simply go back to doing wholesale, and so the costs of trial and error were fairly low for them.

Few people did Kuaishou at first, albeit the platform provided huge traffic. Yet, why were Taozi's, Damengzi, Super Dan, and Xu Xiaomi the only ones who stood out? This was because their personas were good. For example, Taozi's has a forthright personality, and so many people liked her.

Our company started out with six livestreamers, among which a few were sifted out halfway, leaving only Xiaomi and "Dingding's Outfits." We added a few more livestreamers later, such as Xiaomi's disciple, Ruizi. Xiaomi's sales make up 80 percent of our total sales, amounting to more than 4 million yuan per day. Although Dingding started at the same time as Xiaomi, the gap between them is huge. At present, Xiaomi has 6.5 million-odd followers, while Dingding has 500,000-odd followers (as of November 2020) and has not been improving in sales performance. In all honesty, I have always provided for them equally in terms of product matching, team operations, and logistical services. Therefore, it is the individual that is most important—despite promoting the same goods, their results have been vastly different.

Many people have asked me how I trained Xu Xiaomi. To be honest, I don't know either. However, I feel that she has come so far because of two reasons: firstly, she has seized the opportunity that is livestreaming, and secondly, she is indeed extremely well-suited to being a livestreamer.

I feel that her calling in life is precisely to be a livestreamer. Firstly, she is extroverted, warm, likable, and kind and gentle in appearance. More importantly, she is sincere—followers can sense whether a livestreamer is being devious. You can put on an act for one or two days, but certainly not for a year. Xiaomi never "acts," which is just like myself—when I am angry, I show that I am angry. This kind of genuine temperament is instead well-liked by many people. Mentality is also very important; Xiaomi is patient, resolute, and not bothered by criticism.

In June 2020, Xiaomi's mental strength went up a notch. In the past, she cared a lot about the number of viewers she got. There was a period when she constantly drew 30,000-odd viewers to her livestream channel; in particular, she kept drawing 60,000 to 70,000 viewers after taking part in Kuaishou's "Pamper- Your-Followers Day" event on June 16th. Subsequently, however, she often felt like ending the livestream whenever her number of viewers dropped into the 20,000s. I talked sense into her, and she eventually got her head on straight—once when promoting cosmetic products, she did not end the livestream even though there were only 6,000 viewers left on her channel. From then on, she changed her tempo and introduced her products in deeper detail. Today, she can sell 3,000 pieces of a product of which she previously could only sell 1,000 pieces.

Livestreamers must learn from the pros and rely on technology to sell their products. There are some livestreamers who rely on passion to sell their products and are unable to explain their products clearly. For example, a noodles-promoting livestreamer might simply say, "These noodles are delicious, come and buy them!" Instead, a pro would explain things such as whether the wheat was produced in Shandong or northeast China, how long it was placed in the sun, and how it was made into noodles.

Team Composition: 178 People Serve Xu Xiaomi

The core of livestream e-commerce is sales, and the core of sales is livestreamers. Xu Xiaomi's livestream studio employs a dozen-odd people, such as an assistant supervisor, a photography team, livestream assistants, backend assistants, and goods assistants. Outsiders might see more of Xu herself, but internally speaking, the individual capabilities of a livestreamer only make up 40 percent of the company. The most important segment of the company lies in product selection, which is 50 percent of the company in terms of significance; other management and logistical work make up the remaining 10 percent.

At first, we treated livestream e-commerce as a business and made plans for Ricearth Network as a company; we were more standardizing institutionally and more detailed in the division of work. Suppliers often do not know who to engage with when supplying goods to other livestreamers, but in our company, men's clothing and women's clothing have separate procurement teams; the division of responsibilities is very clear. We place importance on team building and enterprise planning, and this has to do with my personal experiences—I used to work in enterprise marketing planning. A livestreamer starts out by relying on luck to earn money, but as time goes on, they have to rely on their own ability to earn money; they must have an entrepreneurial mindset, management capabilities, and operational capabilities.

Kuaishou is continuously growing, and we are growing along with it. When we have developed to a certain size, some of our departments would have to be split into different departments.

The first is product selection. The first good decision that I made fairly early on was to build a product selection team. Many of Linyi's livestreamers are husband- and-wife duos who do not dare to hire anyone but their parents or siblings as their procurement team. Because product selection and procurement are fairly sensitive work, livestreamers would worry about whether their products are the lowest in cost and whether their procurement team is taking kickbacks. Regarding this issue, I am slightly better than others; I believe that my procurement team would not take kickbacks.

The first department in my company to become independent was the procurement department, which is further split into four divisions that are responsible for four major categories: clothing, cosmetics, food, and daily necessities. The department, which now has 20 employees, has very stringent demands when it comes to product selection, and has separate standards for each product category.

The second is warehousing. We have a self-built warehouse and also collaborate with a cloud warehouse. Our warehouse is 10,000 square meters in area and is located at B1 of Shunhe Livestreaming Technology Industrial Park. The cloud warehouse offers me 6,000 square meters in space and is located in the west of Linyi. The reason for using a cloud warehouse is that our own warehouse has limited storage space; nowadays, I would store a few standard parts and simple goods in the cloud warehouse.

Before Singles' Day of 2019, we invested more than 1 million yuan to install a Jushuitan system. This system is relatively intelligent and can guide our employees in their work. It took me nearly a month to get it up and running by making it mandatory—without it, our future development would definitely be limited.

The warehousing department also had to be split up, such as into a goods inspection team and an information team. After the goods arrive, all of their information must be entered into the Jushuitan system.

There is also an order-printing team; all deliveries have to be given an order form and verified. After the order forms have been printed, the goods-picking team would prepare the goods according to the orders. Subsequently, the packing team would take over. It consists of many people—Xiaomi alone has 36 packers.

After the goods have been packed, it would be time for the delivery phase. The couriers would come to the warehouse to collect the goods. We currently collaborate with four delivery companies, namely STO Express, ZTO Express, Best Express, and EMS. We ship 50,000 orders per day on average; Xiaomi sold 280,000 orders on April 28, 2020, and two million orders on November 2 of the same year.

After the goods have been shipped, it would be time for the aftersales phase. Our aftersales department has a Kuaishou Store backend team that communicates with our customers via text. We also have a hotline and thus a hotline team.

We accept "returns without reason;" although the return rate is very low, our high volume means that we need people to sort, unpack, and inspect the returned goods every day. Defective goods would be placed in a special warehouse for defective goods, returned to the suppliers, or disposed of by ourselves. Returned goods that are not defective and can be resold, such as those that were returned because they were the wrong size, must be sorted and put into storage a second time.

Our warehousing department has also set up a post called the "goods manager," which specializes in sorting out the warehouse.

There will always be a handful of unsold goods, so what should we do with them? If they take up a storage slot, our space costs would increase. Hence, the goods manager would carry out centralized sorting of long-tail goods and single products, and then transfer them to the bulk goods zone. The goods in this zone have no quality issues, but they have to be disposed of by selling them at a loss— we use them to incubate new livestreamers, who are unable to sell much initially anyway.

We also have two returns teams—one sorts out returned clothing while the other sorts out other returned products. There is also a team in charge of putting returned goods back in their original storage slot.

The third is operations. We only built up an operations department in 2020, while many other livestreaming teams have not set up such a department to this day. At first, we had no one to teach us what to do; we simply invested money to increase our followers and never calculated our costs. All we looked at was our sales volume and traffic. However, the traffic on any platform will inevitably become more and more expensive, while the costs of increasing our followers on Kuaishou are also increasing. In August 2020, we invested 4.59 million yuan to increase our followers by 890,000, which means that each new follower cost us 5 yuan. Moreover, their repurchase rate and conversion rate are far higher than followers on other platforms.

The most important function of the operations department is data analysis. We often perform a few adjustments according to the results of data analysis. The first analysis is on our daily price structure. We have divided our prices into five tiers: 0–30 yuan, 30–50 yuan, 50–100 yuan, 100–200 yuan, and 200 yuan and above. Through our data analysis, we have discovered that whenever Xu Xiaomi performed well, she would definitely have a few products in the "100–200 yuan" and "200 yuan and above" tiers, and they would make up a large proportion of her performance. In the past, livestreamers dared not sell expensive things, that is, anything that cost above 100 yuan. On August 16, 2020, Xiaomi sold 2,500 pieces of a 688-yuan clothing design; her total sales for this product alone amounted to more than a million yuan. We have also done a price test: there is a suit that we used to sell at 390 yuan instead of its usual price of 490 yuan in order to increase sales, but this time, I gave Xiaomi 1,000 pieces of it and told her to try selling it at its usual price—she eventually sold all of them. This shows that Kuaishou's price per customer and the purchasing power of its followers are changing.

In addition, we have also discovered a few patterns via product structure analysis. For example, Xiaomi performs better when she has products in all four categories (clothing, cosmetics, food, and daily necessities), especially the last mentioned.

Over the past two years, we have grown from a team of a dozen-odd people to more than 300 people, including six livestreamers. The team that serves Xiaomi alone consists of 178 people (as of April 29, 2020, see Figure 3.2). Xiaomi is continually growing, and her team

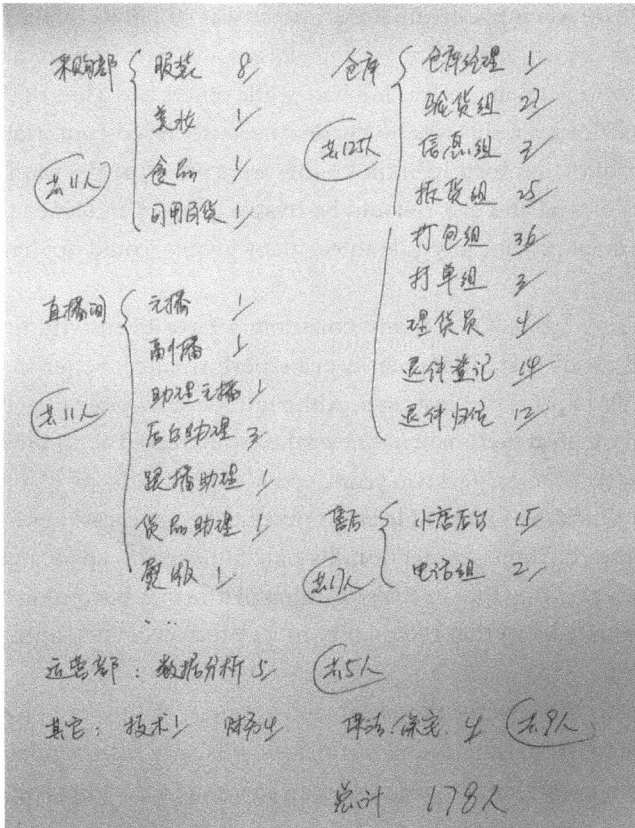

Figure 3.2 The Service Team That Ricearth Network Arranged for Xu Xiaomi (April 29, 2020)

composition is also continually changing—for example, her product selection personnel only had a dozen-odd people in April 2020, but that increased to more than 20 people by August of that year.

Product Selection and Quality Inspection Have to Go Through Three Passes

The market is always changing. I feel that, starting from 2020, people in the livestreaming industry ought to think deeply about product positioning.

In 2018, when livestream e-commerce was still in its infancy, everyone had a can-try mentality, buying clothes at 9.9 or 19.9 yuan a piece. Some people felt that this was not bad, while others had a less positive experience. However, this was no big deal because the costs of trial and error were fairly low. Instead, if the clothes were priced at 195 yuan a piece, the costs of trial and error would be relatively high, and since the platforms did not provide any guarantee, many people would not have given it a try.

Starting from 2020, many consumers have been willing to buy branded goods that are higher in price-performance, better in quality, and higher in price per customer. Although Xiaomi's price per customer is not very high at present, it has nevertheless increased continuously and significantly over the past two years.

The Kuaishou platform is also introducing a succession of policies to increase consumer protection. Its official team has advocated seven standards, showing that its livestreaming platform is becoming increasingly regulated and that the quality of its products is becoming better and better.

In fact, the stricter the platform becomes, the more beneficial it would be to livestreamers and businesses. It is only with regulated platforms that livestream e-commerce can succeed in the long run.

I have always emphasized that our products must change in accordance with market changes. We have not fallen behind in terms of product positioning and have always been progressing at the same pace as Kuaishou.

This is why Ricearth Network has been able to survive to this day and is even overtaking its competitors. To ensure product quality, we have set up a three-run quality inspection process.

The first run is carried out when the clothing has reached our warehouse and is being examined; quantity verification is secondary to quality inspection. Are there any problems with the colors or fabrics? Is there any discolored clothing? The quality inspectors have to pick out the defective goods and put them in the "defective goods warehouse." Our quality inspectors are very skilled—they are able to spot a piece of clothing that has slightly different-colored sleeves. Our packers also play a role in quality inspection. Once, a packer was packing sweaters when he felt that a sweater was slightly lighter than the others just by weighing it in his hand. Upon inspection, he discovered that it was indeed not like the others—a low- necked sweater had been accidentally mixed in with the high-necked sweaters. The quality inspectors had overlooked it because the 500 sweaters in the shipment were all black in color.

Aside from performing quality inspection, we also give every piece of clothing an identification. Although the manufacturers would have provided a tag, our warehouse would affix an additional identification label on the clothes.

After completing the first run, the list of goods would be handed to the information personnel to carry out goods storage. For example, for 1,000 incoming pieces of clothing, the product information of the 900 satisfactory pieces would be entered into the system to generate 900 barcode labels, which serve as our identification labels. Then, more than 20 people would perform another round of inspection while affixing the barcode labels. In other words, our goods must go through two rounds of inspection prior to sales.

Of our company's 300 employees, more than 100 are warehouse workers, among whom 20–25 are specifically responsible for quality inspection—this is a segment with very high manpower costs.

The goods are ready to be sold after passing two rounds of quality inspection. After they are sent to a livestream studio, the livestreamer would carry out another round of quality control when looking at the products, to see if the mass goods are the same as the samples. We would also have someone to carry out sampling inspection and choose samples for the livestreamer to wear. At the same time, we have an ironer who would iron and hang up the clothes before the livestreamer uses them.

Some customers might suspect that what a livestreamer wears is different from what they sell. However, that is absolutely impossible here because the samples worn by our livestreamers are taken at random from the mass goods. If a livestreamer feels that a sample is different from the goods when wearing it, we would call off the promotion immediately—I would rather not sell a particular design than deceive consumers. The livestreamer's try-on phase is actually our third run of quality inspection.

After a livestream, the goods would be prepared according to the orders, followed by packing and shipping—with that, the entire process would be completed. What we ship is what the livestreamer wore; there would not be a case of the goods being different from the samples.

Like quality inspection, our product selection also has to go through three passes.

The first pass is the initial screening of each procurement category, followed by a round of screening by the procurement head, and finally another round of screening by the livestreaming team. When products are sent to Xiaomi, basically only 20 percent of them are able to pass. Moreover, when sorting the products, the livestreaming assistants would directly contact the procurement department to drop a product if they discovered quality issues such as loose threads. And if Xiaomi does not feel good about a piece of clothing that she wears on her livestream, she would tell her followers not to buy it.

Because of our stringent phases of quality inspection and product selection, our costs are much higher than those of other livestreamers. The profit margin of clothing has always been very small, yet our operating costs take up 20 percent of it— this is why we have been losing money over the past few months.

If there is one thing we are very proud of, it is the fact that suppliers dare to supply us with their good products. Although good products are certainly high in cost, we would rather pay high costs than not have good products to sell.

When I am choosing product combinations, my priority is definitely quality, followed by the seller's service capabilities, and only lastly profitability. Were we to prioritize profitability, we would likely overlook quality and the seller's service capabilities. Without a doubt, products are central to whether a livestream e-commerce business can keep on growing. When customers place orders, it is because they like and trust you; if they discover quality issues with the goods after receiving them, your persona and trustworthiness would be diminished. A livestream e-commerce business must be product-oriented; the

Table 3.1 Ricearth Network's Quality Inspection and Product Selection Processes

Quality Inspection Process	First Inspection	Products mainly undergo quality inspection when they reach the warehouse. The quality inspectors would pick out the defective goods and put them in the "defective goods warehouse".
	Second Inspection	Ricearth Network would give every piece of clothing an identification. A second quality inspection is carried out when affixing the identification label on the clothes.
	Third Inspection	After the goods are sent to a livestream studio, the livestreamer would carry out another round of quality control when looking at the products, so as to see if the mass goods are the same as the samples. There would also be someone to carry out sampling inspection.
Product Selection Process	First Selection	An initial screening of each procurement category is carried out.
	Second Selection	The procurement head picks out products that can be displayed on the livestream channel.
	Third Selection	The livestreamer makes the final decision on which products to promote on-stream. The pass rate is usually 20%.

trust relationship between livestreamers and their followers is built on products and services. Table 3.1 shows Ricearth Network's processes of quality inspection and product selection.

How Livestream E-commerce Has Changed the Traditional Means of Production and Marketing

Livestreaming is changing the traditional means of production and marketing. For example, on April 28, 2020, Xu Xiaomi sold a total of 280,000 orders, among which hair dryers made up 6,000 to 7,000 of the orders. At times, we are also able to sell more than 10,000 orders of our ironing machines. It is very difficult for wholesale businesses to have so much stock, and even the manufacturers do not.

We once helped to promote goods for a brand owner. Having long run a traditional e-commerce business, he claimed that he was very experienced at e-commerce and simply wanted to see how Xu Xiaomi would fare selling his products. Xiaomi ended up selling more than 20,000 orders, causing him great distress because he could not fulfill so many orders. Although both traditional e-commerce businesses and livestream e-commerce businesses have to ship orders, the former usually ships 100 orders in one go, whereas the latter often has to ship 20,000 orders in one go.

In a traditional sales model, manufacturers seek distributors and agents in different places via offline channels. Distributors work on an order system; those that deal in daily necessities and home appliances are multi-category distributors who act on behalf of many brands, albeit they would not carry too many goods for each brand. For example, if Xiaomi sells 10,000 to 20,000 pieces in one go, their service would be unable to keep up. And that is a considerably small figure—on November 2, 2020, Xiaomi sold more than two million orders that amounted to more than 100 million yuan, which is even more inconceivable in traditional e-commerce.

Aside from having large order volumes, livestream e-commerce businesses launch a large number of product varieties on a daily basis, which was also unheard of in the past. A product can be sold for a month or even a year or two in a traditional online store, but this is not possible on Kuaishou. Many new products must be offered every day, and they can change at any time.

The need to launch new products every day is a characteristic of livestream e-commerce. If no new products are offered, the popularity and sales of a livestreamer would diminish, at least judging from our experience of doing Kuaishou for over a year.

Firstly, the multi-SKU product structure of livestream e-commerce has driven sales for many source factories.

Secondly, because of their need to launch new products every day, livestream e-commerce businesses are in turn forcing manufacturers to keep on innovating and developing more, better, and newer products.

At first, one or two factories were all it took to satisfy the demands of an online store. Nowadays, however, a single livestreamer can drive the production of many factories.

Taking clothing for example, Xu Xiaomi features approximately 80 different designs in every livestream session. Moreover, the number of SKUs is greater than the number of designs because each clothing design comes in four different colors and three different sizes, which means 12 SKUs. In the past, the product change cycle was very long and there were fewer varieties; but nowadays, products have to be readily modified according to the consumers' demands, and so the number of varieties has greatly increased and the product change cycle has greatly shortened as compared to the past.

I personally guarantee the quantity of Xiaomi's new products by prohibiting any fashionable clothing from appearing on her livestreams more than three times. Each clothing design is usually shown two times, and up to three times at most. After a clothing design has been promoted twice, she would not be allowed to sell the remaining stock, which would usually be given to her disciples to sell at discounted prices.

In the past, selling clothing was just selling clothing, but nowadays, selling clothing means selling cosmetics, food, daily necessities, furniture, and houses at the same time—everything can be sold on-stream. Wu Jun from Linyi Guihe Trading originally sold clothing on-stream, but he later invested in an integrated housing project and sold the houses through livestreaming. Business was so good that he could barely manage. I believe that Xiaomi is also capable of selling sofas and houses—she just has not tried.

Timeliness and interactivity are two very important characteristics of livestreaming, and they represent a huge change. In the old economic age, consumers' demands were inhibited to a certain extent, but in the age of livestream e-commerce, consumers can interact with livestreamers face-to-face and get their demands fully satisfied. If a livestreamer conveys the information from the consumers to the manufacturer, the variety of products would be greatly enriched and the speed of product update and iteration would increase.

This is the C2M (consumer-to-manufacturer model), whereby consumer-end demands compel manufacturers to innovate products and increase product quality.

Livestream e-commerce is actually about on-demand production. We choose products according to consumers' demands. Followers can comment on what they need at any time; the livestreamer will interact with them, while we have a specialized team to analyze the information they provide.

We have realized that a livestreamer is akin to a shopping mall. The approach that livestream e-commerce businesses adopt when it comes to the various demands of followers is completely different from that adopted by traditional e-commerce businesses. We used to work on a single product and focus on depth, whereas we now have to focus on breadth and on becoming 360°, such that we are able to sell any kind of product. I believe that Xiaomi will be able to sell cars in the future. Didn't "Second Brother of Shenyang" manage to sell 288 cars on a livestream once? This amazing figure is comparable to the sales of a 4S car shop. I feel that livestreaming has infinite possibilities—it is a tool that simply depends on who uses it.

Livestreaming has exceeded everyone's imagination; a single person can create as much value as a company. In Linyi, there are few enterprises that generate daily sales of tens or even hundreds of millions of yuan just like Xiaomi.

The Commercial Revolution Has Entered the Next Phase

For the healthy development of livestream e-commerce, there must be competition. Xu Xiaomi is actually no miracle; if she does not improve, others would catch up with her very quickly.

Liu Yilin, president of the Linyi Federation of Industry and Commerce's Short Video and Livestreaming Chamber of Commerce, was considered an industry pioneer during the age of traditional commerce. In 2003, he achieved something noteworthy— back then, the county seat's cinema was in a slump but was well-located, and so he rented it and transformed it into a clothing marketplace. He was the first person in Linyi to establish a clothing marketplace. At nearly 3,000 m2 in area, this market-place in Linyi has generated up to 45 million yuan in annual sales, which is certainly no mean feat.

At that time, location was equivalent to traffic—everyone went to the malls in the city to buy their things, and so traffic was in the malls. From a spatial perspective, Liu's marketplace was well-located and high in traffic, and so he was the Xu Xiaomi, or the Internet celebrity, of that era. However, as the age of livestreaming is despatialized, the location advantages of brick-and-mortar stores have greatly diminished. The marketplace business model is past its golden age, and the commercial revolution has entered its next phase. Taozi's, Damengzi, and Super Dan have become the industry pioneers in the age of livestream e-commerce.

Liu, too, started out as a street vendor and a wholesale merchant, and does not have extraordinary management capabilities. It was also by chance that he opened a clothing store in a Linyi cinema; the truth was that anyone who opened a store there would have made money. However, he is lucky, daring, and good at seizing opportunities. Moreover, he managed to replicate this model in other places—he has concurrently run more than 100 malls before, with a total annual turnover of 1 billion yuan. However, with the arrival of the new age, he has also begun to face unprecedented challenges.

The age of livestream e-commerce is similar; I believe that the batch of livestreamers who started out in 2018–2019, including Xu Xiaomi, relied on luck more than anything else. Back then, platform traffic was high and competition was not so intense, and so anyone who became a livestreamer with just the basic skills and capabilities—such as supply chain and management capabilities—would not fare too poorly as long as they did things steadily. As the market changes, however, everyone must make a few adjustments; businesses have to change in accordance with changes in consumer demands.

Any industry would have a very fast speed of change during its infancy. Because new changes would occur every month, they have to be taken note of every month or even every day, and fine adjustments would then have to be correspondingly made. In 2019, some people did not notice the upward changes in their followers' demands, and when such changes intensified the following year, those who could not keep up with these changes began to fall behind. When a company reaches a critical mass, it would have to make big adjustments, such as in team-building. For example, when daily sales increase from 500,000 yuan to 1.5 million yuan, a team would have to make adjustments in its organizational structure and functional departments, such as by entering goods into an ERP (enterprise resource planning) system rather than simply leaving them to be handled by family members.

Although Xu Xiaomi began doing Kuaishou E-commerce due to the influence of Damengzi, her growth has in turn spurred the development of Damengzi and other top livestreamers. When she first started out, she only had 10 followers, whereas Taozi's and Damengzi already had 4,000 to 5,000 or even more than 10,000 followers at that time. Nowadays, Xiaomi's livestream channel gets more than 10,000 concurrent viewers on average, and her order volume has also exceeded theirs. On August 16, 2020, she livestreamed for more than six hours and made 21.75 million yuan in sales. Her popularity has always remained very consistent at 60,000 to 70,000 followers.

How did Xiaomi overtake the other two in just over a year? This sort of competition has caused them to think deeply and prompted them to make a few changes, such as by paying greater attention to quality control, aftersales, customer service, employee management, team building, and so on. It is competition that will drive this industry to become better and better.

I feel that livestream e-commerce has already entered a new phase. In 2020, a few business owners from traditional industries joined Kuaishou. For example, Linyi's top clothing marketplace magnates have entered livestream e-commerce and jointly established the Maibo Group.

Although the entry of these magnates might change the ecosystem of livestream e-commerce, they will nevertheless suffer initial losses just like everyone else. Livestream e-commerce is completely different in gameplay and logic from traditional commerce, and thus the industry is still lacking in education and training. I feel that in the next one or two years, the livestreaming education sector will gain a lot of market space.

New "Xu Xiaomis" Will Emerge in the Future

If you ask me whether there will be a new "Xu Xiaomi" in the future, my answer would be that there definitely will be.

To give an example, a certain cultural company in Linyi has signed a contract with a livestreamer who does mixing and matching of clothing. She originally worked on her own and generated sales of 30,000 to 50,000 yuan every day. But after signing the contract, she broke through 100,000 yuan on her first livestream and usually made 500,000 to 600,000 yuan per day. On August 16, 2020, she conducted an event and made 1.4 million yuan in sales.

Previously, this livestreamer did not have much of a team or any funds and did not carry out product selection. As a result, her business's finances, logistics, shipping, and goods were poorly handled. The cultural company applied differential positioning on her products and called them "light luxury fashion." Although some clothing does not look good on a particular person, this livestreamer was a great match with such a positioning.

Fashion is divided into many types. Xiaomi's positioning today is "mass fashion," while Taozi's and Damengzi's positioning is "mass leisure." The fashion of this livestreamer is slightly more refined. She has a small face, refined features, and a fairly thin figure, hence the kind of clothes that suit her often do not suit people who are on the fatter side.

Based on positioning, every product category will produce new kinds of livestreamers. The livestreamer that I have just mentioned was able to succeed because she has obtained a sufficient amount of goods that suit her from the company. Due to the large number of consumers in her category, her output has surpassed that of the average livestreamer.

According to Xiaomi's original "pit output," her livestream channel was only able to make 100,000 to 200,000 yuan per 1,000 viewers at first. However, this livestreamer's livestream channel generates a pit output of 400,000 yuan to 500,000 yuan per night from 1,500 viewers. This is firstly because she has a high price per customer, and secondly because she has "depth," which is down to a livestreamer's persona. Furthermore, she is able to explain her products fairly well, and her followers' structure as a group is extremely vertical.

There are many fields that have not been deeply explored in today's livestreams. I believe that, in the future, new livestreamers with different positioning will develop and even surpass Xiaomi.

At the same time, I am quite worried about one thing—given the heights that Xiaomi has achieved, I wonder how she will make further breakthroughs. I have always remained vigilant by doing some work in organization-building and corporate culture construction. I have also engaged a manpower company from Shanghai to analyze the obstacles that we will face in our upcoming development.

I feel that this is an irreversible age. In the next three to five years, nothing will displace livestreaming at the retail level. In particular, as 5G becomes universalized, the faster transmission speeds will mean clearer and more realistic videos. This is similar to how Kuaishou only came about thanks to 4G—it is the entry of the grassroots that will give impetus to the livestream e-commerce market. The magnates of today's traditional industries will definitely enter the livestream e-commerce industry. Looking around us, Dong Mingzhu has begun doing livestreams, and so too have the mayors and county heads in different regions. Due to its long duration, the 2020 pandemic has changed many people's habits. It might not seem like much when a person does livestream shopping once, but their consumption habits over the subsequent months would be unconsciously formed. During the SARS pandemic in 2003, people's acceptance of online shopping increased, and so that proved to be a turning point for e-commerce.

Similarly, the 2020 pandemic is a turning point for livestream e-commerce.

Good things always come after the bad; in the midst of every crisis lies great opportunity.

TIP

How I Select Products for Xu Xiaomi

Kaili is one of the two heads of Ricearth Network's product selection department, and she serves Xu Xiaomi exclusively. The following is an account by her:

Clothing has extremely high demands on product selection; the three aspects of design, quality, and price must all be taken into consideration. Livestreamers have to sell things that are suitable for the range and age span of their followers.

The clothing that Xu Xiaomi sells comes from Guangzhou, Hangzhou, Wuhan, Zhengzhou, and Hebei Province and northeast China. Among them, Guangzhou provides the most goods because the fashion and designs from there are quickly upgraded and are high in price-performance. When it comes to the clothing sector, Xu Xiaomi's selection of goods differs from that of other livestreamers in two important ways.

Firstly, we search purposefully for things that suit her style, which is more fashion- oriented. When Kuaishou first started doing clothing, many people sold casual-style clothing. Xu Xiaomi's image is slightly more feminine; thus she has taken on a more fashionable style and has greater demands on quality. For example, a white t-shirt might come in different fabrics and prices but ultimately does not vary too much. However, fashionable clothing must look good and have a sense of design; demands are very strict on details such as knit binding and waistline height.

Secondly, our focus remains on product quality. We will not choose products that are mediocre in quality even if they suit Xu Xiaomi in style and design. We demand perfection in the details because that is the key to customer satisfaction. It is through quality that Xiaomi convinces her customers. Our profits are very low, and in fact, we lost some money when we first started doing Kuaishou because the costs of delivery, labor, and so on exceeded our budget.

In the cosmetics sector, we only do first- and second-tier domestic brands, and a few international brands. Branded cosmetics tend not to vary much in quality. There are several hundred categories of cosmetics; some are suitable for people 30 years old and below, while others are suitable for people 25 years old and below. We have to select products according to the age group of our followers.

For daily necessities and furniture, we would also choose source products that are top-quality and branded, and that come with a fair bit of their own traffic. For home appliances, we usually choose products manufactured in the Cixi area of Ningbo, Zhejiang Province.

Our product selection department often travels to various parts of China to look for goods, especially clothing. This is because clothes are non-standard products; every designer has their own style and offers unique designs. Clothing has a fast "update" speed, such that new products are launched every day. Conversely, cosmetics and daily necessities are more often standard products. It is not possible for new cosmetic products to be launched every day; in fact, a few branded products have been sold for decades.

The reality is that the entire livestream e-commerce industry lacks good-quality products; this applies to us and more so to less popular livestreamers. Why is that so? Products do not have a ceiling and supply chains do not have standards; there is no such thing as best-quality, only better.

CHAPTER FOUR

WUHAN: A RISING CLUSTER OF QUICK-RESPONSE FACTORIES

- A simple cotton jacket can be manufactured in 130 seconds. Why are Wuhan's factories the best in China when it comes to quick-response capabilities?

THE RISE OF WUHAN: WHEN CHINA'S BEST QUICK-RESPONSE CITY MET LIVESTREAM E-COMMERCE

Key Points

- A piece of clothing takes seven days from design to delivery; a factory can manufacture 100,000 direct-fill down jackets in 15 days; a simple cotton jacket can be manufactured in 130 seconds. Today, Wuhan's factories are the best in China when it comes to quick-response capabilities.

- Thanks to its large-scale quick-response capabilities, Wuhan has become a main source of goods for livestream e-commerce. Sixty percent of the winter apparel for nationwide livestream

The author of this text is Li Zhao, senior researcher, and Zhen Xu, research assistant, both at Kuaishou Research Institute.

e-commerce, including cotton jackets, down jackets, and windbreakers, are manufactured in Hubei factories.

- Wuhan has the basic conditions for quick response—its people (manufacturers) dare to stock up on spot goods, its transportation system is well-developed, and it has many young industrial workers. That its response is so quick also has to do with its factories' adoption of the JIT one-piece flow production model.

Many people do not know that Wuhan is the largest production base for woven clothing in China and a main source of goods for livestream e-commerce. Sixty percent of the winter apparel for nationwide livestream e-commerce, including cotton jackets, down jackets, and windbreakers, are manufactured in Hubei factories.

Unbeknownst to even more people is the astonishing production speed of Wuhan's clothing industry: a piece of clothing takes seven days from design to delivery; a factory can manufacture 100,000 direct-fill down jackets in 15 days; and a simple cotton or down jacket can be manufactured in 130 seconds. Wuhan is currently the best in China when it comes to such quick-response capabilities for large-scale production.

◎ *The following is an account by Ke Faliang, founder of Dongganyizu.*

. . .

Wuhan Is a Main Source of Goods for Livestream E-commerce

I am from Shishi and have been in the clothing industry for 25 years. In 2012, I came to Hanzheng Street in Wuhan to further my career and founded Hubei Dongganyizu Clothing Weaving Co., Ltd. The company is developing quite well these days and has created its own brands—the brand for men's clothing is called "Dongganyizu," while the brand for women's clothing is called "Youshi." We are a relatively large clothing enterprise on

Hanzheng Street, with offices and factories in Hubei, Jiangxi, Fujian, and Guangdong Provinces.

Our factories in Guangdong manufacture clothing in the tens of millions. They are mainly focused on spring and summer wear such as T-shirts and one- piece dresses, which belong to the knitted type and are relatively low in price. On the other hand, our factories in Hubei manufacture several million pieces of clothing per year and are mainly focused on autumn and winter wear such as cotton jackets, down jackets, and windbreakers, which belong to the woven type and are relatively high in price.

From morning until night today, we have shipped more than 40,000 pieces of clothing from our warehouses in Hanchuan, Hubei Province, to various parts of China. Some of these goods are shipped to chain stores, shopping malls, and supermarkets, while some of them are OEM goods for brand enterprises such as Fastfish, Champion, Semir, Guirenniao, and Deerway. We have also made shipments to goods-promoting livestreamers, among whom Kuaishou livestreamers constitute the majority.

We supply goods to a certain top livestreamer on Kuaishou. He has bought more than 20,000 pieces of a down jacket design that we manufactured several days ago. Recently, he has taken a fancy to two down jacket designs and a windbreaker design from our "Lantian Baiyun" series, which is very high in price-performance.

Many people believe that Pinghu, Zhejiang Province, produces the best down jackets. This is because Pinghu began manufacturing down jackets earlier than Wuhan. In particular, by providing OEM products for brands such as Heilan Home, Bosideng, and Uniqlo, it has established quality control domestically and secured a foothold in the down jacket market.

However, Wuhan supplies far more down jackets for livestream e-commerce as compared to Pinghu. Wuhan is on an upward trajectory— its production volume and quality are increasing, and its supporting facilities are becoming more complete. This is why Wuhan has become one of the main sources of goods for livestream e-commerce. Today, approximately 60 percent of the winter apparel for livestream e-commerce, such as cotton jackets, down jackets, and windbreakers, are manufactured in Hubei factories. In addition, the vast majority of down jackets sold on

Kuaishou in the price range of 199–299 yuan are also manufactured in Hubei.

While livestreamers can host their livestreams in Hangzhou, Guangzhou, or Linyi, they certainly must go to Wuhan to procure their goods. This is firstly because Wuhan has very strong manufacturing capabilities. Figures from the Hanzheng Street Management Committee have shown that Hanzheng Street makes up 40 percent of the nationwide market for fashionable men's clothing and is ranked first in China for the production capacity and sales of woven clothing. Secondly, this is because Wuhan is extremely fast in manufacturing speed and is top-rate in quick-response capabilities domestically.

How did Wuhan acquire its quick-response capabilities?

Quick Response Originated From the "One-piece Flow" Production Model

In Hanchuan, factories can begin manufacturing a certain design in the morning and complete the manufacturing process by the afternoon. The goods can then be shipped to a warehouse on the same day. A simple cotton or down jacket can be manufactured in 130 seconds, while a factory can manufacture 100,000 direct-fill down jackets in 15 days.

Why are we able to achieve such speeds? This has to do with our factories' adoption of the "one-piece flow" production model.

Dongganyizu's garment workshop in Xiantao has more than 20 production lines, with a JIT (just-in-time) one-piece flow production signboard in front of each production line. Figures such as the target production volume, the per-capita production volume, and the remaining production time are recorded on this signboard. When the remaining production time, which is calculated in seconds, reaches zero, a piece of clothing would be completed. The countdown is then reset and restarted.

Traditional clothing production lines adopt a "batch flow model" whereby a worker produces many pieces and then bundles and hands them to the next worker to continue production. To give an example, if a production line wants to produce 20 pieces of clothing today, the first worker would be responsible for 10 production procedures and would hand 20 pieces of clothing over to the next worker after they have completed their part.

In the batch flow model, a worker hands a bundle of pieces over to the next worker. Conversely, in the one-piece flow model, a worker hands a single piece over to the next worker. And this task is repetitive—if the first worker is unable to complete their part, the flow would be impeded.

In the batch flow model, a worker might be given three days to hand over their part; there is great flexibility and no sense of urgency among the workers. Instead, in the one-piece flow model, a worker would be urged to hand over their part every three seconds, and so they have no choice but to hurry. Which model do you think has greater efficiency?

In order to adapt to the one-piece flow model and increase our production speed, we have divided the production flow of a piece of clothing into dozens or even a hundred-odd procedures, with each worker on the assembly line responsible for one or several procedures that they have to complete within the stipulated time before quickly handing their parts over to the next worker. Table 4.1 shows the production procedure table for down jackets in one of our factories in Hubei.

The number of production lines per factory and the number of workers per production line can be flexibly allocated according to the complexity of the designs and work procedures. For example, a down jacket with a complex design might have 120 work procedures; if each production line is allocated 25 workers or so, then each worker would be responsible for four or five work procedures.

Using the one-piece flow model, our factory in Xiantao is able to produce, per production line, a simple pair of trousers in 50 seconds and a complex one in 60 seconds; a windbreaker in 80 seconds; and a simple cotton or down jacket in 130 seconds and a complex one in 180 seconds. New workers would need a little more time, at approximately 200-odd seconds.

Furthermore, to prevent disruptions to production whenever a worker takes leave, an "omnipotent worker" who is skilled at every procedure would replace them. As one-piece flow is high in production intensity, only young people are able to handle it. Needless to say, the production capacity is also high.

Table 4.1 The Production Procedure Table for Down Jackets in One of Our Factories in Hubei

款号: 2022-1 薄款   数量: 件   特殊时期上浮10%   组号: 21/22/23组

序号	工序	单价	序号	工序	单价
1	分片/验片/拿框/配片/拿片		58	车面帽侧棉*2	
2	黄平面里门筒*2		59	车面帽中棉*1	
3	前袋上贴贴衬/黄衬*2		60	车面帽中缝及放条带*2	
4	里袋唇/袖带盖贴衬/黄衬*4		61	车面帽中缝0.6线*2	
5	拉链缩水*1		62	车面帽沿棉*1	
6	度位剪弹力绳*1		63	上面帽沿及留弹力绳位*2	
7	前下节口袋位扫粉*2		64	穿弹簧扣一端*1	
8	袖排扫粉*2		65	穿弹力绳弹簧扣一端及打位*2	
9	车前中于前下及压0.1线*2		66	车面帽头棉*1	
10	车前中于前中及压0.1线*2		67	车面帽头于面侧	
11	模板车车拉链袋及放垫布*1		68	车帽里中缝*2	
12	剪开拉链袋唇角*1		69	车帽沿面里及打刀口 *6	
13	车拉链于拉链袋布*1		70	定帽带条及翻帽	
14	刊拉链袋0.1线一圈及折放垫布*1		71	合拼面侧缝走对位*2	
15	前袋面拉省*4		72	拼接下摆内贴及放棉走定*1	
16	前袋里拉省*4		73	比位上下摆内贴及压0.1线*1	
17	车前袋插色拼块*2		74	比位上面帽*1 (有棉)	
18	车前袋上贴袋布*2		75	上拉链及对位*1	
19	落实样版画前袋*2		76	车里门筒面里及放棉*1	
20	按实样线放衬布车前袋面里及窗口*2		77	修翻里门*1	
21	翻前袋及挑角*2		78	里门筒压0.6线*1	
22	压前袋口 0.1明线*2		79	上里门筒*1	
23	车前袋于前片及留袋口位*2		80	上面袖及对位*2	
24	模板车车前袋盖及放棉*2		81	订商标四方*1	
25	修翻前袋盖*2		82	车商标贴里*1	
26	前袋盖压0.6线*2		83	翻压面标贴0.1线*1	
27	前袋盖走定宽度实样线及修剪*2		84	车里袋唇/袋贴*2	
28	车前袋盖于前片及压 0.6线*2		85	开里袋成型及夹商标贴及剪*1	
29	车后中于后下节及压0.1线*1		86	车里挂胸棉*2	
30	车后上于后中及压0.1线*1		87	车里挂里门里及压0.1线*1	
31	折订袖袋织带*1		88	写剪洗水唛*1	
32	模板车车袖袋盖及放织带*1		89	合拼里肩侧缝及夹洗水唛*2	
33	修翻袖袋盖*2		90	车里袖底缝*2及窗口	
34	袖袋盖压0.6线*1		91	上里袖及放带条*4 (有棉)	
35	袖袋盖走宽度实样线及修剪*1		92	拼接拉挂耳及剪*1	
36	车袖袋盖及压0.6线*1		93	套里帽领及夹挂耳*1	
37	面袖袋拉省*2		94	套里下摆*1	
38	里袖袋拉省*2		95	套里摆及修剪*2	
39	车里袖袋插色拼块*1		96	走定面里领*1	
40	车里袖袋面里四方及窗口 *1		97	肩侧缝定位*4	
41	翻袖袋及挑角*1		98	里袖口打折*2	
42	车袖袋口宽度线*1		99	套袖口 *2	
43	车袖袋于面袖及定三角线*1		100	翻衣服*1	
44	车面袖插色拼块及打刀口*4 (24个刀口)		101	压门摆0.1线*2	
45	面袖拼块缝压0.1线*4		102	转角压袖0.1线*1	
46	车袖底缝*2		103	转角压帽沿宽度线*1	
47	模板车车袖袢及放棉*2		104	双针车收下摆*1	
48	修翻袖袢*2		105	车里门筒面里及放棉*1	
49	压袖袢0.6线及落版清剪*2		106	修翻里门筒*1	
50	折车袖排异色拼块*2		107	压里门筒0.6线*1	
51	袖排异色拼块折压0.1线四方*2		108	里门筒走定宽度实样线*1	
52	合压袖排0.1线及放棉*2		109	面门筒切止口 *1	
53	订袖袢*2		110	上里门筒及压0.6线*1	
54	车袖排缝及包袖排*2		111	里袖封口及反车一段*1 (有棉)	
55	走定袖排一圈及翻*2		112	落实样版画面袖袋*1	
56	面袖口打折*2		113	面袖袋袋口扫粉*1	
57	上袖排*2 (注意宽窄)		114		

厂长签名: 总经理签名:

Although work is tough for the workers on the assembly line, their income is also much higher than before. Their monthly salary is around 7,000 yuan on average and as high as 10,000 yuan. In Hanchuan, many factories are compounds with their own workshops and dormitories. The workers there generally drive to and from work; cars are inexpensive and affordable for workers.

Quick Response Goes Hand in Hand with Wuhan People's Bravery to Stock up on Spot Goods

The number one trait of the people of Wuhan is that they are fast in production, speed, and response. Their number two trait is that they are brave; they dare to stock up on spot goods.

Wuhan is well-known as a market for spot goods in China. Customers do not have to order goods in advance; instead, they can purchase spot goods at any time as long as they have the money. Guangzhou and Hangzhou mainly adopt a made-to-order model whereby goods are manufactured according to the order volume. As spot goods are not always available, customers must make orders in advance, and so the cycle is very long. This is why Wuhan gets many orders for spot goods.

Since 2014, the men's clothing markets in Wuhan have grown rapidly. Manufacturers there dare to stock up on spot goods and are confident in selling them. This has led to the formation of quick-response capabilities for spot goods.

A spot-goods model presents serious inventory risks. Although a made-to-order model also has inventory, the inventory of a spot-goods model is much more difficult to control. When there is excess inventory, should the goods be sold off? If so, new goods cannot be sold, but if not, the goods would continue to be piled up and orders for new goods cannot be placed, forming a cycle of death. When a manufacturer is unable to put up with excess inventory, they would think about how to keep inventory at the lowest level—this is why a spot-goods model has forced Wuhan's factories to develop quick-response capabilities.

If a client wants 5,000 pieces of goods, should 5,000 pieces be manufactured and deposited in a warehouse in one go, or should 5,000 pieces of goods be placed on the assembly line with a daily production rate of 1,000 pieces? The answer is definitely to place them on the assembly line and carry out quick response. If you place an order today, the goods can be shipped within three to five days; the goods are actually on the production line.

Wuhan's quick-response capabilities naturally complement its people's bravery to stock up on spot goods. This is something especially suitable for livestream e-commerce because there is a limited time (of several days) for delivering goods, yet also a great deal of uncertainty. Firstly, before a livestream, the livestreamer does not know how many goods they will end up selling. Secondly, the livestreamer does not know how many goods will be returned. If not enough goods are stocked, shipments might not be made in time, leading to complaints by the consumers. Yet if too many goods are stocked, inventory pressures might arise, causing cash flow problems. However, Wuhan is not like that. On the day of a livestream, the relevant factory would already have begun production. At the same time, pushbacks can be made according to the return rate. The batch order quantity can be flexibly decided, then supplemented later according to the livestreamer's sales volume. Therefore, quick response is a very good way of solving the issues of the entire livestream supply chain; it can solve not only the inventory issues of a factory but also those of a livestreamer.

Quick response also serves as a test of the supply of production materials, including their matching with production lines. Once a production line has been started, it would require tens of thousands of meters of fabric per day. Without stocked goods, it would certainly not be fast enough. If there is greige fabric, the production cycle would require at least seven days, otherwise problems would arise. However, things would be worse without greige fabric—all subsequent production cannot be carried out.

Wuhan has an advantage in this regard—there are many suppliers of clothing fabrics and accessories on Hanzheng Street, and so processing factories can procure materials conveniently. Factories with inventories can procure the materials and supply them to the production line in different portions over a few days, thereby realizing quick response. Wuhan's fabric industry is also connected to the nationwide clothing industrial chain; fabric orders can be shipped from Keqiao District, Zhejiang Province, within two days.

The reason for the decline of the clothing industry in my hometown of Shishi has to do with its lack of quick-response capabilities. Unlike cotton jacket manufacturers in Wuhan, those in Shishi might stockpile 30,000 to 50,000 jackets each. At the same time, they are often quick to make orders for fabrics but would then return the fabrics if the colors are poor, causing the production cycle to be stalled by the fabrics. There is also the case of the sports brands of Jinjiang County, Fujian Province. In the past, their production cycles were usually half a year; orders placed in March would be shipped in the second half of the year. Thus, whenever there was a hot-selling product, they did not have the quick-response capabilities to increase its production. That is why Jinjiang's brands—aside from Anta Sports—are on a downward trajectory and many enterprises have closed down.

Quick Response Has to Do with Wuhan's Excellent Geographical Location

Wuhan's bravery in stocking up on spot goods and its development of quick-response production also have to do with its excellent geographical location.

Located in the heart of China, Wuhan is the hub of the country's high-speed rail network. It is convenient in transportation and well-developed logistically, and so shipping is fast and convenient whether by air, sea, or land.

On November 1, 2020, the first high-speed freight train in China set off from Hankou Station. This journey was especially for e-commerce shipments, and it reached Beijing in just four hours or so (see Figure 4.1).

Transportation within the entire province of Hubei is also highly convenient. It takes only two to three hours to drive from Hanzheng Street to the nearby factories and warehouses. Many supporting factories of the businesses on Hanzheng Street are located in satellite cities within 100 kilometers of Wuhan and mainly to its west, such as Hanchuan, Qianjiang, Xiantao, Tianmen, and Jianli. Among them,

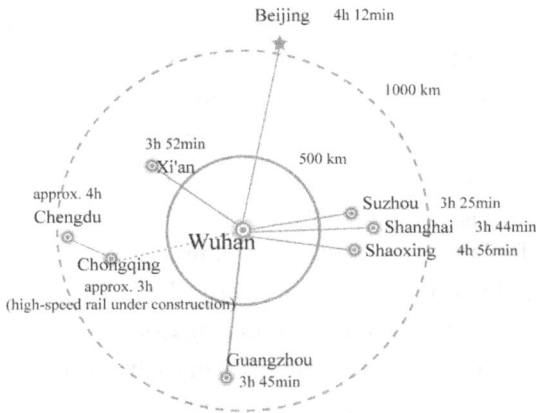

Figure 4.1 The High-speed Rail Network of Wuhan and Major Chinese Cities, Forming a "Half-day Circle of Life"

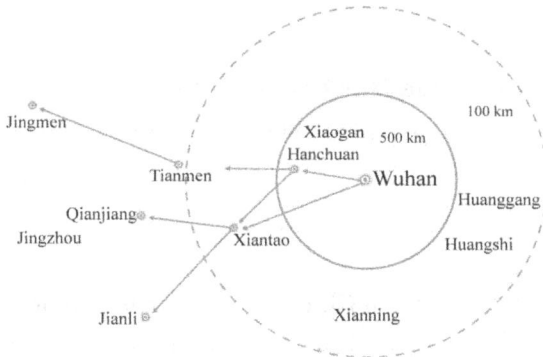

Figure 4.2 The Distribution of Quick Response Factories Within 100 Kilometers or so of Wuhan

Xinhe Town in Hanchuan has 4,400 factories alone (see Figure 4.2). The supporting warehouses are mainly concentrated in Hanchuan, which is 40 kilometers west of Wuhan. This includes the warehouses of Dongganyizu and more than 80 other businesses.

Quick response cannot do without raw materials. Although Hubei does not produce fabrics, it is very close to the places that produce or distribute fabrics. For example, we can get quick shipments of fabrics from Shengze Town in Suzhou, Keqiao District in Shaoxing, and Guangzhou. Wang Junlin is the "king of fabrics" on Hanzheng Street. Like me, he is also from Shishi, and he came to Wuhan to further his career way back in 2003. He procures his woven materials from Shengze Town—shipments made at 10 p.m. over there can reach Wuhan by 9 a.m. the next day. Other materials also take only a day or so to be delivered.

Transportation has become so well-developed in China that most businesses are nationwide in nature. As long as goods can flow, it does not matter whether a livestreamer is in Guangzhou or Hangzhou—Wuhan is able to supply goods to them regardless. Our company has a livestream base in Jiubao District, Hangzhou; many of the clothes there were produced and shipped from Wuhan.

Millions of Workers Provide Adequate Labor for Quick Response

Quick response requires a large number of youthful laborers, and it just so happens that Hubei is able to meet this condition.

There are more than one million workers in the clothing industry throughout Hubei, among which nearly 400,000 are in Hanchuan, 150,000 are in Xiantao, and 120,000 are in Qianjiang. Tianmen and Jingmen also have significant concentrations of workers. Xinhe Town, where our warehouse in Hanchuan is located, has more than 300,000 workers alone. The scene on payday is most spectacular over there— virtually the entire town would be caught in a traffic jam.

In terms of the work efficiency of workers, Hubei fares better than other places. The workers in Hubei's clothing processing factories are mostly 20 to 35 years old. Furthermore, many young people there are learning how to make clothing nowadays. For the same clothing designs, the workers in other regions might only be able to produce 60 percent or even 30 percent of the volume produced there.

Hubei has a clothing industry belt and a foundation of industry workers. The factories in Qianjiang are large in scale, and the industry is relatively complete over there, with several factories consisting of thousands of workers. In Xiantao, there are also many factories with tens or hundreds of workers.

Xingfu Group, which is located in Zhangjin Town, Qianjiang, is the birthplace of Hubei's clothing industry. This group was previously very famous throughout China already, and many of Hubei's clothing factory owners have worked there before. The Group is large in scale, comprehensive in system, and good at quality control. It has provided OEM products for Semir; in fact, it was in Qianjiang where Semir's business took off. The factories and workers that used to manufacture OEM products for Xingfu Group have gradually prospered in Xiantao.

As coastal labor-intensive industries in China are shifting inland, many Hubei natives have returned to work in their hometowns. The relocation of the clothing industry began with factories moving from Fujian, Guangdong, Jiangsu, and Zhejiang Provinces to Wuhan, then continued with them moving from Gutian Road, Qiaokou District, to Panlongcheng, Huangpi District, and ended with them moving from the outskirts of Wuhan to satellite cities such as Hanchuan (approx. 40 kilometers away from downtown Wuhan) and Xiantao (80 kilometers away), as well as cities to the west of Wuhan such as Tianmen, Qianjiang, and Jingmen— they have basically relocated right at the doorsteps of the workers' native homes.

Today, all of the workers in Hubei's processing factories come from the e peripheral cities. They can thus drive home when the factories close for the weekend. In addition, Wuhan also has a very big commercial district on Hanzheng Street. With a carrier and market, industries are certainly able to develop.

THE ORIGIN OF HUBEI'S ONE-PIECE FLOW MODEL

Key Points

- Wuhan's quick-response factories did not form overnight. Langliqi is a typical representative of quick-response factories in Wuhan that transformed from a traditional batch flow production model to a one-piece flow production model.

- From large clothing wholesale markets to nationally renowned first-tier wholesale markets for men's clothing, livestream e-commerce in Wuhan still has a lot of room for development.

Langliqi: A Pioneer in Adopting a One-piece Flow Production Model

Hubei Langliqi Clothing Co., Ltd. is a relatively large clothing enterprise on Hanzheng Street, with its headquarters located in Ruby Tower, No. 1 Longteng Avenue, Hanzheng Street, Wuhan, while its warehouses are in Hanchuan, Hubei Province. Its factories—which employ a thousand-odd workers and are distributed across various places such as Hanchuan, Qianjiang, and Dongxihu District, Wuhan—were among the first in Hubei to successfully transform from a traditional batch flow production model to a one-piece flow production model.

◎ *The following is an account by Zheng Baoping, general manager of Hubei Langliqi Clothing Co., Ltd.*

. . .

Our factories originally adopted a batch flow model. Back then, it took us several days to produce a piece of clothing, and so we lost money every day. Around six or seven years ago, I visited another company's processing factory and was astonished by its assembly line production. This factory was one of the first in Hubei to adopt a just-in-time one-piece flow production model and was able to produce a piece of clothing in less than a minute. Unfortunately, it is no longer around.

After the visit, I immediately changed the production model of my own clothing factories. The first factory I changed was the Langliqi factory located in Dongxihu District, Wuhan. Consequently, its efficiency nearly doubled. Whereas a production line for frayed windbreakers could only produce eight or nine pieces in the past, it can now produce 17 or 18 pieces per worker.

Having successfully reformed the first factory, we began to spread the one-piece flow model to all our factories. Throughout 2014, I worked with consulting firms to reform all 60 or 70 of Langliqi's production lines. Today, we manufacture more than five million pieces of winter apparel and more than two million pairs of trousers annually.

Seeing the rapid improvements in efficiency brought about by our reformation, other factories in Hubei also followed suit. Today, more than 60 percent of the factories in Hubei have adopted the one-piece flow production model.

Wuhan Must Seize the Opportunities Afforded by Livestreaming in Order to Break Through Its Development Bottleneck

No. 1 Longteng Avenue is a large clothing wholesale mall developed by Wuhan Longteng Real Estate Co., Ltd. It is a nationally renowned first-tier wholesale market for men's clothing, especially in the mid-range and high-end categories. There are approximately 1,100 businesses in the mall, and they are distributed across Gold Tower, Silver Tower, Ruby Tower, Sapphire Tower, and so on.

◎ *The following is an account by Huang Xiaoyu, head of merchant management at No. 1 Longteng Avenue.*

· · ·

I used to work in marketing operations and investment attraction. In 2010, I left Qianjiang Group to join No. 1 Longteng Avenue. Back then, good-looking and fashionable men's clothing made up one-sixth of the market, while the rest were undergarments, children's clothing, and sports accessories.

As the saying goes, there is business to be made wherever there is room for survival. When it comes to the undergarment business, Wuhan is a second-tier market, which generally has poor survivability and results. For this reason, we instead decided to focus on men's clothing and dropped all other categories. It took us three years to reform and upgrade the entire market.

Today, there are around 1,500 enterprises in Wuhan that deal in fashionable men's clothing, providing an assortment of quality levels. Among them, 1,100 enterprises are located at No. 1 Longteng Avenue, which focuses on the mid-range and high-end categories and makes up four-fifths of the market share, thereby becoming a nationally renowned first-tier wholesale market for men's clothing. Every one of these enterprises has its own source production factories, most of which were self-founded, while some are collaboration-based.

Kuaishou E-commerce has astutely grabbed hold of this bunch of people who deal in fashionable men's clothing on Hanzheng Street. Be it in terms of production, cost, price, or design, they are certainly irreplaceable.

Every platform is built up on the back of a supply chain. Being production-focused, Wuhan has a strong supply chain but lacks e-commerce talent and means of selling goods. Wuhan's clothing market has reached a bottleneck period, and the only way of making a breakthrough is livestream e-commerce. From another perspective, this also signifies that livestream e-commerce in Wuhan has a lot of room for development.

PART TWO

CASE STUDIES FROM DIFFERENT INDUSTRIES

CHAPTER FIVE

LIVESTREAMING + AGRICULTURAL PRODUCTS

- By drawing on its advantages in logistics, e-commerce talent, and other areas, Wugong County of Shaanxi Province is currently exploring a "buy from the northwest, livestream to the whole of China" model. Through livestreaming, it markets fresh fruits from various parts of northwest China to the entire country, repeatedly creating hot-selling products.

- Livestreaming of agricultural products is pushing Wugong's supply chains, warehousing, logistics, etc. to develop in ways that better suit livestream e-commerce.

THE CASE OF WUGONG COUNTY, SHAANXI PROVINCE: "BUY FROM THE NORTHWEST, LIVESTREAM TO THE WHOLE OF CHINA"

Key Points

- Livestreaming of fresh fruits places high demands on infrastructure investment, requiring specialized fresh food warehouses

---

This chapter is authored by Yang Rui, a researcher at Kuaishou Research Institute, and Chen Yiqi and Zhen Xu, research assistants at Kuaishou Research Institute.

and facilities that can carry out automated sorting and effectively achieve the standardization of fresh fruits to reduce return rates.

- Livestream e-commerce has shorter chains than traditional e-commerce; its supply chains converge procedures such as "procurement from the farmland," warehousing, sorting, packaging, and delivery.

- Northwest China has a lack of good livestreamers. Unearthing livestreamers has to be done on multiple fronts: training one's own customer service team to become shopstreamers, developing training programs for incubating livestreamers, signing livestreaming contracts with local farmers and returning university students, and establishing company-wide engagement with external livestreamers.

There are many other livestreamers who have ventured out of their hometowns to look for goods, and all of them coincidentally chose to visit Wugong.

Wugong County, Xianyang, Shaanxi Province is close to the geographic center of China's territory and was once an important commercial center along the ancient Silk Road. Beginning from the Han Dynasty, the "South Path"—one of the two main paths of the Silk Road in Xianyang—set out from Chang'an and passed through Xianyang, Xingping, Wugong, Fengxiang, and Longxian to reach Lanzhou and subsequently the Hexi Corridor, where it then connected to various states in the Western Regions. Since 2013, due to its development of the "buy from the northwest, sell to the whole of China" e-commerce model, Wugong County has gradually gained fame and become a springboard for selling agricultural products from Xinjiang and other parts of northwest China, especially dried fruits, to the central and eastern coastal regions of China. At the same time, sorting lines, warehouses, logistics, e-commerce talent, and other essential elements have continually grown in numbers here. What was once an agricultural county with little industrial development has since become an "e-commerce county."

Today, as e-commerce enters the age of livestreaming, Wugong is once again ahead of its peers in the northwestern region by working hard on livestream e-commerce and social media e-commerce. Aside from dried goods, many fresh products from the northwest have also become hot selling on livestreaming platforms. Honeydew melons from Minqin, kiwi fruit from Wugong, and winter jujubes from Dali have all seen explosive sales growth, creating a sales miracle among the fresh fruit industry.

Wugong's rapid development in the livestream e-commerce field is due to its time-honored e-commerce genes and more so to its hard work in "striking the pulse of the times" and rapidly iterating and upgrading.

Among the northwest region, Wugong has a relative concentration of e-commerce talent, high-quality goods from Xinjiang, Gansu, and other places, attractive logistics, and warehousing advantages. However, compared to traditional e-commerce, livestreaming also has its own logic—high demands on livestreamers, fast upswings in sales for single products, and stringent testing on backend supply chains. Accordingly, the local government has actively built and developed a support system for livestream e-commerce. On June 21, 2020, the Northwestern Internet Celebrity Livestream Base, which is sponsored by the Shaanxi Fruit Industry Center and the Wugong County government, was launched. Xiyumeinong, a leading enterprise in the field of agricultural product e-commerce, specially established a subsidiary called Shaanxi Huinong E-commerce Co., Ltd. and invested 10 million yuan to undertake the operations of the base. This was the first livestream base in the northwest region.

On the day of its launch, a three-day series of activities called "The Rural Flavors on Kuaishou—Northwest China," which was jointly sponsored by the Wugong County government, Kuaishou Technology, and Shaanxi Huinong, was simultaneously launched. Several Kuaishou livestreamers with a million fans or more, such as "Shaanxi Father-Son Duo, Old Qiao and Little Qiao," "Durian Uncle," "Fruit Uncle," and "Sister Yingying the Cooking Lover" shared their experiences of promoting goods on-stream.

Starting With "Absolutely Nothing"

Prior to becoming "the first e-commerce county in the northwest," Wugong had "absolutely nothing." In the locals' own words, they "lacked products, technology, and atmosphere."

In 2013, this state of affairs changed when the newly appointed county head proposed building Wugong into "the first e-commerce county in the northwest" by making use of several of its basic conditions. The first condition was its geographic advantage of being close to China's geometric center and being an important node in the Belt and Road Initiative, and its strong traffic protection capabilities for internal and surrounding railways, highways, and airways. The second condition was the industrial foundation of its agricultural industry, especially the seasonal fruits of certain places. The third condition was its various handicraft industries that have historical and cultural characteristics. The fourth condition was its large number of returning entrepreneurial talents, being a significant labor-exporting county.

Back then, many Wugong locals could barely explain what e-commerce was, let alone how to do it. That year, Li Chunwang, a merchant who once ran an online store in Xinjiang, made a solo field trip with a backpack to Wugong after seeing its new plan.

On this trip, Li was hoping to find a place that could accommodate everything from procurement and warehousing to production and sales for his company, Xiyumeinong. He had previously already relocated from Xinjiang to Xi'an because the long winters in Xinjiang meant that the roads would be blocked whenever it snowed, and thus goods often could not be shipped for a week. Instead, the hinterland of the Guanzhong region was nearly the geographic center of China's territory, and thus there were great geographic advantages to be had by shipping over and storing dried fruits from Xinjiang here before shipping them throughout the country. However, Li was ultimately unable to find a suitable warehouse in Xi'an, and so he cast his eyes upon Wugong, which was seeking to bring in businesses at that time.

Most of Wugong's industrial parks were completely unoccupied back then. To attract businesses to join, the county government came up with generous incentive policies. In April 2014, Xiyumeinong's production and warehousing logistics center officially opened in Wugong.

Under Li's lead, a bunch of dried fruit enterprises from Xinjiang soon decided to relocate to Wugong. However, just as many people today do not understand livestreaming, Wugong's plans to develop itself into the first e-commerce county in the northwest were met with considerable resistance. Many people felt that the new county head was derelict in his proper duties because he was spending all his time having meetings with e-commerce enterprises that sold jujubes and walnuts, instead of doing more important things.

The opposing voices would soon die down. According to statistics from Alibaba's sales platform, the growth in trade of Wugong's agricultural products ranked 11th among China's county-level e-commerce businesses in 2014. That year, Wugong's total sales of agricultural products exceeded 200 million yuan, ranking first in sales of jujubes, walnuts, dried apricots, and dates, and fifth in sales of dried goods. Overnight, it had become the top seller of agricultural products among the counties of Shaanxi.

In this way, Wugong became an unavoidable stop in the sale of goods from Xinjiang to the rest of China.

"Buy from the Northwest, Sell to the Whole of China"

Wugong's strategy of "buying from the northwest and selling to the whole of China" has to do with Li's personal experiences. During his school days, the Anhui native once served as a volunteer teacher in Qinghai, and thus developed deep feelings for produce from Qinghai. After graduating from college, he was assigned to the Karamay Oil Field in Xinjiang as a project manager, and so he lived in Xinjiang for years. In 2008, he opened a Taobao store that specialized in Xinjiang's local specialties, hoping to get more people to find out about the good stuff from Xinjiang. However, due to the excessive number of uncontrollable factors regarding Xinjiang's logistics and other aspects, he had no choice but to turn toward Xi'an and eventually relocate to Wugong.

After putting down roots in Wugong, Li continued to bring his procurement team on trips around the northwest region. He discovered that, aside from Xinjiang, the other northwestern provinces—Gansu, Shaanxi, and Qinghai—also had a lot of "good stuff" that was unknown to most people, such as the black rice from Yangxian and the millet from Mizhi County.

In this way, Li gathered many specialty agricultural products, such as apples, pomegranates, and walnuts from the Weibei region of Shaanxi, jujubes and coarse cereals from northern Shaanxi, melons, fresh fruits, and dried fruits from Xinjiang, and yak meat from Tibet. Wugong drove the e-commerce trade of more than 400 specialty agricultural products from Shaanxi Province and the entire northwest region of China, while e-commerce in turn provided new momentum for the economic development of Wugong County.

The key to "buying" from the northwest is to understand the goods, whereas "selling" to the whole of China requires paying attention to the construction of a logistics system. Wugong made use of incentive policies to bring in express delivery enterprises, thereby gradually developing logistical advantages.

Because e-commerce enterprises are able to ensure consistent shipment volume, they thus have bargaining power with express delivery enterprises. The price that Xiyumeinong is quoted by logistics providers has fallen to 1.60 yuan for 1.2 kg or less, and 2.20 yuan for 3 kg or less. This price is even shocking to merchants in the Zhejiang area, who certainly have not imagined that logistical costs are so low in the northwest region. Figure 5.1 shows Wugong's "buy from the northwest, sell to the whole of China" model.

It takes five to six days to ship Korla fragrant pears from Xinjiang to other provinces, whereas it takes only a day or so to ship a truckload of pears from Xinjiang to Wugong. Due to the high shipment volume, the unit transportation cost would also fall. After reaching Wugong, the pears would be quickly put into cold storage. Because Wugong is close to the geographic center of China and is relatively well-developed in transportation by rail, road, and air, it generally takes only two to three days to ship goods to other places.

Figure 5.1 Wugong County's "Buy from the Northwest, Sell to the Whole of China" Model

As of July 2020, Wugong had 328 e-commerce enterprises, more than 40 logistics and express delivery enterprises, 105 Taobao Villages, more than 1,200 online individual training stores, and more than 3,000 WeChat businesses. In total, more than 40,000 people were employed in the industry. In 2019, the county's total e-commerce sales exceeded 4.122 billion yuan, contributing more than 10 percent of the county's GDP and increasing the county's income per capita by 862 yuan.

The Northwestern Internet Celebrity Livestream Base

In recent years, Wugong has also been exploring a "buy from the northwest, livestream to the whole of China" model on top of its original "buy from the northwest, sell to the whole of China" model.

Xiyumeinong got into livestreaming as early as 2015, when it ran internal livestreaming tests on Taobao. However, because the results of goods promotion were paltry and there was not yet a strong livestreaming atmosphere, things stagnated for some time. It was only in August or September 2019 that Xiyumeinong began doing livestreams on their Taobao store and engaged a few notable livestreamers. In early 2020, they realized that these livestreamers were beginning to livestream on Kuaishou and other short video platforms.

At the start of May 2020, Li brought the leaders of Wugong County to visit places such as Hangzhou and Yiwu. After they returned, they renovated the disused "Northwestern Agricultural Product Experience City" into 18 livestream studios. Within 20 days or so, the construction of the Northwestern Internet Celebrity Livestream Base was basically completed. On June 21, the base was officially launched.

As traditional e-commerce platforms find it increasingly difficult to acquire traffic and increasingly expensive to acquire customers, livestreaming is becoming ever-more appealing to them. "We are an e-commerce company that sells agricultural products, so we definitely need to find various channels for our products. Platforms such as Kuaishou get huge traffic on their own and have become low-cost. Just by creating short videos and hosting promotional livestreams ourselves, we have gained high viewership and free exposure without having to engage top livestreamers," said Li Xiujuan, head of the Northwestern Internet Celebrity Livestream Base. Table 5.2 shows the changes in circulation mode that livestreaming has brought to the fruit trade.

Table 5.2 Fruit Livestreaming Changes in Circulation Mode

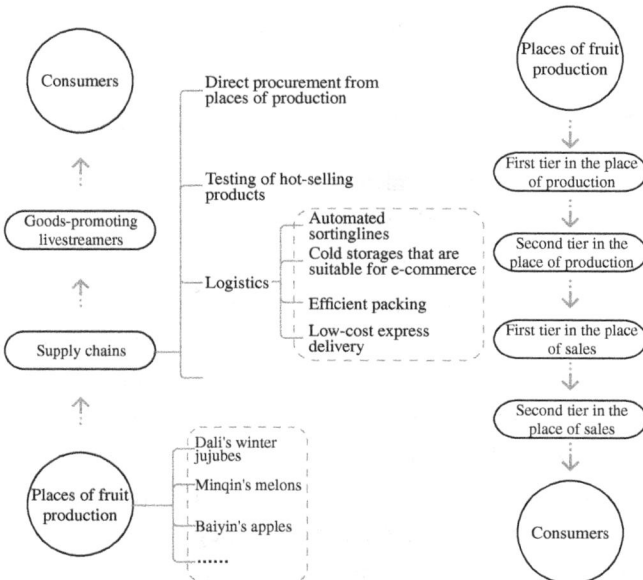

Located in an industrial park in Wugong, the Northwestern Internet Celebrity Livestream Base of today was originally just an exhibition hall for northwestern agricultural products.

Standing at the doors of the livestream base is a roll-up banner that reads "zero- cost tenancy for businesses". The hall is designed after a marketplace and showcases products from places such as Shaanxi, Xinjiang, and Qinghai. All northwestern enterprises and brands that are relatively well-known may enjoy free tenancy here. They mainly sell agricultural products, such as native fruits and an Internet celebrity product from Shaanxi called the "Sanqin Combo" (rolled noodles, Chinese hamburger, and Ice Peak soda). Around the hall, one would find 18 livestream studios, a training center, a supply chain center, and other functional sections. This is the first professional platform for training "agricultural-product Internet celebrities" and running livestream e-commerce operations and services.

Xiyumeinong has three different forms of engagement with livestreamers: its online shop has its own shopstreamers, who are mainly full-time livestreamers trained from its customer service team; its supply chain is able to engage with all kinds of livestreamers and has had collaborations with top-tier, middle-tier, and bottom-tier livestreamers, particularly in the promotion of fresh food products, where it is skilled at direct procurement from places of production and creating hot-selling products; its incubation base has also signed contracts with a few people from nearby villagers so as to incubate them into Wugong's local livestreamers.

In total, Xiyumeinong has 50 full-time livestreamers and operating staff, including its Taobao shopstreamers, JD shopstreamers, and Pinduoduo shopstreamers. Shopstreamers are akin to online salespersons; they have to livestream for eight hours or more every day. Because Xiyumeinong's customer service staff is quite familiar with the overall business of the company, since 2019, it has picked a few people from its customer service team and trained them to become shopstreamers.

Shelves-of-goods e-commerce platforms tend to have accurate consumers. Because livestreams are more intuitive than picture-and-text presentations, shopstreamers have become indispensable. However, the problem with Taobao shopstreamers lies in the fact that the growth in sales generated by them is relatively slow and would not surge by the tens of thousands. That is unless they collaborate with top Taobao livestreamers; for example, Weiya once promoted Xiyumeinong's Chinese hamburgers, while Li Jiaqi once promoted rolled noodles—both of them generated tens of thousands of orders and caused the factories to go into overdrive for several days. Aside from its full-time livestreamers, the Northwestern Internet Celebrity Livestream Base has also signed contracts with a few people from nearby villages and brought them to film clips and conduct livestreams in the fields. At this time, the base serves like an MCN by helping farmer-livestreamers to perform positioning, planning, and editing, to find supply chains, and to negotiate prices with local agents.

For example, a livestreamer might have to pay agent fees that correspond to how many fruits she picks.

The livestream base has a message group for the village livestream schedule. For example, when the "Yellow River sweet potatoes" of Kaifeng, Henan Province, are about to ripen, a message would be posted in the group. After the company has arranged transport, any livestreamer who wants to go to the fields to film clips or conduct livestreams can simply sign up in the group. Generally speaking, there would be five to ten livestreamers traveling together and discussing ideas with each other on each trip. The online accounts of these livestreamers are all related to Xiyumeinong. Although they do their own filming, Xiyumeinong would help them with editing and traffic acquisition and would eventually pay them a commission.

There are currently more than 30 livestreamers on such agreements. Most of them are local villagers, while a dozen or so of them are from Xi'an. Among the farmer-livestreamers incubated by the livestream base, the more successful ones can earn tens of thousands of yuan in commission every month. This has served to increase the income levels of the villagers, thereby contributing toward "alleviating poverty and helping farmers."

For instance, livestreamer A'yuan has only 4,000-odd followers on a certain short video platform but has generated more than 8,000 orders for agricultural products. Hailing from Puji Town, Wugong County, she has been earning a significantly higher income ever since the number of orders has surged. Another livestreamer, Xiaoyang, is a university student whose Kuaishou account already has more than 60,000 followers. Xiyumeinong has signed contracts with them and pays them a basic salary.

Xiyumeinong also has collaborations with Kuaishou's top livestreamers, such as "Sister Cat," a food-promoting livestreamer. Some top livestreamers have also sought out Xiyumeinong on their own initiative after seeing the surge in popularity of food products such as Chinese chestnuts and sweet potatoes. The company has also had collaborations with "Mimi Has Opened a Clothing Factory in Guangzhou," "Little Shenlong," and so on. These livestreamers would include a link to Xiyumeinong's flagship store on their promotional livestreams.

Kuaishou livestreamer "Daxuan's Fashion Mix-and-match" has also promoted goods for Xiyumeinong before, generating more than 10,000 orders for jujubes and more than 2,000 orders for apples. Meanwhile, the vertical livestreamer "Durian Uncle" has also single-handedly generated tens of thousands of orders for garlic on Kuaishou.

The Northwestern Internet Celebrity Livestream Base is running two incubation programs for more than 1,000 people each. One of them is the "Thousand Talents Incubation Project." It is jointly organized with the Wugong county government, which has instructed the deputy mayor of each town and village to enroll people to learn how to do livestream e-commerce. The program adopts a "2+1" model, that is, two days of theory and one day of practice every week.

The other is the "Baiqianwan Program," which has recruited more than 1,300 people province-wide. "Bai" (hundred) refers to the entry of 100 provincial fruit industry cadres into livestreaming, "qian" (thousand) refers to the training of 1,000 fruit industry practitioners, and "wan" (ten thousand) refers to the assisted conducting of 10,000 livestream sessions in 2020.

In 2015, Xiyumeinong established a specialized e-commerce academy that provides training in various counties on how to run Taobao shops, WeChat businesses, and "community e-commerce" businesses. With a livestream base today, many people from far and wide have expressed their interest in coming to attend livestream courses. It is for this reason that the livestream base has specially developed a series of courses on short video operations, livestream incubation, and so on.

In addition, many places in the northwest have a high demand for training. Nowadays, the Northwestern Internet Celebrity Livestream Base is already running livestream e-commerce training programs in Lantian County and Zhenba County of Shaanxi Province, Ping'an County of Qinghai Province, and Taibus Banner of Inner Mongolia. Aside from providing training, Xiyumeinong is also screening suitable candidates to sign contracts with and develop into livestreamers, subsequently providing them with backend support and high-quality supply chains. On livestreaming platforms, Xiyumeinong would also help them to generate traffic and increase their followers via livestreams and short videos. Figure 5.3 shows how Xiyumeinong finds good livestreamers.

Table 5.3 How Xiyumeinong Finds Good Livestreamers

THE EXPERIENCE OF GOODS-PROMOTING LIVESTREAMERS IN A NUTSHELL: SUPPLY CHAINS ARE THE CORE CAPABILITIES

Key Points

- When the sales volume of a livestream channel rapidly rises to peak values, it would be a great test for the enterprise's supply

This chapter is authored by Yang Rui, a researcher at Kuaishou Research Institute, and Chen Yiqi and Zhen Xu, research assistants at Kuaishou Research Institute.

chains, quick-response capabilities, team coordination, logistics, and cash flow.

- Capabilities in logistics, warehousing, and human resources that were developed in traditional e-commerce can also be used in livestream e-commerce, albeit livestream e-commerce demands faster speeds and greater explosiveness.

- Fresh food products are highly seasonal and might only have two to three weeks of shelf life. Before a new product is shelved, it can be tested by delivering 1,000 to 2,000 orders of it to regular customers. If the feedback is good, it should continue to be invested in, but if not, it should be reoptimized.

Liu Xinjuan is a first-generation employee at Xiyumeinong, having joined the company in 2013. She is currently responsible for the movement and storage of goods for the entire company. She has a deep understanding— and has done deep research on—the characteristics of livestream e-commerce, as well as the tests that it puts on backend supply chains.

◎ *The following is an account by Liu Xinjuan, chief supply chain officer at Xiyumeinong.*

· · ·

On-stream Promotion of Goods Has a Greater Need for a Complete Supply Chain Than Traditional E-commerce

Fresh-food livestreaming places extremely high demands on supply chains because surges in orders take place very quickly during a livestream.

When we were doing traditional e-commerce, creating a hot-selling product required going through a process. For example, an online shop had to be slowly built up by accumulating sales and good reviews; its trajectory was a gradual upward curve. However, creating a hot-selling product on a livestreaming platform does not follow the same logic. Sales might peak at the very start and then rapidly drop. Therefore, when sales suddenly peak, an enterprise's supply chain capabilities, response capabilities, and team co-ordination would be tested. For example, if I receive a steady 50 to 100 orders every day but that suddenly increases to 10,000 orders one day, my supply chain capabilities would be tested to the utmost.

Take sweet potatoes for instance. To sell 2.5 kg of sweet potatoes, I would need adhesive tape, a carton, and foam, and would also have to pay for the packing staff and express delivery—these are the most basic back-end demands. When all of these have been prepared, I would still need the goods from the places of production.

The places of production themselves might not have these resources, which are required for online sales. I might be able to make do if there are only 50 orders per day, but that would not be possible if there are 10,000 orders in one day. We came up with the "buy from the northwest, sell to the whole of China" model precisely because it allows us to deploy workers or couriers to anywhere in the northwest where they are lacking in numbers. However, outside of the northwest, we are unable to perform such resource allocation at the moment.

Here's a more intuitive example. Last year, we sold Minqin melons for the first time. Things were especially difficult at that time, and we encountered many problems. The Minqin area is covered in sand and belted by powerful sandstorms, and the environment there is extremely dry. In the past, the Minqin people had their mouths full of sand every day. The first year we were there, conditions were very poor and so we found it hard to adapt. However, the Hami melons from Minqin were extremely delicious and had extremely high potential to be hot-selling products.

While in Minqin, we did not have any packers. Lacking awareness about e-commerce, the farmers there did not understand what packing was. In fact, things like cartons and adhesive tape were unavailable there. Moreover, express deliveries had to transit through Lanzhou before reaching Xi'an. To solve this problem, we directly contacted an express delivery van to ship the required materials from Xi'an to Minqin, and subsequently to ship the goods from Minqin to the transit point in Xi'an. In this way, we were able to save a few days' worth of time. If the supply chain is inadequate, goods cannot be shipped when a livestream generates a surge in orders.

On short video platforms, there are a few users who underwent "barbaric growth"—they built up their accounts by making use of the bonus traffic offered during the platform's early stages, then began selling goods. However, judging from their business practices, they are unprofessional. Instead, we have positioned ourselves as a "professional army" for goods promotion because we have a complete and high-quality supply chain.

Take, for instance, Dali County's sweet potatoes, which also experienced a sudden surge in popularity on livestreaming platforms. Because Dali is very close to Wugong, our procurement team traveled to the place of production to collect the goods and subsequently shipped them to Wugong, where we have ready-made workers and production lines, as well as our own carton factory. The cartons can be produced overnight and used to pack the goods the next day. Few supply chains are able to achieve such standards.

A supply chain must not only be very strong logistically but also have products and consistent personnel. Furthermore, it requires adequate financial resources; not every livestream e-commerce business can collect 3,000 tons of apples in a short period of time just like Xiyumeinong did. In terms of human resources, material resources, and financial resources, Xiyumeinong is already sufficiently well-equipped and thus surges can take place very quickly.

Many people wonder how Xiyumeinong can become so successful at selling fresh food within a year despite only selling nuts in the past. Today, Xiyumeinong's sales of fresh food are equal in value to its sales of nuts.

Summer is the off-season for nuts. In former years, Xiyumeinong would incur losses during the off-season, such as from June to August. However, we instead turned a profit in the off-season of 2020 because the sales of fresh food offset our losses.

Compared to the hot-selling products in traditional e-commerce, products for livestreaming must be better in quality. This would ensure a livestreamer's continued willingness to promote your products. Even if a livestreamer has relatively high "follower stickiness," they often face a lack of products— fortunately, we have high-quality products that they would certainly like.

Our KA (key account) department has done extremely well. Once, we brought a livestreamer to a "Dalieba bread" workshop, where he sold more than 10,000 loaves of bread in one livestream session. After the session, he asked us—on his own initiative—if we had other goods to sell. Therefore, although it might be us seeking out livestreamers at first, the livestreamers often end up seeking us out eventually. If the customer feedback is positive, they would naturally trust us.

It is often said that "without aftersales, fresh food cannot be sold." Nevertheless, a strong supply chain is able to maintain aftersales at a certain proportion. Our customer service team consists of more than 80 people and is thus able to keep up even when a lot of aftersales are required. As a result, livestreamers do not have much to worry about when collaborating with us.

The Logic Behind Creating a Hot-selling Product: Early-stage Testing + Frontend and Backend Coordination

We have long been trying to sell fresh food, but vigorous development in this area only began in 2019. When the company determines that something must be done in the current year, the front and back ends of our entire operations system would go all out to do it.

As Li Chunwang said, the apples from the banks of the Yellow River in Gansu Province and the apples from Inner Mongolia are no worse in taste than those from Aksu, Xinjiang—they are also "rock candy apples" and are very cheap in price. He has personally gone on week-long visits to their places of production to see and taste the apples for himself. Having resided in Xinjiang for so long, he has gained a deep understanding of Aksu.

Back then, we hoped to get this product done right because it was great in taste and reasonable in price. We swiftly gathered 3,000 tons of apples from the production areas of Baiyin, Gansu Province—this was certainly huge volume for an online sales channel. Moreover, the price was 4 yuan per kilogram, and so we had to invest a considerable sum.

We eventually made this product into a hot-selling one. During the Singles' Day period, we had to ship hundreds of thousands of orders in one day. Our warehouse was packed full of apple trucks from the doorway to the road; a dozen or so trucks were waiting to unload their goods.

This is our strategy for all of our products. We are not "two-way merchants" when it comes to agricultural products; instead, we go down to the places of production to collect and ship the goods ourselves. We gather the goods once per season; were we to gather them only when we needed them, others would have snapped them up before us—as the saying goes, if the goods aren't in my warehouse, they are in someone else's warehouse. Subsequently, I would also purchase goods from other people's warehouses, often at much higher prices.

It is on these grounds that we usually control the entire supply chain at the source. After collecting the apples, we are also extremely picky during the shipment process and would exercise strict quality control. Our machines would divide the apples according to their size and weight before manual selection is done, and only then would the apples be shipped. While some people have thought about selling these apples as "Xinjiang apples" because there is little difference in taste between them, we are not willing to do such a thing.

When we want to do something, nothing can faze us. When we were selling Fuping pancakes, we did not know a thing about them and so we sent our staff to learn from the locals for a few months. Because none of us had professional training in making these pancakes, we had to learn and ask questions.

Therefore, our hot-selling products can be said to be those that the company concentrates all its resources on before waiting for them to explode in popularity. After the apples reach our warehouse, we would take turns organizing events on platforms such as JD, Kuaishou, and Taobao. Consequently, our warehouse would not get any rest.

We also have many products that were unsuccessfully tested after development, and so we did not gather them in bulk. However, fruits are too "fast-paced" for any such trial and error. For example, our "Gala apples" were not selling well in 2020. As it was raining a lot back then, we focused heavily on gathering these apples at first. However, after the rain stopped, all kinds of water-caused damages—which were invisible to the naked eye during the collection process—appeared on the surface of the apples, and so we found many rotten apples while preparing the shipments.

For any product, the first shipment batch would determine whether it can be done in the long term. After shipping the first batch of goods, we would not dare to continue selling a product if the aftersales indicators were poor; otherwise, our business might "die."

Our company has a new media department that is like a band of elite soldiers who are highly knowledgeable about our regular customers. Before a new product is launched, we would get the new media department to conduct a round of promotion—they would usually end up generating one to two thousand orders. Because these orders are made by our regular customers and furthermore because we provide good quality at highly suitable prices, we are able to receive feedback very quickly. The new media department is our fastest department at launching and selling products, and so they would promptly give us the feedback regarding this batch of goods. If the feedback is poor, we would perform re-optimization and re-testing, but if the feedback is good, we would proceed.

Because fresh foods have a very short storage time and are highly seasonal, they might be shelved for only two to three weeks and, unlike nuts, are not available all year round. They have extremely high demands, be it on product quality or our entire team.

Separate Departmental Accounting and Company-wide Engagement with Livestreamers

The year 2020 is our fourth year keeping separate accounts for our departments. Practically our entire company engages with Internet celebrities and livestreamers. We have sold more than 100,000 orders for garlic on Kuaishou; hundreds of thousands of orders for sweet potatoes and pumpkins on Kuaishou and other platforms; and have also seen surges in orders for onions, melting- flesh peaches, and Minqin melons before.

Our sale of Minqin melons is handled by a young lady from our supply chain department. If the livestreamers she engages sell a large number of goods, she would earn a generous commission. However, we have an internal policy that we would not "hijack" livestreamers and platforms that others have already engaged.

Our supply chain department would prepare a name list of livestreamers and then seek them out one by one. The livestreamers are then asked to promote our more presentable products. For example, the "red fragrant pears" that we have been promoting over the past two days can be sold without much effort because we have already developed this business in earlier years. We had originally planned to sell 200 tons of them but ended up selling 600 tons by accident, and eventually ran out of stock. This pear variety has a very low aftersales rate and a 98–99 percent "good review" rate. It is a hybrid variety of the "Xinjiang pear" and a Shaanxi pear variety. Although it is slightly worse in taste than the Korla pear, it is nevertheless rather sweet and crunchy yet inexpensive, and so it is considered good value for the money.

The people in our supply chain department, such as the young lady I mentioned, are nearly always bringing livestreamers to different places of production. They began doing livestreaming fairly early on and have sold the most goods. Their initial idea was to integrate procurement and sales and create a supply chain through livestreaming; this would allow them to supply goods to both Xiyumeinong and livestreamers.

The Northwestern Internet Celebrity Livestream Base is also dedicated to handling the work of livestreaming; both its customer service department and supply chain department have personnel responsible for engaging livestreamers. There is an ongoing competition among the different departments of our company.

THE INFRASTRUCTURE NECESSARY FOR LIVESTREAMING FRESH FOOD, USING KIWIFRUIT AS AN EXAMPLE

Key Points

- The keys to promoting fresh fruits are quality control and after-sale services.

- The automation of sorting and packing would improve consumers' purchasing experience.

This chapter is authored by Yang Rui, a researcher at Kuaishou Research Institute, and Chen Yiqi and Zhen Xu, research assistants at Kuaishou Research Institute.

- The e-commercialization of logistical designs and cold storages can increase supply chain efficiency.

Aside from e-commerce trade based on the "buy from the northwest, sell to the whole of China" model, kiwifruit from Wugong has also gradually built up a market nationwide.

Today, kiwifruit plantations cover approximately 2,670 square kilometers of land worldwide, with China, New Zealand, Australia, and Chile being the biggest producers of kiwifruit. Kiwifruit plantations in China make up more than half of the aforementioned land area. Among them, plantations in Sichuan cover approximately 467 square kilometers of land and mainly produce red-heart kiwifruit and yellow-heart kiwifruit, while plantations in Mei, Wugong, and Zhouzhi Counties of Shaanxi Province together cover approximately 600 square kilometers of land and mainly produce green-heart kiwifruit.

To the south of the Qin Mountains, the area of the Mei and Zhouzhi Counties is geographically suitable for planting kiwifruit and is the main production area of kiwifruit in Shaanxi Province. Between the two counties, Zhouzhi County began producing kiwifruit earlier on, whereas Mei County has a bigger plantation area. Wugong is the county with the highest population density in Shaanxi Province and is the latest among the three counties to begin producing kiwifruit.

There are more than 10 different varieties of kiwifruit, and they generally take three to five years to bear fruit. Although Wugong has the shortest history of producing kiwifruit, it pretty much only produces the latest varieties such as Cuixiang and Xuxiang, which are especially good and sweet in taste right off the tree. It thus enjoys a late-mover advantage. As of the end of 2019, Wugong's kiwifruit plantations covered approximately 84 square kilometers of land, and it had the largest cold storage cluster in the Guanzhong region.

Green-heart kiwifruit can be sub-divided into several varieties, the newest ones being Hayward, Xuxiang, and Cuixiang. They are picked every year starting from the end of August, and by November, there are none left on the trees. Ripened kiwifruit will spoil if they are not picked in time and must be put into cold storage after they are picked.

The shipment period of kiwifruit is divided into the stock period and the storage period. The stock period lasts only 50 days or so, whereas the storage period can last from the end of October until March of the next year.

Plantations for agricultural products, particularly kiwifruit, have attracted a bunch of "trend-setters" from the fresh food industry to join.

Luo Xiangfeng is the general manager of the Shaanxi Co-op Cainiao Northwestern Fresh Produce Warehouse. He has had 10 years of experience running a kiwifruit business in Xianyang. According to him, Wugong's e-commerce industry consisted mainly of dried fruits and foodstuffs at first, and it was his company that popularized the selling of fresh fruits. The purpose of building a warehouse was to gather goods from places such as Xinjiang, Gansu, and Ningxia in Wugong before shipping them throughout China, and the goal was to turn "non-standard fruit products" into "standard fruit products"—in the same vein as fast-moving consumer goods— through grading, classification, and packaging, thereby turning raw fruits into commercial fruit products.

The Shaanxi Co-op Cainiao Northwestern Fresh Produce Warehouse made its soft opening at the end of 2017 and officially opened in April 2018. It has 11,700 square meters of physical space and can store up to 3,000 tons. Its services cover every segment of the fresh food supply chain—it provides "cross-temperature" warehouse allocation services in the three forms of "room temperature, chilled, and frozen," and caters to the sales of fruits and fast-moving consumer goods from places such as Shaanxi, Gansu, Ningxia, Qinghai, Inner Mongolia, and Xinjiang. In 2019, its shipment volume exceeded 6.5 million pieces, totaling 160 million yuan in sales. Its second-phase construction, which covers approximately 16,700 square meters in area and is slated for completion in November 2021, will provide better support for the flow of northwestern agricultural products to the rest of China.

The company currently has two Tmall stores, namely "Qinpinyuan" and "Guoyuanwai." The annual turnover of its independent fruit e-commerce business is more than 200 million yuan. At the same time, it is responsible for the online operations of Haichijia, a popular "hot and sour noodle" brand. It is also incubating four Kuaishou livestreaming accounts, including "Direct Fruit Shipment–Beibei" and "Haichijia Xiaobai." For 2020, these four accounts have set a sales target of 60 million yuan.

◎ *The following is an account by Luo Xiangfeng.*

. . .

Quality Control Is Fundamental; Infrastructure Investment Is Large

We started out as a local kiwifruit business and have been doing e-commerce sales for 10 years already. Together with Cainiao, we have built in Wugong the most professional fresh food warehouse in the entire northwest region. In 2021, we plan to build an additional warehouse that specializes in fruit storage—the total construction area is more than 30,000 square meters.

In reality, on-site livestreams that showcase the process of picking, packing, and shipping are more effective for selling kiwifruit. With more than 60,000 followers, the Kuaishou livestreamer "Beibei" can sell more than 4,600 orders every day by livestreaming from a warehouse. Her livestream channel gets up to 1,000 concurrent viewers and at least 200 to 300 viewers.

The keys to promoting fresh fruits are quality control and aftersale services. For example, there are a few buyer-style fruit livestreamers who do not understand the goods they are selling, such as regarding the shelving and unshelving time, quality control, and aftersale issues. No matter which platform they are on, they would meet their Waterloo sooner or later.

Fresh food products cannot simply be promoted in a livestream base. The livestreaming strategy for fresh food products is different from that for other categories, requiring large investments in infrastructure, land, hardware equipment, and so on. You need a professional fresh food warehouse that can ensure food quality and check the shape and surface of fruits through grading and classification. While products such as cosmetics and clothing can be promoted in clusters for industrial products and fast-moving consumer goods, this is far from enough for fresh foods and fruits.

When selling goods on Kuaishou, the order volume is highly unstable. For example, a Tmall store tends to get a very consistent number of orders per day, whereas on Kuaishou we may suddenly get tens of thousands of orders after a period of few orders. Thus, if we are unprepared, we would be unable to ship the goods.

The advantage of our supply chain lies in its ability to ensure basic conditions while providing room for maneuvering. For example, it can prepare 50,000 orders in advance, but if the livestreamer only sells 30,000 orders, the remainder can be diverted to Tmall's regular channels. Otherwise, such a sudden drop-off would spell big losses for smaller-sized supply chains. On the other hand, if a livestreamer sells hundreds of thousands of orders in one go but is unable to ship the goods or runs into logistical problems, huge losses would also be incurred. With a warehouse and cold storage that are more than 30,000 square meters in area, we are flexible in operations and unpressured by order volume.

The biggest problems faced by fresh food livestreamers are: whether their infrastructure can keep up, whether their supply chain is able to ship the required amount of goods, and after the goods have been shipped, whether their quality control can keep up and whether they are able to provide good aftersales services.

Having invested tens of millions of yuan in infrastructure, we do not dare to damage our own brand. Given our huge volume of goods, we have to check the weather forecast every day and stockpile goods in time. While farmers who sell their own homegrown fruits can close up shop if there are no ripe fruits or if it is raining on a particular day, we are different— even if it is "raining knives," we must ship orders within 48 hours, as per our promise to customers.

The Automation of Sorting and Packing

Nowadays, our warehouse is very well-equipped; sorting and packing have all become automated. For example, our sorting equipment has a brushing machine at the very front. The surface of a kiwifruit is full of trichomes, and so if a customer opens a pack of handpicked kiwifruit, they will get trichomes all over their hand. We thus installed an automated brushing machine at the front to ensure that consumers get clean and sleek kiwifruit.

In addition, we have a specialized machine for taking 108 photos of each fruit from all angles. Fruits that do not meet the shape requirements would be automatically weeded out from the "Discarded" production line during the selection phase. The machine is able to detect fruits that have spots, bumps, or abnormal shapes. The purpose of shape detection is to eliminate the blind spots of manual selection, which are often invisible to the naked eye. In this way, we can ensure that consumers get beautiful fruits and a good purchasing experience.

Apples and kiwifruit have different classification standards. Apples are measured according to diameter; for example, 60 means that an apple is 60 millimeters in diameter, while 80 means that an apple is 80 millimeters in diameter. Kiwifruit is instead measured according to weight; for example, 90–100 means that a kiwifruit is 90–100 grams.

Thus, the process goes like this: apples of different diameters would flow out from different outlets on the conveyor belt, while cartons would also be conveyed via an upper conveyor belt. The workers standing on both sides would take the cartons down, pack the apples into them, and leave them in place. Each carton—consisting of three kilograms of apples—would then be automatically sealed.

The E-commercialization of Logistical Designs and Cold Storages

Our warehouses are all designed according to the demands of e-commerce sales on storage and shipment and are specially created for fruit e-commerce. Instead, some traditional cold storages are able to accommodate 10,000 tons of goods but only have two unloading outlets.

We now have 11 cold storages that provide a total of 22 outlets when each is opened on both sides. They can be adjusted according to the volume to be unloaded. When the unloading volume is large, especially for e-commerce, all 22 outlets can be simultaneously opened. The goods can be packed as soon as they are unloaded—with 22 packing outlets, efficiency is high and loss is little.

Ordinary storages are only able to unload up to 20,000 orders per day, whereas ours, which take up 11,000 square meters of space, can unload up to 100,000 orders per day—with a bit of overtime—during peak periods. We thus have absolutely no problems dealing with surges in orders during a livestream. Figure 5.4 shows our sorting lines and cold storages, which are designed with the characteristics of e-commerce sales in mind.

Wugong has the cheapest logistics and the largest order volume in the entire northwest region of China. Many express delivery companies such as SF Express have collaborations with us. We ship 14 million orders every year; thanks to the scale effect, we can effectively lower the fees we pay to express delivery companies.

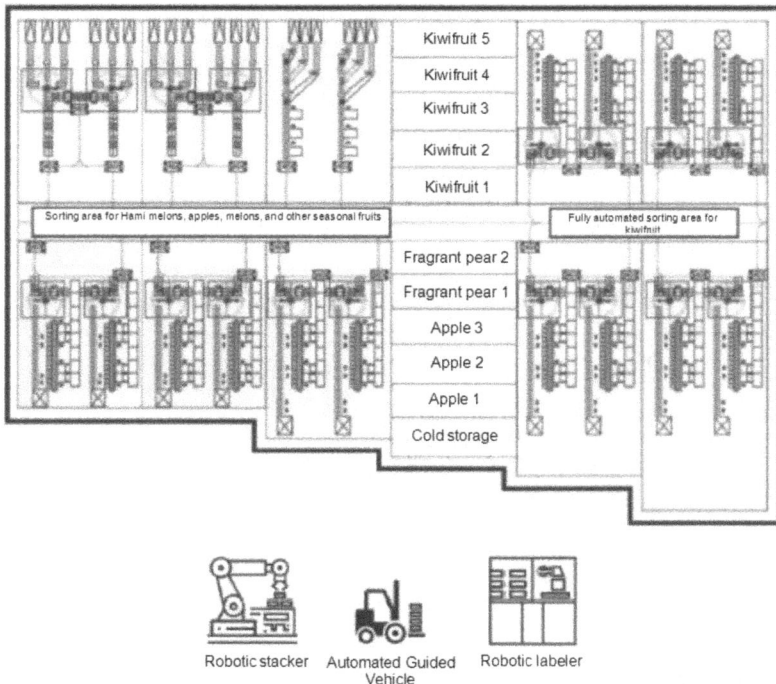

Figure 5.4 Cold Storages and Production Lines That Are Designed with the Characteristics of E-commerce Sales in Mind

Note: The warehouse has 11 cold storages with a total of 22 outlets. On both sides of the cold storages are automated sorting lines for kiwifruit, apples, and other fresh fruits. Such a design can greatly increase the efficiency of sorting, packing, and shipping.

Provided that grading, classification, and packaging are done well, we can keep the aftersales rate of kiwifruit within 0.5 percent, which is a very low figure. Firstly, this is because kiwifruit is a hard and climacteric fruit, and thus only ripens after it has been kept for a period of time. Secondly, this is because it is easy to package. For instance, mangoes are difficult to package, whereas kiwifruit and apples are not. Now that our kiwifruit supply chain has a strong foundation, the problem is finding excellent livestreamers to sell our fruits on- stream.

CHAPTER **SIX**

LIVESTREAMING + EDUCATION

- Livestreaming offers students outside of first-tier and second-tier cities the opportunity to receive personalized and accurate educational services, and at a lower price than before.

YUANDINGHUI: CREATING EDUCATIONAL CLOSED LOOPS USING KUAISHOU LIVESTREAMS

Key Points

- Large educational organizations tend to exercise centralized teaching and research, which means that many students cannot receive personalized services. This gives localized online schools an opening.

- After completing his self-study at night, a student with mediocre results would rush to join a livestream channel and listen to the lecture enthusiastically. This anecdote embodies the true essence of Kuaishou Education.

- Yuandinghui plans to use a technology center to serve 10,000 teachers in 2021.

The author of this chapter is Yang Rui, a researcher at Kuaishou Research Institute.

The founding of Yuandinghui was "forced" by the pandemic. Yuandinghui's parent company is called "Yuanding," which mainly provides a class management platform tool for primary and secondary school teachers. During the pandemic in 2020, when Yuanding's team members in Wuhan were quarantined at home, a strange combination of factors led to the creation of an educational MCN called "Yuandinghui." It has gone all-in on the Kuaishou platform and seems to be fairly successful so far.

The experts whom Yuandinghui has signed contracts with are all ordinary teachers with teaching experience and not celebrity teachers. Many of them come from fourth- or fifth-tier cities and county seats. Although their number of followers is only in the tens of thousands, their livestream channels consistently draw several hundred students. Aside from being experienced in teaching, they are also very professional and dedicated to their job. To accommodate their students' schooling schedule, some of them have chosen to start their livestream lectures in the mornings at 5:40 a.m.

The founder of Yuandinghui, Wang Xu, has lofty ambitions. He hopes to build a localized online school that provides lectures via livestream channels. His goal for 2021 is to train 10,000 KOCs, thereby forming a livestreaming matrix.

◎ *The following is an account by Wang Xu, founder of Yuandinghui.*

. . .

"Yuanding" started out by developing a K-12 (pre-school education to high school education) class management tool. Its product is mainly divided into three modules: learning, physical exercise, and class management. For example, after a teacher has handwritten the academic transcripts of the entire class, information visualization can then be realized simply by taking a photo. At the same time, dynamic data analysis can be carried out on the students' results. We have to process around 20,000 such photos every day.

There are approximately 338 cities in China that are fifth-tier and above, of which Yuanding provides coverage in 329. Our official account and mini- program have accumulated 3,000,000 to 4,000,000 user groups and get nearly two million daily active users, among which are 300,000 primary and secondary school teachers.

New Species: MCN + Local Online School

During the 2020 pandemic, the Kuaishou Education Ecosystem team and EdBeta Fund created a WeChat group for online education to help education entrepreneurs find startup opportunities on Kuaishou. After joining the group and learning from it, we found that MCNs had rather interesting relations of production and thus held many internal discussions on them.

Things also developed due to a strange combination of circumstances. Yuanding's Wuhan team was originally in charge of introducing products to schools, but when the pandemic struck, they became quarantined at home and thus decided that they might as well start a Kuaishou MCN. In April 2020, we officially opened for business.

Unlike traditional MCNs, we are not part of the Internet celebrity economy but are instead an "MCN + Local Online School." Let me break down and explain this concept.

Firstly, we believe that what MCNs solve are the problems regarding relations of production—this is their core purpose.

Previously, in order to market their courses, many educational organizations bought traffic on Yuanding's official account or miniprogram to do advertising. I have long thought about whether we can sell our own courses instead of simply relying on this form of commercial monetization.

The reason we did not do so was that I felt that recruiting teachers to carry out centralized teaching and research was low in ROI and fairly high in risk. Earlier on, a few IT-based projects like ours had recruited many teachers to prepare lessons, but they were high in manpower costs yet low in conversion. They served as a warning to us.

However, according to the MCN model, our relations with teachers are partnerships and thus no fixed costs such as teachers' base salaries would be incurred. What we have to bear are the costs of our own middle-end operations, which are included in Yuanding's business scope.

Therefore, this new type of relations of production is a very important reason why we are able to establish an MCN.

Secondly, the logic of a localized online school.

Large educational organizations usually adopt a centralized model of teaching and research. In other words, they would recruit talented people and focus on developing the best possible system of teaching and research with unified standards. Although this is a very good thing, its shortcoming is a lack of variation; by and large, different teachers would provide lectures on the same set of content.

However, with the opening up of China's education market, we have gradually reached users in different circles and discovered that centralized teaching and research do not suit everyone.

To give a simple example, a student who often scores 40 or 50 marks on examinations might find it difficult to understand the solution to a Math Olympiad problem, whereas the top students in Beijing's key secondary schools might find the same solution too simple. Therefore, suitability is a huge issue.

In addition, we can also see that, since 2019, a few startup projects on local online schools have emerged. For example, "Salt Chamber" from Fujian Province has expanded to six provinces throughout China.

Furthermore, China's college and high school entrance examinations are divided by region, and the market also has great regionality. For example, if the best school with the best teachers in Guangdong Province works on a centralized project of teaching and research, it would be able to cover Guangzhou, Shenzhen, and so on; parents and students would be willing to pay for it because every city in Guangdong Province uses the same editions of teaching material. Such local online schools are higher in suitability than nationwide educational organizations. For parents, localized teachers are also the most practical choice because local big name schools are very highly recognized.

This is the reason we chose to work on an "MCN + local online school." Our teachers are not celebrities but simply "teachers on a platform" instead, and we develop KOCs rather than KOLs. Most of them are ordinary workers in the education industry and not Internet celebrities or superstar teachers. We hope to offer a localized teaching and research online school to local students in the 300-odd cities that Yuanding already provides coverage in, as well as those in the broader market that Kuaishou provides coverage in.

Such an online school is defined as localized rather than nationwide. For example, a teacher in Jintang County, Chengdu, would not give lectures to students in Shanghai; he or she would only serve local students. Correspondingly, we place emphasis on the "Same City" module on Kuaishou. The teaching circles in some places are the same; for example, Shuangliu District, which is only a few dozen kilometers away from Jintang County, has similar academic standards to the latter, and so the teachers in Jintang County are also able to provide coverage in this district.

Creating a KOC Livestreaming Matrix

The teachers whom Yuandinghui currently has contracts with mainly come from three sources: first, teachers who were originally already Yuanding users; second, "native knowledge livestreamers" who developed on Kuaishou, such as "Granny Ganlu's Math Olympiad Lectures" and "Brother A'chai"—they know how to teach via livestreaming but are not good at promoting themselves and accumulating followers, and so that is where we come in; and third, teachers from other channels.

Granny Ganlu is 58 years old and has researched on elementary-level Math Olympiad for 13 years. Although she has only 40,000-plus followers, her livestream channel consistently draws around 300 concurrent viewers. "Junior High School Math Teacher Madam Gui" is a teacher in her 30s from Liuzhou, Guangxi Province; she has more than 170,000 followers and gets more than 700 concurrent viewers on her livestream channel. There is also "Learn English with Tsinghua's Gao Yuanyuan," whose real name is Shasha; she was a top student at Tsinghua University and is now an English teacher in one of Beijing's key secondary schools. As of November 2020, her livestream channel draws more than 20,000 viewers every day, with more than 2,000 concurrent viewers at its peak.

KOCs do not have as many followers as the top livestreamers and superstar teachers. Taking a fifth-tier city as an example, its population is 800,000 to 1.2 million people, of which K-12 students make up 10–12 percent, meaning that it has approximately 100,000 K-12 students. These students are the target servees of our KOCs. When Yuandinghui's teachers accumulate 100,000 followers, we would let this number grow on its own.

We have completed all the closed loops on Kuaishou. Using "Tsinghua's Gao Yuanyuan," Shasha, as an example, she only provides lectures on Kuaishou and charges a fee for them. Kuaishou has begun to offer paid livestreams, and so we use it to offer big online classes. Nowadays, a paid livestream lesson would get 200 to 300 buyers.

The price per customer of a paid livestream is anywhere from 3 to 9 yuan. During the 2020 summer holidays, Shasha provided 40 days of lessons, with one lesson per day. These 40 lessons were not sold as a package but separately instead. The short videos we upload every day include a link to the paid livestream lesson for that day or the next day; the lesson provided each day is different.

Following those 40 days, Shasha's livestream channel began to stabilize in terms of number of viewers. We split the profits 50–50, which is a pretty good deal for teachers. In August 2020, Shasha's account earned 60,000 to 70,000 yuan. Nowadays, many of Yuandinghui's teachers expect to earn 50,000 to 100,000 yuan by livestreaming.

We choose KOCs according to very simple logic. For instance, in a county seat, we would find teachers from schools that Yuanding already provides coverage. Alternatively, we would recruit teachers on Kuaishou. To give a hypothetical example, we would find a good teacher from a county's number one middle school. The number one middle school of a county is usually one of the better local schools, and so this teacher would be at a high enough standard to provide coverage for the students in his/her circle. We would work with him/her to create livestream lessons on Kuaishou, thereby enabling him/her to build up a personal brand on Kuaishou and generate a considerable income.

Be it in terms of the number of followers or the number of concurrent viewers, a single KOC is certainly no match for a KOL. However, we aim to develop KOLs on a large scale. Yuandinghui's goal for 2021 is to create 10,000 accounts—each with 100,000 followers, more than 100 concurrent viewers, and a monthly GMV of 10,000 yuan per person.

Earning the Business of Loyal Followers: "Creating Goods" Instead of "Letting the Goods Find Customers"

As of today, many people from the education industry who have Kuaishou accounts are still at version 1.0 of understanding, i.e., how to accumulate followers. I believe that we are at version 2.0, and this is mainly based on our livestreaming figures. During the 2021 winter holidays, our livestreaming matrix drew nearly 20,000 concurrent viewers.

This has to do with the guidance that the Kuaishou Education Ecosystem team has offered us and our understanding of the overall efficiency, as well as with our mindset of buckling down to get things done. I have never believed that having a lot of followers is all that it takes; many teachers with a million followers only get a few dozen viewers on their livestream channels. And without viewers, monetization is impossible.

There is a core underlying logic at work here—exactly whose business are you looking to earn? Is it your loyal followers or new followers?

The biggest difference between education and e-commerce lies in the fact that many of the things sold in e-commerce are fast-moving consumer goods that can be sold every day. Conversely, the SKUs of educational products are not updated as frequently, and it is possible for the same product to be sold over a long period of time.

We have observed that the livestream channels of certain livestreamers are able to generate GMVs of tens or hundreds of thousands of yuan just by selling a single course. However, they often run out of steam and are unable to sell courses for a long time subsequently, and this is because they use up all possible groups in one go. As their business is targeted at new followers, they must rely on short videos to attract followers.

Instead, our business is targeted at loyal followers. For example, when a teacher starts giving livestream lectures, 100 people are willing to spend 3 yuan a day to attend these lectures, and so the daily revenue is 300 yuan, meaning a monthly revenue of nearly 10,000 yuan. These 100 people are willing to spend time attending lectures on the livestream channel every day, and thus are called loyal followers.

We do not care whether a KOC teacher has 10,000 or 50,000 followers— as long as their livestream channel is able to maintain 100 concurrent viewers every day, that would be good enough for us. The people who watch short videos and those who watch livestreams are two different groups of people; only those who are truly willing to spend time listening to lectures attentively on a livestream channel are true followers.

Creating popular short videos alone would not draw followers to a livestream channel. One of the essential aspects of Kuaishou is the strong stickiness and sense of trust of its followers. When they find a teacher that they really like, they would be willing to attend lectures on the teacher's livestream channel every day.

Nearly 40 percent of Granny Ganlu's followers are left-behind children. These students come to her livestream channel every day not just to learn but also to satisfy their emotional needs. Often, they would comment on her livestream channel that their teachers at school do not care about them, and their parents are not with them. As luck would have it, they have now found a teacher who calls them her darlings and cares for them. Therefore, we believe that students in less-developed regions have emotional needs, and this precisely reflects the stickiness of Kuaishou's followers.

During the summer holidays, Shasha would begin her livestreams at seven or eight in the morning. When school reopens, however, her viewers would decrease very quickly. Some of them have given feedback, saying, "Teacher, we have to reach school by 6:30, so can you begin your lessons at 5:40?" Because of these followers, Shasha wakes up even earlier in the morning to begin her livestreams.

This embodies yet another essential aspect of Kuaishou that separates it from other platforms. Most people within the industry are working on standardized education, whereby a group of people develops a centralized curriculum before going to various platforms to find users. This is similar to e-commerce, in which goods are manufactured before seeking buyers on the market.

However, the true logic of Kuaishou is about "creating goods," as shown by a few of Kuaishou's influential livestreamers who would use their own capabilities to "create" whatever their followers want. Their teaching content is determined by the needs of their followers (students). This has greatly overturned our understanding.

Moreover, our statistics have found that 46 percent of Shasha's students for her 40-lesson summer course did not miss a single day of class. This greatly exceeded our expectations. Many people believe that Kuaishou's followers are here to play rather than to learn. However, this figure proves that Kuaishou's users are willing to continue learning on the platform if they find a good teacher.

For example, "Brother A'chai" livestreams on Kuaishou at around 10 p.m. every day. Why has he chosen this time slot? This is because many junior high school students in Guangdong Province have to conduct self-study in the evenings. He would begin his livestream at around 9:50 p.m., and by 10 p.m. or so, his livestream channel would have 300 to 400 viewers—that is when everyone has finished their self-study and is able to attend his lecture.

His students mostly score 60 to 70 marks on their examinations, which is considered below average. It might be hard to imagine that students with such mediocre results would be willing to attend online lessons after their self- study, but this shows that they like the teacher and thus do not find the online lessons excruciating.

Therefore, to succeed on Kuaishou, you first must be interesting and get followers to like you. I feel that the true essence of Kuaishou is about "creating goods." For those students who genuinely like you, you should offer them whatever they need—this is the art of doing business with loyal followers.

Restructuring the Chain of the Education Industry Using Livestreams

What is the sales conversion process of an educational organization usually like? Firstly, it is about putting goods on the market to create exposure. The advertisements we see on various apps and WeChat official accounts or on television are all directed by ad delivery departments.

These departments would place users in a CPA (cost per action) pool, which can take different forms: it can either be completely free or require paying a few yuan to enter a group in which lessons would be provided. These lessons, which can be bought at a very low price, are essentially trial lessons.

There is also a list-based method. For example, the on-screen ads that you see are CPM (cost per mille) ads. When users click on them, the system would get them to enter their phone numbers. Subsequently, marketers would call up the users and arrange lessons with them. This is a form of accurate marketing.

During this process, it is the CPS (cost per sales) that truly matters. This refers to the users who spend 2,000 to 3,000 yuan to purchase a course at its full price. The underlying logic is the need to carry out sales conversion.

As we started out with Yuanding, we can see the real internal data of any online education project no matter how they promote themselves externally. The conversion rate from leads to full-price lessons is only 20 percent at most, while some channels only get one-fourths or one-thirds of this figure, i.e., 5 percent to 7 percent.

For example, WeChat group marketing was originally carried out on a weekly cycle. Generally speaking, ad delivery would commence on Wednesdays or Thursdays, followed by three to four days of trial lessons. The marketing and operations teams would then wait for users to join a specified WeChat group. After accumulating 5,000 people, four days of lessons would begin. At the same time, the teacher would persuade students—who had initially only paid 9 yuan for a financial management course—to purchases courses at their full price. Every company would have its own sales pitch.

Table 6.1 The Delivery and Conversion of Online Educational Projects

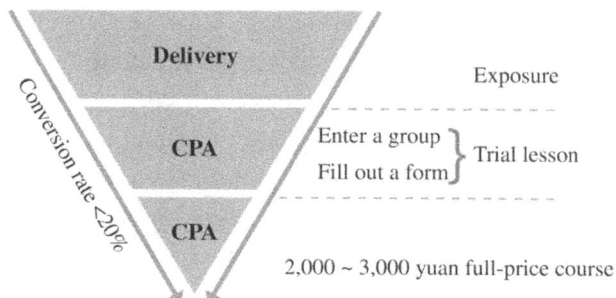

In reality, 5,000 people are accumulated via trial lessons, among whom 20 percent are converted into buyers of full-price courses over three or four days. This gives approximately 1,500 to 1,600 orders, which is a highly impressive result. The implementation cycle of such an operation is always carried out on a weekly basis; the manpower and time costs are too high for it to be done daily.

However, our paid livestream courses are actually sold in the form of admission tickets, thereby reconstructing the sales logic. One way of selling a 60-lesson summer course would be to sell it for several hundred yuan in a package; this is essentially no different from the old sales conversion process, whereby the teacher needs to be considerably skilled at promoting goods. However, livestreamers in the education industry are different from those in the clothing, cosmetics, and other industries; as teachers, they often feel uncomfortable about having to persuade their students to buy courses.

Another way is to sell each of the 60 lessons individually. Although there is a course syllabus, the lesson content for the next day can be adjusted according to the progress made today. Thus, each 3-yuan lesson is equivalent to an entrance ticket to a self-study room.

However, this method faces a huge challenge—it demands efficient sales conversion every day. Instead, the traditional form of sales conversion simply requires focusing on selling the course in one go, and its sales logic cannot support a price of 3 yuan per lesson. Its supply chain—which is made up of teachers, a production team, a sales team, an operations team, and a delivery team—is very long and is completely unable to support the costs of these teams.

Our teachers rarely film video clips, and besides, our short videos are mainly based on the teaching content and are thus a little dry. We are also rather slow at increasing our followers. Two days ago, we created an inspirational clip that has caused our number of followers to surge. However, the number of new followers is just a virtual number to us; it only solves the problem of exposure. To achieve actual conversion, livestreaming remains necessary. I believe that livestreaming has restructured the sales conversion process, making it possible for sales to be made every day and at a flat price of 3 yuan.

Some large educational organizations merely regard Kuaishou as a tool for acquiring traffic and attracting users to their WeChat groups. This is essentially no different from treating a Kuaishou account as a WeChat official account. However, what is the point of simply repeating on Kuaishou what has already been done on WeChat? Since the idea is to conduct livestream lessons, why lead people elsewhere? Why not conduct lessons on Kuaishou instead? We want to create closed loops on Kuaishou.

The core of Kuaishou's product logic lies in communities and associations. We now have nearly 20 Kuaishou communities and have to manage them every day.

We do not just want to follow the approach of MCNs, which is to sign contracts with a lot of teachers and conduct courses in every part of China. The core of the Internet celebrity economy is the promotion of goods, such as the full-price courses and textbooks of other educational organizations. We only conduct courses and do not promote goods, be it for trial lessons, paid livestream lessons, or recorded courses. However, our core products are paid livestream lessons, which are conducted by 80 percent of Yuandinghui's teachers nowadays.

Firstly, I believe that recorded courses cannot meet the demands of teaching because the stickiness between teachers and followers is not so high. It can be observed that there is a huge difference between the number of people who buy a recorded course and the number of people who actually complete the course. And without completing the course, a student would not have gotten to enjoy the teacher's services. It is only when a student buys a course, attends the lessons, and gains knowledge that they would make more purchases in the future—this is easier to achieve through paid livestream lessons.

Secondly, it is difficult for recorded courses to create connections among followers, whereas on a livestream channel, the interaction among followers is very important. An atmosphere of learning makes it easier for the course to be effective.

How to Serve 10,000 KOCs

We have incubated 200 to 300 Kuaishou accounts so far, and our goal for 2021 is to incubate 10,000 of them. Hence, we need to finalize the entire process and recruit successive batches of teachers, thereby turning the entire operation into an assembly line of sorts.

We will scale up by relying on our middle-end. In the past, MCNs usually served teachers by signing a contract with a top influencer and providing them with a team to assist them in writing scripts and filming and editing videos. This team could consist of anywhere from two to six people and would serve three to five teachers on average. A superstar teacher might, however, require several dozen people to serve them alone.

Instead, we have signed contracts with KOCs and intend to build a technology center that will empower teachers in two major ways: the first is to increase their followers as we place great emphasis on the number of followers that their livestream channels have; and the second is for them to earn an income by teaching.

Our incubation process basically takes eight weeks of time to help teachers increase their number of followers to 10,000 or more. The increase from 10,000 to 100,000 would then take an additional three to four weeks. For the initial training camp and the subsequent eight weeks, we would break up the work tasks for each week to facilitate operation and implementation.

As suggested by the Kuaishou Education Ecosystem team, we have divided Yuandinghui's team into six groups to serve the entire process. So far, we have formed five groups already.

Group A is in charge of the frontend recruitment of teachers.

Group B is in charge of teacher management, which is of central importance to us. They have to keep in touch with our teachers on a daily basis via phone and WeChat groups and tell them what they must do for that day. They are somewhat like celebrity assistants, and each of them can serve up to 40 teachers.

The managers in Group B mainly provide psychological guidance. For example, they would help a teacher who has recently gained a lot of followers to reflect on their experience and discuss areas that they can still improve in. Or, they would console and provide support to a teacher who has not gained new followers for a few days, and also help to figure out the problem and think of solutions.

However, the output of Group B requires the support of the other groups.

Therefore, we have created an independent Group B1 that is only in charge of the script library and does not deal with teachers. This library is very useful to teachers. We will help teachers prepare a rich variety of filming materials. Teachers can search for materials in the script library according to their number of followers and the stage that their account is at. Every script is a sample that contains information including the number of different scenes, the topic for the day, what to film for the first three seconds and the subsequent four seconds of a scene, what kind of facial expression to show, and so on.

There are suitable scripts in the script library, be it whether the teacher wants to provide lectures toward a screen, toward a blackboard, toward a PowerPoint presentation, or via a skit. We have classified these scripts into different categories from which teachers can choose.

The materials in the script library come from popular precedents across the Internet, while some were developed by ourselves. There are some teachers who cannot quite understand that the platform is algorithm-driven by nature. Without those indicators of gameplay and interaction rate, a video would not get sufficient exposure. Hence, we have to adjust the structure of videos and use algorithms to carry out matching.

We also carry out data analysis by using our own videos as well as those of other people. After assessing and publishing a video, Kuaishou's algorithm would push it into the next pool within a few minutes. The indicators are very impressive for our videos; on average, the click-through rate of a video cover is 30 percent or more, the interaction rate is 10 percent, and the new follower rate is 1 percent.

Group C is in charge of livestream operations for all teachers. A teacher has to meet certain standards before they are allowed to begin livestreaming. As our teachers' followers are considerably "vertical," a teacher may begin livestreaming after accumulating more than 6,000 followers or 180 people in their Kuaishou group. After they have acquired the basics of livestreaming, we would offer them professional training. They would then give their debut livestream and conduct a review on it. Subsequently, they may officially provide livestream lectures. At every stage of a teacher's growth from the time that they join Yuandinghui, they would be guided by a corresponding team according to the standard procedures.

Livestream operations require scene control, community management, and event planning, all of which are handled by Group C. During a goods-promoting livestream, a scene controller has to be present to alter prices and set the atmosphere. Likewise, during a livestream lecture, it would be ideal if the scene controller and the teacher can both be present in the livestream studio. However, this is hard to achieve because our teachers are scattered across the entire country.

A teacher's livestreams are relatively simple—they are all lessons. Therefore, we would place a few sales segments on the public channel. The scene controller is usually an administrator or a teaching assistant.

Group E is in charge of data. How have we made it possible for one person to serve 40 teachers? This is due to our middle-end system and data dashboard, which allow us to see a teacher's livestream statistics, follower growth, and so on—such real-time data can provide adequate support for our livestream operations.

We are also in the middle of forming Group D, which will be in charge of supply chain standardization. Nowadays, some students want to buy a teacher's lecture notes, and so this requires us to engage with printing houses and logistics companies. Figure 6.2 shows the operations teams that Yuandinghui has formed with ordinary teachers in mind.

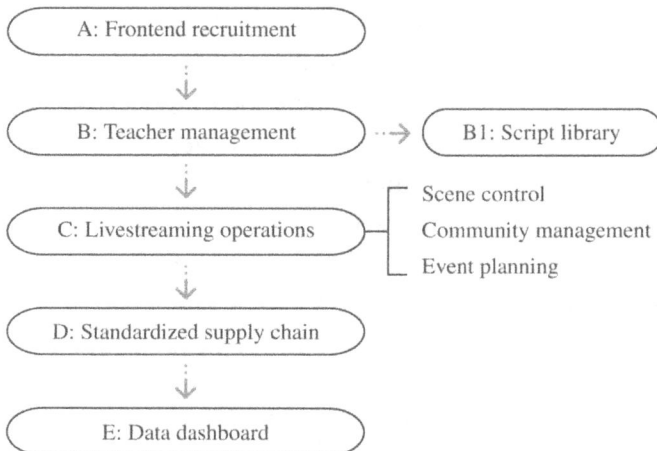

Figure 6.2 The Operations Teams That Yuandinghui Has Formed with Ordinary Teachers in Mind

These are our standard operating procedures in full; they form a completely standardized assembly line and are the outcome of repeated discussions and iterations. The members of the Kuaishou Education Ecosystem team have also offered us plenty of support in this regard. Figure 6.3 shows Yuandinghui's full process for recruiting teachers.

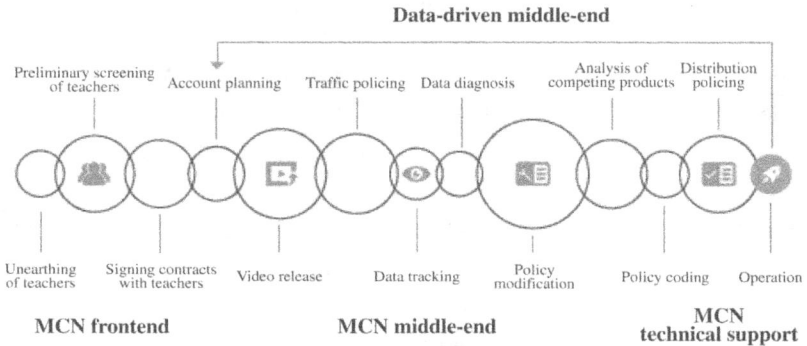

Figure 6.3 Yuandinghui's Teacher Recruitment Process in Full

Winning Together with the Platform and Teachers

When it comes to our relations with traditional online educational organizations, the Kuaishou platform, and the native teachers on Kuaishou, I believe that they can be looked at from the following perspectives:

Firstly, judging from the nature of our educational services, what we are doing is online education. Broadly speaking, our products are in competition with those of established online educational organizations. However, we are taking a different route. Online education is a large category; our business model and target groups are different from those of others.

As mentioned earlier, we have adopted an "MCN + local online school" model. We do not provide centralized teaching and research and are not a labor-intensive enterprise. Instead, through our powerful technology center, we empower a wide range of teachers and form partnerships with them. We have also restructured the sales conversion chain of online education and lowered the costs of customer acquisition.

Secondly, judging from our relations with Kuaishou's native teachers, Kuaishou is essentially an ecosystem or a plot of soil; the role that it plays is fairly low-level, and its function is to bring users online. I feel that our logic is consistent with that of the native teachers in Kuaishou's ecosystem.

I remember that when I had my first phone conversation with Brother A'chai, I realized that Kuaishou's native "knowledge livestreamers" were highly grateful to Kuaishou and also hoped to complete closed loops on the platform. From a platform-based perspective, we all hope to complete teaching closed loops on the Kuaishou platform to retain users.

Thirdly, in terms of methodology, growth trajectory, and overall teaching content, we cause a certain amount of "corrosion" upon the native teachers. This is because they do not have the same large-scale, "assembly-line style" combat capabilities as us. Nevertheless, many teachers are willing to work and win together with us.

Earlier on, we kept promoting separate, individual accounts, but nowadays, we are preparing to do "co-livestreaming" within the same circle. In this way, English teachers and math teachers can have the same followers, thereby forming a true online school. Next, we want to make it such that every teacher has a paid group of 200 to 300 people, giving us a paid group of 500 to 600 unique people when stacked with other groups.

An ideal scenario that we have envisaged is for us to have a few partnering teachers from a county, with each teacher having as many as tens of thousands of followers. These teachers are able to cover various subjects, including Chinese, English, math, physics, and chemistry.

ENABLING EVERY STUDENT TO FIND SUITABLE EDUCATIONAL PRODUCTS

—Wang Xu
Founder of Yuandinghui

Key Points

- True inclusivity is about enabling every student to find suitable educational products and enjoy the charm of education.

- Kuaishou's inclusive algorithm and dual-column logic can help grassroots teachers build their own small private domain traffic.

- We will enable more and more users from low-tier regions to participate in online education.

Editor's note: Be it as tools of communication or production, short videos and livestreams have provided extraordinary value in terms of innovation and efficiency. Based on increasing efficiency in the education field, they put a greater test on our team's understanding of "content professionalism" and "teaching service professionalism." Moreover, this understanding has to be backed up by "inclusive values."

Hence, the Kuaishou Education Ecosystem team has held a conversation on the idea of "inclusive values" with their friends at Yuandinghui, with Wang Xu taking the minutes. This article talks about Yuandinghui's understanding of what supports and drives them to act, to innovate, and to put into practice.

Reunderstanding Inclusivity After Starting a Business

A few years ago, when we were promoting Yuanding nationwide, we encountered many schools, teachers, and students from less-developed regions, including primary schools in town centers and remote villages. Some of these schools only had one subject teacher and one pastoral teacher, and mixed students from all grades into the same class. This is an actual situation that exists in education. From then on, having come into contact with a broader scope of education in China, many of our deep-rooted ideas were shattered.

We had originally believed that we would be able to help students in these regions simply by providing them with better learning tools and a more modernized information system. However, during the process of implementation, we discovered that what these students actually need are teachers who can provide them with guidance on their shortcomings.

This is the first level of inclusive education that I understand. We hope that there will be more people to take care of more students, especially those from less-developed regions, so that they can enjoy the same education as urban students. In other words, we intend to spread high-quality educational resources more widely than before.

When we first started doing Kuaishou, we hoped to bring in a group of excellent teachers who would deliver high-quality content to more users by using Kuaishou's "short video + livestreaming" model. However, during the actual process of livestreaming, we discovered an unexpected phenomenon: when our teachers used the supposedly excellent teaching methods from top schools to carry out teaching, many students on our livestream channels could neither understand nor grasp these methods quickly.

When our teachers are preparing lessons, their expectation is for more students to score 90 marks. However, we discovered that many of the children on our livestream channels merely hoped to improve their scores from 40 to 60 marks. Therefore, a problem arises: does our supposedly "excellent" curriculum suit all our students?

This is the second level of inclusive education that I understand: high-end educational products are not always the best. True inclusivity lies in enabling every student to find suitable educational products and enjoy the charm of education.

Kuaishou knowledge livestreamer "Brother A'chai" begins his livestreams at 10 p.m. every night because his students have to conduct self-study in the evenings. When I saw how his students would rush onto his livestream channel to continue learning after completing their self-study, Kuaishou once again shattered my original understanding. These students, traditionally seen as "marginal students" who get bad grades and are poor in learning ability, would actually give up their rest time at night for the sake of learning—this is something that we absolutely never imagined.

Hence, we have discovered that good education ought to be interesting and useful. Truly inclusive education is about enabling more people to develop an interest in learning itself and thereby produce an inner drive to keep on learning. The significance of inclusivity lies in the transmission of knowledge using methods that are more acceptable to the masses; it is only when learning is interesting and useful that more people would partake in it.

Understanding Kuaishou's Inclusive Education from the Supply and Demand Ends

Education is divided into two ends. The first is regarding who the providers of good content are, while the other is regarding who the learners are. Yuandinghui's trials run on Kuaishou Education mainly sought to reflect its inclusive values from these two ends.

On one end, the providers of educational content have achieved unprecedented variety on Kuaishou.

When we were looking for native teachers to collaborate with on Kuaishou, we discovered to our surprise that Kuaishou already had a large number of teacher-livestreamer accounts. Moreover, we were able to find teachers for any academic term, subject, and textbook edition. These teachers came from different circles and used a large amount of time to run their own Kuaishou accounts.

Kuaishou's inclusive algorithm and dual-column logic are also able to effectively help grassroots teachers build up their own private domain traffic. Kuaishou Education has enabled these KOC teachers to enjoy equal opportunities; instead of merely serving as a foil for superstar teachers, they are now able to provide more benefits to more ordinary educational creators.

The joining of many grassroots teachers has also expanded the scope of educational services. In line with this principle, Yuandinghui has, since the beginning, fixed Kuaishou's native grassroots teachers and the relevant teachers from less-developed areas on Yuanding as its recruitment targets.

Hailing from the countryside of Guangdong Province, "Master Yu's Chinese Lectures" is a teacher who has enjoyed reading classical literature since his youth. Due to various reasons, he never had the opportunity to teach the traditional poetry and "Big Chinese" content that he enjoyed most while serving as a schoolteacher previously. Hence, he began to create his own educational content on Kuaishou. At first, he merely hoped to use his spare time to teach Big Chinese for a while and thereby fulfill one of his dreams. Little did he expect that his Big Chinese course would prove to be an instant hit—in just a month, he became a famous

Big Chinese teacher who had 50,000 followers. Today, he works full-time on Kuaishou, thereby fulfilling his dream and enabling more people to comprehend the beauty of ancient poetry.

On the other end, i.e., the perspectives of the course-attending students or their parents, we discovered that more users from less-developed areas are partaking in the process of learning today.

Previously, these users might not have come into contact with online educational products at all or had some contact but ultimately never bought a full-price course. Today, through Kuaishou short videos and livestreams, they have come into contact with large online classes that are delivered in the form of livestreams.

The father of one of our students has a Kuaishou account called "Drifting Without Trace." When browsing Kuaishou one day, he inadvertently discovered Teacher Shasha's English short videos. Shasha is not only beautiful in appearance but also provides her lectures in fluent, idiomatic English, which is a rarity in classrooms across China. Hence, this parent became a loyal follower of Shasha.

He has also shared Shasha's works in his own Kuaishou groups, WeChat groups, and QQ groups. He once said that he hoped more of Kuaishou's loyal followers would see that there is such a good teacher on Kuaishou. Today, "Drifting Without Trace" has become an administrator of the Kuaishou follower group of "Tsinghua's Gao Yuanyuan" and a fully-deserving opinion leader among those hundreds of thousands of followers. He said that he would continue to share Shasha's works so that more people in China would find a truly good teacher on Kuaishou.

For Kuaishou's loyal followers, the advantages of inclusive education are reflected in two aspects: on the one hand, they can obtain online educational content at a low price or even for free. On the other hand, they can find teachers that they like and courses that they can understand, thereby completing their final educational deliverables on the Kuaishou platform.

As of today, the followers of the accounts of Yuandinghui's teachers come from more than 300 cities across China.

Based on the distribution of Yuandinghui's followers, we can see that more and more users from low-tier regions are partaking in online education. At the same time, more and more of the loyal followers mentioned by "Drifting Without Trace" are beginning to learn attentively and continuously on Kuaishou instead of simply seeking entertainment on the platform.

In compliance with her followers' demands, Shasha has adjusted the time of her livestreams to 5:40 in the morning. The number of her daily viewers has exceeded 20,000, while the number of her peak concurrent viewers has exceeded 2,000.

The unwavering persistence of her followers every morning has shown us that they will become an emerging force in the online education market of the future. Kuaishou's algorithm has created better interpersonal connections within the ecosystem and redefined the notion of "people, goods, and place."

Yuandinghui's Goal Regarding Inclusive Education

In creating Yuandinghui, we hoped to better unearth teachers throughout China and help them maximize their value. Yuandinghui's vision is to liberate every teacher in the world.

In our opinion, liberation takes place on three levels:

Firstly, we provide teachers with better tools to liberate them from their tedious daily schedules.

Secondly, we use more efficient methods to help teachers share their own teaching experiences and build their own independent brands.

Thirdly, we help teachers earn an income that matches their efforts.

Many grassroots teachers do not understand the techniques of producing short videos and hosting livestreams. Despite spending a lot of time on filming short videos, they are unable to achieve the desired results. However, because they are frontline teachers who understand children well, we are willing to provide them with more assistance in growing and monetizing their accounts. We want to help people who are willing givers to get their due rewards and recognition of their value.

In the future, we hope to find on Kuaishou 10,000 grassroots teachers from the 300-odd cities in which we provide coverage. We want to help them become educational livestreamers that have hundreds of thousands or even millions of followers and ensure that their livestream channels consistently draw 100 concurrent viewers, thereby enabling them to earn a stable income and influence hundreds of millions of people.

We will enable these grassroots teachers to offer everyone teaching methods that are more practical, teaching content that is more suitable, and product prices that are more affordable. This will allow more consumers to partake in Kuaishou's ecosystem. Together, we will work hard to build better connections among teachers, content, students, and parents, and fulfill even more dreams. Ultimately, we will achieve the true value of inclusivity.

CHAPTER SEVEN

LIVESTREAMING + JEWELRY

- In the brick-and-mortar store retail model, the markup rate of jadeite is as high as 1,000 percent. But livestreaming is making the prices of jadeite increasingly transparent. Using Sihui as a case study, this chapter looks at how livestreaming is bringing new opportunities to the traditional jadeite industry.

SIHUI, GUANGDONG PROVINCE: A NEVER-SLEEPING CITY OF JADE AND JEWELRY

Key Points

- Livestreaming has changed the sales chain and made prices transparent. Customers can now buy authentic source goods on livestream channels.

- Once predominated by "walkstreamers" and "sitstreamers," Sihui has gradually become predominated by shopstreamers. At the same time, businesses with enterprise operations have emerged here.

- Jadeite livestreaming has boosted employment and spending in Sihui.

This chapter is authored by Yang Rui, a researcher at Kuaishou Research Institute, and Zhen Xu, a research assistant at Kuaishou Research Institute.

When we first went to Sihui, a small county-level city in Guangdong Province, to conduct a survey and research, we often heard fresh yet unfamiliar terms being spoken by those surveyed—"meter-high counters," "goods owner," "appointment number," "glass-type," "green jadeite," "unpolished jadeite," and so on. These terms are either jargon in the jadeite industry or new professions and phenomena born of jadeite livestreaming.

Sihui is located within Zhaoqing, Guangdong Province, and is often called the "city of jadeware." Only a half hour drive from Guangzhou Baiyun Airport, this county-level city is the biggest processing and distribution center of nephrite and jadeite in China. Seventy percent of its annual expenditure of raw nephrite and jadeite comes from Myanmar, and it produces 80 percent of China's total annual output of nephrite and jadeite products.

With the advent of the livestreaming era, Sihui has also been nicknamed the "city of jadeware livestreaming." As early as 2016, there were already some young people shuttling among the stalls of Sihui's jadeite wholesale markets with their mobile phones in hand, helping their followers haggle with stallholders and make quick purchases. As the livestreaming ecosystem gradually evolved, Fang Guoying, founder of Wanxinglong Jadeite City, spotted a business opportunity—he built a livestreaming city in the northern district of Wanxinglong, thereby bringing Sihui's jadeite industry onto the express lane of livestreaming. There are many doubts regarding the compatibility of jadeware and livestreaming. For example, every piece of jadeite in the world is unique, and so people often say that "gold has a price whereas jade is priceless." Conversely, many people understand livestream e-commerce to be synonymous with bulk sales and hot-selling products. Hence, how did the jadeite industry, which is so removed from the idea of hot-selling products, become a trend in livestreaming?

Furthermore, jadeite is popularly seen as something expensive. Thus, what kind of people would buy a product with such a high price per customer via a livestream channel? Why is the repurchase rate of jadeite so high on livestream channels? How did livestreamers establish a high degree of trust with their followers? Why Sihui of all places? And what kind of influence has the jadeite industry had on the production and sales chains?

Some of this confusion might be cleared up by reading through the following interview.

Let me first do a summary of it. Every piece of jadeite carries a tremendous amount of information—just identifying its type, translucency, and color puts a huge test on one's eyesight and experience. Inside a jadeware wholesale market, you would see many people holding a powerful flashlight in their hand. This is because the experts require a flashlight to examine a piece of jadeite's degree of perfection, which is determined by its density, its translucency, its coloration, the number of "cotton spots," the presence of fractures, and so on. During the old era of picture and text, a photo or even a video was unable to convey so much information, but livestreaming has made it possible to do so.

Livestreaming has reduced the costs of communication in the jadeite trade. Sihui's jadeite industry has gone through the era of WeChat Business, and until today, many people are still running WeChat businesses. However, WeChat businesses find it very difficult to perform real-time communication with buyers during the processes of bargaining with stallholders, receiving payment from buyers, and handling returns. On a livestream channel, the livestreamer serves as a spokesperson for their followers by helping them bargain with goods owners. If a follower takes a fancy to a certain product, they can tell the livestreamer to point the camera at it, and they can then enter "1" to buy it.

Livestreaming has also reduced the barriers to entering the jadeite industry. Anyone with a mobile phone can conduct livestreams. From sales to shipment to aftersales, all the processes can be completed by a single person. This is something unimaginable to many of the old guard in the jadeite industry. Originally, anyone who wanted to enter the jadeite industry had to serve as an apprentice for three to five years before starting their own business step by step. Alternatively, they would need to have huge capital on their hands. Nowadays, however, countless empty-handed young people can enter the industry with nothing but warm blood in their veins.

Livestreaming has changed the sales chain and made prices transparent. Perhaps many of you readers have had experiences of buying jadeite in a brick-and-mortar store and realizing that the better-quality ones tend not to be cheap in price. In reality, from a raw stone to the finished product, jadeite has to pass through a factory, a "first-tier" market in Sihui, a "second-tier" market in Hualin, and a brick-and-mortar store before finally reaching consumers. As it passes through each of these phases, its price would usually double. But now, livestreaming has practically eliminated all these intermediate phases,

causing the chain to become "raw stone → factory → goods owner → livestream channel → consumer." At the same time, livestreaming has made the prices of jadeite transparent (see Figure 7.1).

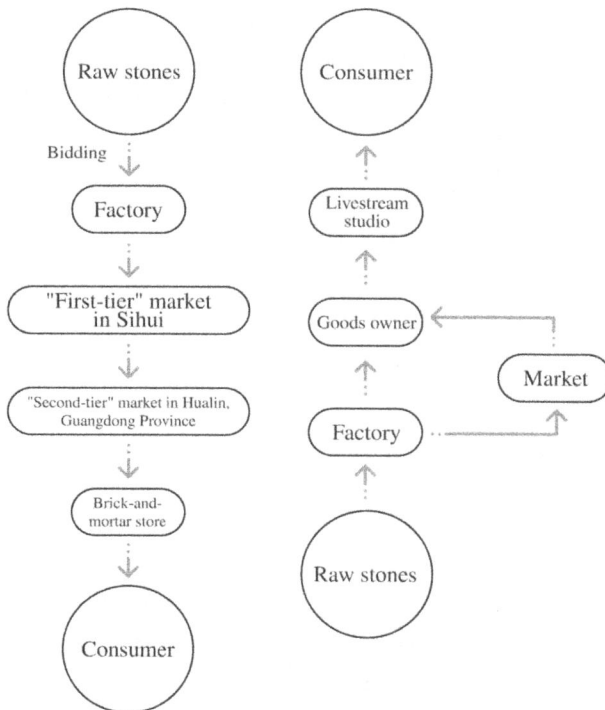

Figure 7.1 How Livestreaming Has Changed the Sales Chain of Jadeite

This explains why Sihui's livestream ecosystem has become so hot. As China's source of jadeite processing, Sihui has an absolute advantage in price performance. The personal experiences of Kuaishou livestreamer Boss Li fully encapsulate this point. She started out by procuring goods from Yiwu, but later discovered that Guangzhou had many sources of high-quality goods. By chance, she later got on a bus heading toward Sihui, where she discovered an even bigger world.

Livestreaming has increased the visibility of the jadeite industry. On a livestream channel nowadays, unpolished jadeite can be exhibited, the process of polishing can be shown, and even the upstream trade of raw stones can be displayed. As the visibility of the upstream segments of the jadeite industry chain has been greatly increased, jadeite is also gradually becoming seen by more people. Through our survey and research, we have discovered that many livestreamers are newcomers to the jadeite industry. They, too, had decided to enter the industry after watching a few livestreams and feeling that this was a highly profitable industry. The increasing visibility of the industry is also reflected in the breakdown of the existing social circle among businesses. As a livestreamer from Sihui said, "WeChat businesses can only reach their friends on WeChat because that is the enclosed space of a private domain. On the other hand, livestreams can obtain customer traffic from public domains; people from all over the world can enter a livestream channel."

Furthermore, livestreaming has increased the penetration of jadeite. In the past, jadeite was only sold in brick-and-mortar stores of large cities—and often only at special counters. However, because livestreams are accessible by users all over China, people in regions where jadeite previously did not reach and was not sold are now also able to buy jadeite. Besides, even in brick-and-mortar stores, only a limited number of products can be seen; in comparison, livestreams are able to showcase a far greater number of SKUs.

A Mix of Walkstreamers, Sitstreamers, and Shopstreamers

Sihui has 13 jade trading centers, among which livestreaming is most prevalent in Tianguangxu, Yubo City, and the Wanxinglong area.

Livestream studios can be found everywhere, be it in an inconspicuous alley or a fashionable high-rise building. At the same time, there is a dense distribution of inlaying shops and small processing workshops. The livestreaming industry in this area can be said to be made up of walkstreamers, sitstreamers, and shopstreamers.

Tianguangxu is one of the most famous jadeware wholesale markets in Sihui. Nowadays, it sells finished jadeite products by day and unpolished jadeite by night. Inside each of the many stalls scattered throughout the market, jadeite is exhibited on "meter-high counters." The stallholders sit behind the counters, allowing customers to freely wander among different stalls.

In Tianguangxu Market, there are also "walkstreamers," i.e., livestreamers who use their phones to show their followers the process of them finding goods among the stalls. When they see a piece of jade that they like, they stop to admire it for a while. With their camera facing it, they shine a light on it to check its translucency. If a follower becomes interested in buying it, the streamer may then haggle with the stallholder.

Walkstreaming is one of the earliest forms of jadeite livestreaming. A few livestreamers recall that when they first started doing it, many stallholders were unreceptive to them. When they used their phones to film videos of the goods in a stall, the owner would ask, "What are you filming?" Gradually, however, the stallholders realized that these livestreamers were really able to sell their goods on their behalf, and thus their initial coldness eventually turned into compliance.

Over time, most of these individual livestreamers have disappeared.

Sitstreaming is another form. In Jincuibao Jadeite and Jadeware City, which is situated next to Tianguangxu, we saw this extant form of livestreaming. The livestreamer sits behind the meter-high counter, with the store owner sitting on the opposite side. The change from walkstreaming to sitstreaming is actually the transformation from "livestreamers looking for goods" to "goods owners supplying goods."

This transformation also has to do with the followers' sense of experience. During a walkstream, the walkstreamer's camera would constantly wobble. Furthermore, there is a chance that the walkstreamer would be driven away by the stallholder. As a result, consumers are not guaranteed a good experience and might wonder if there would be quality issues with the things they buy. Instead, during a sitstream, each piece of jadeite is introduced one by one, affording consumers the time to look at each piece carefully. Compared to walkstreamers, sitstreamers offer consumers a greater sense of trust, a more intuitive display of the jadeite, and a less time-constrained experience.

The "livestream studio + goods owners supply goods" model is another form that evolved from sitstreaming. Today, 90 percent of Sihui's livestreams have switched to this model. Inside the Wanxinglong Livestream Base, which is one of Kuaishou's service providers in Sihui, there is a dense distribution of fixed livestream studios and livestreamers. Goods owners supply goods to the livestream studios via "appointments." If it is said that the livestream studios and goods in Hangzhou's supply chain bases are fixed in place waiting for the livestreamers to come and conduct special livestreams, then in Sihui's supply chain bases, it is the livestream studios and the livestreamers that are fixed in place while the goods owners and goods are mobile.

Such livestream studios, which are similar to livestream shops, get a fairly consistent amount of traffic and give less weight to the livestreamer's persona, instead relying more on the products to get ahead of the competition.

The livestreamer generally takes a "plate of goods" from the goods owner and sells each piece of jade one by one. The goods owner sits opposite the livestreamer, who then tries to strike a bargain with them. If a viewer on the livestream channel likes a particular piece, they can type in the secret code given by the livestreamer. For example, if the livestreamer says, "enter one if you like this," the viewer would enter "one" on the public channel. Subsequently, the livestreamer would write down the name of the first viewer to "enter one" on a small flashcard together with the product price. They would then use a vernier caliper to measure the size of the jadeite on-stream, and then write down details such as the thickness, length, width, and height of the jadeite on the flashcard. If the product is a ring or a bracelet, the circumference must also be noted. After the viewer has made payment, the jadeite would then be shipped.

Sihui has thousands if not tens of thousands of goods owners of all sizes who supply goods to the various livestream studios. The studios oversee sales while the suppliers handle all goods and returns. The goods owners usually spend their daytime collecting goods from factories and markets, and their nighttime conducting livestreams in the livestream studios.

Most goods owners know very well which livestream studios mainly sell pendants or inlaid gems, and which cities their products are mainly sold to. If they are unclear on these things, they can scan a WeChat QR code pasted on the door of the livestream studio to find out. Some goods owners would send photos of their products, while others would bring their goods to the livestream studio to inquire directly. If a livestream studio takes a fancy to their goods, it would arrange a schedule with them.

Jadeite is usually made into pendants, inlaid gems, bracelets, rings, and so on. Most of the time, the goods sold by a livestream studio would bear its unique style and label, and would be categorized into low-quality, medium-quality, and high-quality. Each livestream studio would consolidate its product line according to its followers. For example, if a livestream studio known for selling "high-quality goods" suddenly sells "low-quality goods," its followers would usually be dissatisfied. Similarly, if a livestream studio known for selling "medium- and low-quality goods" starts to sell "high-quality goods," these high-quality goods would usually not sell well.

A few companies with enterprise operations have already established departments for livestreamer training, presales, aftersales, and logistics. They also have a new media department that is specially in charge of filming video clips, and a marketing department that oversees engaging with goods owners. Because such companies tend to have huge daily shipment volumes, they would certainly have negotiated a price with the logistics companies and thus enjoy a price advantage.

From the moment a follower places an order for a product in a livestream channel until the product is retrieved by the courier, the company would monitor the entire process via camera. This is because jadeite is relatively expensive and so there is a need to apportion liability appropriately in the event that something goes wrong.

Livestreaming Has Bred New Professions in the Jadeite Industry

"The young people here in Sihui are standing on an unprecedented trend in history." Shen Li, head of operations at the Wanxinglong Livestream Base, suddenly made this comment while bringing us around the livestream city. Inside the base, we heard the voices of livestreamers haggling with goods owners coming from the livestream studios every now and then. At the entrance of the livestream studios, two types of roll-up banners are commonly seen: the first is employment advertisements, while the second is a QR code for taking an appointment number.

Many new professions have emerged in Sihui thanks to jadeite livestreaming, including livestreamer, goods owner, assistant livestreamer, customer service officer, and operator.

Anyone who has some knowledge of the jadeite industry may apply to become a livestreamer. The goods owners, who understand their own products best, would teach the livestreamers how to appraise their products, including the selling points. There are also some livestream studios that provide training to livestreamers. Shen Li said that the monthly salary of a livestreamer is upward of 10,000 yuan, with additional commission based on their sales performance—the livestreamers who perform well earn at least 20,000 to 30,000 yuan every month.

Sihui has gathered people from all over China. Kuaishou livestreamer "Haifeng Jewelry"—who has more than 1.4 million followers as of early January 2021—is from Jilin and was formerly an excavator operator. In 2017, he went to Ruili, Yunnan Province, to do jadeite livestreaming. During that time, he uploaded on Kuaishou a video clip of himself haggling with Burmese traders. The clip made it on to the Trending page and brought him many new followers. Thereafter, he entered the jadeite industry, and he has now come to Sihui to seek riches. Wang Zhi, owner of the Kuaishou account "Wangwang Jadeite," is from Hunan Province. In 2016, he heard that someone from his hometown had made a good sum of money by selling jadeite, and so he headed to Yunnan himself. In April 2018, he went to Sihui, opened his own Kuaishou account, and slowly built his own team. There are many other young people with similar stories.

A goods owner is another new profession. Just like jadeite hunters, they search for products in factories and markets, using their sharp eyes to assess the value of different pieces of jadeite and then striking a bargain. After procuring the goods that they like, they supply these goods to livestream studios. To be an excellent goods owner, one must "understand goods, prices, and the market situation."

The goods supplied by goods owners have propped up Sihui's livestream studios of varying sizes. To a certain extent, goods owners are also helping the livestream studios bear some of their risks and pressures. Goods owners must have capital strength; if the livestream studios fail to sell their goods, the goods are stuck in their hands. Therefore, aside from having professional acumen and bargaining skills, goods owners must also be astute at assessing consumers' preferences.

Sihui's livestreaming industry offers much higher salaries than those in most industries. For example, a restaurant waiter earns approximately 2,500 yuan per month, whereas a livestreamer's base salary is approximately 10,000 yuan per month. Even a customer service officer in the livestreaming industry earns upward of 4,000 yuan per month.

Shen Li explained that there are currently 300 livestream studios in the Wanxinglong Livestream Base, and they have directly and indirectly driven the employment of tens of thousands of people. Taking Kuaishou livestreamer "Wangwang Jadeite" for example, his team only consisted of him and his wife when they first arrived in Sihui in 2017, but it has now expanded to 50 people, among whom are a dozen-odd livestreamers and a dozen-odd customer service officers. A few livestream studios that have completed the enterprization of their operations have teams consisting of hundreds or even thousands of people.

During the course of bringing more people on board Kuaishou, Kuaishou's service providers have discovered that there are a few elderly stallholders who find it difficult to accept the new business format, do not know how to do livestreaming, and lack a strong will for it in any case. As a result, their businesses languished during the pandemic.

Jadeite's Breakout Has Stimulated Consumption

The livestreaming scene in Sihui has experienced the iteration of different platforms. In 2020, the scene became more fragmented than ever before. Optimistic about the potential of jadeite livestreaming, many major platforms decided to enter Sihui. Aside from integrated platforms, they also include jadeite livestreaming platforms that are more vertical in nature.

Shen Li explained that, before 2017, Sihui's livestreaming scene mainly sold "stock goods." Although those cheap things that were sold for a few dozen yuan each were also jadeite, they were seen as not good enough in quality by industry insiders. Therefore, the price per customer was only a few dozen yuan at first.

As promotional livestreams became popular, the quality of jadeite on offer increased within just a few months, thereby causing the price per customer to increase to several hundred yuan. As of today, it has risen to over a thousand yuan. For some Kuaishou businesses, the price per customer has exceeded 40,000 yuan.

As the tastes of consumers evolve, jadeite designs are becoming increasingly diverse, and the speed of update is also increasing. Livestreaming has sped up the circulation of jadeite and the updating of designs, while businesses respond according to the market demand. The role of the goods owners is also speeding up the update process; this is because overstocking is their biggest headache, and thus they must seize trends quickly and choose products that best suit the tastes of livestream channel viewers.

To satisfy the new demands of consumers, jadeite designs with higher price-performance have been developed. In the past, the popular demand was for jadeite designs that portrayed an artistic conception of mountains and waters, but now, more and more followers are willing to spend several hundred yuan on small jadeite ornaments. Jadeite is becoming a part of the lives of the common folk.

During the era of brick-and-mortar store retail, only a limited number of people understood jadeite. However, livestreaming is currently causing jadeite to "break out" of this circle and connect with potential consumers. When Kuaishou livestreamer Boss Li was running a brick-and-mortar store in Hangzhou, her customers were mostly locals. Today, however, her followers come from all over China and even overseas.

Back in the day when jadeite was sold via brick-and-mortar stores, a store could only accommodate 20 or so people at the same time. But a livestream channel can accommodate thousands of concurrent viewers. As soon as they encountered the new sales channel that is livestreaming, those people who previously could not afford to buy jadeite worth hundreds of thousands or millions of yuan in brick-and-mortar stores discovered that there were actually jadeite products that they could afford, and they were thus likely to place orders. This is because livestream channels offer higher price-performance than what is possible in brick-and-mortar stores.

Moreover, brick-and-mortar stores cannot keep up with livestream channels in terms of price, design, and variety. Fashion trends for jadeite would change with the seasons. To give an example, for customers from northern China where temperatures get cold by autumn, gilded jadeite does not sell well during autumn because it feels cold on the skin.

Several new trends have also emerged in Sihui's jadeite livestreaming scene. Many expert-type livestreamers who were originally based in Yunnan Province have relocated to Sihui.

On the one hand, this is because Yunnan Jade City Market was temporarily closed after two imported cases of COVID-19 were found in Ruili on September 13, 2020. Furthermore, due to the severe epidemic situation in Myanmar, the bidding process for raw jade materials was postponed and thus new materials could not be imported into China. Facing an extreme shortage of goods, the livestreamers in Ruili came over to Sihui to look for goods.

On the other hand, this is also because several of these livestreamers discovered that the price-performance of jadeite in Sihui is higher than that in Ruili. Logistics is one of the contributing factors. A Kuaishou livestreamer who had relocated from Ruili to Sihui explained that the latter is superior in logistics to the former—in Sihui, the logistical costs are only 2.7 to 3 yuan per order.

Perhaps because more and more jadeite experts have relocated to Sihui, exchanges and collision of information are now taking place in the city. These days, Sihui's livestream bases and jadeite businesses are considering the idea of making standard products.

The International Jadeware City Livestream Base, which is one of Kuaishou's service providers in Sihui, is also planning to build a product selection center. Aside from jadeite, it would also deal with chalcedony, agate, and nephrite, as well as gemstones, moissanite, gilded jade, silver-inlaid jade, and other varieties. The center is mainly focused on standard products and is equipped with livestream studios and scenario spaces. When livestreamers arrive at the base, they only have to focus on livestreaming; all the follow-up work would be handled by the center.

WANXINGLONG LIVESTREAM BASE: THE FUSION OF ONLINE AND OFFLINE

Key Points

- As a service provider in the jadeite industrial belt, the Wanxinglong Livestream Base bears responsibilities for serving the industrial belt, incubating businesses, regulating the behaviors of offline businesses, and so on.

- Wanxinglong Jadeite City began cracking down on counterfeit goods as early as the old market era, laying the foundations for its subsequent regulation of the operations of livestream e-commerce businesses.

- Wanxinglong Jadeite City has opened a livestream city, providing businesses with a physical space for livestreaming.

- In August 2019, the "Kuaishou Jadeite Industrial Belt Base" was officially established in Wanxinglong.

This chapter is authored by Yang Rui, a researcher at Kuaishou Research Institute, and Zhen Xu, a research assistant at Kuaishou Research Institute.

Wanxinglong Livestream City belongs to a species that developed from offline wholesale markets. Such livestream bases, which are situated within an industrial belt, must carry out offline management of businesses that livestream online.

For "high-stakes" industries such as the jadeite industry, professional acumen is necessary to carry out appraisal. Because regulation is fairly difficult, a good market can serve the functions of regulating businesses and cracking down on counterfeit goods. These functions were already available during the old era of wholesale markets; what has to be done now is to bring them "from offline to online." Sihui's livestream ecosystem was not built in a day. As one of the earliest livestream bases in the jadeite industry, Wanxinglong's "industrial belt + livestream base" developed one step at a time. It started out by accommodating the novelty that was livestreaming with an open mind and subsequently created a better physical space for livestreaming, thereby achieving the integration of online and offline (see Figure 7.2).

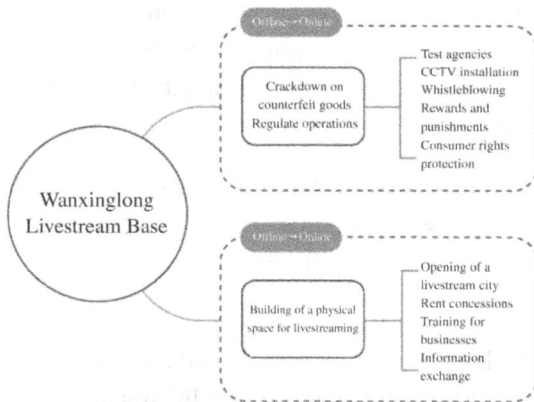

Figure 7.2 The Functions of the Wanxinglong Livestream Base as an Industrial Belt Service Provider

◎ *The following is an account by Fang Guoying, founder of the Wanxinglong Livestream Base.*

· · ·

The Beginnings of Wanxinglong Market

I am from Putian, Fujian Province, the hometown of China's national arts and crafts. All of my ancestors were woodcarvers. During the '90s, people of my father's generation left Putian and came to Sihui together to establish a jade sculpture processing factory. From then on, Fujianese people began to take root in Sihui.

In 2001, I came to Sihui to work as a jade carver. Back then, Sihui was fairly active in the nationwide jadeware processing industry. There are a significant number of jadeite processing factories here; many Yunnanese people would bring the raw jadeite stones they bought back home to Sihui to do the processing work. People from Guangzhou would also come to Sihui to buy unpolished jadeite that they would then resell back home.

Jadeite is so fascinating because every one of its phases is high-stakes. At the factory phase, the gamble is on the cutting of the raw materials. At the polishing phase, the gamble is on the positions and grade of the coloration. When polished, some pieces of jadeite do not gain translucency and thus "lose the gamble." All of these have to be assessed using professional acumen.

From 2003 to 2008, the jadeite industry gradually entered the development stage. Just like livestream e-commerce today, it enjoyed strong market demand and high profits. However, things were much easier back then. All we had to do was buy the raw jadeite stones, do some simple designing, and then wait for customers to place orders at high prices. Hence, we accumulated a large sum of money at a very young age.

Most of the jadeite in China's markets comes from Myanmar, where a bidding process is held three times a year. After the raw jadeite stones are auctioned off in Myanmar, a second bidding process would be carried out in China, causing the prices to increase. The better materials would go to Jieyang and Pingzhou, and only the remainder would be transported to Sihui for processing. Hence, before we went to Myanmar ourselves, most of the raw jadeite stones that we bought at auctions came from Pingzhou, Foshan.

I am probably part of the first batch of people to bring my fellow "provincemates" from Fujian Province to buy raw stones in Myanmar. In

2004, I went to Myanmar alone to do a preliminary survey. I felt that it was not right to "make a fortune by myself in silence," and thus I asked a few of my provincemates to accompany me. Back then, communications were extremely poor; my mobile plan could not be used in Myanmar and so I could only make calls using a landline telephone while there. I remember that the cost was $8 USD per minute. On one particular trip, I brought 21 of my provincemates to buy raw jadeite stones in Myanmar and hired a minibus to transport us to the quarry.

Upon reaching the jadeite market in Myanmar, everyone felt an indescribable sense of happiness. That was because jadeite was very cheap in Myanmar back then—a kilogram of ice-type jadeite (jadeite is classified as bead-type, waxy-type, ice-type, and glass-type, in increasing order of quality) cost only 1,500 to 1,600 yuan, which meant that we could earn huge profits just by buying and reselling them back in China. However, prices have increased a lot since then; today, a kilogram of ice-type jadeite would cost at least tens of thousands of yuan.

It was after 2008 that China's jadeite markets truly entered a stage of rapid development. At that time, the jadeite industry practically never faced a lack of demand; buyers would form a queue at the doorsteps of stone-cutters on their own initiative. By 2012, when the industry had matured in development, there were more than 30,000 Fujianese in Sihui, while the Fujian Chamber of Commerce was the chamber of commerce with the most employees in Sihui.

Back then, Tianguangxu was the biggest wholesale market in Sihui. Although its market hardware left much to be desired, its long history, good location, and large source of customers meant that everyone was desperate to get in. As a result, conflicts often arose over stalls and rental costs.

To ease such conflicts, the Fujian Chamber of Commerce made plans to open a new marketplace. After an intense process of planning and site selection, we finalized the site of Wanxinglong's market project at the end of 2012. Furthermore, at a fully attended meeting of the chamber of commerce, I was elected as the founder of Wanxinglong Jadeite City even though I had only ever managed a few dozen people and did not have any professional experience in market operations. From being a sculptor, I was forced to become a sublandlord, and thus had to bring myself to focus on running this large yet precarious market.

Cracking Down on Counterfeit Goods and Regulating Operations

At that time, there was nothing but a half-completed building in the vicinity of Wanxinglong. This area used to be very out-of-the-way and deserted; everyone instead headed in the direction of Tianguangxu and Yubo City. Figure 7.3 shows the distribution of Sihui's jadeite wholesale markets and livestream ecosystem.

The jadeite industry was in very good shape back then. However, the phenomenon of dishonest merchants secretly peddling counterfeit jadeite was also quite rampant. The issue of counterfeit jadeite appearing in Sihui was even exposed in the mainstream media. Cracking down

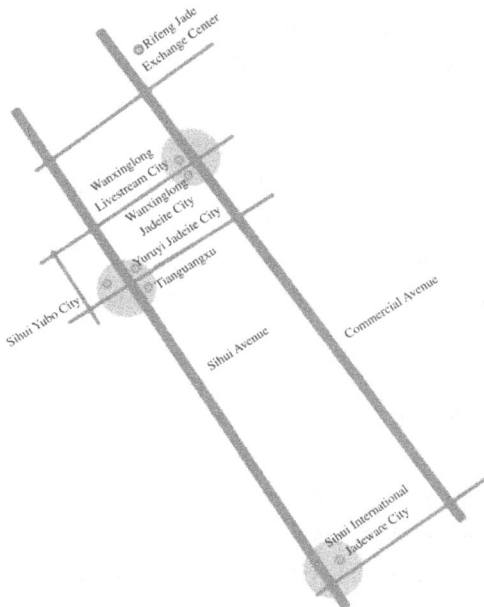

Figure 7.3 Distribution Map of Sihui's Jadeite Wholesale Markets and Livestream Ecosystem

on counterfeit goods thus became the top priority of Sihui's jadeite industry. Back then, out of my own initiative, I proposed to Sihui's municipal government to announce a promise of good-faith management using the words: "All goods are authentic; any counterfeit goods found will be compensated tenfold," with Wanxinglong serving as the endorsing body. Should anyone have the misfortune of buying counterfeit goods in Wanxinglong Jadeite City, the market—acting as the first person responsible—would compensate them 10 times the amount paid.

In little time, the Sihui government provided us with positive response and support. As a precaution, the relevant authorities approved a temporary individual business license with a half-year validity for us. It stipulated that Wanxinglong would have to close if we breached the promise within half a year.

Having gone through so many years of development in Sihui, the Fujian Chamber of Commerce enjoys a very high social standing and industry reputation. On October 8, 2012, we began to seek tenants and within two days, filled up the vacancies. Most of our tenants were of Fujianese descent; in total, more than 1,000 tenants paid a deposit, and so we collected more than 10 million yuan in cash.

On December 1, 2020, Wanxinglong began to be furnished. From that day on, I stayed permanently on-site until the furnishing was complete. The following Spring Festival was the first time I did not return to my hometown to celebrate the Lunar New Year—I was still busy on-site on the morning of New Year's Eve. On March 3, 2020, the market officially opened for business; it had taken only three months from start to finish.

While we had brought in the tenants, we still had to figure out how to bring in the customers. Back then, "traffic" was still not a popular term; our focus was on attracting customers.

At that time, Sihui's first-tier wholesale markets mainly did the wholesale of finished products and semi-finished products. Since 80 percent of our goods were sold to businesses in Hualin International, a shopping mall in Guangzhou, I felt that we should bring in customers from the source. Hence, we paid a huge sum of money to establish a regular bus service that ran directly from Hualin International in Guangzhou to

Wanxinglong in Sihui. There were 27 buses every day, with the first bus setting off at 1:10 a.m. From March to June, passengers did not have to pay for their tickets as long as they got on at Hualin International and got off at Wanxinglong.

However, there were some people whose purpose of taking a bus to Sihui was to collect goods from Tianguangxu. In order to save on the 25-yuan bus fare, they would take our free bus and then walk over to Tianguangxu after getting off. Hence, I thought of an idea: a free breakfast, consisting of a steamed bun, a cup of soybean milk, a fried dough stick, and a meat bun, would be provided at the entrance of Wanxinglong.

Having brought in both businesses and customers, our next step was to keep our promise of cracking down on counterfeit goods. We encountered many problems right from the start. Due to our lack of management experience, a few individual dishonest merchants were able to find and exploit loopholes. This led some of our customers to purchase counterfeit goods in our market, and so we ended up compensating them more than a million yuan in total.

Later, we established a Party market administration branch, which would hold meetings with businesses. Because we had stallholders from all over China, we divided them by region and allowed them to choose the Party members whom they wanted to serve as the members of the Party branch's mediation committee. We warned them in the strongest terms not to pass off counterfeit goods as authentic ones and told them that tenants who performed well would be granted free rent for as long as they operated.

More than 600 cameras were installed throughout the market. Aside from the restrooms, practically everywhere was within view of a camera. We made a rule: if a customer has the misfortune of purchasing counterfeit goods in Wanxinglong, we would not only deal with the errant merchant for breach of contract but would also publicly expose their practice of selling counterfeit goods—this would bring a lot of shame upon them.

We also instituted mutual supervision among the stall merchants. This was because some of the stalls in our market were run by two different stallholders: one in the morning and another in the afternoon. They would change over at 11 a.m., but this provided an interval which often got seized upon to sell counterfeit goods. Due to the high mobility of these people, it was difficult to spot such practices. Hence, we instituted "supervision by the masses" and encouraged whistleblowing. Once verified, the whistleblower would be rewarded with 30,000 yuan.

By carrying out our management model consisting of high rewards and strict measures, the entire market began to practice good-faith management. Over so many years of entrenching this model, Wanxinglong has become universally recognized as a "market with no counterfeit goods." In fact, there are practically no counterfeit goods in any of Sihui's markets these days.

At the end of 2014, the jadeite industry reached the peak of its development. I expanded the market to a total of 5,600 tenants, causing all 40,000 square meters to become even more packed than before.

The Growth of a Livestream Base

In 2015, the operation of brick-and-mortar stores in the jadeite industry began to decline. Back then, seeing that many people were doing WeChat Business, I advised our stallholders to seize this opportunity as well. However, the jadeite industry is a strange one—even if a customer has been purchasing goods from the same stall for a year, the stallholder would not know their name or phone number. Therefore, goods could not be bought on credit.

During our annual business conference in April, I suggested to the 1,000-odd attendees: "WeChat is not only for browsing WeChat Moments or watching video clips. All of you must start doing business on WeChat." While most stallholders continued to use their phones just to watch TV shows and chit-chat, a few people took my advice and eventually did very well on WeChat Business.

As the jadeite industry continued to decline in 2016, the south zone of our market remained fairly stable, whereas the north zone suffered a serious case of businesses winding up, leaving only a handful remaining. I had no choice but to convert a part of the north zone into a farmers' market and supermarket. Around that time, a foot massage city opened close to Wanxinglong.

Business was fairly hot; it raked in two to 3 million yuan every month. A friend thus advised me to remake the north zone into a foot massage city as well. To be honest, I was a little enthused by the idea at first, but I decided otherwise after mulling it over for a few days. This was because I saw myself as a sculptor and jeweler, and thus felt that opening a foot massage city would be a little inconsistent with my persona. As a result, many parts of the north zone remained vacant.

In the second half of 2016, I saw people livestreaming with their phones in the market. This was a truly refreshing sight at that time. After all, jadeite being traditionally a luxury product, there had only ever been two ways of entering the industry. The first was to start out as an apprentice, move up to become the owner of a small factory, and then slowly build up one's own business. The second was to come from a rich family and pour in millions of yuan all at once. However, these young people were able to sell jadeite simply by walking about the market with their phones in their hands and constantly haggling with sellers—this truly upended the traditional notions of the industry.

After a period of observation, I discovered that these people had very high mobility and did not have a fixed place of business. This method of "constantly moving about" was highly prone to operational risks. Consider this: how can a stranger who sells goods using a phone guarantee the quality of the goods sold? How can they provide aftersale services? How can the goods owner get payment security? Herein lay a series of questions that needed to be urgently solved, such as regarding trust endorsement.

Nevertheless, I felt that livestreaming could be done and would be the next big trend. This is because livestreaming is more intuitive than WeChat Business, which only allows the display of images, textual information, and prices. Moreover, there have been many cases of goods not matching their online depiction and refunds not being issued after the goods had been returned. WeChat businesses have extremely high communication costs, whereas livestreaming allows direct communication.

In the second half of 2016, many livestreaming platforms gained popularity. However, trust had not been established regarding the supply of goods, and thus many businesses remained leery of livestreaming. I came forward and told them to hand their goods to livestreamers without fear, and that I would pay them myself if the livestreamers defaulted.

Subsequently, we held discussions with livestreamers. We told them that it would be very difficult for them to gain the trust of suppliers if they did not have a fixed place for livestreaming, and that we would provide them with 1,000 square meters of space in Wanxinglong for free, so that all they would have to do was livestream while sitting in front of a stall. However, I also requested them to submit a copy of their identity cards and business licenses, pay the deposit, and get certification in livestreaming. In this way, those former walkstreamers became sitstreamers, and we created the predecessor of the livestream studio.

In 2017, more and more people became livestreamers. We thus converted the building originally occupied by a farmers' market and supermarket into a livestream city. As many newcomers could not afford the rent, we halved the rental price. Consequently, we not only failed to make a profit for the year ahead but even had to shell out a million yuan to cover the rent. Of course, upon hearing about the tremendous support that we provided, many livestream businesses from all over China decided to move there.

Today, Wanxinglong Livestream City has been partitioned into many separate livestream studios to spread out the noise and appear more organized. Now that the livestream businesses are concentrated in one place, the goods owners have done likewise—they can conveniently head over to a different livestream studio after they have completed the livestream in another. The jadeite livestreaming ecosystem of Wanxinglong has turned for the better and become complete in no time at all.

The New "Industrial Belt + Livestream Base" Model

Wanxinglong can be considered the first "industrial belt + livestream base" for jadeite and jade in China.

When Taobao Live first started, we wrote a proposal to Taobao's official team, hoping that they would come to Sihui to set up a base there and improve their offline services. Back then, we did not have a concept of what a base or a service provider should be.

After they received the proposal, they looked into our backend figures and were astonished to see that the order volume, price per customer, conversion rate, broadcast duration, etc. were all so high in Sihui.

In 2018, Taobao sent a team to visit Sihui. They were surprised to see that so many people were livestreaming there. Selling jadeite was just as easy as selling cabbages, while anyone could livestream with just a mobile phone. Feeling incredulous, they believed that such an ecosystem ought to be promoted. This new retail model was an example of the "industrial belt + livestream base" for which they had long been looking.

In August 2019, the "Kuaishou Jadeite Industrial Belt Base" was officially established in Wanxinglong. As of October 2020, more than 700 businesses have taken up tenancy in the base.

My understanding of "industrial belt + livestream base" is about how to display products in the industrial belt to consumers in a more intuitive way.

The question is, who should be the one to establish a livestream base in an industrial belt? Led by markets, platforms, and the government, a local industrial base organization can be established to serve the industrial base, incubate businesses, regulate the behaviors of offline businesses, and provide functions such as aftersales, trust endorsement, and rule-setting.

Our identity today has become that of the offline managers of an online platform. For example, it is very difficult for Kuaishou Live to face thousands of businesses directly, and so our livestream base would carry out online management using the methods that were previously used for offline management, thereby helping Kuaishou better manage the businesses on the platform.

Nowadays, most of the businesses in our base are from Sihui, and they account for 90 percent of our total GMV. Only a small handful of the businesses are from places around Sihui. We are only able to regulate those businesses that stay within the base, and thus it would be impractical for us to have businesses from Yunnan or Hubei Provinces. We only grant tenancy to businesses that everyone approves.

We still have to work hard to get our traffic and services done right. For example, we will help livestream studios engage with a few supply chains.

In 2017, we also established an e-commerce association and formulated many rules that must be strictly observed in carrying out livestream operations.

At present, we have positioned Wanxinglong as a cradle for incubating new businesses. This is a gathering place for middle- and bottom-tier businesses, as well as small, growth-oriented livestream studios. Wanxinglong's ecosystem is highly capable of satisfying the survival and developmental needs of these small livestream studios. For example, goods owners can collect goods from Wanxinglong Market in the morning and then make appointments with many livestream studios. At night, they would be able to sell their goods via livestreams. In one night, a small livestream studio can have appointments with many goods owners who would take turns to sell their goods. The concentration of goods and resources in Wanxinglong is very advantageous to the growth of new businesses, which was my original intention in building a livestream city.

Non-standard products such as jadeite have to be introduced one by one on-stream. I have been thinking about whether jadeite can be made into a standard product with a low price per customer and whether we can collaborate with big brands such as Lao Feng Xiang and Zhou Liu Fu to conduct "brand livestreams."

In any case, the market will become even more finely partitioned in the future. For jewelry, it is better to create standard products with a low price per customer and engage jewelry experts to promote them. Take for instance high-end products such as the "Zhuang Jadeite" brand; they do not need too much traffic and simply require accurate matching with the demand side.

In the future, platforms will have an increasingly complete set of rules. I personally believe that the shopstreaming model is still the most well-done among the existing livestreaming models. However, business models will continue to change. In my opinion, jadeite livestreaming is still at the "grass-planting stage" (where buying desire is induced via word-of-mouth recommendation), and its price per customer will continue to increase. And when a large amount of stickiness has been created between livestreamers and their followers, there would be a shift toward private domains.

PART THREE

CASE STUDIES FROM
DIFFERENT INDUSTRIES

CHAPTER EIGHT

BUILDING THE PLATFORM INFRASTRUCTURE

- How does Kuaishou E-commerce differ from other e-commerce platforms?

- How can businesses with few followers increase their followers and sell their goods?

- How can brands build private domains on Kuaishou?

WHAT IS KUAISHOU E-COMMERCE?

—Xiao Gu
Senior Vice President of Kuaishou Technology and
Head of Kuaishou E-commerce

Key Points

- E-commerce naturally developed from the community ecosystem of Kuaishou users. In compliance with its users' demands, Kuaishou regulates transactions and provides a series of transaction tools and e-commerce infrastructure, including Kuaishou Store, Store Access, Distribution Library, User Ratings, Shop Ratings, and Kuaishou Service Provider. In 2019, we became the second-largest livestream e-commerce platform in the world in terms of the total value of goods transactions.

- Kuaishou E-commerce stands for shopping with fun, choosing products with trust, and buying products with peace of mind. At present, it mainly satisfies the indefinite needs of its users. The market for semi-definite demands is a huge slice of the pie; if e-commerce livestreaming can resolve such demands, it would be able to catch up with shelves-of-goods e-commerce.

- Kuaishou is an "experiential e-commerce business," and its demands on the platform are greater than those of traditional e-commerce. E-commerce platform governance is a concept from traditional e-commerce, whereas livestream e-commerce places greater emphasis on experience. "Governance" looks at whether the basic needs are met, whereas "experience" looks at whether the higher needs of users can be satisfied.

The development of Kuaishou E-commerce can be divided into two phases. From May 2018 until just before the Spring Festival of 2020, we mainly worked on its foundations and refined our own products—this was a period of steady development. After the Spring Festival of 2020, the pandemic caused e-commerce livestreaming to surge in popularity, and thus Kuaishou E-commerce entered a period of rapid growth.

In 2019, we became the second-largest livestream e-commerce platform in the world in terms of the total value of goods transactions.

In May 2018, when Kuaishou established its e-commerce department, it only had one product manager and one operations manager. Prior to this, many people had already bought stuff on Kuaishou. In 2018, we published a statistic: more than 1.9 million comments regarding a demand for transaction were posted on Kuaishou every day.

Because there was such a demand and also buyers and sellers on the platform, the market was already there regardless of whether Kuaishou went into e-commerce or not. Initially, the buyers and sellers would perform transactions via third-party payment software, but we considered such software to be informal channels. This can be likened to the discovery of street vendors by law enforcers, who can then adopt one of two possible attitudes: the first is to clear them out, the second is to regulate them. Regulation would mean to stipulate an authorized venue and time and to formulate rules.

We chose the latter option because such a large transaction demand could not be cracked down on completely, nor should it be—this was a huge opportunity for us. Therefore, in conformity with the trend, Kuaishou provided a series of transaction tools and e-commerce infrastructure that enabled everyone to feel more at ease while carrying out transactions. This was how Kuaishou E-commerce came about.

Launching Yellow Cart to Cater to Demands

The first step of Kuaishou E-commerce was about achieving compliance, while its first action was to launch the transaction tool called "Yellow Cart" in June 2018.

Licenseless street vendors often present the problem of unsafe transactions. Prior to the launch of Yellow Cart, there were similar problems on Kuaishou. Some people were scammed after making a payment via a third-party payment software, while others received "goods not as described" or did not receive their orders at all. When they tried to reason with the seller, they ended up getting blocked, and thus they had no choice but to contact the platform and put the blame on us.

We launched Yellow Cart because of two reasons: firstly, we had discovered that there was a demand for transactions on Kuaishou, and secondly, we had discovered that various problems occurred during transactions. Yellow Cart enables compliant transactions to be made, thereby increasing businesses' and consumers' degree of trust toward transactions. Back when Kuaishou only provided information matching services and thus buyers and sellers had to perform transactions via other channels, we were completely unable to trace transaction information, distinguish honest transactions from dishonest ones, and regulate the unlawful behaviors of buyers and sellers.

Taobao was the first to be connected to Yellow Cart, followed by Mockuai, Youzan, and so on. Back then, Kuaishou did not have to handle transactions, escrows, and customer service; all it did was direct traffic, albeit it practically did not have any capabilities on its own. This was why we created Kuaishou Store. Even though it only accounted for 1 percent of our overall GMV at that time, we assigned more than 90 percent of our team to work on it.

In July and August 2019, Kuaishou made a series of adjustments. From being purely dependent on external platforms, Kuaishou became equipped with SaaS (software as a service) tools such as Kuaishou Store, as well as those provided by Mockuai and Youzan. The tools provided by Mockuai and Youzan completed our transaction closed loops during the initial construction phase of Kuaishou Store.

The policies that we set for third-party platforms are all equal; users and businesses can choose whichever transaction platform they want. However, Kuaishou Store is currently the predominant platform. Firstly, the on-site transaction conversion rate is definitely higher than the jump transaction rate, and thus sellers will choose this method on their own. Secondly, Alipay must be used for payment when buying stuff on Taobao, but what if our loyal followers do not have Alipay? This is why we required Kuaishou Store to support many payment methods.

Kuaishou Store was built from scratch; its transaction system, mechanism construction, and connection with third-party platforms were all completed during the first phase.

"116 Shopping Carnival" and "Good Source Things"

After the first phase was completed, Kuaishou held the "116 Shopping Carnival" event for the first time in 2018. During this event, Kuaishou livestreamer Brother Sanda generated sales worth 160 million yuan on one livestream. Subsequently, Kuaishou E-commerce became known to more users and businesses. Many businesses have said that it was seeing the case of Brother Sanda that spurred them to begin their own path in e-commerce.

Previously, there had been a heated debate within the company over whether to hold the "116 Shopping Carnival" event. We were mainly afraid of the Matthew effect it might bring about—whereby the top businesses would consolidate their superiority—and the pressure that the event would put on our operations. Nevertheless, I felt that holding the event was a good thing; it could increase our influence and help everyone understand the importance of livestream e-commerce.

On the whole, Kuaishou is very restrained about creating festivals. At present, the "616 Quality Shopping Festival" and the "116 Shopping Carnival" are the only large shopping festivals that the platform holds. The other festivals are held by individual industries and vertical categories, such as the monthly "Pamper-Your-Followers Day" and the Jewelry Championship, which we see as smaller-scale events.

By the time we hosted the second "116 Shopping Carnival" in 2019, we had more or less determined the direction of Kuaishou E-commerce's operations, which is to produce "good source things." We did not emphasize "goods" because this word has been used excessively and felt too common, hence we proposed "things" instead. Industrial belts are the source; we had used this very concept of "good source things" when promoting and recommending many business owners, such as Kuaishou livestreamer "Xiaoxu the Jadesmith," in an industrial belt. Having determined the direction, we will generally not change it any further; what we must do is keep advancing in this direction.

Affected by the pandemic in 2020, many businesses were unable to resume work and production and thus had to do business via livestreaming. As a result, many new producers and brands came to Kuaishou. In the past, Kuaishou gave people the impression that it mostly sold unbranded products, but the six months following the Spring Festival of 2020 proved to be a period of rapid growth for brands.

In the final analysis, a platform cannot do without brands. Besides, Kuaishou's loyal followers do not merely consume unbranded products; they, too, have a natural demand for brands. This is why Kuaishou has carried out many operations on brand projects. Be it in terms of product quality or quantity, the supply side is rapidly growing, causing Kuaishou E-commerce to enter its second phase of development.

What Is Kuaishou E-commerce?

What is Kuaishou E-commerce? We believe that it is out of the ordinary; it stands for shopping with fun, choosing products with trust, and buying products with peace of mind.

Everyone has a few shopping apps installed on their phone; which of these apps to open or not open depends on the users themselves. Every e-commerce shopping platform is unique, but on closer inspection, it can be seen that there are several platforms that have more or less the same products that sell well—instead, what they are competing over is the frequency at which users open their apps, and so they feed their users with diversity, convenience, and low prices.

Kuaishou's advantage is quite apparent: we are an "interesting" video platform. For users, Kuaishou is first and foremost an ecosystem or community and not just an e-commerce platform. Users browse Kuaishou mainly because they find our content highly interesting; shopping and transactions take place merely in passing. This is why Kuaishou is opened more frequently than pure e-commerce platforms. While people do not necessarily buy things every day, they need to get their news, recreation, and entertainment every day, and one common way of doing that is to watch videos.

Kuaishou's disadvantage stems from the same point. Because we are a video community, traffic comes in very easily. However, because we are not purely an e-commerce platform, a core issue that we must solve—which is a very difficult thing to do—is how to accurately find and distribute business information so that people with shopping needs can find livestreamers they like and products they want, while people with no shopping needs would not see such business information. If Taobao does not display products and simply plays a bunch of videos instead, it would probably lose most of its users. Conversely, most people come to Kuaishou as a pastime; were we to focus on getting our users to buy things, we would probably lose users, as well. Of course, that is unless a user's original intention was to shop and to watch the promotions of the livestreamers they follow.

I don't really agree with calling Kuaishou "livestream e-commerce;" it should be called "e-commerce livestreaming" instead. The subject of livestream e-commerce is "e-commerce," whereas the subject of e-commerce livestreaming is "livestreaming." This is the essential difference that separates Kuaishou from Taobao and JD. Kuaishou is not purely an e-commerce platform, but it can be called a livestreaming platform.

How to Satisfy Three Different Types of Demands

The relationship between Kuaishou and shelves-of-goods e-commerce is not a competitive one, and that is because the user demands that they satisfy are fairly different.

I believe that the demands of our users can be divided into three types: definite demands, indefinite demands, and semi-definite demands.

An example of a definite demand is when a user wants to buy a 50-inch television of a certain brand. In most cases, they would not come to Kuaishou to buy it, but would instead prefer to buy it from shelves-of-goods e-commerce businesses such as Taobao, JD, and Pinduoduo, all of which seek to satisfy this type of demand.

An example of an indefinite demand is when a user has no intention of buying things but, upon seeing something that catches their eye on a livestream channel, makes a purchase in passing. At present, Kuaishou E-commerce satisfies this type of demand. E-commerce livestreaming is still at an early stage, and so the market for indefinite demands is not yet as big as that for definite demands. It goes without saying that a person's budget for buying things in passing is not as big as that for buying things that they set out to buy.

What, then, are semi-definite demands? An example of this is when a user wants to buy a new bed quilt after their old one has been torn, but does not know which brand is good or how to compare prices. At present, the market for satisfying semi-definite demands is mainly offline. To make such purchases, people would usually go to bazaars, supermarkets, or shopping malls, or they might also go on Taobao, JD, or Pinduoduo. Of course, they might also come to Kuaishou to watch livestreams and short videos, and then make a purchase from a livestreamer.

The market for semi-definite demands is a huge slice of the pie and is not much smaller than that for definite demands or indefinite demands.

In fact, it might eventually catch up with the market for definite demands in terms of size. All e-commerce businesses are currently competing among themselves—and also with offline brick-and-mortar stores—for this market. The leading businesses in this regard are not livestreaming platforms such as Kuaishou but rather shelves-of-goods e-commerce businesses such as Taobao and Pinduoduo, and that is because they can display a lot of products with the help of accurate searches, making it seem just as if a user has entered the quilt section of a shopping mall and can choose any brand of quilt they like. Instead, on a livestreaming platform, users would not know who is selling quilts at the moment.

I believe that e-commerce livestreaming can catch up with shelves-of- goods e-commerce in this regard if it can solve such demands and create a scene similar to window-shopping—this can be done by grouping together all livestream channels that are currently selling quilts and forming a "quilt street." Although shelves-of-goods e-commerce businesses can display products to consumers, they have too many homogeneous products and do not clearly explain a product's pros and cons to consumers. As a result, consumers are often left in confusion and do not know how to choose.

The Platform of Choice for Non-standard Products

The Kuaishou platform is highly suitable for selling non-standard products because such products are presentable and not easy to compare in price. If users feel a need to carry out a price comparison on the things sold on livestream channels, then the conversion efficiency would fall. Livestreaming is characterized by high efficiency and stickiness; although expensive standard products can also be sold via livestreaming, it would be very difficult for users to come back to a livestream channel if they do a price comparison and realize that they can get it cheaper elsewhere. Hence, products which prices can be compared may be sold, but they must be offered at a cheaper price than elsewhere. Instead, as non-standard products are not easy to compare in price, users would keep on buying them on a livestream channel as long as they are deemed to be good. Therefore, a decision-making environment like a livestream channel is more suitable for selling non-standard products that cannot be compared in price.

Non-standard products can also be divided into branded products and unbranded products. While we do sell branded products, we mainly sell non-standard unbranded products at our current stage. Non-standard unbranded products need to be backed up by the credibility of a livestreamer. As a livestreaming platform that also has private domains, our content-based environment is suitable for selling non-standard products, and this forms a virtuous cycle. I hope that Kuaishou will become the platform of choice for buying non-standard products. Jewelry, jade, and clothing are all highly typical non-standard products.

We also hope to progress from selling unbranded products to selling branded products. Kuai brands are one way of doing so. Kuaishou livestreamer Xu Xiaomi's "Jiangnan Impression" and 77 Sister Ying's "Call of Spring" are both native brands of Kuaishou, and they both adopt the OEM production method. These livestreamer-owned cosmetic brands offer non-standard products and had developed from non-brands into Kuai brands. Thus, they cannot be compared in price and yet possess a certain brand effect. Kuai brands will gradually evolve; at first, they might be developed and sold only by an individual livestreamer, but after the livestreamer has built up a team, they can be sold throughout the Internet. A process is required for brands to change the minds of users. For example, the ClIiCK Toothpaste brand founded by Chen Rihe is showing a trend of brandification.

Brand Livestreaming and the Partner Model

Nowadays, the biggest problem encountered by brands that are planning to do livestreaming on Kuaishou is the difficulty of finding help and receiving guidance. In the past, brands also decided against entering Taobao because it required building a team, carrying out operations, and buying Taobao Express (pay-per-click advertising), which were too much for them to handle. For this reason, Taobao launched Taobao Partner (third-party companies that provides operational services). Although Kuaishou has a similar program called Kuaishou

Partner, it is nevertheless much more complicated for brands to operate on as compared to shelves-of-goods e-commerce platforms. On a livestreaming platform, brands must create content first, and so they need to have a very strong content team.

At present, a few brands including "Perfect Diary" already have a well- developed livestreaming content team. However, most businesses and brands have yet to build their own livestreaming teams and are also unable to find suitable teams to help them out. This is the pickle that brands would encounter when they enter Kuaishou these days.

Our suggestion to large brands is not to come over to Kuaishou and start selling goods right away. Instead, they should first create an account to do brand publicity, and only start selling goods subsequently. However, many brands acted rather impatiently when they first joined Kuaishou—they wanted to conduct livestreams and sell their goods immediately. They merely regarded Kuaishou as a sales channel and were unwilling to knuckle down to create content. This was a problematic attitude to have.

It is perhaps a testament to the excellence of Kuaishou E-commerce that these brands were so deeply impressed by the sales performance of several top livestreamers that they thought they could come over and start selling goods right away. However, not everyone can become a livestreamer, and not every livestream is able to sell goods well; becoming a livestreamer and promoting goods on-stream are highly professional affairs.

When entering Taobao, most brands would elect to go with the Taobao Partner model. Baozun is one such enterprise that provides brands with services such as store operation and digital marketing. However, there are currently still not many of such enterprises on Kuaishou. The ecosystem of Kuaishou E-commerce is not yet robust enough; brand service providers are still somewhat lacking in diversity. At present, the better-known ones are Yowant, Kmeila, and Mockuai.

Kuaishou is currently creating its own traffic management system and provides commercial tools such as "Follower Stories" and "Store Access." Store Access is an excellent traffic delivery tool that has basically replaced "Miaobang." A few years ago, Yowant was an important client of Miaobang, but this is no longer the case because of the emergence of

Store Access, which also costs money but does not require engaging top livestreamers. I feel that this is a good thing.

The Alliance of Good Things

Kuaishou has also created the "Alliance of Good Things," which is a distribution library system that has brought in the goods of many brands and distributors, thereby providing livestreamers with goods to sell and solving their shortage of goods.

As the threshold for joining the "Alliance of Good Things" is not high, many businesses have willingly joined, especially domestic brands. Today, it consists of nearly 200 brands that have a monthly GMV of more than 1 million yuan, including China Gold, Koushuiwa, Three Squirrels, Snow Flying, Yaya, Haier, and Royalstar. Every month, we have to collaborate with several thousand businesses that are seeking to join the distribution library and supply livestreamers with goods.

We decided to create the "Alliance of Good Things" because we realized that a livestreamer's work of selling goods is very complicated, requiring product selection, livestream studio arrangement, customer service management, logistics, and so on. While everyone wishes to be capable of opening a shopping mall on their own, the barriers to entry are clearly too high. We hope to use the distributor model to free livestreamers from these tasks so that they would only have to focus on how to create good content and how to sell the goods.

Why the distributor model? For example, when a livestreamer has grown to 500,000 followers, they would definitely have to sell different categories of products. Supposing that they only sold apples initially, they would usually only be able to generate sales for one season every year. Hence, they would have to sell other things during the following season, and so they would begin to distribute other products. Besides, livestreamers often want to upgrade their supply chains and sell branded products; they cannot keep on reducing their prices. The distributor model can be used to address the two core demands that are cross-category sales and sales of branded products.

In the past, some people felt that distribution libraries were useful to small-time livestreamers but not to big-name livestreamers. However, this is no longer the case. We have found that the top livestreamers also have very strong demands on products.

The problem faced by entertainment-type influencers is very obvious: their business solicitation teams are not professional enough. Although some of them have tens of millions of followers, their conversion rate might not even be as high as e-commerce livestreamers with just 10 million followers. For such influencers, we help them refine their supply from the perspective of a platform, using branded products that are high in quality yet low in price to replace the products that they originally sold.

For example, some entertainment-type influencers previously promoted products using external links. However, the customer attrition rate is very high for this method because the users might not have installed the necessary third-party shopping app. Nowadays, these influencers feel that creating a "Store of Good Things" is a very good method that can form a closed loop and would not cause an excessive loss of followers. Therefore, from the perspective of supply, the Alliance of Good Things provides the top livestreamers with high-quality supplies.

From the perspective of efficiency, entertainment-type influencers cannot afford to spend too much energy on handling products. Moreover, as soon as there is a problem with their products, their accounts would be suspended and they might never be able to come back, and so they are highly protective of their reputations. Therefore, they would love to have the support of a professional product selection team or a brand that would bear responsibility for any problems.

Aside from entertainment-type influencers, several professional e-commerce livestreamers also need this sort of risk-sharing. For example, if a big-name clothing livestreamer in Shijiazhuang wants to sell home appliances, their business solicitation team would go to various places across China to find products. However, the service provided by agents and scalpers is inconsistent in quality. If the Kuaishou official team supplies them with a few products and helps them with product selection, they would actually be very willing to promote products across different categories.

Livestreamers do not lack goods, which can be found throughout shopping malls and wholesale markets. Instead, what they lack are goods that are truly good in quality and low in price. All livestreamers lack these kind of goods, including the top livestreamers.

The problems that the Alliance of Good Things helps brands to solve are very obvious. For example, if brands wanted to sell goods on Kuaishou in the past, they would have to engage livestreamers and list their goods in the livestreamers' stores. Hence, instead of entrenching their own users and followers, they only entrenched the livestreamers's followers. But now, brands simply have to open another store. Every livestreamer adopts the distributor model, and thus their followers will develop a connection with the brands' stores. Similar to Tmall's "shelves of goods," brands can not only entrench their own users but also accumulate product reviews and sales.

Moreover, the distribution library adopts the rebate model and does not charge a promotion fee, while settlements are automatically made by the official system. As brands can control prices, they are very willing to use it.

As of today, the order volume of the Alliance of Good Things already makes up a significant proportion of the overall order volume of Kuaishou E-commerce. We have also set a target amounting to tens of billions for 2021. At this stage, distribution has already become an important growth engine for Kuaishou E-commerce.

"Experiential E-commerce Business" and Platform Governance

Business Grading. At present, Kuaishou's customer complaint rate is 0.03 percent to 0.05 percent, which is similar to that of most e-commerce platforms.

Businesses have to achieve three passes on Kuaishou's platform: the first is in product quality, the second is in service, and the third is in after-sales. They must reply to questions from consumers as soon as possible and must facilitate return requests without delay. We impose the highest standards on the businesses on our platform.

Kuaishou takes a few measures to ensure that users get a good experience, such as using a crowd-sourcing method to invite users to participate in an assessment of whether a livestreamer is conducting false advertising on their channel. We often display pop-ups on livestream channels or send screenshots to users, asking them whether a particular description counts as false advertising. We have made it convenient for users to make complaints by simplifying the various complaint channels.

Compared to pure shelves-of-goods e-commerce, livestream e-commerce requires livestreamers to provide an additional level of product description. To reduce the difference between user expectation and reality and improve the user experience, we must start out from the perspective of national standards and strive to achieve demands that are a level above these standards. The pursuit of a perfect experience is an endless one; we will never stop striving to provide our users with a higher level of experience.

Kuaishou's Service Provider System

Kuaishou engages two types of service providers: operational service providers and technical service providers. We usually call the latter type ISVs (independent software vendors) rather than service providers.

There are five kinds of operational service providers: MCNs, third-party service providers, brand service providers, training service providers, and industrial belts.

MCNs provide content creators with services such as persona building, content production, and integrated marketing, all of which serve to expand their scale. Third-party service providers must be able to solve problems related to product sales and services on behalf of goods owners, such as Internet marketing, store operations, and customer service. Brand service providers must not only solve the aforementioned problems for brands but also help platforms bring in brands that meet industry requirements and expand the scale of brands. Training service providers must provide high-quality lecturer resources and help newly joined goods owners and creators complete

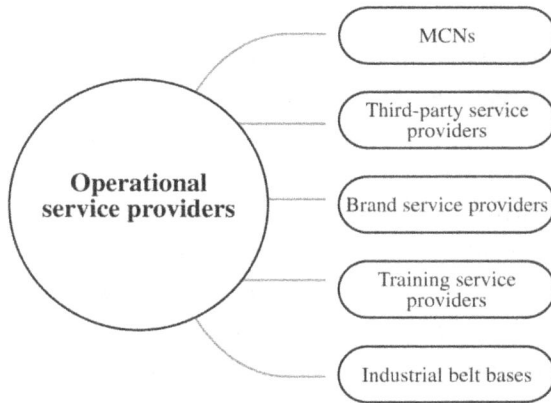

Figure 8.1 The Five Types of Operational Service Providers

their introductory training. Industrial belt bases have to manage both people (livestreamers) and goods (good source things). These five kinds of service providers are mutually complementary.

What are technical service providers? Kuaishou is supported by a few types of basic work, such as auditing, security, operations, maintenance, third-party payment software connection, logistics, and order printing, all of which require corresponding service providers because Kuaishou cannot meet all their demands on its own. The infrastructure of Kuaishou Store serves as an inner core with an ISV ring around it, forming a transaction setup. The simplest examples are ERP systems; all businesses have ready-made management systems such as Jushuitan and Kuaidadan. Jushuitan counts as an ISV that can be connected to the Kuaishou Store system.

Kuaishou's transaction system is more complicated than on other platforms—it consists of Kuaishou Store, Mockuai, Taobao, Youzan, and so on. Mockuai is on the same level as Kuaishou's transaction system and does not count as an ISV as far as Kuaishou is concerned. Instead, it is a separate platform that is connected to the Kuaishou platform; it, too, has external ISVs, of which many are also engaged by Kuaishou. In a sense, they are also seen as ISVs by Kuaishou, albeit we regard them as four parallel transaction platforms that have their own

ISVs. Our transaction platform has an inner core, and that is Kuaishou Store; the other platforms serve as supplements for improving transactions and satisfying the different needs of businesses.

The entire transaction system consists of four areas from the inside out: content flow, product flow, capital flow, and logistics. The first is content flow, which is the level that livestreaming is; Kuaishou is a tool that in itself provides content production and content consumption. At the level of product flow, we mainly do a few things related to auditing and user protection. In terms of capital flow, the few things that we do are mainly done via WeChat or Alipay. And in terms of logistics, we also do not do much other than collaborating with delivery companies such as SF Express and ZTO Express.

A Huge Opportunity for Supply Chains

The rise of Kuaishou E-commerce has had a huge transformative and driving effect on both the production end and consumption end of products.

E-commerce livestreaming is characterized by a need for a large number of SKUs; new products must be launched every day. Livestreamers cannot afford to sell just one product per day, otherwise they would quickly lose all their followers. Kuaishou livestreamer Xu Xiaomi launches 50 to 80 SKUs every day and sells each SKU a maximum of three times.

However, on the production end, the manufacturing of many SKUs by a factory runs counter to the patterns of industrial production. A factory would very much like to manufacture one million pieces of a single product model instead. The fewer the SKUs, the higher the production volume, and the lower the unit cost of a product, the greater the eventual profits would be.

Therefore, in this sense, factories and livestreaming platforms are naturally contradictory to each other. The way to address a factory's demand for a large quantity of a single SKU is to increase the number of livestream studios; although the sales volume of a livestream studio is relatively small, the total sales volume of many livestream studios would add up considerably. Similarly, the way to address a livestream studio's demand for a large number of SKUs is to increase the number of factories; even if each factory only manufactures one SKU, having hundreds or even thousands of factories would result in a large number of SKUs. Therefore, the relationship between livestreamers and factories can be depicted as an N-to-N matrix, with a supply chain serving as a go-between link.

The N-to-N approach is a little like the S2B2C (an e-commerce marketing model that gets suppliers to collectively empower channel partners and serve customers; wherein S refers to suppliers, B refers to channel partners, and C refers to customers) concept. When the demands of N number of livestreamers are concentrated in the supply chain, the factories would be able to ensure that the production volume is sufficiently large; the larger the volume, the lower the costs of a single SKU and the cheaper its price would be. On the other end, when N number of factories are concentrated in the supply chain, the livestreamers would be able to choose from many SKUs. Otherwise, they would face a shortage of products, and this is because it is unrealistic to rely solely on them to find their own products—they have neither the professionalism nor energy to do so (see Figure 8.2).

Many factories are gathered, giving livestreamers more SKU choices

Supply chain

Many livestream studios are gathered, reducing the factories' cost per SKU

Figure 8.2 The N-to-N Matrix

In short, although livestream studios and factories may appear to be mutually contradictory, they nevertheless present a huge opportunity for supply chains as long as the intermediate links are gotten right.

STORE ACCESS: PROVIDING BUSINESSES WITH AN ASSURED PATH OF GROWTH

—Feng Chao
head of Kuaishou's commercial e-commerce marketing services

Key Points

- To do business on Kuaishou, businesses must establish consistent traffic. Store Access, which is a tool for scaling up traffic acquired from public domains, provides businesses with an assured path of growth.

- After Kuaishou's public and private domain traffic are interconnected, a huge force would be produced. Traffic is acquired from public domains to be managed in private domains, which would then repay the public domains after they are up and running. This forms a complete chain, or in other words, a "snowball effect."

- Store Access is also lowering the threshold for opening an account. In the future, it will be more friendly toward small and medium-sized businesses. With the development of Kuaishou Store, it can serve more virtual products such as educational courses.

Businesses need certainty in order to do business. If 100,000 orders are shipped on the first day but only a handful of orders are shipped three days later, such a business cannot be sustained for long.

This holds true on Kuaishou, as well. Businesses need consistent traffic and different ways of acquiring traffic. If a business is experienced in doing advertising, it should focus on advertising, or if it is familiar with the "Natural Boost" feature of Follower Stories, it should focus on Follower Stories. On our part, we need to purposefully develop various traffic tools that can empower businesses.

The emergence of Store Access has offered our clients traffic that is more accurate. What we provide is an assured path of growth; all that businesses must do is spend time working on delivery optimization (materials, audience targeting, bidding, and objectives).

From the Jinniu Platform to Store Access

It was while we were working on the Jinniu platform that we came up with the idea for Store Access.

At first, we wanted to satisfy our clients' demands at every level. Some of them wanted to sell goods directly, some wanted to increase their followers, while others wanted to do livestreaming. Through a step-by-step analysis, we figured out that the first thing we should do was create a "type-2" e-commerce platform that allowed goods to be sold directly. "Type-2" e-commerce is no longer the same as it was initially; it has become a way for businesses to sell goods even if they have zero followers.

In September 2019, we launched the Jinniu platform, allowing businesses to sell goods in public domains.

Initially, Jinniu was a cash-on-delivery platform. Its clients could look at the product displayed in a news feed advertisement, enter the landing page, and then fill in their address and mobile number if they liked the product. Payment was only made upon delivery. Cash-on-delivery usually has a low acceptance rate because low-priced products are very hard to sell.

Affected by the pandemic following the Spring Festival of 2020, the platform saw a decrease in clients for two to three months. At that time, we wanted to provide our clients with a few more online payment features as that would increase the number of product categories and thereby boost sales of lowpriced products. After developing such online payment features, the acceptance rate indeed increased greatly, while our client coverage also expanded.

In addition, we tried our best to guide everyone to follow the accounts of the businesses on the platform. In March 2020, a few clients that delivered news feed advertisements began to do livestreaming, selling 20 to 30 orders per livestream. Realizing that a huge force would be produced after Kuaishou's public and private domain traffic were interconnected, we set out to develop Store Access.

In May 2020, I officially took charge of Store Access. At that time, I hoped to develop three features: one for bidding for orders during the first phase, one for bidding for new followers during the second phase, and one for bidding for livestream channels during the third phase.

In July 2020, Store Access officially went online. At that time, it only attracted a handful of clients, but beginning from the end of July, the client growth curve gradually turned into an ascending straight line. Within three months of its official launch, Store Access had accumulated thousands of clients.

Opening Up the Chain of Public and Private Domains

Back when we were working on the Jinniu platform, we discovered that the people who did livestreaming had absolutely no understanding of how to use public domain traffic, while the people who used public domain traffic had absolutely no understanding of how to use private domain traffic. These two groups of people were "isolated" from each other. There was a client who bid for orders on the Jinniu platform—over three days, he poured in 2 million yuan and accumulated more than 300,000 followers. However, because he had been focusing on news feed advertising previously, he did not know how to manage these followers.

Before public domains and private domains are interconnected, some people have made use of the information gap to bring in a bunch of followers, albeit they do not have a long-term management strategy. From our perspective, it would be beneficial to everyone if these two groups of people could move in the same direction and focus on doing long-term business.

For clients who want to sell goods while having zero followers, we can use public domain traffic to help them sell some goods initially, draw in attention, and accumulate followers. If their goods are able to sell well, we can publish a few "works" to increase their followers, and then deliver livestream traffic when they begin livestreaming. In this way, a complete chain is formed: traffic is acquired from public domains to be managed in private domains, which would then repay the public domains after they are up and running.

For platforms, goods adulteration is a highly burdensome problem. Once public domains and private domains have been interconnected, such a phenomenon would rarely manifest. This is because when a business has to manage its followers, it delivers only good-quality goods to its customers. If a business does not have to manage its followers, does not have a system for managing its goods strictly, and does not provide a way to comment on its goods, then quality assurance is very difficult to achieve. After public and private domains are interconnected, poor-quality goods are prevented from being mixed within public domains, while at the same time, private domains gain an additional way of delivering traffic to public domains.

For businesses, getting a good return on their investment would be most reassuring. However, adopting face-swiping technology, depending on business connections, and running advertisements all come with uncertainties. Businesses must think about which platform they want to mainly concentrate on for the next few years. With the emergence of Store Access, businesses can keep on investing money in exchange for consistent traffic as long as they comply with Kuaishou's rules. This is a model that is highly welcome by businesses that have "learned a lesson" from traditional e-commerce.

In the past, Kuaishou's lack of public domains caused many users to shun it when choosing a delivery platform. Businesses are generally inclined to choose platforms of which they have a certain understanding. This can be remedied with the launch of Store Access.

Some time ago, a few businesses that mainly focused on traditional e-commerce wanted to use Kuaishou as a traffic portal that merely directed traffic. Through our guidance in policies, operations, and sales, we slowly attract businesses to open a Kuaishou Store. Firstly, when businesses use Kuaishou to direct traffic, it means that they must invest in Kuaishou. Secondly, businesses that do not have livestreaming capabilities can start out by working on "Type-2" e-commerce, as offered by the Jinniu platform. The costs of bidding for orders are relatively low, and goods can be sold without a need for livestreaming. Thirdly, after a business has acquired livestreaming capabilities, it can bid for livestreams and new followers.

By habit, Kuaishou's loyal followers usually follow the accounts of the businesses where they make purchases. Therefore, from the off-site direction of traffic to the selling of goods through public domain traffic and then to the management of private domain traffic, a complete chain is formed. After the chain has been established, the next thing to do is stratify operations. We have many operational methods of giving different types of businesses a boost, especially for the growth of small and medium businesses, as long as they have the necessary tools and capabilities.

The Three Core Capabilities of Store Access

Store Access is a product for acquiring traffic from public domains on a large scale. As distinct from naturally promoted commercial advertisements, its objectives are to empower businesses, to make all kinds of business easier to do, and to increase the certainty of businesses' path of growth.

Store Access has three core capabilities: strategy empowerment, chain empowerment, and data empowerment.

Firstly, strategy empowerment. Store Access can provide coverage for the diversified and personalized scenarios marketed by users at all levels. From daily short video promotions to livestream promotions, and from the conversion of public domain traffic to the development of private domain traffic, it offers corresponding marketing objectives that are refined and personalized to livestreamers at all tiers, as well as new livestreamers.

Store Access has three optimization objectives: to optimize the increase in followers, to optimize order payment, and to optimize traffic direction via livestreaming. Businesses of any type can use Store Access to find a method and path of growth that is suitable for them.

New livestreamers and businesses have a very difficult time during the cold-start phase. This is because they must spend every day carrying out refined operations on their accounts, editing the scripts of their short videos, and building their own personas, all to keep on accumulating followers. With Store Access, new businesses can first bid for the sales target of "Order Payment." For example, a business can bid for a hook product that is high in price-performance on Store Access to obtain the customer base for this product. After users have bought this product, they would follow the business's account in passing. In this way, new businesses would be able to sell their products while having zero followers; this helps them get through the cold-start phase successfully and also gain followers.

Middle-tier businesses have a pain point, which is how to increase their followers after they have established their personas. Most of the time, they can bid for Store Access's sales target to "Increase Followers." Based on the positioning of the account and its product selection, Store Access would perform targeted and refined audience group deliveries, enabling the livestreamer to quickly find accurate followers and achieve rapid growth.

The pain point of the top livestreamers with millions or tens of millions of followers is regarding how to achieve an even greater breakthrough in every event given their existing follower bases. What they can do is bid for the sales target of "Direct Traffic via Livestreaming." Store Access can rapidly direct traffic to livestream channels, bringing in an endless stream of users. Given the efficient operational capabilities of the top livestreamers and the support provided by their product selection teams, these users can be rapidly converted in the livestream channels, breaking through the bottleneck period.

Secondly, chain empowerment. The conversion chain of Store Access is very short, such that it can be completed in just one or two steps. In the past, conversion chains were very long; after entering a short video or a livestream channel, users first had to find the Follow button, then click on the avatar to enter the livestreamer's personal homepage. It took at least three steps for an order to be generated, with some loss of user conversion at each step. Store Access has shortened the conversion chain, thereby reducing the churn rate and increasing the conversion efficiency on Kuaishou.

Thirdly, data empowerment. A precondition for good business is to understand data. Products that are promoted via Store Access have a corresponding professional data platform—Business Access. On this platform, businesses can see the effects of the money they spent, be it on their products, stores, user groups, followers, or traffic. During the subsequent delivery process, businesses can then carry out strategic optimization on their livestream channels' operations, product selection, and persona-building, as well as the ad delivery chain, in accordance with this data.

Business Access: An Intelligent E-commerce Tool

Business Access is an intelligent data-based tool that helps in business decision-making. In other words, it uses data—including traffic data, marketing data, livestreaming data, goods and transaction data, and aftersales data—to help businesses do business better. It basically provides coverage for all data related to short video traffic and livestreaming traffic, as well as the data of all the phases required during the operational processes of the e-commerce industry.

Firstly, traffic data. Its value mainly lies in rapidly tracking the sources of traffic and determining the optimal path of delivery. On the one hand, which channels do users come in from, and what is their conversion efficiency? For example, did the users come in from livestream channels, product pages, or short videos? These segments are intuitively presented in the form of a funnel, and through comparison, a decision can be made on which segments need to be optimized and refined. The objectives can then be optimized during the subsequent processes of marketing and operations.

On the other hand, traffic portraits. Does the traffic come from new customers or regular customers? Which specific products do they buy? This can provide businesses with data support and a basis when optimizing the orientational segments, audience group segments, and bidding segments during subsequent ad deliveries.

Secondly, marketing data. Its main value lies in analyzing delivery results and helping businesses reduce costs and increase efficiency. Kuaishou has two products for increasing followers: Follower Stories and Store Access. However, they have rather different product marketing scenarios. Follower Stories is more for consumer-end deliveries, and thus it differs from Store Access in terms of the location and pattern of traffic conversion and the deliverable products.

Through an overview of the marketing data, every sum of money bid on Store Access and Follower Stories can be seen. For each case of traffic output and conversion, there is a highly detailed data comparison that can be used to assess the kinds of products that should be delivered in different scenarios and marketing phases, and the kinds of optimization that should be performed on different products at different segments.

Thirdly, livestreaming data. During the process of livestreaming, many livestreamers are confounded by their livestream channels' perpetual failure to take off in popularity, and do not know what kinds of marketing activities they should carry out at different points in time in order to achieve the best results. Business Access has a real-time livestreaming data feature that can help livestreamers instantly adjust their e-commerce marketing strategies.

An overview of the real-time livestreaming data is useful in three ways. Firstly, it helps businesses promptly understand the livestreaming results and the marketing situation to rapidly adjust the tempo of promoting goods on-stream and continuously optimize the livestreaming results. Secondly, it gives businesses a good grasp of the historical livestreaming results, thereby providing ample data reference for subsequent livestream promotions. Thirdly, it helps businesses to understand the conversion results, audience portraits, and sales volume of each promotional livestream in detail, to keep on optimizing the livestreaming segments, and to adjust their e-commerce marketing strategies.

Fourthly, product and transaction data. Many businesses do not have a very clear understanding of their own stores, as well as the traffic and conversion results of their products. Business Access offers a highly professional interpretation of product and transaction data and is able to promptly feedback the conversion results and increase the efficiency of operations optimization. The product overview data helps businesses in the growth phase to achieve efficient product marketing and visible and real-time product monitoring, thereby improving the optimization of product operations such as the allocation of goods and the adjustment of prices. The one-stop product sales data analysis helps businesses to deal with the sales situation of their stores, to rapidly adjust their operations strategy, and to improve their e-commerce results. Businesses can assess the conversion results of their products in accordance with the conversion data. They can then expand the product traffic with good results, optimize the product traffic with poor results, customize their product marketing methods such as by creating vouchers or repricing their products, continuously even out and fix the shortcomings of their products, strengthen the advantages of their products, and continuously optimize the overall conversion results of their products. Through the store transaction data, they can see the overall conversion results of their store and find out which products are suitable for which groups of people. Subsequently, they are able to optimize their orientation and the ad delivery strategy for their audience groups, continuously search for their store's target consumers, and optimize their store's figures.

Lastly, customer service data and aftersales data. These two types of data are related to a business's services, and they also reflect a business's supply chain capabilities. For example, the aftersales dispute data and the product evaluation data reflect a product's competitiveness in the market. If a business has a relatively high aftersales dispute rate for a product as compared to other stores, it should consider changing the product's supply chain and optimizing its upstream segments. By looking at their customer service's inquiry figures, reply rate, duration figures, and so on, businesses can optimize the capabilities of their entire customer service team, arrange the work shifts of their customer service personnel in a mechanized and personalized fashion, satisfy the demands of their customers' complaints and inquiries as much as possible, and increase their store's competitiveness in terms of service and quality.

Our Core Purpose Is to Empower Small and Medium-sized Businesses

We want to build a complete sales, operations, and product system that serves the needs of our clients at all levels. We are working on programs for influencers, middle-tier and low-tier clients, external clients, and vertical clients. However, this system will favor small and medium-sized businesses in the future.

At present, many livestreamers with different ranges of followers have shown vigorous development. For example, top Kuaishou livestreamers Xu Xiaomi, 77 Sister Ying, and Sister Mi are all seeing steady increases in their number of followers, while cases of accounts with zero followers gaining 100,000 followers in one month are springing up endlessly.

We know very well that the vitality of a platform mainly depends on whether there are new people joining. When choosing a traffic tool, clients would look at the height of the threshold; hence, simply by lowering our threshold, we would be able to bring in many small and medium-sized businesses. Our core mission is none other than to empower small and medium-sized livestreamers and businesses and to develop an awareness in them.

It is very important for newcomers to be able to sell goods even while having zero followers. Nowadays, this is mainly done via the Jinniu platform, and also via Store Access. The Jinniu platform has built its own news feed advertising platform, while Kuaishou Store also has its own news feed advertising platform. After the public and private domains have been fully interconnected, we focus on publicizing the idea of being able to sell goods just by bidding for orders, while having zero followers. We want our traffic tool to favor small and medium-sized businesses, and this is something that can be achieved very quickly.

Soon, cases of small and medium-sized businesses successfully increasing their followers will emerge on a large scale. At present, several cases of businesses increasing their number of followers from zero to the tens of thousands have already sprung up in different parts of China. There is a company in Wuhan, consisting of a dozen-odd livestreamers, that was informed by an agent that Kuaishou currently has a tool similar to Taobao Express. After making a few trial deliveries, they realized that the ROI was not bad. Most of these livestreamers now have more than 100,000 followers, and they are still making deliveries every day. In general, they would bid 3,000 to 5,000 yuan per day, with their ROI around 200 percent to 300 percent. Having this kind of certainty allows businesses to feel most at ease. With the increase in livestreamer supply chains and product SKUs, businesses can expand their deliveries one step at a time.

Henceforth, we will focus most of our work on promoting the growth of small and medium-sized businesses. While we have already done a couple of things, we will fork over a substantial sum of money to provide these businesses with actual subsidies in the future.

We are also lowering the threshold for opening an account on Store Access. Currently, Store Access still does not allow deliveries to be made upon filling in one's identification information, mobile number, and account name. Opening an account requires a lot of credentials to be provided, and the threshold is rather high. We will soon build a team that exclusively serves small and medium-sized businesses to empower them. At the same time, we will promote self-services, thereby allowing clients to make deliveries on their own and satisfying the needs of clients at different levels. As long as the threshold for opening an account is lowered such that anyone can make trial deliveries, Store Access should quickly spread among all businesses.

At present, Store Access mainly serves Kuaishou Store. However, with a few minor changes, it would be able to serve more vertical categories, including industries such as gaming and education.

Among our numerous goals, our priority is to scale Store Access and then to serve all kinds of businesses—especially small and medium-sized businesses—in a practical manner.

NEW ORGANIZATIONS, NEW MODELS

- Let's see what the founders of four service organizations that grew up in the Kuaishou ecosystem—Yowant, Mockuai, Kmeila, and Star-Station—have to say.

XIE RUDONG, FOUNDER OF YOWANT: RETAINING AN AWE FOR BRANDS

Key Points

- Yowant refers to four dimensions when selecting non-celebrity livestreamers: professionalism, looks, diligence, and Internet sense.

- By making use of its livestreamer-related advantages, Yowant helps brands sell goods. It also feeds back to brands the data and consumer demands it obtains during the process of livestreaming.

- Yowant made use of its supply chain advantages to open a livestream e-commerce base in Linyi.

The authors of this text are researcher Yang Rui, senior researcher Li Zhao, and research assistant Mao Yirong, all from Kuaishou Research Institute.

Yowant Network plays an important role in the field of livestream e-commerce. In December 2018, Yowant Network Co., Ltd. was acquired by Foshan Saturday Shoes (002291) and became listed on the stock market. This identity gave it much more "ammunition" to face its competition.

Yowant is constantly "advancing against the wind." In 2014, Yowant started out by doing Internet marketing and advertising and later shifted its sights to mobile game promotion, becoming tops in the industry after four months of hard work. In 2016, it joined the trend of operating WeChat official accounts— it operated several thousand official accounts and collected 400 to 500 million yuan in ad revenue.

During Kuaishou's "116 Shopping Carnival" in 2018, livestreamer Brother Sanda generated sales of 160 million yuan in one day. Sniffing a new opportunity, Yowant held a project meeting the very next day and decided to take part in "11/11 Kuaishou E-commerce Festival." Giving up some inside details, Yowant's CEO Fang Jian said, "We did not have our own livestreamers back then. Based on our number of followers, we decided to engage more than 20 livestreamers, and eventually found "Living Stone," "Yao Yongchun," and others. Our project group was also put together at the last minute. The company converted all of its offices into livestream studios—even my office had to be taken."

"In the end, we suffered losses of more than a million yuan. This was mainly because the fees for the livestreamers were fairly high. Nevertheless, we believe that this loss was well worth it," Fang recalls.

Subsequently, Yowant upped its investment and signed celebrities such as Wang Zulan and Wang Yaoqing. It also began to incubate its own non-celebrity livestreamers. In 2019, Yowant ranked first among Kuaishou's MCNs for consecutive months. When Yowant is mentioned in the livestreaming circle these days, the two livestreamers that come to mind are Master Yuda and Li Xuanzhuo, who have become walking advertisements for Yowant.

◎ *The following is an account by Xie Rudong, chairman of Yowant Network.*

· · ·

GETTING STARTED: UNEARTHING THE GOODS-PROMOTING CAPABILITIES OF WANG ZULAN AND OTHER CELEBRITIES

When we first entered Kuaishou in 2018, we still did not understand livestreamers deeply enough. We contacted every Kuaishou livestreamer who had roughly 10 million followers but almost none of them responded to us. Back then, we felt that the process of incubating our own livestreamers was too slow and thus sought collaborations with celebrities. The first celebrity we found was Wang Zulan.

Why Wang Zulan? Firstly, his follower base on Kuaishou is huge. He had entered Kuaishou very early. When we were signing the contract with him, his Kuaishou account already had more than 13 million followers. Secondly, he is highly popular. In 2018, he was a permanent guest on one of China's most well-received variety shows, and thus he would bring in a fair amount of traffic. Thirdly, he does not have "idol baggage" and has a natural "Internet sense."

During our first meeting, I only asked him two questions. Firstly, I asked him whether he understood on-stream shopping—he replied that it was pretty much the same as TV shopping. Secondly, I asked him whether he could sell facial masks—he replied that he could. Hearing his replies, I felt assured that we could succeed in this.

The growth of goods-promoting livestreamers requires a process, and celebrities are no different. It took us a long time of trial and error before we found a suitable model for collaborating with celebrities. Celebrities have a lot of engagements, and so they have a very limited amount of time to put into livestream e-commerce. However, their greatest advantage is the high and sustainable traffic that they bring. Outside of livestream channels, they can maintain talk about them and expand their influence through variety shows, television series, and movies.

The celebrities who have collaborated with us, such as Wang Zulan and Wan Yaoqing, have all accumulated large numbers of followers on Kuaishou, and the results of their livestream promotions are very impressive. For example, we spent two months helping Wang Yaoqing's Kuaishou account grow to six million followers. On September 19, 2020, his follower count was 8,092,900, and his promotion on that day generated 234,900 orders. As of September 30, 2020, he had 29,043,000 followers on Kuaishou, more than twice what he had when he signed the contract with us.

We believe that now is a good opportunity for celebrities to enter livestream e-commerce. Compared to other platforms, Kuaishou's sales volume is relatively consistent; doing Kuaishou E-commerce is a form of long-term investment and returns.

MCN Yowant's Four Dimensions for "Creating Stars"

From August to September 2019, we officially incubated our own livestreamers. Our first batch of non-celebrity livestreamers consisted of eight women and two men. Today, only the two men remain— Master Yuda and Li Xuanzhuo. They have also become walking advertisements for Yowant. During Kuaishou's "616 Quality Shopping Festival" in 2020, Li Xuanzhuo's livestream generated more than 100 million yuan in sales. On November 5, 2020, Master Yuda went one better and achieved a GMV of more than 368 million yuan in a single livestream.

Our criteria for choosing non-celebrity livestreamers mainly consist of four dimensions: professionalism, looks, diligence, and Internet sense.

Professionalism means that we require our livestreamers to be highly familiar with their products.

When we were training Li Xuanzhuo to become a livestreamer, we specially hired a wine-tasting master to taste wine with him every day. Over a long period of being influenced by the master, he became increasingly knowledgeable about wine. Nowadays, his livestream studio would be filled with the smell of wine even when he is not livestreaming. In this way, his persona as "Kuaishou's wine immortal" has been cemented.

Master Yuda was originally an etiquette trainer, and when he first came to Yowant, he was in charge of training livestreamers in etiquette. He has an understanding of cosmetics from earlier times, and having livestreamed for so long, he has also gradually broadened his horizons when it comes to cosmetics. Nowadays, we also hire teachers from brand companies to help him deepen his understanding of clothing, jewelry, home appliances, and so on. We hope that he can branch out from cosmetics to become an all-category livestreamer.

It is a trend in the livestreaming industry to emphasize looks. If a handsome guy or pretty girl is livestreaming, everyone would pay a little more attention. When the company first recruited Li Xuanzhuo, his looks convinced us at first glance.

Diligence is also something very important for a livestreamer. Being in this industry basically means having no rest days throughout the year. Every day, as soon as the camera is on, a livestreamer would have to start working until late at night.

The last thing is Internet sense. For example, there are no secrets to making it on to the Trending page; it simply depends on one's storytelling ability. The main aspect of an Internet sense is none other than the ability to attract followers using stories. Stories frequently used by big livestreamers include marriage proposals, marriages, childbirths, and first-month birthdays. Yowant is likewise; the context of our stories can be the company's founding anniversary, IPO anniversary, and so on.

Nowadays, we prefer to incubate those livestreamers who already have the basics. For example, even if a livestreamer has less than 10,000 followers, we would collaborate with them if they are familiar with the process of selling goods and understand the livestream e-commerce market.

For those livestreamers with strong influence among their followers, we can enter into a joint venture with them. What we would do is transplant Yowant's resources to them, helping them increase their followers by tenfold and their livestreaming turnover by fivefold.

Currently, our model for collaborating with livestreamers is mainly to create a joint account and share the profits. After signing a contract with a livestreamer, we would fork over money to build them up. All profits would be split according to the agreement.

We would provide every livestreamer with a specialized operations team that is divided into front-end and back-end. The front-end team mainly handles the livestream studio's operations, such as goods management, platform management, content, filming, and editing, on behalf of the livestreamer. The middle and background teams of the backend are shared; for example, a product selection team, a customer service team, and an aftersales team. The operations team that serves each livestreamer consists of at least four or five and up to a dozen or so people. At present, our operations teams consist of more than 400 people in total.

TIP

The New Model of Collaboration Between Yowant and Kuaishou Livestreamer "Big Oranges"

The New Model of Collaboration Between Yowant and Kuaishou Livestreamer "Big Oranges"

In March 2020, Yang Tao and his wife, who own a clothing factory in Hangzhou, opened an account called "Big Oranges" on Kuaishou. The account accumulated 1.23 million followers within seven months.

The couple had been involved in both offline and online sales in their past working experiences. While running a Taobao store and later a WeChat business, they created many hot-selling products. They have also run two wholesale stalls in Wenzhou and Guangzhou, where they were highly demanding on clothing quality. In 2016, they opened a clothing factory in Hangzhou.

Many years of e-commerce experience have given Yang Tao the ability to analyze different platforms. It took him only one glance to see the potential in Kuaishou's private domain traffic. "Private domain traffic is what I have been looking for. This type of traffic can be used repeatedly, and, unlike public domain traffic, it does not follow a logic of pure delivery," he said.

In 2020, Yowant became a shareholder of Big Oranges' factory. Compared to non-celebrity livestreamers who started from scratch, Big Oranges is already a well- developed livestreaming channel with sources of goods for women's clothing. "While he has invested in me, I am still the majority shareholder. We have complementary advantages," said Yang. According to Xie Rudong, this model of collaboration has only been adopted by Big Oranges alone. Yowant's understanding of non-standard products such as women's clothing is not as deep as its understanding of standard products, and thus it currently gives Big Oranges great freedom to develop on its own.

What made Big Oranges accept Yowant's investment? Firstly, Yowant can provide it with standard products. Previously, Yowant had done the mixing and matching of goods for many of Kuaishou's top livestreamers, and thus it has many supply chain resources and ample experience in handling standard products. Instead, Big Oranges has mainly dealt in women's clothing all along, and so its collaboration with Yowant has given it a stable supply chain for standard products.

Secondly, Yowant can provide its factory with financial support. In Yang's words, "Internet businesses have very high burn rates."

Thirdly, Yowant's enterprise operations and management have an absolute advantage in the field of livestream e-commerce in terms of information and operations. Compared to solo livestreamers, Yowant's team is diverse in services, fast enough in obtaining industry information, and professional enough in its operations.

Moreover, Yang's goods can be sold via the channels controlled by Yowant. Through mutual collaboration, quick-response capabilities can also be developed. The factory would develop new products, manufacture samples, and then deliver them to the livestreamers' studios. After each studio places their orders, the factory would then carry out templating and manufacturing.

Retaining an Awe for Brands

Yowant's core competitiveness lies in its supply chain and brand. Today, we maintain long-term and stable partnerships with hundreds of well-known brands, such as L'Oréal, KANS, PROYA, Be & Cheery, and Three Squirrels.

Our long-held principle is to sell good-quality goods and only branded goods. I believe that we should have a reverent attitude toward brands—the premium on brands is well-deserved because they carry out selection and classification on products. When consumers see a brand, they would instantly know what its quality is like and thus would be willing to buy it.

Brands are very powerful. Why do Li Jiaqi and Weiya want to sell branded goods? This is because brands empower livestreamers to sell goods more easily than before. Through our own operational capabilities, we can expand the market space for brands, thereby earning ourselves greater room for negotiation. For example, Florasis initially supplied their loose powder to us at a unit price that was 20 yuan more than they quoted for Li Jiaqi, and we accepted it. After livestreaming for a month, we showed them the livestreaming results and brought down the unit price by 10 yuan through renegotiation. Once again, we accepted this and continued to work hard. After livestreaming for another two months, we finally negotiated the same unit price as Li Jiaqi.

This was the most difficult brand that we successfully negotiated with— negotiations lasted three months. Back then, when a supplier was finding goods for us, they told us that Florasis was fairly difficult to negotiate with because the company had incurred many market expenses and thus offered less room for negotiation. I understood this very well; if a brand has established a firm foothold in its industry and then offers us a product at a suitable price, this product would definitely sell well on a livestream channel.

In reality, with the increase in users' spending power, people have an ever-increasing demand on quality of life, causing consumption levels to rise very quickly. Things that are low in price and quality can perhaps be sold a few times, but cannot be sold in the long run. When a consumer has bought a high-quality product from a good livestreamer, they would no longer fancy products that are low-quality.

Among our current brand clients, OLEVA has been particularly successful in doing Kuaishou livestream e-commerce. This is a cosmetics enterprise that has been around for nearly 20 years, and its products were mainly sold in Sephora and Watson's in the past. Nowadays, its sales in livestream e-commerce make up more than 50 percent of its total annual sales. We have participated extensively in its phases of categorization and R&D.

Yowant does for OLEVA what Li Jiaqi does for Florasis. Yowant's livestreamers can help OLEVA make tens of millions of yuan in monthly sales. On October 13, 2020, Master Yuda's livestream channel sold 5 million yuan worth of a caviar set. This was a freshly arrived batch of goods, yet all 30,000-odd pieces were sold out in a flash. When we relayed the news to OLEVA, they decided to step up production.

The value that we provide for OLEVA mainly lies in the two aspects of product selection and product mixing-and-matching. Although design and R&D are carried out by OLEVA themselves, we would inform them about the categories of goods that Yowant's channels need, and what level of packaging is needed. This is because we are more familiar with the selling of goods—after all, livestreamers are the closest to the market and consumers.

We would inform OLEVA about the figures and consumer demands obtained during the course of livestreaming, and they would then carry out R&D based on this information. At times, they would develop a few products for us to choose from. If, after testing, we find these products to be suitable in quality and price, we would place large orders for them. The other thing we do is the mixing-and-matching of products into sale bundles. In addition, we would also help OLEVA to train livestreamers and to sign one or two livestreamers to do livestreaming for OLEVA's flagship store on each of the different platforms.

Our collaboration with PROYA takes on a different model. As their own model is fairly well-developed, they do not need us to carry out product selection and mixing-and-matching. Instead, we would help them connect with livestreamers. We can also help them maintain their sales volume on livestream e-commerce channels throughout the year. Like an exclusive distributor, we would engage external livestreamers to sell out the goods as stipulated if our own livestreamers are unable to do so.

Unlike PROYA, most large enterprises and brands would not allow us to become so deeply involved in product selection and manufacturing. They would usually have their own specialized data departments and would greatly trust their own judgment in product category selection. They are very high in fault tolerance and have a lot of leeway for adjustment. Instead, brands like PROYA are relatively small and do not have much leeway for adjustment, and so their losses would be huge if they are unable to sell their products well. Hence, they offer us more room in which to play a role.

Deep Collaboration with Brands: Joint Ventures and Joint Constructions

We have models for even deeper collaboration with brands. For example, we have established a joint venture with Renhe Pharmacy. The joint venture would underwrite goods for them, with Yowant guaranteeing its sales volume. In addition, we have also made Renhe Pharmacy's sanitary pads a hot-selling product. It basically took Master Yuda one livestream session to sell out its monthly production volume.

To give another example, OSM is a traditional brand that had an unsuccessful series of personal care products. We thus helped make this series of products a hot- selling one. The plan we came up with was to engage livestreamers to promote OSM's shampoo and body wash products on their livestream channels every day. In this way, sales slowly increased.

Why are brands willing to collaborate so deeply with us? Firstly, Yowant can help them ship their goods and increase their sales volumes. Renhe and PROYA are both listed companies, and so are we; there is a certain interactivity among listed companies. Some securities researchers from the new retail industry would also conduct survey and research on us and our partnering brands. The collaboration between us is built based on standardized operations, good quality, low return rates, and so on. To a certain extent, we help each other succeed.

Secondly, Yowant can relay the latest information from the livestream e-commerce industry to brands and can also help them train livestreamers. We mainly do these things for brands that are deeply bound to us. As long as Yowant is able to sell well, the products of these brands would be highly sought-after when sold in other channels because the market has already been verified by us.

Thirdly, Yowant has a complete market layout and diverse sources of income. We do not earn money solely from the goods side. This is what separates us from other top MCNs and makes brands feel more at ease about having long-term and stable collaboration with us.

Extending Our Tentacles to Linyi

One day in 2019, I found out through the news that there were many livestreamers in Linyi. This gave me an idea to bring our partnering brands to Linyi. It took only a year for my idea to turn into action. In 2020, when Yowant had a few branded products that had not been sold out, I wanted to send someone to Linyi to bring livestreamers from there over to Hangzhou to conduct walkstreams. However, after thinking things through from a long-term perspective, I decided instead to build a base in Linyi.

On September 20, 2020, we officially signed a contract with Shandong Province Linyi City Hedong District Dongcheng Construction Investment Group Co., Ltd. to build the Yowant Livestream E-commerce Base in Linyi. This will become the first brand mall in China to be open 24 hours a day. Livestreamers will simply have to conduct livestreams in the specialty stores of this commercial complex. This model follows the same logic as the supply chain bases in Hangzhou's Jiubao District. However, the problem with the Jiubao model is that it lacks its own livestreamers and thus cannot control the livestreamers' schedules.

Nowadays, Linyi's livestreams consist of many unbranded products. We hope to introduce a few of Yowant's brand resources to help brand exhibitions achieve autonomous operation.

This is also the first livestream industry base built under the leadership of Linyi's local government. Hedong District's government intends to invest a lot of capital in the construction and furnishing of the base. Yowant and the Hedong District Dongcheng Construction Investment Group have jointly established a base operations company, with Yowant serving as the majority shareholder and taking charge of the actual operations of this livestream base.

In the future, Yowant will bring in more enterprises from the livestream industry chain and, through business solicitation, introduce partnering brands as well as brands that suit the local customs and traditions.

Why did we choose Linyi? Firstly, Linyi has many livestreamers with strong goods-promoting capabilities. Through a third-party data platform, we discovered that Linyi indeed has numerous livestreamers, among which are 4,000 to 5,000 livestreamers who have transaction figures. Moreover, a good number of them have 200,000 to 300,000 followers and generate a five-figure sales amount through livestreaming every day. In addition, the cities on the periphery of Shandong Province, such as Qingdao, Jining, and Jinan, have livestreamer resources that ought to be further unearthed.

We had previously supplied goods to Taozi's, one of Linyi's top livestreamers, as part of two trials, and discovered that the results of the goods promotion were excellent. In a later trial, most of the goods were also sold by livestreamers from Linyi. We wasted no time forming a business team to engage with Linyi's livestreams locally.

Secondly, Linyi has a lack of good-quality branded goods. Due to a lack of goods, a few of Linyi's local livestreamers have brought their teams around China to find goods. After building a livestream base in Linyi, we will bring in resources from Yowant's partnering brands. Brands value a livestreamer's goods-promoting ability above all—as long as a livestreamer is able to promote goods and generate hot-selling products, they would be very willing to provide their resources. In this way, Linyi's livestreamers can access brand resources right at home, saving them time and increasing their efficiency greatly.

Thirdly, Linyi's top livestreamers are seeking transformation from a low to a high price per customer, and from unbranded to branded goods.

In the past, Linyi's livestreamers were able to achieve impressive figures in their promotion of goods, but many of them sold miscellaneous goods or unbranded goods that were relatively low in price and high in order volume. However, with the upgrading of users' consumption levels today, this type of business is on the decline. Moreover, it is very difficult for these types of goods to fetch a high price per customer.

While Linyi's livestreamers are seeking to transform and upgrade, our resources and advantages are just able to fulfill their needs. Therefore, together, we are able to achieve win-win cooperation and play to each other's strengths.

At present, we are negotiating the construction of similar livestream bases in Shanghai and Wuhan, albeit the positioning of these bases will be different. The base in Linyi will mainly be B2B, whereas the base in Shanghai will mainly be B2C. We also intend to try out a combination of online and offline.

XIAO FEI, FOUNDER OF KMEILA: FOCUSING ON PROVIDING SUPPLY CHAINS TO SMALL AND MEDIUM-SIZED LIVESTREAMERS

Key Points

- Kmeila is an e-commerce supply chain platform in Hangzhou that mainly helps small and medium-sized livestreamers solve the problem of a lack of goods.

- Kmeila has connected more than 30,000 small and medium-sized livestreamers with more than 3,000 factories, brands, and suppliers in a highly efficient manner.

- The data system developed by Kmeila can track the whole course of every order—this is a core capability of a supply chain.

The author of this text is Li Zhao, senior researcher, and Zhen Xu, research assistant, both at Kuaishou Research Institute.

Kmeila is an e-commerce supply chain platform in Hangzhou that provides goods to small and medium-sized livestreamers through an e-commerce service system.

Approximately 70 percent of Kmeila's business comes from Kuaishou E-commerce—it currently has engagements with more than 30,000 Kuaishou livestreamers. Kmeila was among the first batch of service providers to be added to Kuaishou's API and also among the first batch of business solicitation heads for Kuaishou's Alliance of Good Things.

In October 2020, less than three months after joining the Alliance of Good Things, Kmeila achieved nearly 4,000 percent growth in turnover.

◎ *The following is an account by Xiao Fei, founder of Kmeila.*

. . .

Why did Kmeila want to create a supply chain for content-based e-commerce? This is because, in 2017, we discovered that for many platforms that relied on content to attract traffic, an inability to monetize was the main reason that the experts called it quits. Therefore, intending to serve these experts, we began to work on a supply chain so that they could monetize by promoting goods.

We developed an entire e-commerce service system, including an e-commerce service middle-end and an app called Hongrenbanlv, as well as a supplier system in which livestreamers can complete orders directly. In 2018, we realized that there were a few people whose figures for promoting goods were highly impressive, and upon closer investigation, further realized that most of them were Kuaishou livestreamers. Hence, we immediately set all out to provide supply chain services to Kuaishou livestreamers.

At first, we also served the big livestreamers, but later on, we slowly focused our service on small and medium-sized livestreamers. This is because small and medium-sized livestreamers are like a spring of "fresh water"—there is a steady stream of newcomers every day.

We currently collaborate with more than 30,000 livestreamers, with their follower counts mainly in the 100,000–1,000,000 range. There are relatively few of them with less than 100,000 followers; on the other hand, those with more than a million followers have greater demands for collaboration and thus are not stable either.

In September 2020, Kuaishou launched the Alliance of Good Things. We applied to become a business solicitation head for the Alliance. Thanks to the virtuous cycle engendered by our high-quality supply chain resources and livestreamer resources, it took Kmeila less than three months to achieve a nearly 4,000 percent growth in turnover. In July and August 2020, our monthly turnover was around 1 million yuan—this rose to more than 10 million yuan in September and nearly 40 million yuan in October of that year. This shows that our path of collaborating with small and medium-sized livestreamers was a correct one.

Why We Focus on Serving Small and Medium-sized Livestreamers

Big livestreamers are better able to find goods on their own as compared to small and medium-sized livestreamers, who are thus more in need of service. We have found that several businesses nowadays only offer products that are very low in price-performance to small and medium-sized livestreamers. They only care about the big channels and are only willing to carry out "one-click distribution" for the big livestreamers.

Small and medium-sized livestreamers have a very strong need for high-quality supply chains; all of them have a need for monetization. Among the various means of monetization, e-commerce is the most stable.

Small and medium-sized livestreamers are not professional e-commerce sellers. While a significant number of them can possibly be full-time content creators, very few of them can be full-time goods sellers. Just like long-haul truck drivers who are on the road 24 hours a day, they do not have the time to stock up on goods themselves. Although they are good at creating content, they do not understand goods and more so inventory, EPR, turnover, and stock.

They must pay high costs to find goods on their own and are very likely to incur losses for stockpiling, shipments, and such. Among them, very few people are conscious of procuring goods from proper channels.

Instead, they are often only able to find small workshops and have to bear responsibility for any problems that arise.

For example, when a Kuaishou livestreamer from Lianyungang wanted to sell crayfish, what did he do? He found a crayfish supplier from Qianjiang, Hubei Province, over the Internet. He ended up getting scammed, receiving goods that were not as described. I asked him why he did not seek out the farmers' professional cooperatives in Qianjiang or the local e-commerce association, to which he replied that he tried but could not find them. In reality, many livestreamers do not have this kind of awareness; even though he earns 10 million yuan per month, his supply chains are mostly handled by his relatives and friends, and he is unable to recruit any talents.

Later, he set up a 5,000 m2 warehouse in his own home and bought a big truck with which he personally journeyed to Qianjiang to purchase goods with cold, hard cash. After hauling the goods to Lianyungang on a fully-monitored journey, he kept them frozen in the warehouse and subsequently did the packing and shipment on his own. During this process, a great deal of wastage was incurred. Unbeknownst to him, Qianjiang is very well-developed logistically speaking and has many local enterprises that provide shipping services. Hence, it was a severe case of information asymmetry that led to this outcome.

This sort of information asymmetry creates a huge market space. Nowadays, there are a few MCNs that claim to be in service of small and medium-sized livestreamers but are actually trying to turn them into Internet celebrity livestreamers. They would take all of these livestreamers under their name, yet only serve the more successful ones.

The only way to truly serve small and medium-sized livestreamers is to scale. Firstly, the greater the number of livestreamers, the lower the marginal costs and the higher the earnings. Secondly, this serves to increase the bargaining power against the suppliers. Individual livestreamers would not be taken seriously by suppliers, whereas the thousands if not tens of thousands of livestreamers that Kmeila represents have an amplifying effect.

The ceiling for Kuaishou's small and medium-sized livestreamers is high enough, and they are large enough in numbers. We have discovered that there are many livestreamers on Kuaishou with around a million followers; they outnumber the livestreamers with around 10 million followers by hundreds of times. Similarly, the livestreamers with around 100,000 followers outnumber those with around a million followers by hundreds of times and are in turn outnumbered by those with around 10,000 followers. Therefore, the lower the follower count, the more the livestreamers in that range. This is an exponential increase that can be represented by a pyramid; the lower one goes, the more stable the numbers.

At present, we will first work on the livestreamers in the range of 100,000 followers while improving our own service capabilities and efficiency. After serving this batch of livestreamers, the system would have collected even more data, enabling us to serve those livestreamers with 10,000 or even 1,000 followers.

Connecting the Two Ends of People and Goods

Kmeila's operations mainly rely on our self-developed e-commerce service system, the core of which is to find the right "people" and "goods." Nowadays, there is a very large chasm between people and goods. Livestreamers might have traffic, but they cannot get good-quality goods to sell; many factories have goods, but they are unable to sell these goods. Kmeila seeks to connect livestreamers with factories and brands.

We provide sources of goods to livestreamers and carry out "one-click distribution." We also handle aftersales and customer service, allowing livestreamers to create content with peace of mind. We assess every livestreamer's goods-selling capabilities according to the system data and recommend to them the goods that suit them most.

Kmeila's team now consists of around 150 people, with the business development team taking up more than half of this number. The business development team is divided into the two directions of "business solicitation and goods selection" and "livestreamer development."

The business solicitation and goods selection team is in charge of searching for sources of goods all across China. Most of them have been in the industry for a decade or two and thus know very clearly where the source manufacturers of the goods are. The team is divided into different categories, with the people in each category traveling to different regions of China. For example, those in the cosmetics category go to Guangzhou, while those in the food category go to Henan Province.

Source factories are what we are looking for; their one-click distribution capabilities are very important to us. If we are unable to find suppliers with uch capabilities, we would find a suitably priced agent to procure the goods.

During the initial phase of a collaboration with a supplier, it is necessary to inspect the goods and carry out preliminary evaluation and only allow the supplier to continue supplying goods after building up trust. We have a quality control team to inspect the quality of the goods. Moreover, if there are aftersale problems, the supplier would be subjected to our rules—for example, if there are many customer complaints, we would deduct the supplier's deposit.

Clothing is very high in variation; there are hundreds of designs for each type of clothing, and hence it is impractical to procure every single design.

What we would look at is whether there were problems with the supplier's earlier shipments. If there were no problems with the 100,000 pieces that they supplied at first, they would only have to ship samples over the next time. In this way, shipments can be made very quickly.

The livestreamer development team oversees looking for a large number of livestreamers. What we do is to check the Livestream Square every day and take note of any good livestreamers. Then, we contact them via different channels. Alternatively, we get recommendations from livestreamers or go to livestreamer hotspots to look for them.

We collaborate with livestreamers who have developed on Kuaishou and have the potential to monetize and the ability to promote goods. We mainly look at their follower counts and viewer counts, which are figures that are officially provided by Kuaishou and are unlikely to be wrong. At the moment, we do not collaborate with livestreamers who only have a few thousand followers. This is because our starting point is goods; we enable livestreamers to make money by selling goods. If they have neither followers nor a follower persona, it would be very difficult for us to serve them via the system, and more so to guarantee that they can make money on Kmeila.

What we calculate is a livestreamer's efficiency of making money. We have also come up with a "follower order power" coefficient for selecting livestreamers, i.e., the ratio of a livestreamer's follower count to their order count or turnover.

At first, we signed e-commerce agreements with livestreamers that required them to sell our goods, but we later realized that this was not very feasible. Nowadays, Kmeila no longer restricts livestreamers but instead lets them choose us through our services.

Finding All Sources of Good-quality Goods in China

Goods are the essence of livestream e-commerce. Due to the mutual competition among livestreamers, they do not share their sources of goods with one another, and thus small and medium-sized vertical-category livestreamers are unable to get high-quality goods. Our strong suit is none other than to find factories—using the food industry for example, we first find stores with huge sales volumes that have set up shop on traditional e-commerce platforms, then find their supporting factories to sign formal contracts with, and make business-to-business payments. The cost for livestreamers to procure goods from Kmeila is less than 10 percent higher than the cost for them to find their own goods, yet this saves them a huge amount of time and energy.

We hope to find all sources of high-quality goods in China and turn them into a "plate of goods." We then pick out the best ones and give them to the most suitable livestreamers.

For example, we have collaborations with 100 factories to sell water, but only the products of three factories appear on our app's product selection interface. It is not possible for us to give every single product to the livestreamers; we only deal in products with the highest price-performance and profitability for livestreamers and usually only choose the very best at that. The reason that we choose products from three different factories is that they are divided into the three levels of high-, middle-, and low-end, and thus we would pick the most reliable factory for each level.

We impose high demands on and manage our suppliers strictly; they must comply with our service guidelines. The eventual degree of exposure that a supplier's products get depends entirely on their own value. We subject our suppliers to great constraints; the goods that they ship must be consistent with the samples they give us.

Our goods cover all categories and consist of tens of thousands of SKUs. Cosmetics, personal care products, food products, and general merchandise have the highest proportions. For clothing, we mainly do exclusive brand livestreams with very high turnovers. Because of the particularity of the quality requirements for food products, we also prefer branded products. For general merchandise, we mainly collaborate with source factories.

On the whole, our goods are mainly fast-moving consumer goods with high repurchase rates. We sell anything that is needed in daily life and do not sell products that are eye-catching but useless.

Relying on Data to Drive Services

We serve thousands if not tens of thousands of small and medium-sized livestreamers using a unified system. On our platform, livestreamers can simply click on a product to sell it on Kuaishou immediately. Their orders automatically enter the system, which can determine which supplier the goods come from. After the supplier has shipped the goods, the system displays the relevant information. No manual operation is required throughout this process.

On the system, livestreamers can see their sales figures such as follower activity, repurchase rate, and livestream conversion. They can also have two mobile phones, with one for selling goods and the other for looking at the figures. Suppliers may also enter the system to check the various figures, albeit they do not know which followers bought their products and cannot export the livestreamers' follower data. By using the system, we have also gained a grasp of the real sales figures of all livestreamers; we know very clearly who sold what things at what time, which things were sold the most, and which things were sold the least.

What most livestreamers see are the products recommended on the home page, which are high in price-performance and are suitable for them to sell. Everyone sees a unique set of recommendations; we recommend products to them according to their content tags, follower personas, turnovers, and other figures, or according to the sales of Internet celebrity livestreamers who have similar content tags and follower personas as them. This is because people groups and the products they sell have a certain degree of similarity. In doing so, we have increased the livestreamers' monetization efficiency.

Based on the figures for the livestreaming orders that we have accumulated over the past two years, we have developed an aftersales data board that can track the entire course of every order. This is a core capability in supply chain organization, and it is certainly brought about by data and intelligence.

Hence, we are essentially a data-driven company. The more people we serve, the more data we accumulate, and thus the more accurate the products we recommend to livestreamers.

The Virtuous Cycle Between Internet Celebrities and Platforms

Aside from small and medium-sized livestreamers, vertical-category livestreamers also need us to provide differentiated supply. They are proficient in a single category or in even more vertical categories. For example, while some livestreamers promote different types of women's clothing, others only promote dresses or t-shirts. Although these livestreamers go very deep into a certain field, they do not have the energy to research other directions.

However, followers cannot possibly buy from a single category only. Most shoppers on Kuaishou do not have a clear buying purpose; instead, they simply buy whatever they fancy. Therefore, while a vertical-category livestreamer can focus on their own products initially, as they slowly develop, they would grow anxious about their followers leaving them upon seeing their followers shopping on other people's livestream channels. Hence, they need to add new product categories and sources of goods. For example, approximately 50 percent of the products sold by Shandong livestreamer Xiaofoye on her livestreams are not her own; she mainly sells clothing, while we provide her with food products and cosmetic products.

Big livestreamers need us to help them galvanize their followers. For example, while they can sell wine, tea leaves, and cosmetics at very high profits, they need a few products with fairly high price-performance to give to their followers as a benefit. Sure enough, our products have high price-performance and thus are well-received by their followers.

We have a great need for platforms like Kuaishou; it was all thanks to Kuaishou that we could be established. In turn, we can also help Kuaishou develop in a healthier way.

TIP

Kmeila's Nationwide Supply Chain Base Plan

At present, Kmeila has built supply chain bases in Hangzhou and Huzhou, Zhejiang Province. Next, we are going to build supply chain bases in Haitou, Jiangsu Province, Linyi, Shandong Province, and Shijiazhuang, Hebei Province, concurrently, thereby spreading our bases throughout China. We will also enter other clusters of Kuaishou livestreamers, such as in Shenyang, Zhengzhou, and Guangzhou. We do not need these bases to be very large in scale; each of them will only require a few people to operate. We will mainly still depend on the technologies, products, and supply chains of our headquarters in Hangzhou.

Why do we have to build local bases? This is because it would be very difficult for us to gain the trust of livestreamers if we just say that our factories are in Hangzhou. By building these bases, we can understand the needs of local livestreamers more clearly and swiftly, and do not have to travel all about every day.

For example, our local team in Lianyungang can visit the livestreamers over there and livestream together with them every day, thereby understanding their needs, what they are selling, and what they lack, which we immediately help them find. Our supply chains in various parts of China are akin to a shop window that displays goods from all over the country; their main purpose is not to supply goods. If a livestreamer wants crayfish from Qianjiang, Hubei Province, we can ship directly from Qianjiang.

Why did we choose to build a base in Huzhou? Firstly, Huzhou's municipal government has good policies. Secondly, Huzhou is close to Hangzhou and has cheap land prices. Thirdly, Huzhou has cosmetics towns where many brands and supply chains are gathered. In this way, livestreamers can take a flight from wherever they are to Huzhou, spend a week there, and promote many brands on-stream in one go.

ZHU FENG, FOUNDER OF STAR-STATION: THE THINKING BEHIND TRADITIONAL AD DELIVERY NEEDS TO BE CHANGED

Key Points

- Kuaishou has pioneered functional livestreaming, greatly unleashing the forces of production innate to various industries. This has also made it possible for products to reach even more users in an inclusive manner.

The authors of this text are researcher Li Yuchao and research assistant Cai Yuhui, both at Kuaishou Research Institute.

- The Star-Station model is a new species that grew up in Kuaishou's ecosystem. For enterprises to emerge victorious, they need to be content-, operations-, and data-driven.

- To seize the opportunities in livestreaming, an enterprise must personally lay out and establish an internal MCN department to gain middle-end capabilities.

Zhu Feng, founder of Star-Station TV, is a graduate from Tsinghua University and an entrepreneur born in the '90s. On Kuaishou, Star-Station's account and the accounts of their clients have more than 200 million followers combined.

A case that Zhu Feng often mentions is that of "Lady Penguin's Tavern." She is a seller of red wine and opened two accounts in succession on Kuaishou. The first account had 10 followers, while the second had more than 700 followers. However, she gave up subsequently. Later, Star-Station helped her operate an account. Today, her account has more than a million followers and generates 7 million yuan in monthly sales. It previously ranked among the top five in Kuaishou's cuisine rankings, and often sells out its stock in one night.

Zhu Feng believes that livestreaming is becoming a means of production that will enter every person's life, just like water, electricity, and gas. Livestreaming has brought about opportunities for entrepreneurs to transform their businesses. In the future, an up-to-date enterprise must grasp the system of livestream operations in its own hands and possess middle-end capabilities.

◎ *The following is an account by Zhu Feng, founder of Star-Station.*

. . .

The Decisive Transformation of an Internet Celebrity

I became an entrepreneur after completing my undergraduate studies at Tsinghua University's School of Journalism and Communication. My partners and I made it onto the "Forbes 30 Under 30 Asia 2017" list and are also among the youngest members of the Tsinghua Entrepreneur and Executive Club. On Kuaishou, our account and our clients' accounts have more than 200 million followers combined.

At the end of 2016, people mainly watched videos on Youku and iQIYI. Back then, I was considered an Internet celebrity who did football commentary and was ranked first in Youku's entertainment category. Later, I discovered a problem: my followers stopped interacting with me on Youku—and even "ceased to exist" on Youku—but instead interacted with me on Tieba and in QQ groups. Hence, I made my first transformation—I began looking for a new platform and found Kuaishou.

Although I could not understand Kuaishou at that time, I realized that Kuaishou's follower stickiness and interactivity were far higher than those of other platforms—it is less of a medium and more of a social platform. We made a very important decision to cut off all content on other platforms and all our revenue from advertising, filming promos, etc., and focus fully on Kuaishou.

Livestreaming Has Changed the Relations of Production in Society

We are not an MCN but rather a new species that grew up in Kuaishou's environment. We are an industrial belt base authenticated by Kuaishou's official team, and one of Kuaishou's bigger third-party service providers for brands.

Why did we choose Kuaishou? This was because I believed that short videos and livestreams are essentially changing the relations of production in society. In the past, most livestreams were "showtime livestreams;" they were a stage for singing, dancing, and other forms of performance. During a sharing session for entrepreneurs at that time, I introduced myself on-stage as an Internet celebrity, causing a hubbub among the audience—they had some preconception of the term "Internet celebrity" and felt that all Internet celebrities had come from talent shows. However, we later realized that livestreaming has changed things, and this sort of change began from Kuaishou.

Today, livestreams have changed from "showtime livestreams" to "functional livestreams." Why are they called "functional livestreams?" This means that the relations of production in society can be changed using short videos and livestreams. For instance, even the most capable teacher can only teach up to a few dozen students in one lesson, but on Kuaishou these days, a teacher can influence hundreds of people in one lesson. Hence, a teacher's forces of production have been unleashed. To give another example, instead of goods-promoting livestreamers, the people who sold goods in the past were counter salespersons or wholesale merchants, but the availability of short videos and livestreams nowadays has greatly unleashed the original forces of production in sales.

As far as the eye can see, China is a country with great economic depth. Given its huge population, how can we make it possible for people in remote regions to buy high-quality goods? I felt full of excitement when I was thinking about this back in the day. I thought to myself, "My goodness! There are far too many things that can be done in our country." Hence, I needed a platform that could help me reach these people. Kuaishou is an inclusive tool that can reach every ordinary person, enabling us to see that the livestream ecosystem is slowly moving in a better direction.

Previously, Dong Mingzhu livestreamed for three hours on Kuaishou and generated 310 million yuan in sales. On Singles' Day in 2019, a certain top livestreamer's team generated more than 2 billion yuan in sales. Were they able to sell so well because they organized an event for this Singles' Day? The answer is no—they have always been selling well in Kuaishou's ecosystem. The traffic entrenched here can bring about continuous and consistent growth in sales, and that was why I settled on this platform.

Livestreaming Has Brought About Transformation Opportunities for Enterprises

Entrepreneurs are now presented with an opportunity brought about by the changing of the times. As we have seen, short videos and livestreams are becoming a means of production that will enter every person's life, just like water, electricity, and gas.

During the old era of the PC Internet, we had to conduct promotions and bid for ads, and after doing so, the platform would put my ads on the homepage. The platform thus served as a center that influenced the nodes on the periphery. However, things are different these days. The transmission model that we face today consists of distributed traffic and multi-node transmission. Every user is a node that can carry out content distribution; every dispersed node has its influence.

To give an example, I once saw a video on Kuaishou promoting road rollers. The account had less than 10,000 followers, yet it sold 20 road rollers in a three-hour livestream, with the price per unit of around 400,000 yuan. It was only a very small node, but because it was on a social platform with distributed traffic, the user group that it was able to influence was very accurate, and thus the price of 400,000 yuan per unit did not deter sales.

In another example, there is an account on Kuaishou with more than 200 videos, all of which show the livestreamer fishing, and even the posture of fishing is the same in all of them. Were it on another platform, this account would probably not be popular. I once watched its livestream— throughout its three-hour duration, it simply showed the livestreamer fishing, and not a word was spoken. Nevertheless, the comments below were very lively: "I see the bait." "What model is the fishing rod?" This left me bewildered. Later on, I added this livestreamer as a friend and discovered that he could sell more than 1,000 fishing rods every month, with most of his traffic coming from Kuaishou.

Therefore, distributed nodes are essentially a very interesting community in which one can find many like-minded people and interact with them using short videos. Why short videos? Because the barriers to entry are low. It is highly unlikely for a middle-aged woman from a village to be able to write a 10,000- word essay, but if you give her a mobile phone, she would be able to film her life. This is why Kuaishou stands out.

Being Content-, Operations-, and Data-driven

Perhaps some people still have the preconception that this platform is very old-fashioned. However, I feel that the essence of being "old-fashioned" is an information gap. The greater the information gap in a certain place, the greater the value you can create. Back when China did not have e-commerce, it was by striding over such a huge information gap that Alibaba created tremendous economic value. As of today, we have served more than 100 enterprises, but this is still not enough.

Recently, I visited many places in China and realized that China is indeed vast in territory and rich in resources. Jade from Sihui, seafood from the East China Sea, textiles from Jiangxi Province.... Have you ever thought about what the building blocks of China are? Rather than those big brands, it is actually the countless small and medium-sized businesses. Although many businesses are already selling their goods by livestreaming on short video platforms, there remains a problem, which is the fact that the businesses in China's small-town and rural markets and industrial belts still do not really understand what ROI and data analysis are.

Hence, I created a simple set of tools for businesses; all they have to do is confirm the goals that they want to achieve, and we would take care of everything. Before this, we had already worked out a reproducible set of formulae for creating hot-selling products. We created many accounts and posted many videos on Kuaishou and found out through continuous grayscale testing and A/B testing (making two or more versions of a webpage, API, or process and evaluating the best version) that there are thousands of dimensions that can affect the amount of traffic that a video gets, such as upload time, cover picture, color resolution, saturation, and title font and length. We gradually figured out how to get on to Kuaishou's Trending page.

The way to achieve victory these days is no longer to be "the king of content," and that is because there is far too much excellent content on the platform already. Instead, it is necessary to be content-, operations-, and data- driven. If two people filmed the same clip but carried out different operations and data analysis, the results would be completely different. Hence, we often see accounts that become popular overnight due to their excellent content, but without the support of operations and data analysis, it would be impossible to maintain popularity on the platform in the long run or to create a path of monetization.

During the process of traffic delivery, all of our clients have achieved ROI growth. Before collaborating with us, a livestreamer in the category of jewelry and jade had an ROI of 1 percent, but it has now risen to 800 percent. One of our sports brand clients used to have an ROI of 20 percent, but after we helped him do traffic delivery, he now has an ROI of 1,000 percent. When businesses earn money, so do we—and that is why people say that "businesses are the greatest charity." When you have "run through" a business model, you find that it is essentially a charity that can repeat cyclically and possesses ecosystem capabilities.

The Thinking Behind Traditional Ad Delivery Needs to Be Changed

To deal with their short-video-related needs, a few foreign enterprises and big brands still engage their original suppliers, i.e., traditional advertising companies. Their mindsets have not changed.

The biggest difference between us and advertising agencies lies in algorithms and traffic. Our platform's algorithm-based recommendations can recommend accurate user groups to livestreamers. For example, in terms of packaging technique, a bot will identify accurate user groups according to the livestreamer's cover and overall rhythm and then recommend the livestreamer to them. In such a situation, production experience determines how one is matched with the most suitable audience on a platform that uses algorithm-based recommendations.

In traditional ad delivery, everyone sees the same content. Moreover, advertising agencies basically spend their entire budgets on large scenes, creativity, and copywriting; they rarely think about how to survive on a new platform like Kuaishou.

Therefore, the standards of measurement must be changed, and so must the methods of production. Some time ago, we helped "Wang Doudou's Childhood" deliver a cosmetics livestream—the results were excellent, with the conversion rate of her flagship product as high as 96 percent. During that livestream session, she sold all of the goods she had prepared. Furthermore, I conjectured that she would have sold even more if her inventory was set at a higher level.

We carry out delivery changes according to the real-time sales conversion figures from the backend. For example, when there is an upcoming flash sale for a new product, the number of viewers on the livestream channel must be maximized at that point in time. Hence, we "fired on all cylinders" delivery-wise, helping her increase her number of viewers from the usual 6,000-8,000 to 18,000. As a result, the product gained great publicity and achieved its goals. Subsequently, we reduced the speed of delivery back to the normal level and proceeded with delivering the next product.

Enterprises Must Have Their Own MCN Departments

During the first phase of third-party operations, we helped many enterprises increase their followers. Subsequently, what they must do is sell goods. What is an MCN's value during this process? Its ultimate purpose is to enable enterprises to possess their own middle-end capabilities.

One of our clients has approximately 15,000 salespersons nationwide. Their boss made a request to me, which was to move all their salespersons to Kuaishou. Instead of requesting that we bring them 100,000 followers within 30 days, we were tasked with ensuring that every salesperson has 2,000 followers. In this way, the enterprise would have 30 million followers online.

Enterprises ought to have an official account for brand-building purposes. Subsequently, many sub-accounts can be opened to create different personas and thereby penetrate many different circles. For example, Xueersi's subject matrix and Ximalaya's column matrix were both created by us. Simply put, when a user follows the official account of a certain educational brand, they probably receive more finely divided content from the sub-accounts subsequently. In this way, each and every node is rounded up. After a brand matrix is established, it would be possible to build an online sales system that would eventually be firmly held in the hands of the enterprise itself.

In such a model, every account in the enterprise matrix has a different persona and circle. For example, women's clothing has different styles for different circles, such as elegant style or lolita style. As a third-party operations agency, we can help enterprises create benchmark accounts for different circles.

In the future, an up-to-date enterprise must set up its own MCN department, have a complete set of livestreamer, operations, and filming teams, and take root in the livestream ecosystem to do sales. Given the significant uncertainty of KOLs, enterprises should not always engage them to promote goods. Instead, they should keep a grip on these kinds of teams, and after achieving operational stability, they can further create thousands if not tens of thousands of teams.

Therefore, enterprises ought to have their own middle-end capabilities, and in the future, they should recruit and train even more livestreamers and salespersons. When a framework has been built and media is bought and delivered, all the traffic falls into their traffic pool, thereby forming a link. A cycle is formed by obtaining traffic from Kuaishou and leading it to private domains.

Our main direction for the future is to help enterprises build their own middle-end capabilities. After all, an enterprise cannot allow an external enterprise to take charge of something as important as its growth in the long run.

PART FOUR

KUAISHOU'S ECOSYSTEM (PART 2): THE RISE OF BRANDS

CHAPTER TEN

GROWING KUAI BRANDS

- Just as Taobao has Tao brands, Kuaishou is also growing Kuai brands.

- This chapter provides two case examples: the first is ClIiCK bee venom toothpaste, which became hot-selling thanks to the promotional efforts of a company. The second is the "Call of Spring" brand, which became hot-selling thanks to the promotional efforts of its owner, a livestreamer called "77 Sister Ying."

CLIICK: HOW A BRAND OF BEE VENOM TOOTHPASTE BECAME HOT-SELLING

Key Points

- The underlying logic of the rise of Kuai brands is a change in the main consumers. As new notions of consumption emerge, people born in the '90s and '00s pay greater attention to price-performance.

- By leveraging highly efficient channels such as livestreams and short videos, a group of people who have high-quality goods

---

The authors of this text are Kuaishou Research Institute senior researcher Li Zhao and research assistant Cai Yuhui.

but no more opportunities in traditional e-commerce eco-systems and the WeChat Business ecosystem have found new opportunities.

- A hot-selling product is a prerequisite for building a brand. However, to become a true brand, a brand must be rolled out on all channels to leverage the supply chain.

n 2020, ClIiCK Toothpaste was awarded the champion toothpaste product for monthly sales on the Kuaishou platform. Previously, this product was unable to get sales going in traditional channels; it was only on Kuaishou that it surged in popularity. Chen Rihe, founder of ClIiCK bee venom toothpaste, has worked hard in the industry for many years. He specializes in research on bee venom products and recipes, laying a high-quality foundation for his products.

An important driver of ClIiCK Toothpaste's popularity is a company called "Mockuai." It is located in Hangzhou and was established in 2015.

To find out how ClIiCK Toothpaste seized the opportunities in the era of livestreaming and became a successful example of a Kuai brand, let's see what Chen Rihe, founder of ClIiCK Toothpaste, and Xiaofei (Wang Yulin), founder of Mockuai, have to say.

◎ *The following is an account by Chen Rihe, founder of ClIiCK Toothpaste and chairman of Rihetang Medical Technology Co., Ltd.*

· · ·

The Birth and Growth of "Bee Venom Toothpaste"

I worked in marketing for the Kao Corporation, Bawang International Group, and 999 Group, in that order, and later on, I set up my own cosmetics factory. However, I lost a lot of money because I did not understand technology. In 2008, I founded Rihetang, and in 2016, I began to combine the concept of "bee venom" with toothpaste. I have studied bee venom for a decade or so and have also worked on the ClIiCK brand for 10 years now. Bee venom is a type of traditional Chinese medicine (TCM), and so bee venom toothpaste is an example of the modernization and "productization" of TCM.

Our bee venom products also include facial cream, shower gel, plasters, and so on, for a total of about 10 products. We have been selling bee venom plasters for many years through professional channels of beauty and healthcare, and they enjoy an excellent rep. On Kuaishou, we mainly sell products such as toothpaste, shower gel, and soap.

In China, there is a very well-known TCM toothpaste brand—Yunnan Baiyao Toothpaste. It was the inspiration for my research and development of bee venom toothpaste. In accordance with my long-term tracking and study of Yunnan Baiyao Toothpaste, I positioned bee venom toothpaste as an all-in- one type of toothpaste. In particular, it has an obvious effect on stomatitis; my assessment was that there was a market demand for this.

In 2017, we set the price of our toothpaste at 38 yuan per tube on traditional e-commerce channels, which is not much different from the price of Yunnan Baiyao Toothpaste. In the first year, we sold approximately 100,000 tubes; we had failed to open the market, causing several million tubes of toothpaste to pile up in the warehouse. It was at this time when we decided to reduce the price. After reducing the price to 10 yuan or so per tube, we were able to sell several hundred thousand tubes in one year.

In June or July 2019, we reached an agreement for collaboration with Mockuai. Based on their understanding of our product, Mockuai positioned us as "the glory of domestic products" and reckoned that we could not compete with the big toothpaste brands such as Yunnan Baiyao Toothpaste at a high price point, and thus suggested selling our product at a low price point of 8 yuan per tube. Low-priced functional toothpaste products are usually sold at around 11 yuan per tube, and so by setting our price at 8 yuan per tube, we would not have any competitors in this field.

I had previously assessed that if our product was able to sell well at a low price point and benefit the common folk, it would not be a bad positioning either. Hence, I agreed to hold a trial promotion on the Mockuai platform. To my surprise, one million tubes were sold in the first month, and this increased to several million tubes in some of the following months. From September 2019 to the autumn of 2020, sales were very stable—a total of 10 to 20 million tubes were sold on channels such as Kuaishou and Tmall, ranking among the top few toothpaste products in domestic sales.

The Key Factor for a Product to Remain Hot-selling Is Ultra-high Price-performance

We objectively assessed that our toothpaste product was indeed built up on the Kuaishou platform, with the promotions carried out by Internet celebrities during the early days playing a huge role. As bee venom is something very conceptualized and rarely understood, we had to engage eloquent speakers to introduce and demonstrate it in order for it to become understood and gain the trust of consumers.

At first, Mockuai recommended our bee venom toothpaste to several Kuaishou livestreamers with fairly high follower counts. After they generated good sales and spread its influence, a few other Kuaishou livestreamers began selling it as well. Had there not been so many Kuaishou livestreamers promoting it and generating a surge in sales during the early days, it would not have enjoyed continuous development later on. After bee venom toothpaste became highly popular on Kuaishou, we gradually expanded to other platforms.

As sales increased, the production layout of our factories also changed. Rather than putting all production in the same basket, we now have two factories supplying goods. In this way, I can balance out any disturbances and control risks. From my experiences and lessons learned, I know that there would be a huge problem if we have only one factory supplying goods and it is unable to manufacture enough goods at a critical point in time.

Based on my analysis, Internet celebrity products can develop continuously and steadily if they can reach the later stages. The key factor remains an ultra-high price-performance; at this price point, it is very difficult to buy this kind of functional toothpaste.

We are the pioneers of bee venom toothpaste in China. Sixty or 70 years ago, a type of bee venom toothpaste had appeared in Italy, but it was only made as a concept and was not actually sold. Today, our toothpaste product has many effects, such as anti-inflammation, painkilling, stop-bleeding, oral ulcer-healing, breath-freshening, and sensitive-teeth prevention. It took us 20 months to create its recipe. One of its flavorings was specially researched and developed for our bee venom toothpaste by the engineers of a Swiss company. It was custom-made to be combined with the TCM extracts that we produced ourselves. It can keep one feeling refreshed for several hours; consumers would feel a highly obvious feeling on their very first use.

Its effects cannot be the least bit fake because the assessment is not done by ourselves. As of today, our toothpaste has received several million reviews on various platforms, with a positive review rate of 97 percent or higher, which is impressive enough. After working on it for more than a year, we came to the understanding that the product is the most important of all; if a product that is good and cheap meets the right opportunity, it would probably sell like hotcakes.

I believe that the concept of bee venom has a huge effect because it is very novel. There are also a few small aspects, such as the packaging design, where we are unconventional. At first, people felt that the packaging of our toothpaste looked like that for shoe polish. Many of my friends in the industry told me that my toothpaste would either sell out or be a complete flop. However, I persisted with this style, and in consideration of subsequent development, I applied for the protection of the related patents and copyrights.

Besides, toothpaste has to be used throughout the year, regardless of the season. On top of that, the teeth-brushing habits of Chinese citizens have improved a lot over the years; even people in remote regions have gradually grown used to brushing their teeth twice a day. And with the popularization of the Internet, everyone's health notions and lifestyles are improving, while their consumption habits have already changed tremendously.

As an accidental factor, the coronavirus pandemic in 2020 stimulated online sales greatly. During the pandemic, most offline stores could not open for business, and thus sales could not be made through traditional channels. Conversely, the problem of opening for business does not exist for online channels; livestream e-commerce was instead presented with new opportunities. It was from December 2019 to the pandemic period that our sales volume surged.

Success consists of many comprehensive factors. This is generally what I have surmised: Firstly, the core factors are definitely product efficacy and ultra-high price-performance. Secondly, the promotional role played by livestreamers on the Kuaishou platform is also very crucial. Thirdly, periodic factors; mainly because of the pandemic, online spending has increased. Nowadays, the repurchase rate of our toothpaste is as high as 20 percent to 30 percent, which is considered very high even among the top-tier toothpaste brands in China.

The Brand-Driven Modernization of Traditional Chinese Medicine

Leveraging the power of platforms and organizations and prioritizing sales volume are the principles of a new brand model. Nowadays, we have a tight-knit collaboration with Mockuai; our product development and various promotional events are all carried out in accordance with their suggestions. At present, the goal that we and Mockuai have set is to hit 50 million tubes in annual sales. Meanwhile, they also hope that we would carry out product upgrading and develop a few new types of bee venom toothpaste and children's toothpaste to suit the needs of different consumer groups.

For a brand to truly develop and achieve a certain scale and popularity, it cannot rely on a single platform. Instead, it should seek to build up its product line on all platforms, including a comprehensive online and offline layout. At the moment, we are still not so well-rounded; our sales volume on Kuaishou accounts for 60 percent to 70 percent of our overall sales volume, and we have not touched on many other channels. In the future, we hope to engage spokespersons— possibly from among the top livestreamers on various platforms—to help us establish ourselves on multiple platforms. At the same time, offline promotions are also included in our development plan.

For now, what we can do is to make full use of "Internet Plus," especially the trend that is livestream e-commerce. Otherwise, we would not be able to develop as quickly as expected. We have established an Internet company, with a team specially in charge of livestreaming, to study the operations of various platforms. I am deeply confident that, sooner and later, ClIiCK bee venom toothpaste will secure a place in China's market for TCM toothpaste, becoming a functional toothpaste product that is loved by and affordable for the common folk.

Of course, my long-term goals are not just limited to ClIiCK Toothpaste. I also want to create a big platform for TCM and industrialize the good things from our traditions, or in other words, to modernize TCM. At present, bee venom has not been truly industrialized; its future prospects are still wide open.

It is necessary for a human to have some dreams; what if they actually come true?

◎ *The following is an account by Xiaofei (Wang Yulin), founder and CEO of Mockuai.*

· · ·

There are a few stories to tell when talking about how we built up ClIiCK bee venom toothpaste.

Mockuai has a specialized department for brand incubation, in which personnel have mostly been involved in products for many years. After going all over China in search of products that have the potential to become hot- selling, they eventually found Mr. Chen Rihe, who has been doing R&D throughout his career, in Guangzhou. A type of toothpaste that he researched and developed is notable for its painkilling and anti-inflammatory properties, its bee venom content, and the refreshing feeling it gives after being used for brushing teeth.

Back then, he was facing difficulties with sales of this product. He had 800,000 tubes in stock and wanted to sell them via WeChat Business, but eventually found himself unable to do so. We took a look at a few samples and felt that the product was pretty amazing, and thus we began to promote it on Kuaishou. In no time, it began to sell like hotcakes. In 2020, tens of millions of tubes were sold across several major platforms.

This type of toothpaste has several characteristics. Firstly, it is really good to use; many large factories have tried to reverse-engineer its formula but none of them have managed to replicate its feeling. Secondly, its packaging looks neat. The brand has been around for many years but had simply failed to take off.

Our strategy at that time was to first engage a few of the top livestreamers to try it out and only begin promoting it if they were impressed by it. Later, we also engaged with small and medium-sized livestreamers. After understanding and trying the product, they quickly decided to sell it together. In addition, there were a few other livestreamers who began promoting it after having a positive experience of using it themselves. At this time, it seemed to Kuaishou's users that everyone was using ClIiCK Toothpaste.

While we were working on ClIiCK Toothpaste, we realized that after the product made progress on Kuaishou, its sales volume in its Taobao flagship store and many other channels also picked up. Moreover, most of these sales had spilled over from Kuaishou. For example, many people have bought ClIiCK Toothpaste on Kuaishou, but when they wanted to buy it a second time, they searched for it on Taobao. As the search volume increased, the Taobao store received more orders. There are also some people who first saw the product on Kuaishou and then saw it again in other online communities. Upon realizing that it was a hot-selling product, they rushed to buy it. By encountering this kind of information on multiple occasions in multiple channels, consumers would build up brand awareness.

How Long Is the Path from a Hot-selling Product to a Brand?

A hot-selling product is a prerequisite for building a brand. Aside from large sales volumes, a brand also needs to have high repurchase rates, low costs of purchase decision-making, and high conversion rates.

Chen was always quite a capable person. His product was very well done and simply lacked channels. By leveraging highly efficient channels such as livestreams and short videos to integrate several elements, a foundation was laid for the birth of this brand.

We have discovered that, on Kuaishou, businesses can not only sell branded goods but also build Kuai brands with high efficiency. When businesses have established themselves on a platform, they would attract and unearth a new batch of supply resources. These businesses might have no opportunities left in traditional e-commerce ecosystems and the WeChat Business ecosystem, but because their products are good in quality, they would gain new opportunities as soon as they find new channels.

Kuai brands are just like Tao brands, except that they were incubated in Kuaishou's ecosystem.

At present, there are still not many Kuai brands on Kuaishou, but there are many opportunities for such brands to develop. Their underlying logic lies in the consumer groups; having become the main consumers, the '90s-born and '00s-born generations are neither familiar with nor mindful of the earlier brands, but instead pay greater attention to price-performance and other new ideas.

As a service provider with close ties to Kuaishou, Mockuai is familiar with Kuaishou's ecosystem and maintains excellent relations with the top livestreamers. Hence, we can engage these livestreamers when we want to promote a certain product. On top of that, Mockuai provides services to a few small and medium-sized livestreamers and can give priority to them when finding livestreamers to promote a certain brand.

Previously, we wanted to do "C2 Internet celebrity 2M"—in other words, to collect the demands and data of the consumer end via Internet celebrities, summarize them, and then reform the upstream production. In this way, the efficiency might be higher. However, we later discovered that this path is relatively difficult to take at the moment. It is not easy for a livestreamer to create their own brands because the volume is too small to support the bargaining space of the factory. Besides, if a livestreamer creates their own brands, it is unlikely that other livestreamers would help them promote their goods.

A true brand requires a very large scale in order to leverage the supply chain to create better quality and charge higher prices. Moreover, it must be rolled out on all channels; in addition to Kuaishou, it must also be sold on Taobao and JD.

Another method is co-branding between a livestreamer and a brand. For example, Longrich Toothpaste and a certain livestreamer have jointly launched a series that can be considered dual-branded. Longrich is a widely recognized brand, while the livestreamer provides further endorsement. I feel that there are also opportunities for such promotions.

CALL OF SPRING: THE VERTICAL-CATEGORY CULTIVATION OF YIWU LIVESTREAMER "77 SISTER YING"

Key Points

- On the second anniversary of her debut on Kuaishou, "77 Sister Ying" livestreamed for nearly 16 hours and generated more than 37 million yuan in sales.

- Rejecting various temptations to generate surges in orders, Sister Ying persisted in working on the vertical cosmetics category, and eventually took the lead among Yiwu's numerous

- livestreamers.

- By building "Call of Spring" as a Kuai brand, the price per customer is set relatively high and a price war is avoided. Attention is placed on the effects of its products.

September 7, 2020, was the second anniversary of "77 Sister Ying's" debut on Kuaishou. That day, she livestreamed for nearly 16 hours on Kuaishou, generating more than 37 million yuan in sales.

Sister Ying and her husband built up their Kuaishou business in Yiwu and are part of a batch of people who started doing livestream e-commerce on Kuaishou fairly early on. Like many of their peers in the industry, they

The authors of this text are Kuaishou Research Institute senior researcher Li Zhao and research assistant Cai Yuhui.

focused on vertical categories and persisted in creating a brand, beginning version 2.0 of "Yiwu e-commerce."

◎ *The following is an account by Liu Yan, husband of "77 Sister Ying"*
and founder of the company.

. . .

I was born in northeast China and moved to Qingdao, Shandong Province, when I was in my teens. After learning martial arts for a few years at Shaolin Temple, I opened a gym in Qingdao but achieved nothing in those three years aside from marrying Sister Ying. Her full name is Xu Xiaoying, and she is from Weifang, Shandong Province.

After we got married, we could no longer ask our families for money, and so we became street vendors together with a few friends. We set up stalls from Qingdao to Yangzhou, covering the entirety of Jiangsu Province at different points in time. Later on, it became a saying that you have to go to Yiwu if you want to ship goods throughout China. So, in December 2013, we packed our bags and went moneyless to Yiwu, where we stayed in Beixiazhu Village.

Influenced by Yan Bo, we began doing Kuaishou. Back then, he was the first person from Beixiazhu Village to do Kuaishou. After learning from him for some time, Sister Ying conducted her first Kuaishou livestream on September 7, 2018. (For Yan Bo's case example, refer to *The Power of Being Seen—What Is Kuaishou*, published by Kuaishou Research Institute.)

Initially, like many of Yiwu's livestreamers, Sister Ying mainly sold clothing and general merchandise instead of focusing on cosmetics. At that time, she felt that cosmetic products could neither be seen nor touched because they were applied on the face, and thus she was afraid that people would be distrustful of using them.

After a few months of livestreaming, we could no longer generate sales for general merchandise, while our clothing was also a little out of season, causing our business to wane. And when the return rates for leggings and cashmere coats rose to 30–35 percent, we decided to give cosmetics a try. We quickly realized that our loyal followers could accept cosmetic products, and the return rate was only 8–10 percent. Sister Ying had been exposed to the cosmetics industry early on and had also worked in supply chains, and so we crossed over to cosmetics at the end of 2018. This category can increase in output value and would definitely be much stronger than general merchandise when done right.

The Origins of Kuai Brand "Call of Spring"

Every platform can produce a few good brands. For example, HSTYLE is a Tao brand, while CIIiCK Toothpaste is a Kuai brand. On the Kuaishou platform, our "Call of Spring" can also be considered a Kuai brand today.

There are currently three factories that serve as OEMs for us, and they are mainly situated in Baiyun District, Guangzhou. Before we turned to livestreaming, we already had close-knit collaborations with these factories. In the past, they mainly supplied goods to beauty parlors and other such channels and did not have their own trademarks and brands. The inspiration that doing livestream e-commerce has given us is that we must create a brand of our own. Our collaborating factories mainly manufacture products for beauty parlors. In the cosmetics industry, the beauty parlor line of products requires more specialized knowledge and more effective products as compared to the daily chemical line of products. The formulae for products in the beauty parlor line vary according to the customers, whereas the formulae for products in the daily chemical line are universal—the same shampoo can become any brand depending on its label, and thus can be mass-produced.

Therefore, the quality of the beauty parlor line of products is generally higher than that of the daily chemical line of products. For example, the content of active ingredients must be high because beauty parlors have a need to ensure that customers can see the post-usage effects. If you buy a bottle of facial cream or water cream in a supermarket and the effects are poor, you would stop using it at worst. However, this is not the case for beauty parlors; to attract customers to sign up as members, they must first gain people's approval by choosing products that have obvious effects, such as making one's complexion ruddy and glossy or improving one's outward elegance. If there are no effects after one or two months, a beauty parlor would not be able to keep operating.

For the quality of our products to be good, the costs cannot possibly be too low, and thus we are unable to fight a price war with other livestreamers; all we can do is to let the effects of our products speak for themselves, hence the need to build up our brand. During an event held on September 7, 2020, the average price per customer was only 401 yuan, yet it was very well- received by users and thus we made more than 37 million yuan in revenue that day. For this event, we also invited people such as the general counsel and the chief production engineer of "Call of Spring's" R&D team to promote the products together.

Why Persist in Working on Vertical Categories and Brands

There are money-making opportunities to be found in every category; having decided to work on cosmetic products, we dropped all other categories. What we have figured out over so many years of ups and downs in this industry is that a livestreamer must persist in working on vertical categories. This sense of direction comes from practical experience rather than profound ideology. To do something, you must be focused and not all over the shop, otherwise, your followers would end up not knowing what you are actually good at.

In Yiwu, the livestreamers with hundreds of thousands of followers are often easily swayed; they would sell this one moment and sell that the next, depending on whatever is trending. If a livestreamer who originally sold bags is unable to make it on the Trending page after filming videos on bags for a month, then suddenly discovers that someone else has made it on to Trending by filming videos on fruits, he might be tempted to film videos on fruits, as well. What he does not know, however, is that that someone might have spent several months filming those videos before making it on to Trending. After realizing that it is also not easy to make it on to Trending by filming videos on fruits, he might then jump over to children's clothing. All this teetering about puts the account at risk of becoming useless. This is because the bag videos attracted a couple of bag lovers and the fruit videos attracted a couple of fruit lovers, and so when he jumped over to children's clothing, the followers accumulated from the previous two categories would no longer be relevant.

Following trends is simple; all you have to do is to copy what the people in front are doing. However, if you are working on vertical categories, there is no one to help you do research, and so you have to figure things out on your own. This is something very painstaking and endurance-testing; it has actually been very mentally tormenting on us to work on vertical categories.

Although Yiwu's market for small goods has been very successful, few of the people who do livestream e-commerce here have persisted in working on vertical categories. This might have to do with the genes of this place: goods and people.

Firstly, the goods-centered mindset of Yiwu's livestreamers is relatively acute, and thus they often neglect persona-building. Yiwu has far too many products; the back-end factories of every one of the more than 70,000 businesses here have many products. This overabundance of products makes it very difficult for businesses to focus on a particular category, but when their accounts are new, this makes it possible for them to quickly make it on to Trending.

Instead, were they to persist in working on vertical categories, it would usually take very long before they made it on to Trending.

Secondly, many of the livestreamers who have come to Yiwu to set up a business here had started out from the grassroots. Having been completely broke or even deeply in debt at first, they enjoy making quick money and chasing trends. They might have been convinced of the fine future prospects offered by vertical categories, yet if they do not make money for an entire month, they might not even be able to afford food. Hence, to make ends meet, they would rather follow trends and make it on to Trending first. If they fail to generate a surge in sales, they would be unable to afford their living expenses for the next month and thus would have to leave Yiwu.

It is very difficult to become a big livestreamer without working on vertical categories. Although everyone understands this principle, it is actually not easy to commit to. This might be because one's economic conditions forbid it, or because one is unable to resist various temptations.

The Kuaishou platform is actually very suitable for steady, persistent, and tenacious people to work on brands. On Kuaishou, growth during the early days is often not very fast but absolutely steady. This is because Kuaishou values a livestreamer's private domain traffic, which is a unique advantage of Kuaishou that provides a good opportunity to take root on Kuaishou and work toward brandification. It would not be worth it to instead lose one's head just because other platforms provide traffic support and bring in new followers quickly.

In particular, after Kuaishou launched Store Access, public and private domains became interconnected. Thanks to Store Access, Sister Ying's follower count increased rapidly—she had only three-million-odd followers in August 2020, but this increased to nearly eight million followers by November that year. Moreover, her followers are very high in stickiness. Our daily turnover is very consistent, albeit higher when we conduct events.

It would usually take a very long and painful period of time for a livestreamer to shift from a low price per customer to a high price per customer. This is because, over time, the spending power of one's followers would be concentrated at a certain price point. Kuaishou seeks to help vertical-category livestreamers establish their brands, thereby setting benchmarks.

Sister Ying positions herself differently from other people; she only does her own brands, does not supply goods to other people, and does not sell other people's goods. We mainly focus on the effects, the science, and the technology of our products. Nowadays, there is an intense price war in all categories and not just in the cosmetics industry. Going forward, we will persist in our own direction and quality, thereby ensuring that we would not get dragged into a price war.

The Chain of Livestreaming: From Factories in Guangzhou to Markets in Yiwu

These days, I basically spend half of every month in Guangzhou to expedite our goods and develop new products.

During the event held on September 7, 2020, there were many summer products on offer. After the event, new products had to be developed.

Summer products tend to be more refreshing, whereas moisturizing products must be developed for autumn and winter because these seasons are windy, dusty, and dry-air.

After having discussions with my R&D engineers in Guangzhou, we established that they would adjust the formulae for new products according to my demands, create samples for me to test, and then finalize a product if testing is successful. Subsequently, manufacturing would begin after the boxes and bottles have been prepared. This is a set of routine procedures.

Just as clothing has different designs for spring and autumn, cosmetic products come in two different styles—refreshing and moisturizing—for different seasons. Our factories, which specialize in customized products, can carry out production in accordance with our clients' demands.

Taobao and Tmall are e-commerce businesses, and so are livestreaming platforms. However, there is a huge disparity among different platforms; they are different in nature, different in terms of the age groups and levels of spending power that each brand corresponds to, and different in terms of the notions of consumption among urban and rural dwellers. Brands are likewise; although the products of a domestic brand and several products of "Call of Spring" are manufactured in the same factory, the same products get vastly different sales volumes in different channels. The products that this domestic brand sells well in other channels would not necessarily sell well on a livestream channel. At times, they are unable to sell the products that we are able to sell well.

Moreover, different livestreamers face different follower groups. The color cosmetics of Sister Ying and another livestreamer are manufactured in the same factory, yet our color cosmetics do not sell as well as those of the other livestreamer. This is because Sister Ying's followers are mainly above 30 years old, whereas those of the other livestreamer are mainly below 25 years old. Young women have a higher usage of color cosmetics, whereas older women have a greater need for systemic skincare, such as wrinkle-treating or anti-aging products.

Sister Ying speaks in a soft yet enchanting voice—every word she speaks would imprint itself on your heart. This characteristic has to do with the characteristics of our products; because our products have a high price per customer, the livestreamer must be a bit more detailed in explaining their features, ingredients, and benefits to justify their high price. For such products, passionate speeches would be futile; they are not like shopping mall promotions where passionate speeches are delivered to get everyone to think that they would lose out if they do not snap up the products quickly. This kind of atmosphere-setting method is useless for us; we have to use data rather than rely on emotions to prove that our products are good.

Our goods are shipped from Guangzhou and Yiwu. Between them, we ship relatively more goods from Yiwu because we get more timely information when we ship goods ourselves. In Guangzhou, we ship goods using a cloud warehouse—because it belongs to a third party, we have to send and receive the relevant shipment information to and from them, thereby reducing the shipment speed. And when errors occur, verification is difficult due to their huge shipment volume. Moreover, the cloud warehouse only earns a small fee yet will incur high costs if they have to expend manpower on tracking, hence coordination is limited. Instead, when we do our own shipment, we would get it done right even if it means losing money, otherwise our rating and our followers' experience would be affected—no matter the costs, we must get our aftersales done well. Nevertheless, cloud warehouses also have their advantages; they can ship a lot of goods within a short amount of time, and so when our shipment volume is large, they can reduce the pressure on us and increase our shipment speed.

Since our factories are in Guangzhou, why did we choose to remain in Yiwu? This is mainly because we started out in Yiwu and it has been seven years now, hence our friends and circles are all here. Were we to relocate and spend another seven years building up a relationship circle, there would be hidden costs required. That is why we will not relocate so readily.

Furthermore, there are special advantages to being in Yiwu and having the backing of such a huge and active market for small goods. Although Guangzhou has a strong supply chain system, a well-developed manufacturing industry, and superior prices of goods, it is slower than Yiwu in terms of information awareness. Yiwu's advantages are that its markets are extremely sensitive and the transmission of information is extremely fast—it is usually first to know about the latest business model or strategy.

To give an example, in March and April 2019, we brought a group of livestreamers to Guangzhou by coach to film video clips. Many factories forbade us from filming their interiors—only the most daring or forward-looking factory owners knew that this was free advertising for them. When we visited Guangzhou again in April and May 2020, many factories prepared banners in advance and displayed the message "Welcome, XX's livestreaming team from Yiwu" on an electronic screen. Factories in Guangzhou were a little slower to get started on livestreaming, albeit they are gradually changing and becoming more and more aware of Kuaishou.

In addition, from a business perspective, we have made money in Yiwu and so it might very well be our "auspicious land" and the place that is suitable for us— that is why we have chosen to remain in Yiwu.

CHAPTER ELEVEN

A NEW MARKET FOR OLD BRANDS

- How did three brand enterprises from three different industries seize the opportunities provided by livestreaming and open up a new field?

HOMEKOO: THE LOGIC BEHIND THE HUGE INCREASE IN ORDERS DURING THE PANDEMIC

Key Points

- Homekoo made plans for the short video industry in advance. As early as 2018, it already had hundreds of millions of followers throughout the Internet. It has self- incubated "A'shuang the Designer," "Wuli the Designer," and more than 10 other livestreamers in the home furnishing category.

- Homekoo has achieved explosive growth since 2019. In 2020, the order volume brought about by short videos and livestreams was 200–300 percent more than that of the previous year.

The authors of this text are senior researcher Li Zhao and researcher Yang Rui of Kuaishou Research Institute.

- This text introduces the organizational framework of the experts incubated by Homekoo MCN, as well as the marketing strategy of "leaving leads online, completing transactions offline."

Homekoo is a leading enterprise in bespoke furniture. Established in 2007, this wholly owned subsidiary of Shangpin Home Collection Group uses network design platforms and virtual reality technologies to integrate industry chain resources and provide its clients with personalized and bespoke services, creating an O2O (online to offline) + C2B business model that combines Internet direct marketing with large-scale digital customization.

Homekoo MCN, an arm of Homekoo, is a high-quality content platform that is targeted at the leading MCNs throughout the home furnishing industry. It has self-incubated and signed contracts with more than 300 home furnishing experts, and counts "A'shuang the Designer," "Design Help You," and "Wuli the Designer" among its top IPs. As part of its commitment to "making all furnishing work easy," it produces and disseminates high-quality content to provide consumers with high-quality decision-making content that helps them perform better furnishing.

◎ *The following is an account by Zhong Dingxin, head of Homekoo MCN.*

. . .

Gaining 40 Million New Followers and Increasing Year-on-year Monetization by 200-300 percent in 2020

As early as 2017, we had already proposed a strategy for "videofication." Back then, our main consideration was the stubbornly high costs of customer acquisition that were common to all channels, hence we wanted to explore new models to see if these costs could be reduced.

Short video was a new path that only a handful of enterprises in the home furnishing industry had ventured into at that time. After finding out via big data that the short video industry was growing very quickly and that users were spending more and more time on Kuaishou and other platforms, we decided to turn toward short videos, as well.

At the end of 2017, we officially formed a team for creating short videos. We were probably the first enterprise in the furnishing and furniture industry to form a team consisting of dozens of people to create short videos. We were just in time for the Spring Festival of 2018 when the popularity of short videos grew rapidly—we had barely produced a few videos when one of them became highly popular. The first video we produced has accumulated tens of millions of likes, while the fourth video we produced has accumulated three to four million likes.

Back then, each video that we filmed could bring us up to one million new followers. For an enterprise, this was far too exciting and shocking. Consequently, we believed that we should ramp up our intensity and expedite our roll-out on Kuaishou and other platforms. Since March 2018, we have basically gained six million new followers every month, and there was even a month when we gained 10 million new followers.

Throughout 2018, we accumulated nearly 100 million followers on Kuaishou and other platforms. And since 2019, our overall state can be said to be explosive growth. In the bespoke furniture industry, commercial monetization is usually assessed according to volume; in other words, anyone whom the designer creates a visual plan for and gives a specific quotation to is considered a client. Based on this calculation method, our monetization of short videos and livestreams for 2020 was 200–300 percent more than that of 2019. That year, we gained more than 40 million new followers and have since maintained a growth of two million new followers every month.

Why are we able to attract so many followers on short video platforms?

We have internally come up with three reasons for this. The first reason is our early start. Back then, there was very little content related to furnishing on short video platforms, albeit users were highly interested in such content. The second reason is that we have accumulated a lot of high-quality content. When we converted picture-and-text content that had more than 100,000 views for that year into videos, we realized that the results were great, with many videos quickly becoming popular. The third reason is our advocacy of innovation, which is a very important culture in our enterprise. Our teams compete among themselves on the number of followers they bring in and the number of videos they produce; this state of trying to outdo each other quickly normalized the work of producing short videos.

In terms of content, our short videos are either the knowledge-transmitting type, i.e., they teach users how to carry out furnishing and design, using knowledge transmission to draw traffic, or are the highly enjoyable type, i.e., followers would broaden their horizons and feel good after watching these videos and thus would naturally leave likes.

Taking "A'shuang the Designer" for example, she has more than 10 million followers on Kuaishou (as of February 2021), and this number continues to grow every month. Her videos appear similar to one another—they would first mention a pain point in furnishing and design, such as how to make a 20 m2 apartment feel like a 60 m2 apartment, before teaching you the specific actions to take. They are very well-received by her followers because the actual results are shown in a clear and easily understandable manner.

A'shuang's videos draw anywhere from 300,000 to 1,500,000 views—all of which come from natural growth rather than paid promotions.

Self-incubating Experts from Scratch: Organizational Framework and Related Systems

Internally, Homekoo has 13 expert accounts similar to "A'shuang the Designer." From account creation, naming, positioning, and expert-selection to content creation as well as the subsequent series of operations, every expert was incubated from scratch. For example, we had begun planning for "A'shuang the Designer" since the end of 2017, and it was only in March of the following year that she made her official debut.

In terms of organizational structure, Homekoo has divided content among two major centers, namely the content marketing center and the content operations center. The content marketing center is in charge of the frontend creation of content, the management of experts, and the building of the expert matrix, as well as the frontend commercialization. The content operations center is instead in charge of follower monetization for Shangpin Home Collection and Wayes (including its overall furnishing services); it obtains the contact information of their followers, converts the traffic into private domain traffic, and then further upgrades the followers into customers with direct demand.

These two centers each consist of many departments. For example, the content marketing center has seven departments, the first of which is the short video team, which has approximately 70 people. This team is further divided into many studios, such as the studio for "A'shuang the Designer" or "Wuli the Designer." Generally speaking, all of the experts with many followers have their own studios.

Figure 11.1 shows the content organizational structure of Homekoo. A'shuang's "A'shuang the Designer" is currently the company's biggest account and thus it is allocated its own studio with a relatively large staff.

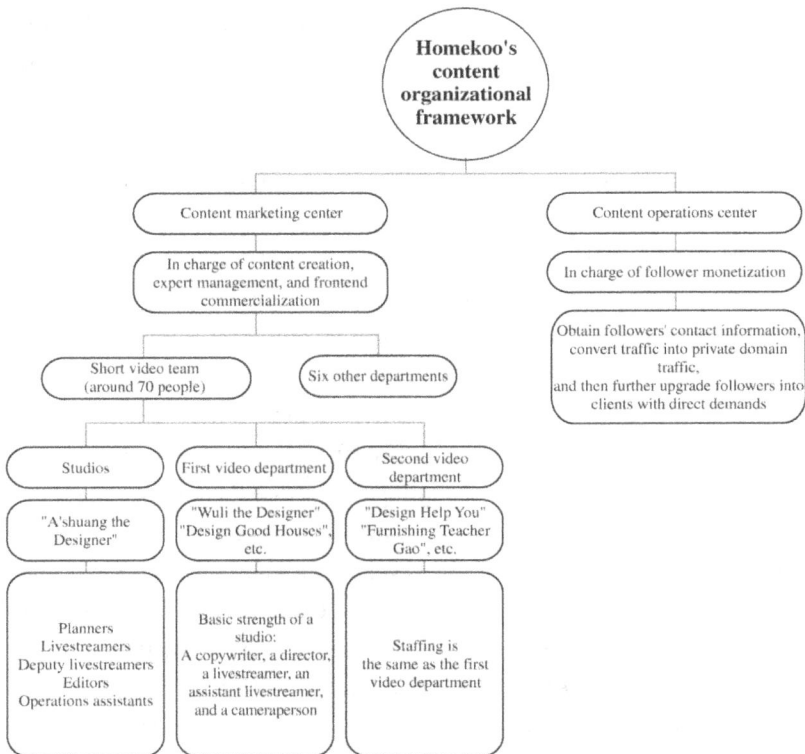

Figure 11.1 Homekoo's Content Organizational Framework

Although the other accounts are also allocated studios, they are given a smaller staff and are collectively managed by two short video departments. The staff allocated to each account generally consists of a copywriter, a director, a livestreamer, an assistant livestreamer, and a cameraperson.

A'shuang, too, started out from scratch. During her exploration phase, she changed her name several times, and because her positioning was not so accurate initially, she did not manage to accumulate enough followers. We have made constant adjustments to get to where we are. After A'shuang cut her hair short and dyed it yellow, her entire persona was established as that of a capable and professional designer. Just like her name suggests, her character is very straightforward, and when matched with her professional clothing and her tagline "I love designing more than I love men," it is not hard to see why her videos quickly exploded in popularity. Her followers are attracted to her highly recognizable persona. We have also supported her in terms of manpower and done script planning for her. Nowadays, she gets a very consistent monthly increase in followers. Her account is considered a company asset.

At present, A'shuang's studio consists of 10 or so people, including three planners, two editors, an operations assistant, and two deputy livestreamers.

A'shuang mainly serves as the main livestreamer and a cameraperson, and also does commercial advertising. The usual design work is divided among her assistants, whereas she reviews and amends the plans that they draw up. Although she was just an ordinary employee at first, she has now become an Internet celebrity who gets a lot of traffic.

When she first started out as a Kuaishou livestreamer, she personally wrote the scripts, did the designing, and chose the appropriate home furnishing spaces. We also hired professionals to carry out script optimization and training for her. She is very keen to learn and is passionate about furnishing and design. When she sees a furniture line that is exceptional in beauty, she often shed a few tears; it is only when she really likes it that she can create content that her followers would be interested in. Moreover, her recommendations are, without exception, practical content that can help her followers avoid pitfalls while carrying out furnishing and design.

Before becoming a livestreamer, she was one of our company's approximately 20,000 designers. She joined the company around the time when the company was looking to form a short video team. We have a few criteria for selecting livestreamers: firstly, they must have a high overall score, such as a recognizable appearance; secondly, they must have strong communication and presentation skills; thirdly, they must know a bit of design; and fourthly, they must have unique personal traits.

"Wuli the Designer" was originally a designer, as well. Due to her heavy Guangdong accent, she often mispronounces words in Mandarin. Hence, her personal tagline is "mediocre at Standard Mandarin but exceptional at design."

Nowadays, a studio is usually be allocated two directors and two camerapersons. The groups compete among themselves and work on their respective topic of choice. In addition, they must take part in the planning for a few important monthly or seasonal topics.

To reduce employee outflow, we sign two types of agreements. The first is a prohibition of business strife, while the second is a profit-sharing agreement that ensures our livestreamers earn a sufficient income. Something very special about this industry is the need for ample scenario resources as well as professional teams. Hence, even if our livestreamers remain in the same field after leaving the company, there is no guarantee that they would be able to hold up.

On the one hand, we need many film scenes. We have many clients; on average, we get more than 60,000 clients every month, thus providing us with many film scenes. Many of our film scenes are the homes of our clients. We also have a lot of stores that can be used as film scenes.

On the other hand, short videos cannot be produced by one person alone; they require strong content creation and operations teams. The knowledge points in the home furnishing industry are very fine, and thus it is very difficult to create competitive content without the support of professional talents. Moreover, having followers does not equate to having commercial value; ultimately, monetization still must be carried out. We have very strong monetization and commercialization teams within the industry. Although there have been a few cases of livestreamers leaving us, they were ultimately unable to succeed.

Marketing Strategy: Leave Leads Online, Acquire Experiences Offline

Our studios have three different means of monetization. The first is our main business, that is, monetization via our overall furnishing business. For instance, A'shuang gets thousands of orders per livestream. The second is advertising. Nowadays, many brands would engage livestreamers to conduct livestreams. The experts charge a fee according to their follower count— A'shuang's fee is 300,000 yuan per livestream. Most of the top accounts in this industry are our livestreamers. The third is e-commerce sales, albeit progress in this aspect is rather slow at the moment.

Kuaishou has given us great support. I have talked to Kuaishou's head of real estate and home furnishing before. I told the head that because of the high price per customer in this industry, transactions cannot be completed online, and thus the entire path of monetization must be opened up. I also stated our request in passing: allow followers to leave their contact information on a livestream channel as a lead and portal for customer acquisition and allow enterprises to leave their contact information on their livestreaming accounts.

Around May 2020, Kuaishou added a "Little Bell" feature on its web page. This feature enables quick access to monetization. Users can click on the "Little Bell" to enter their name and contact number, following which they can snap up free online designs, claim free design charts, or watch a livestream and make an appointment for a drop-in made-to-measure design. Nowadays, A'shuang can draw up to 6,000 submissions (leads) per livestream.

Normally, platforms would not want brands to direct traffic offline. Instead, they would usually hope that transactions take place through them because only then would they earn revenue. However, the furnishing and design industry is very special—consumers cannot possibly make a payment of tens of thousands of yuan online, and thus they merely convey their intentions online. After creating a plan, our designers would invite the consumer to go down to a store to look at the plan and the related products. Orders are only made subsequently. This is a marketing method whereby "leads are left online and experiences are acquired offline."

Since February 2020, our model has basically been about using online livestreaming to attract interest, while sales take place at our various store terminals. To be specific, by getting top influencers to conduct livestreams, we give consumers a trust window before guiding them to the 2,000-odd stores of Shangpin Home Collection and Wayes throughout China. After entering a store, consumers may watch livestreams, take part in events, and make purchases.

On March 15, 2020, we hosted a "3.15 Big Brand Livestreaming and Group Buying Festival." We engaged more than 80 experts in the vertical categories of furnishing and design and also mobilized all 10 or so of our top influencers. The main livestream venue was Shangpin Home Collection's experiential store in Dongbao, with more than 80 sub-venues throughout China. During this festival, we gave our followers huge discounts and benefits, providing more than 100 million yuan in subsidies. Furthermore, we conducted flash sales for many hot-selling products—for example, we slashed the prices of sofas by 60–70 percent.

We also partnered with more than 50 big brands, including Fotile, BOSS, Sleemon, TATA, and Haier. We displayed and sold their products on our livestream channels, offering benefits to our followers and clients alike.

We also invited a few bosses as guests on the program, where our livestreamers haggled over prices with them. Eventually, the actual turnover exceeded 130 million yuan.

In addition, we invited our clients to go down to our stores, where they could watch the livestream directly. While they were watching A'shuang livestream, we began handing out discounts and benefits, allowing them to haggle on prices and "crack golden eggs." Our offline designers would tell them that they would gain a chance to "crack a golden egg" if they made a payment in time. The prizes included refrigerators and washing machines worth tens of thousands of yuan, as well as free-of-charge orders.

The endorsement by top influencers, the sufficiently low prices, the experience of watching a livestream in an offline store, and the discounts and benefits offered by our designers for prompt payments made for an atmosphere in which consumers were generally willing to make payment. This was an "online + offline" model. Moreover, our stores attracted many regular customers because these customers knew they would get huge discounts and benefits if they came down to the stores on that day.

We had actually already hosted an on-stream group-buying event on February 22, 2020, albeit it was mainly based on a fixed deposit rather than completed transactions. At that time, there were more than 10,000 orders that paid the deposit—according to a price per customer of 20,000 yuan, this meant that sales amounted to nearly 400 million yuan. However, the actual value of the completed transactions turned out to be an eight-figure sum only. Following this trial, we hosted the "3.15 Big Brand Livestreaming and Group Buying Festival" and reattracted those customers who had not completed a transaction the last time.

Speeding Up During the Pandemic: Increase in Online Demand + AI Empowerment

It is very dangerous for brick-and-mortar industries to not embrace the Internet. Taking the home furnishing industry for example, we saw that a few enterprises that had taken the lead in online livestreaming achieved impressive transaction volumes during the pandemic. Conversely, a few enterprises that had a poor online layout are now experiencing very difficult times. The designers in many furnishing companies have faced salary cuts or even layoffs.

If we take the number of online client applications for free made-to-measure designs as the criteria for monetization, then the number of applications converted from short videos and livestreams between March and May 2020 was 200–300 percent more than that for the same period in 2019. And looking at all channels, our number of client applications was twice that for the whole of 2019.

Since 2018–2019, we have felt a traffic crunch and a rapidly increasing cost of customer acquisition on a yearly basis. In 2020, however, our cost of customer acquisition fell.

There are two main reasons for this. The first is that the pandemic caused a clear increase in demand for a few kinds of online furnishing and design. The second is that our Group launched a new model for online design.

We gathered excellent design cases from the past and created a few standardized schemes using AI technologies, thereby forming a scheme library. Our 20,000 designers throughout China can use this library to quickly find the schemes that they want, greatly improving their work efficiency. Previously, it took them three or four days to come up with a scheme, but they can now do so in a day or even half a day.

As the pandemic gradually subsides, the work of offline made-to-measure design can be successively resumed in various parts of China. Nevertheless, we will continue to take online design as our focus and the direction in which we persist. We will communicate with our clients online, provide them with detailed schemes and quotations, and then invite them down to our stores to make the final payment and check out our showrooms.

Expanding to Wherever There Is Traffic

Homekoo has accompanied the development of the Internet for 14 years now. Figure 11.2 shows the marketing milestones of Shangpin Home Collection.

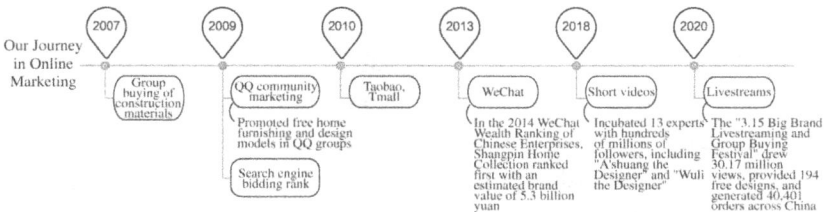

Figure 11.2 The Marketing Milestones of Shangpin Home Collection

When I joined the company in 2009, it was still working on group-buying of building materials. Later on, due to the large number of QQ users, we crossed over to proprietary products and set up (marketing) channels online.

One of these channels was QQ Groups. Back then, we worked out a model of marketing and customer acquisition for QQ Groups: we would join many different QQ Groups and promote free home furnishing and design in them. This served as our form of private domain traffic. Another channel was search engines: we would take part in "Baidu Bidding" and carry out precise advertising, which we would pay for according to the advertising results.

In 2010, we began doing Taobao and Tmall. When Weibo emerged a year later, we began doing it, as well. Then in 2013, we did WeChat. It can be said that we will expand to wherever there is traffic or a new channel.

We also have a habit: if we determine that a channel has huge traffic, we will basically go all-in on it—our entire Group would expend significant financial resources, manpower resources, and technical resources to open it.

Today, Homekoo is working on at least 10 to 20 channels, each of which is allocated several subdivided teams. We would enter any channel that has tens of millions of people or more in traffic.

Homekoo can be considered to have done short videos and livestreams fairly early on in comparison to the entire home furnishing industry. We believe that Kuaishou and Taobao are the better platforms for doing livestream e-commerce.

Kuaishou is about private domain traffic. Judging from our followers' activity levels and our internal operations, Kuaishou's follower stickiness is much greater than that of other e-commerce livestreaming platforms. This has something to do with the "loyal follower culture" advocated by Kuaishou. There are many users on Kuaishou who are very grounded; although they do not have that many followers, their followers' approval of them and the products they recommend, as well as their followers' spending power, are astonishingly high.

The furnishing and furniture industry lacks traffic in itself. Although many brands have formed within the industry, it still has not seen the emergence of an absolute champion brand or even a "100 billion enterprise." This provides an opportunity. Furthermore, every enterprise has to bear the pressure of client traffic, and thus to acquire even more traffic, enterprises would certainly embrace the Internet, short videos, and livestreams. Despite our early start, we nevertheless face great pressure. At present, the growth of our overall traffic, view count, and follower count has already slowed down. This is due to a serious case of homogenization, causing platforms and consumers to suffer from a bit of aesthetic fatigue. We are now trying to add in special effects, showcase our VR capabilities, and upgrade the positioning of our short videos. For us, innovation has practically become an important weekly affair.

Although we do not know what methods would be more well-received by platforms and consumers in the future, any method would rapidly become old even if it is accepted for a period of time. All we can do is race with the times.

At present, what we are trying to do is record the entire furnishing process according to the workflow, starting from the construction site and the unfurnished building. For example, each of A'shuang's videos nowadays only showcases one space and one knowledge point. Next, we want to show consumers how home furnishing is carried out from scratch, how it is designed, and how it is installed. Consequently, they would understand how to furnish their homes. This would make our videos more authentic and real.

As for our monetization model, we will gradually draw our followers on Kuaishou and other platforms into our pool of private domain traffic. We usually regard this pool to be a follower group, which is something also found on Kuaishou. When managing a follower group, we must keep on dispensing furnishing-related knowledge and offering a few discounts and benefits from time to time. Hence, followers can not only obtain knowledge on home furnishing but also enjoy low-priced products, making them willing to remain in the group. Using this method, we will also keep on enhancing our followers' favorable opinion of us so that they would think of us whenever they have to carry out furnishing in the future.

JAC MOTORS: ACHIEVING THE HIGHEST GROWTH RATE IN THE CAR MARKET THROUGH ALL-EMPLOYEE LIVESTREAMING

Key Points

- During the pandemic in 2020, JAC Motors carried out all-employee livestreaming. After trying this out for eight months, its livestreaming matrix accumulated nearly four million followers across 1,475 Kuaishou accounts. Livestreaming accounted for 25–30 percent of their customers. The overall cost of consumer acquisition via livestreaming is lower than that of the 4S store model.

- An introduction of the specific operations of automobile brand livestreaming, including where the livestreamers come from and how the sales leads brought by livestreamers are allocated.

- Livestreaming has reduced the distance between enterprises and consumers. Through livestream channels, many people who do not dare to enter 4S stores have gained an understanding of the relevant knowledge and satisfied their need for a car.

In 2020, the car market suffered an overall downturn, yet JAC Motors became the frontrunner in this market in terms of growth. This was in part because every employee of JAC Motors quickly embraced livestreaming after the pandemic struck.

In October 2020, after eight months of trial, JAC Motors's livestreaming matrix accumulated nearly four million followers across 1,475 Kuaishou accounts. Livestreaming accounted for 25–30 percent of their customers.

The authors of this text are researcher Li Yuchao and contributing researcher Wu Xiaofei, both at Kuaishou Research Institute.

◎ *The following is an account by Huang Kaixin, head of livestreaming and short video projects at JAC Motors.*

·   ·   ·

Livestream Channels Can Sell Cars, Too

In September 2019, JAC vehicles were sold via Kuaishou Live for the first time. This took place at a dealership in Ordos, Inner Mongolia. The Kuaishou account of this store is called "Brother Yang Talks Cars" and it currently has nearly 25,000 followers. While the account was created by the owner of the store, the livestreams are carried out by a young sales consultant who is able to sell a significant number of cars every month via livestreaming. He only introduces the cars on-stream, whereas the follow-up work is done by other people.

After the experience of this store in Ordos was brought up to the company's headquarters, we recommended the idea to our other dealerships. Instead of making it mandatory, we kept it on a voluntary basis.

Subsequently, a dealership in Yunnan Province gave it a try and achieved good results. At first, they got two of their salespersons to conduct the livestreams, but later increased this to every one of their employees.

So far, our company's headquarters believes that this model can be spread throughout China in a more systematic fashion. In October 2019, the company began putting in effort to promote livestreaming. During the launch event for the Jiayue A5, we invited a few outstanding dealership livestreamers to come down and take part in the event. We also invited a few top livestreamers in the hopes that our dealerships would gain a feel of a livestreaming atmosphere and learn from the modus operandi of the top livestreamers. Before the pandemic, we were already running approximately 50 livestreaming accounts. Subsequently, it was thanks to our foundation of all-employee participation that we were able to quickly respond during the pandemic.

After the car market suffered an overall downturn in 2019, the long-awaited peak season of sales during the Spring Festival was unfortunately scuppered by the onset of the pandemic, causing panic among us all.

During the Spring Festival Gala of 2020, a Kuaishou advertisement left a deep impression on the public. Zhang Wengen, general manager of JAC Motors, was the first to think about using Kuaishou Live to sell vehicles. While everyone was still on leave during the Spring Festival of 2020, we put livestreams and short video events on the agenda for our online meetings and requested all our employees to conduct livestreams.

On February 6, 2020, JAC Motors established a project team for livestream sales, with me serving as its head. This project team is operated across departments, with its personnel coming from the digital marketing department, the marketing management department, the training department, and more. It has two main tasks: the first is to take direct part in livestreaming by introducing our products, while the second is to guide the operations of JAC Motors' matrix of Kuaishou accounts, including livestream development, operational flow, and training in livestreaming methods, as well as livestreaming incentives.

Responding to the Pandemic with All-employee Livestreaming

The livestream matrix of JAC Motors was established on February 17, 2020. Back then, we only had 110 Kuaishou accounts. It took us about a week from making our preliminary considerations to mobilizing all our employees. The plan was for us to create a program for training coaches internally and then sending them to our dealerships. In reality, however, we assigned livestreaming tasks to our dealerships before the coaches had been fully trained. Hence, our coaches can be said to have developed together with our dealerships.

Before the pandemic, everyone only participated lightly in the on-stream sale of vehicles. And after the outbreak of the pandemic, we ran into many problems while developing our work in livestreaming. For example, if our employees could not return to work in the stores and did not have cars at home, what could they talk about on-stream?

Kuaishou has a feature called "Livestream Partner." It was mainly used for video game livestreaming at first, but we instead used it to display pictures and video advertisements of our products to our loyal followers on our livestream channels or in our short videos. And when a sales lead appeared, we would make a record of it. Meanwhile, those employees who had a JAC car at home could conduct livestreams showcasing the car from home. At that time, our headquarters' employees returned to the workplace in staggered shifts, and thus they could conduct livestreams on the first floor of the headquarters.

After testing the waters to a certain extent, we got our dealerships throughout China to take part, as well, assigning them two or three livestreaming tasks per day. Be it the company's senior leaders, engineers, researchers, developers, or salespersons, everyone took part in livestreaming. At our peak, we had nearly 100 livestreamers internally.

By means of this sort of all-employee training and coaching, JAC's sales from livestreaming rapidly took off. During the pandemic, we held meetings practically every day. We compiled excellent case examples and innovative methods into a book that we then distributed internally as training material. If a livestreamer did not know what to say, they could simply read off the book, and after they gained sufficient experience, they would be able to exchange ideas with their loyal followers. This kind of trial is in itself a process of audition and elimination.

We have always maintained close contact with Kuaishou's employees in the eastern part of China. Our earliest contact with them was in September 2019, when they explained to us what Kuaishou was and what the on-stream promotion of goods was. Back then, we were confused and could not really understand what they were saying. During the pandemic, we consulted with them on how to sell vehicles on Kuaishou, during which they shared a lot with us and provided training. We have also given them feedback on a few application-related problems.

JAC is probably the first enterprise in the automobile industry to do brand livestreaming. Back then, Kuaishou wanted JAC to become the first company to conduct livestreams in the automobile category, and so they told us that we could try out all of our new products on the platform and give feedback on any issues to them. Hence, we were the first automobile brand to use many of the tools on Kuaishou for livestreaming.

The Specific Operations of Automobile Brand Livestreaming

Eight months after establishing our livestreaming matrix in October 2020, the matrix accumulated more than 3.4 million followers across 1,475 livestreaming accounts, with the follower count of each of our top livestreamers in the hundreds of thousands. In total, we have nearly 100 livestreamers with more than 10,000 followers and draw 1.5 to 2 million views per day. Although the figures of our individual livestreamers may seem fairly unexceptional, when they are specially combined as a brand service, they can practically achieve all-Internet, full-course, and round-the-clock coverage.

At present, the livestreamers in JAC Motors's livestreaming matrix are made up primarily of the employees of our dealerships, secondarily of a few recruits from society—such as university students recruited as part-time livestreamers by the dealerships—and thirdly of the workers in our automotive engine factories. These livestreamers earn a fixed basic salary and a certain commission for leads that are converted into transactions. To encourage sales, we pay a higher commission than most 4S stores.

Social recruitment is something that we encourage our dealerships to do. This is because the employees in 4S stores have their own work duties and often do not have spare time. As for the workers in our engine factories, they mostly undertake the work of demonstration and training.

We generally adopt a principle of "whose lead, whose responsibility" for customer leads provided by livestreamers. If the pertinent livestreamer is not a dealership employee, our principle is to assign the lead based on proximity to the region of the customer source.

After livestreaming for a long period of time, our livestreamers would occasionally co-host livestreams with one another. Hence, they have developed a sense of familiarity among themselves. When assigning resources, we would go according to the trust relationships that they have separately built.

In terms of management, we impose different requirements on different livestreamers. For example, if a livestreamer has 20,000 to 30,000 followers, we would require them to bring in a certain number of views.

We would monitor the backend figures of our matrix and manage our livestreaming accounts using certain methods and mechanisms. We currently have nearly 1,500 livestreaming accounts, with an active proportion of around 45 percent.

Throughout this period of selling vehicles on-stream, we have had to conduct weekly brainstorming meetings and keep in step with the latest Kuaishou strategies, thus producing many marketing innovations such as livestreamer 1v1 battles (similar in style to those on *Your Face Sounds Familiar*), co-hosting of livestreams with top Internet celebrities, and "hundred-sided battles" with the top livestreamers leading the bottom livestreamers. Not only do these events help livestreamers increase their followers, but we also give them a certain amount of traffic as a reward. The livestreamers' eventual earnings mainly come from the conversion of their followers, that is, the number of vehicle orders.

Livestreaming is something that requires the support of dealership owners to be sustained. Firstly, all-employee participation cannot be achieved without their support, and, secondly, be it for livestreams or short videos, a certain outlay must be made for the red envelopes, gifts, and promotions. Our top livestreaming accounts on Kuaishou are generally those of shop owners or investors because they are more willing to invest money in their accounts.

Furthermore, livestreaming cannot rely on the efforts of a single person. Instead, an internal and external atmosphere in which everyone can work together is necessary for it to be sustained in the long run. For example, when we encouraged everyone to livestream during the pandemic, our engine factories took the lead in forming a team to serve as an example and then spurred our dealerships to follow suit. Demonstration is very important, and that is why we found a benchmark from our matrix to further encourage everyone.

The general flow for users to be brought from online to offline goes like this: when consumers see our products on a livestream channel or a short video and want to purchase or further understand a vehicle, they can pass us their contact information via a private message or the "Little Bell" on a livestream channel—this would count as a lead. The actual transaction processes are carried out offline, such as experiencing the product or negotiating a price.

The consumer end's acceptance of on-stream sales has to be slowly cultivated and gradually entrenched over time by means of honest management. So far, it seems that our loyal followers' acceptance of on-stream buying of vehicles is fairly high. We explicitly require on-stream sales to be carried out in good faith; all promises must be fulfilled. Regardless of the price point, livestreamers must introduce their products factually. Many people have paid a deposit without even looking at the vehicle themselves, which is a testament to the trust they have in us. In traditional 4S stores, nobody would pay a deposit without first looking at the vehicle.

In addition, on-stream sales can help many of our loyal followers attain greater respect and understanding. For example, some of our loyal followers on Kuaishou are migrant workers who earn less than 5,000 yuan per month, hence they usually would not dare to visit a 4S store to inquire about the price or details of a vehicle. However, when they are online, nobody would know their salary and spending power, while they themselves would not feel much apprehension—we would answer any question regardless of how simple it is, and even if they do not ask questions, they can find out more information from the questions asked by others. When they realize that they can buy a car priced at 70,000 to 90,000 yuan with just 10,000 yuan on hand, this part of the demand would be stimulated and fulfilled.

After watching our livestreams for a month or two, many people who did not understand cars at first would gain a fair understanding of them, such that they would not need a salesperson to explain the key points to them when they head down to a store.

There are also a few grassroots customers who are diffident about going down to a store to make inquiries or who have long held an intention to buy a car without acting on it. However, livestreaming has prompted them to act on this intention. On-stream interactions also give them a warm feeling and remove their sense of distance. Many loyal followers trust our livestreamers greatly and only buy cars from people whom they approve. This is actually a process of sincere interaction among people.

Of course, we also have a few sales techniques such as offering discounts for online purchases, issuing red envelopes and vouchers, handing out a few peripheral gifts, or allowing refunds even if the deposit has been paid. We would rather work a little harder ourselves if it means satisfying our consumers and achieving a good reputation.

Livestreaming Has Brought Us 30 percent of Our Car-buying Users

When we were working on brands in the past, it was very difficult for us to increase the sales conversion rate directly. However, this is simpler when livestreaming. Through an internal survey, we have found out that the demographic for users who buy cars on-stream is mostly men aged 25 to 30 years old who are mainly distributed across fourth-and fifth-tier cities or county seats in the northwestern, northeastern, and southwestern regions of China. Based on the current figures, the customer acquisition rate for livestreaming is 25–30 percent—in other words, out of every 100 car-buying users, approximately 30 of them gained an understanding of our cars by watching our livestreams.

The overall customer acquisition cost for livestreaming is relatively lower than that for the traditional 4S store model. The Kuaishou platform itself gets a lot of traffic; simply by creating an account, we would acquire the traffic— and thus the customers—that naturally comes with each account. The cost of this is mainly reflected in terms of manpower; the livestreamer has to keep on talking, which is hard work in itself.

The influence of a brand is inextricable from its sales conversion; their effects cannot be looked at separately. However, with the changing of the times, our delivery proportion will become lopsided. In addition, we generally coordinate our various platforms to carry out promotions. Based on a certain plan, we would determine a theme that all our modules would serve and then carry it out both online and offline.

During product launches or important milestone events such as auto shows, we would also engage several top livestreamers or Internet celebrities to perform onstage. For example, "Second Brother's Car Reviews" (4.17 million followers as of February 2021) and "Dake Talks Cars" (7.40 million followers as of February 2021) have yielded impressive results, with their main purpose being to increase the exposure of our products. During a cloud conference previously held by JAC Motors, we also invited "Second Brother's Car Reviews"—that day, we drew 300,000 to 400,000 views, with many followers interacting with our livestreamers and leaving more than 6,000 leads in total.

A livestreaming event that left a deep impression on me was the Chengdu Motor Show that took place in April 2020. Back then, China was still in the final phase of the pandemic, and so there were fewer people in attendance. We chose more than 30 of the top livestreamers from JAC's livestreaming matrix to attend the motor show and conduct a full-day livestream on the newly-launched Jiayue X7. Many of our dealerships also carried out a live 1v1 competition that attracted many viewers and enlivened the atmosphere.

Nowadays, JAC's matrix of livestreaming accounts draw approximately one million livestream views on days when no additional resources are invested, and up to 10 million livestream views on days when additional resources are invested. Our livestreams have attracted many consumers from vertical fields, and with a fairly high conversion rate to boot.

For every one of our launch events nowadays, we would consider whether to hold it online or offline, with online set to become the primary mode in the future. Due to the pandemic, the results of online dissemination have been better than those of offline dissemination. For example, the launch of the Sihao X8 in September 2020 was a combination of online and offline. The results were better than before; the number of online viewers was several hundred times more than previously, and many sales leads were obtained. In terms of costs alone, online dissemination actually does not cut our costs by much because the appearance fees of several top livestreamers are quite significant. However, because there are many more online viewers, the results are better.

The sales model of today has developed from traditional store sales and e-commerce sales to social sales. The promotion of goods by livestreamers is akin to a form of social sales; relationships must be maintained and word- of-mouth is very important. Once an account loses the trust it had built up, it has a tough time continuing.

Sales of large goods in the automobile category ultimately depend on the actual objects (cars). Moreover, unlike home appliances, cars have issues related to aftersales, maintenance, and so on, hence livestream e-commerce cannot completely replace offline automobile stores.

Therefore, we will not give up on traditional offline events. To a certain extent, JAC's brand launches have become follower conferences. In online-only events, there is a certain sense of distance among the people. That is why offline contact is still needed to let followers understand how a car is manufactured—it is only when they meet and have genuine contact with their favorite livestreamers that their feelings can deepen.

Nevertheless, on-stream sales are certainly a huge trend. In the future, automobile sales might not require as many 4S stores as there are today.

At present, we are also striving to create an "automobile lifestyle" and an "automobile ecosystem." In other words, rather than simply selling cars, we are constantly creating their peripheral products. This is similar to the strategy of Xiaomi, which started out by selling mobile phones; these days, they are performing excellently in sales of smart home products. We also provide sales services that are centered around an automobile lifestyle.

TIP

We Actually Tasted the Sweetness of Livestream Traffic Monetization

The following is an account by Zhang Qian (Kuaishou account "Zhang the Beautiful of Mengcheng Hongtong"), general manager of Mengcheng Hongtong Automobiles, a JAC dealership:.

When the pandemic was spreading in February 2020, our automobile manufacturer posted a message in our work group telling us to download Kuaishouand do livestreaming. After undergoing a few training sessions conducted by the manufacturer, we began trying to livestream with our mobile phones from home.

Because every employee of the manufacturer was involved, we felt that livestreaming was a part of our work. Our store has an employee called "Brother Mao" who started using Kuaishou quite early on and was thus rather familiar with livestreaming—he accumulated more than 20,000 followers on his own. Though he was skilled in livestreaming, he was not so good at sales and thus never achieved a satisfactory conversion rate. After the manufacturer started assigning livestreaming tasks to us, we consulted with him on several operations that we did not understand, such as how to begin a livestream, how to offer red envelopes, what to talk about while livestreaming, how to motivate followers to follow us and send us hearts, and what kinds of conversation techniques to use. As the manufacturer can also gain followers after entering JAC's matrix of automobile livestreaming accounts, it provided us with support and guidance.

In Mengcheng County, which is a part of Bozhou, Anhui Province, there are only a handful of stores that are as big as us. Thanks to the manufacturer's encouragement, we were among the earliest stores in the county to do Kuaishou Live, and at a significant outlay at that. During the pandemic, a large number of cars were sold in the county, and as the pandemic reached its final phase, I sold quite a few cars via livestreaming.

At first, livestreaming was just like talking to clients; I introduced myself and the cars, which was simple enough to repeat over and over again. Later, I began introducing the properties and other details of the cars, or information related to car maintenance. Because I livestreamed every day, there was a mix of loyal followers and new followers watching. While keeping the basic content of my livestreams consistent, I would vary some of the content. Later, when my loyal followers began interacting with me and asking questions, I was able to talk about more life-oriented and diverse topics.

Based on my own experiences, persistence is very important. Initially, we only persisted because of the demands made by our manufacturer. Being in a management position, my original purpose is not to sell cars via livestreaming but rather to understand new sales models. Since everyone says that it is presently the era of "InternetPlus," short videos, and livestream traffic, I joined in to find out what these concepts are actually about and how they can be put into practice. Little did I expect that traffic conversion could indeed be brought about in the end.

I remember that the first order that came from Kuaishou was around April 2020. Back then, the pandemic had just ended in China. We had livestreamed every day from February to April, persisting in getting this done. Since April, the orders have poured in— our earlier work could thus be seen as cultivating users.

That first order was not placed by someone from Mengcheng. This is something that Kuaishou adds to offline stores—the consumers are not geographically restricted. The new car owner was from a neighboring county that was a one hour drive away. He said that he wanted to buy a car after watching my livestream. After exchanging contactinformation and conversing, I sent the location of our store to him. At that time, I felt that it was impossible to establish sufficient trust over a mobile phone and thus guessed that he would not come down to our store. To my surprise, however, he actually did come down.

After reaching the store, he said he was looking for "Beautiful Sister," which ismy name on Kuaishou. Upon hearing my voice, he recognized me and identified himself as a loyal follower on Kuaishou. We swiftly entered the offline sales process. He said that he had been following my livestreams for a long time and had acquired a fair understanding of our products. After looking at the colors, he promptly ordered a car— it was the Jiayue A5, which I had introduced on a livestream. Because we had done sufficient preparations early on, the subsequent process proceeded very quickly.

Based on the shopper-to-transaction ratio, the online conversion rate is slightly higher than the offline conversion rate; as long as our online shoppers are able to comedown to our store, there is a high probability that a transaction will be completed. Weare located in an area with many 4S stores—an automobile industrial park—and thus the customer accuracy is fairly high. However, judging from our follower count and the transaction conversion rate, offline is certainly no match for online.

Following the pandemic, our dealerships have had to squeeze time out to do regular tasks but also squeeze time out for livestreaming. At the height of the pandemic, five or six of our store's sales consultants served as livestreamers, and until this day, there are three people including myself who are still doing so.

As far as we are concerned, livestreaming is a form of sales supplementationand support. Judging from the trend, sales will have to be a combination of online and offline in the future. Hence, our marketing work must keep up with the times.

In addition, livestreaming has indeed brought about traffic monetization, and thus we have truly tasted the sweetness of this sales method. At first, there were many people who were unconvinced and uninformed about it and felt that we looked silly babbling oninto our mobile phones. However, we knew what we were doing and made plans to stickit out rather than give up on it as soon as the pandemic ended.

Nowadays, dealerships such as ours bear the costs of livestreaming. Our employees' reward for livestreaming is the commission that they earn from trafficmonetization. I would personally verify and distribute the red envelopes that we hand out on our livestream channel and the rewards and discounts that we offer our followers. Our manufacturer would provide a few traffic-related rewards as a supplement. Asthe yield from livestreaming is not obvious in the short term, we regard the costs of livestreaming and *maintaining our short videos on Kuaishou as money invested in advertising. That we have been able to persist until now is also because our boss has been willing to invest in livestreaming.*

We also have to thank our manufacturer for their guidance and support that have enabled us to do livestreaming on Kuaishou. Their general manager for sales, Zhang Wengen, is someone with a sharp market sense. He is always at the forefront of the market and in touch with the frontline of sales. At the same time, he greatly encourages everyone to innovate new sales methods during market downturns. It was under his guidance that Kuaishou Live was popularized within the JAC hierarchy on a top-down basis. We hope that the livestreaming platform can also organize training regularly to improve our usage of the Kuaishou app. This will help us enrich the content and format of our livestreams, become more familiar with Kuaishou's rules and requirements, and avoid usage barriers caused by information asymmetry. At the same time, it will promote communication and interaction between the platform and its users, thereby contributing to a win-win situation for both sides.

PART FIVE

NEW INFRASTRUCTURE AND INNER LOOP

CHAPTER TWELVE

CONSUMPTION UPGRADE AND EMPLOYMENT CREATION

- Using the case of Linyi, we look at how livestream e-commerce has driven employment.

- Using the case of four users from Xinjiang, we look at how people who are 3,500 km away from Linyi have upgraded their consumption.

A FIRST LOOK AT HOW LIVESTREAMING HAS DRIVEN EMPLOYMENT IN LINYI

Key Points

- In livestream e-commerce, livestreamer teams have rapidly expanded to become a motive force of direct employment.

- Livestream e-commerce has driven employment in supporting industries and the entire employment ecosystem, widening the channels for employment.

The authors of this text are researcher Lu Yajun and research assistants Cai Yuhui and Tian Jiahui of Kuaishou Research Institute.

- Livestream e-commerce provides higher salaries with which to re-cruit professional talents.

How has livestream e-commerce driven employment? In October 2020, we went to Linyi, Shandong Province, to conduct a small investigation, hoping to provide our readers with some intuitive understanding through several case examples.

We discovered that over the past two years, a large number of livestreamers have emerged in Linyi, thus creating many employment op-portunities for livestreamer service teams. The increase in the quantity of orders in livestream e-commerce has also fostered prosperity for support-ing industries such as industrial parks and delivery services. At the same time, the large volume of orders has saved many factories. All of these have worked together to create excellent employment conditions locally.

In addition, salary levels in Linyi's e-commerce industry have increased substantially from the past. In particular, there is a strong demand for top talents, albeit the supply of talent is clearly insufficient.

Livestreaming Has Driven Employment

Kuaishou livestreamer Taozi's: When we first started promoting goods via livestreams, we only had an apartment with three rooms and two lounges, measuring 100 m2 or so in area. But now, our executive floor and livestream studio have a combined area of 3,200 m2, and this does not include our warehouse—measuring more than 10,000 m2 in area—that has been relocated to the outskirts.

Our company now has more than 200 employees, including a livestream studio operations team, an administrative team, an aftersales team, a warehouse logistics team, and a finance team. The biggest among these teams is the warehouse logistics team. Only a handful of people can actually be spotted in the livestream studio, when in fact many people work in the background to serve the livestreamer.

Ricearth Network: Ricearth Network is the company where Kuaishou livestreamer Xu Xiaomi works. We currently have more than 300 employees, including six livestreamers. On average, each livestreamer has five livestream studio assistants who are respectively in charge of video filming and uploading, goods management, ironing, and warehouse returns. Each of the mid-tier livestreamers—who generate sales of around 300,000 yuan per day—is served by approximately 20 warehousing personnel who oversee aftersales, warehousing logistics, procurement, and so on. In our company, Xu Xiaomi brings in the most orders—she can bring in around 80,000 orders per day of livestreaming, and she also has the highest number of people serving her.

Shunhe Industrial Park: Our industrial park has a floor area of 150,000 m2 and is divided into two construction phases. In total, we have more than 200 companies as our tenants. During the peak season, the park gets more than 600,000 orders per day, and assuming a price per customer of 50 yuan, that adds up to nearly 1 billion yuan per month.

Livestream e-commerce has greatly helped in solving employment problems. If a mid-tier livestreamer brings in 5,000 to 6,000 orders per day, the company would have to provide a team of 30–40 people to serve them. Therefore, if 100 of such livestreamers are incubated, many jobs would be created.

At present, Linyi has a population of more than 12 million, and more than eight million registered accounts on Kuaishou. Approximately 8,000 of these accounts each generate 1,000 orders per day.

Before it crossed over from the industry for home building materials, Shunhe Industrial Park had a daily client traffic of 300–500 people. Nowadays, excluding client traffic, there are nearly 2,000 working personnel within the entire industrial park. What's more, even the brick-and-mortar stores in the vicinity have been invigorated by livestream e-commerce.

Supporting Industries Have Boosted Employment

The most direct reflection of the rise of supporting industries, as driven by livestream e-commerce, is the rapid development of the delivery industry. In the first half of 2020 alone, orders received by Linyi amounted to nearly 20 billion yuan, which represented a year-over-year growth of 75 percent and ranked first in Shandong Province. Previously, Linyi did not have cloud warehouses, but due to the increase in delivery volume, the cloud warehouse business has taken off.

Kuaishou livestreamer Taozi's: At first, we only had one courier here, but I now have a dozen couriers or so serving my studio. The most senior courier has become the leader of a three- or four-man team. He used to earn only 5,000 yuan a month, but that has now increased to nearly 10,000 yuan.

Ricearth Network: Nowadays, we engage the services of four delivery companies: STO Express, ZTO Express, Best Express, and China Post. Xu Xiaomi alone sells 80,000 orders a day and thus requires dozens of people to handle shipments. The employment of these people solves the livelihood issues of their families. On November 2, 2020, we made use of the "Kuaishou Shopping Festival" to sell two million orders worth a total of 104 million yuan in one day, causing the delivery companies to be insanely busy.

Shunhe Industrial Park: Our industrial park must ship more than 600,000 orders every month, which is equivalent to the annual shipment volume of STO Express in Linyi. The Shunhe Group has invested in building a smart cloud warehouse that will be fully operational by June 2021. It will be the first fully automated smart cloud warehouse in Linyi, with a maximum daily shipment volume of 200,000 orders. At the same time, in our collaborations with livestreamers and businesses on Kuaishou and other platforms, Shunhe Cloud Warehouse will handle difficult problems related to orders, returns, storage, and second-sales.

Driving Employment Throughout the Ecosystem

Ricearth Network: So far, Xu Xiaomi has sold more than 13 million products. We have more than 500 suppliers, among which are 200 that we have deep collaborations with. Hence, we are driving the entire employment ecosystem. At times, we are even able to save a factory. Some time ago, one of our cosmetics suppliers was on the verge of shutting its factory. It took Xu Xiaomi one livestream session to sell more than 35,000 bottles of its "Youth Original Essence." After that event, many livestreamers also wanted to sell this product but faced a shortage of goods, and so the factory "came back to life" and resumed production.

We have also "satiated" many factories. We have successively given impetus to many factories and an uncountable number of jobs in at least three industries: packing materials, cartons, and cosmetics.

Shunhe Industrial Park: Linyi has more than 130 specialized wholesale markets. The first thing that livestream e-commerce did was bring about changes to more than 400 businesses in a certain market for non-staple foods. When the general manager of this market first established shared livestream studios for businesses to sell their goods via livestreaming, what he did was to convert space within the original site of the market into 10 livestream studios. Later, by making use of products and goods from the stores, he built product selection rooms in which the livestreamers would choose their products before livestreaming. In August 2020, their monthly GMV exceeded 100 million yuan.

Nowadays, many brands want to build product selection rooms and livestream studios in Linyi. For example, the livestream head of "361°" said that they would build a 1,000 m2 exhibition hall in Linyi exclusively for livestreaming at the end of 2020. The entire industry is upgrading.

An Increase in Salary Levels

Kuaishou livestreamer Taozi's: In Linyi, the basic salary of Taobao's customer service officers used to be 2,800–3,000 yuan per month, which could increase to 3,500 yuan per month after two or three years of service. However, the salary of aftersales customer service officers in the livestream e-commerce industry is at least 4,000 yuan per month.

Ricearth Network: Our average monthly salary is approximately 6,000 yuan, while some people can make up to 10,000 or 20,000 yuan. For example, the packing team is paid per piece; their average monthly salary is around 8,000 yuan, while some of them can earn more than 10,000 yuan per month, which is considered quite a high salary in Linyi.

A Strong Demand for Top Professional Talents

Kuaishou livestreamer Taozi's: We have no lack of grassroots employees, but we lack people at the management level, which is the case throughout the entire livestreaming industry in Linyi. Our first executive director was found by a headhunting company that we paid more than 30,000 yuan in fees. His salary standard was quite high and was benchmarked to the salary level in Hangzhou.

Nowadays, we have educational requirements for our aftersales customer service officers. In the past, junior middle school education was enough, but we have now increased the standard to senior middle school and above. They must also be familiar with using a computer, including office systems and software.

To recruit talents, we have also established a branch office in Hangzhou. We have recruited seven livestreamers in Hangzhou, albeit they are still in the training phase. Certain skills are required to become a livestreamer, and they require a substantial amount of time to be honed. The specific amount of training time needed is related to the individual overall ability of each livestreamer.

Shunhe Industrial Park: There is a severe shortage of talents, especially for professional livestream e-commerce talents.

What is most tiring to us is the fact that talent development cannot keep up with our company's speed of development, hence we are often unable to recruit the ideal people even after six months of recruitment. Ever since we began trying to sell goods on-stream, our development has been speeding up, and it has now entered a bottleneck period. This is why we need a professional team to carry out planning, analysis, and management to increase the operational efficiency of the company.

WHO BUYS THE GOODS OF LINYI'S LIVESTREAMERS FROM 3,500 KILOMETERS AWAY: AN INTERVIEW WITH FOUR USERS FROM XINJIANG

Key Points

- Shipping fees remain a pain point for Xinjiang users when shopping online. Several Kuaishou livestreamers, as represented by Taozi's, have implemented free nationwide shipping and are thus very well-received.

- Following the pandemic, more consumers from Xinjiang have chosen to shop online. The spending power of Xinjiang users is very high even though their salaries are not.

- Livestream e-commerce is of great help to users from Tacheng, Karamay, Hotan, and so on. Their local brick-and-mortar stores offer few product choices, a state of affairs that livestream e-commerce has changed.

In October 2020, we conducted an investigation in Linyi, Shandong Province. The livestreamers there mentioned on several occasions that they have many buyers from Xinjiang, who have very high spending power to boot. Xinjiang is approximately 3,500 kilometers away from Linyi. In the past, Linyi's wholesale markets could only reach users within several hundred kilometers, but now, livestreaming has connected Linyi's livestreamers with consumers from all over China.

After interacting with livestreamers in Linyi, we also wanted to look at the other end of transactions, i.e., livestream e-commerce consumers who are far away in Xinjiang. We wanted to find out what changes livestreaming has brought about for them. Unfortunately, the unexpected outbreak of the coronavirus pandemic derailed our plans to visit Xinjiang, and thus we first conversed with four users by phone.

The author of this text is research assistant Guo Senyu of Kuaishou Research Institute.

◎ *The following is an interview with four Kuaishou users from Xinjiang.*

. . .

Interview 1: Ms. He

A Loyal Follower of Livestreamer Taozi's, From Emin County, Tacheng Prefecture, Xinjiang

I have been watching Kuaishou for over a year. It was in June or July 2019 when I began following Kuaishou livestreamer Taozi. For me, what is most attractive about her is her forthright and authentic character. That was why I slowly became her loyal follower.

At first, I could not ascertain the quality of the stuff sold by livestreamers, and so I only bought a few small items to give it a try. After I received the goods, I felt that the quality was pretty good and the price-performance was high. Besides, shipping was free of charge.

When I bought stuff on other e-commerce platforms in the past, Xinjiang was not included within the area for free shipping. Hence, I had to pay shipping fees of about 10–15 yuan. As I shop online quite often, shipping fees are certainly an important factor that I would consider. Taozi's provides free shipping throughout China as well as good aftersales services; whenever I tell them about a problem with the goods, they would reply promptly and display a good attitude while attending to me. That is why I am willing to keep on buying stuff from them.

Due to the pandemic, we rarely visit brick-and-mortar stores these days, and instead purchase many of our things online. Daily necessities are the only things that we continue to buy offline. I feel that online shopping can fulfill most of my living needs; offline shopping takes up time and does not always offer products of the expected quality.

Livestream promotions have stimulated my consumption desire. I would watch such promotions on my mobile phone whenever I feel bored. I have bought many things not because I need them but because they looked appealing on-stream or because I felt that they could be useful after listening to the livestreamer's description of them.

Tacheng Prefecture is a fairly remote place that is inconvenient for the delivery of online purchases. The rise of livestream e-commerce has changed Tacheng greatly. The most intuitive change is the ever-increasing number of delivery collection points. At first, there was only one big collection point in the entire county seat, but now, the county seat has been divided into several zones, with many small collection points set up in each zone.

The major courier companies have all begun operating here. SF Express provides slightly faster service than the other companies, which take a week or so to deliver shipments to us.

Kuaishou has resonated deeply with the people in Tacheng; everyone here uses Kuaishou. The people around me have all begun watching livestream promotions on Kuaishou. At the same time, I would share with them my favorite stores and livestreamers, as well as products that are high in price-performance. As a result, more and more people around me are using Kuaishou to buy stuff.

Interview 2: Ms. Tang

A Loyal Follower of Livestreamers Taozi's and Wawa's, From Dushanzi District, Karamay, Xinjiang

I am a loyal follower of Kuaishou livestreamers Taozi's and Wawa's. I am an old acquaintance of Taozi, and we have constantly kept in touch. When Taozi began selling stuff on Kuaishou in 2018, she invited me to help her out in Shandong. It was at that time that I began using Kuaishou and found out that I could buy things on Kuaishou.

Ten years ago, I had already begun shopping online, albeit in small quantities and only occasionally. That was because I kept on receiving defective or counterfeit goods, and furthermore, making returns from Xinjiang was both difficult and expensive. Hence, I usually bought my things in shopping malls. The people around me are likewise; for a long time, we held the notion that it was easy to get scammed while shopping online, and thus that it was better to buy things from brick-and-mortar stores.

In recent years, however, brick-and-mortar stores in Karamay have fallen into an ever-deeper slump. Taking clothing for example, since 2017, the number of available clothing designs and brands, as well as the rate of new product launches, has fallen substantially. The clothing designs found in the brick-and-mortar stores here are very outdated yet much more expensive than those available online. Other products are also more expensive than elsewhere. Nowadays, the only things that sell well in offline stores here are probably daily necessities and foodstuffs such as fuel, rice, cooking oil, and salt. What I have felt most deeply is the fact that practically nobody here goes shopping anymore; even the large shopping malls do not get many shoppers. Of course, this might have a lot to do with the coronavirus pandemic.

Around 2019, due to Taozi's influence, I began buying things on Kuaishou livestreams and have since kept on increasing my outlay. These days, I spend 4,000 to 5,000 yuan per month on Kuaishou.

Firstly, this is because the things sold on Kuaishou livestreams are not only cheap, but their quality is also guaranteed. Returns are insured, and the attitude of the customer service department is great—these services give me an extremely positive feeling because they were rarely offered when buying things online in the past. Secondly, livestream e-commerce on Kuaishou has saved me a lot of time. On my past weekly shopping trips, I would visit various shopping malls and department stores throughout the city because clothes, shoes, and daily necessities were respectively sold in different places, thereby wasting a tremendous amount of time and energy. However, since livestreaming came about, I have been able to browse and purchase all kinds of products on my mobile phone with great convenience.

The living atmosphere in Xinjiang is extremely comfortable—everyone eats what they want and buys what they want. Everyone likes to buy good stuff without paying too much consideration to other factors. That is why our spending power is very high even though our salaries are not.

I have also observed that there are many fashionable young women here. Because of the difficulty of buying trendy designs offline, they usually buy their clothes online. With the availability of livestream e-commerce on Kuaishou these days, there are many livestreamers who sell clothes and teach their viewers how to mix and match clothes. I am certain that their buyers include those young women.

Interview 3: Ms. Ye

A Loyal Follower of Livestreamer Landuo's, From Toutunhe District, Urumqi, Xinjiang

I have been using Kuaishou for more than three years now. Since July 2020, I have also begun watching livestream promotions. Due to the outbreak of the pandemic in Xinjiang back then, people here in Urumqi could not go outdoors for a very long period of time, and thus we had a lot of spare time. Because I highly admire the product style of Kuaishou livestreamer Landuo's, I have continually bought things from her. I would generally make a purchase every time I watch her livestream and would consolidate several orders to save on the shipping fees.

I feel that the brick-and-mortar stores in Urumqi are pretty good; the prices and variety in the offline shopping malls are fine for me, and thus I do not buy things such as clothes and cosmetics on the Internet. At the very most, I would buy a few small items that are unavailable here. Nowadays, I shop in brick-and-mortar stores more often, but because I like Landuo's, I would often go on Kuaishou to buy things as well. It is inconvenient for us to buy things via e-commerce if free shipping is not provided. Given the objective geographical conditions of Xinjiang, we know why we have to pay shipping fees and are very willing to do so. However, if we make frequent purchases, the total shipping fees would become quite intolerable. This is why the return rate for online purchases has always been very low in the Xinjiang region—it is too troublesome for us.

Furthermore, I do not really like waiting, nor do the people around me. This is because of the slow logistics in Xinjiang. For example, if I consolidate a few orders from Landuo's into a single shipment, it will take more than a month from the time of my first order until I receive the shipment. By the time I receive the clothes, they might no longer imbue a fresh feeling or might even be quickly going out-of- season. Waiting is a very tiring affair for us.

There are a few places more remote than Urumqi that have an even greater demand for livestream e-commerce. This is because all shipments to Xinjiang have to pass through Urumqi, and thus all the things sold in the brick-and-mortar stores of those places are shipped from here. For clothing, the offline stores in those places are far inferior to the stores here. If livestream promotions provide direct shipment of goods from the places of production to users in those places, the benefits to them would be self-explanatory.

Interview 4: Su Su

A Loyal Follower of Livestreamer Landuo's, From Gujiangbage Village, Hotan, Xinjiang

I began using Kuaishou about three or four years ago and made my first purchase on a Kuaishou livestream channel in 2019. I usually only buy cosmetics, clothing, and snacks on livestream channels.

I follow Landuo's because she mixes and matches clothing very tastefully, and also because her clothing is good in quality. I would generally make a purchase every time I watch her livestream. However, I would consolidate my orders from several livestream sessions to save on the shipping fees. What I would usually do is send screenshots to the customer service department and get them to consolidate the orders into one shipment. There are actually a few livestreamers on Kuaishou who do not ship to Xinjiang, let alone provide free shipping. However, Landuo's is willing to ship to Xinjiang and also to do the fiddly work of consolidating the orders. That is why I enjoy buying clothes from her and would spend several thousand yuan each time.

I rarely go shopping in brick-and-mortar stores here in Hotan because the stores here are far behind those in other provinces. The main problem with the stores here is not their prices but rather the lack of designs that I like and the lack of variety to choose from. It is usually only when buying cosmetics that I would go to a brick-and-mortar store to try them out. Before livestream e-commerce on Kuaishou came about, I would usually shop on traditional e-commerce platforms and look for things that come with free shipping. Of course, I am willing to pay a shipping fee of up to 20 yuan if there is something that I need urgently.

Livestream e-commerce has changed many of my spending habits. For example, when watching a Kuaishou livestream on my phone, I would often develop a buying desire even if there is nothing I need. Most of the people around me also watch livestreams on Kuaishou.

After these four interviews, we gained a preliminary understanding of users from Xinjiang and the state of livestream e-commerce over there. Firstly, shipping fees remain a pain point for Xinjiang consumers when they are shopping online. However, a small number of livestreamers on Kuaishou, as represented by Taozi's, have implemented free nationwide shipping and thus are very well-received by Xinjiang consumers. Secondly, due to the continuous impact of the pandemic as well as the rapid development of the express logistics industry, offline brick-and-mortar businesses in Xinjiang (especially regions outside of Urumqi) have slumped. Consumers there have a greater inclination toward online shopping. Livestream e-commerce has made up for the lack of offline stores and greatly stimulated the consumers' demand for shopping. Thirdly, the rise of livestream e-commerce has been of great help to consumers in remote areas such as Tacheng and Karamay. The business model of livestream e-commerce, whereby livestreamers directly interact with consumers, has greatly made up for the inability of consumers in remote areas to purchase good products offline. Fourthly, consumers in Xinjiang are not conservative in terms of spending their money, and thus they have substantial spending power on the whole.

TIP

Editor's Note

Before publishing this book, we invited a few friends to give us their opinions on it. One of them asked us how this interview with four users from Xinjiang is related to consumption upgrade and internal circulation—it was a little puzzling to him.

I personally thought quite the opposite: this chapter might seem uninteresting but is actually extraordinary in meaning. Hence, I wanted to add a few more words.

Tacheng Prefecture, Xinjiang, is the farthest "nerve ending" of China, at approximately 3,500 kilometers from Beijing. These days, users from Tacheng are able to interact "face-to-face" with livestreamers from Linyi, Hangzhou, and Shanghai, and can also purchase clothing directly from these livestreamers.

This means that Tacheng is now "synchronized in real time" with Linyi, Hangzhou, and Shanghai! The most important word in this phrase is "real-time," followed by "synchronized." This is something that was unimaginable in the past.

Real-time synchronization means that: (1) When there is an update in terms of design and style to the things sold by businesses from Hangzhou, Shanghai, and Linyi, the people in Tacheng would find out in sync. (2) When Tacheng is in sync, it means that the whole of China is in sync. (3) When the whole of China is in sync, it means that a "common market" has been formed nationwide and the entire country has actually become "the same city." This is an unprecedented phenomenon.

This is the "internal circulation" brought about by the construction of information infrastructure. This circulation can not only reach the farthest capillaries of the country but also achieve real-time transmission and nationwide synchronization.

Once such a circulation is formed, it would mean that the speed of consumption iteration would greatly increase nationwide—whenever there is something new in any part of China, it would be instantly synchronized nationwide. This is because the popularization of mobile phones, 4G, logistics, and payment has caused a unified and complex market that is extremely fast in update speed to be formed in China. This market, which is one of a kind worldwide, has laid the foundation for innovation and will eventually create tremendous wealth.

In reality, what Internet video has done is merely shorten time and space.

Its principle is essentially the same as the effects of the popularization of automobiles a century ago. Because automobiles became available to the middle class, many villages were absorbed into cities. At first, villages and cities were two different worlds, but the availability of automobiles shortened time and space, causing villages and cities to integrate as one. As a result, urban innovation and consumption could be synchronized to the villages in real time.

This was the internal circulation and consumption upgrade a century ago.

Today, Internet video is an even more powerful information infrastructure—it has truly integrated all 9.6 million km2 of China into one.

This is why we felt that this chapter was of value and thus related it to the concepts of consumption upgrade and internal circulation. The economic growth of China is nowat a new starting point.

CHAPTER THIRTEEN

LIVESTREAMING + POVERTY ALLEVIATION

- Short videos and livestreams enable the produce and beautiful scenery of impoverished regions to be seen by everyone in China.

- This chapter offers two perspectives: the first is the personal experiences of Zhang Fei, a poverty alleviation secretary in Aba, Sichuan Province, in alleviating poverty through livestreaming, while the second is a research paper authored by Yan Yilong, associate dean of the Institute for Contemporary China Studies, Tsinghua University.

THE PATH OF "POVERTY ALLEVIATION VIA LIVESTREAMING" OF THE FIRST SECRETARY OF GANJIAGOU VILLAGE, ABA PREFECTURE

Key Points

- All monetizable resources of a village, such as folk cultures, sceneries, and specialty products, can be converted into sources of income via livestreaming.

The author of this text is research assistant Mao Yirong of Kuaishou Research Institute.

- To promote agricultural products on livestreams, it is necessary to solve problems such as inconsistent product quality, lack of variation, slow logistics, and difficult aftersales.

- The traditional sales method is to sell the agricultural products to stall owners or middlemen in the county seat. The rise of livestream e-commerce has expanded the depth and width of sales, enabling agricultural products to be directly sold to consumers across China.

Mid-October is the viewing season for the Color Forest in Sichuan Province. Many visitors drive westward from Chengdu to Provincial Highway 303—passing Dujiangyan, Balangshan Tunnel, and Wolong National Nature Reserve. Subsequently, they stop at Mount Siguniang in Xiaojin County and look for beautiful scenery.

Were they to check the "Same City" or the "Discover" page on Kuaishou, they might very well find the livestream of the Kuaishou account "Carefree Paradise," where a young man or his wife shows off a beautiful sea of clouds or a plate of mountain cuisine.

The young man is called Zhang Fei. He is a member of the publicity committee for Meixing Town, Xiaojin County, Aba Prefecture, Sichuan Province, and also the first secretary of Ganjiagou Village. Since November 2016, he has been using Kuaishou short videos to record his daily work in poverty alleviation for Ganjiagou Village. In 2017, he began using livestreams to facilitate the sale of cured meat by peasant households. In this way, livestreaming and poverty alleviation have been brought together in an unexpected Way. However, Zhang received mixed feedback for the cured meat sold on his livestream channel. The user opinions prompted him to unify the production segments, provide quality assurance, and standardize the agricultural produce. Because fresh fruits are highly seasonal and limited in quantity, he broadened the categories of his products in order to ensure that he has products to sell on his livestream channel throughout the year.

As a village cadre and a Kuaishou livestreamer, Zhang must not only provide products to consumers but also gather the local agricultural produce into a proper supply chain. While searching for sources of goods, he also formed collaborations with local commission manufacturers and processing enterprises to ensure the scale and quality of his sources of goods.

As his followers increased, he faced increasingly diverse consumer demands. His livestream channel brought about a new model of transaction— he piloted a model in which the consumers could pay for ownership of the black pigs reared in the mountains. In this way, he transformed agricultural byproducts into "future products" that were paid for in advance, satisfying the demand of Kuaishou users for "cyber-rearing of pigs." Enterprise-level transaction orders could also be negotiated on his livestream channel, enabling agricultural products to be sold in bulk via a model of direct procurement.

In the Kuaishou ecosystem, Zhang actively sought out interaction with users in all circles. Early on, he became friends with several Kuaishou livestreamers to pick up filming techniques. Subsequently, he passed these techniques on to the mountain folk by setting up short video training courses, encouraging the local farmers to sell goods via Kuaishou livestreams.

Livestreaming has not only brought agricultural produce out of the mountains but also brought outsiders into the mountains. Thanks to livestreaming, the cuisine and scenery of the mountains became tradable resources, while "Carefree Paradise" gradually transformed from an account for goods promotion into a "geographical name card." In the future, the development of the tourism industry will further galvanize the local economy. Figure 13.1 shows Zhang's path in poverty alleviation.

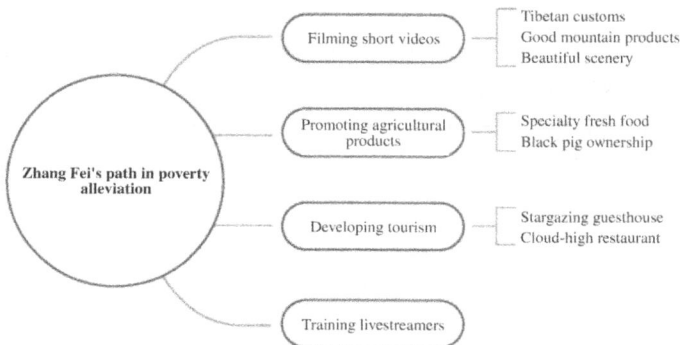

Figure 13.1 Zhang Fei's Path in Poverty Alleviation

◎ *The following is an account by Zhang Fei, first secretary of poverty alleviation in Ganjiagou Village, Xiaojin County, Aba Prefecture.*

. . .

Over these few years of using Kuaishou, I have been most deeply impressed by Kuaishou's ability to connect mountain villages with the outside world, transforming what was "impossible" in the mountains into something "possible."

Kuaishou has been of great help to my rural poverty alleviation work. Firstly, it has broadened my horizons. By using such a new tool, I have done all that I can to help the villagers sell their goods via short videos and livestreams, creating an outlet for selling mountain agricultural produce. Secondly, short videos have connected mountain resources with external capital. The loyal followers on Kuaishou are not only willing to buy local specialties from the mountains but have also visited us as tourists and provided suggestions pertaining to our work of poverty alleviation and village development. Furthermore, they are willing to invest money here. The mountain villagers are also becoming increasingly open-minded— more and more of them are starting to embrace Kuaishou, learning how to film short videos, opening stores on Kuaishou, and selling their goods via livestreams.

Finding out About Kuaishou and Recording My Work in Poverty Alleviation

In 2016, I went to serve as the first secretary of poverty alleviation for Ganjiagou Village. At that time, Ganjiagou had 26 households that were registered as being in poverty. The villagers barely had any source of income; they pretty much lived off the mountains, yet were hardly self-sufficient. In the summer, they would go up the mountains to gather matsutake mushrooms and other wild mushrooms, which they would then sell in the county seat for a bit of money. But when it snowed in the winter, they would have no income and thus find it hard to get by.

Once, when my younger brother came to Xiaojin County to visit me, I brought him on a trip to the village. On the way up the mountain, he got me to download the Kuaishou app. I asked him what the benefits of using Kuaishou were, to which he replied that I could earn an additional income by livestreaming and receiving gifts from viewers, and use this income to aid the poverty-stricken households. After I installed the app, he came up with the nickname "Brother Fei's Sichuan Adventures" for me and helped me bring in 10 initial followers. This was how my story on Kuaishou began.

At the end of November 2016, I uploaded my first short video on Kuaishou. It was very simple in content—I panned the camera from a stone house in the mountains to the scenery in the distance and said, "Hello my friends, this is Ganjiagou Village in Laoying Township, Xiaojin County, Aba Prefecture. From today on, I will record my story in tackling poverty!"

I generally filmed the houses, chickens, and pigs in the village, and the lives of the folk here. However, my footage was very shaky and unclear. Despite persistently uploading two or three videos every day, I received few views and interactions. Back then, I used the same title for every short video: "Ganjiagou Village of Laoying Township! We will not leave poverty to the next generation!" I also followed a few Kuaishou livestreamers to see how they did their filming and to learn how to get on the Trending page.

One day in November 2017, I entered the village and happened to film a video of a cowherd driving cattle. The video made it on to the Trending page, garnering more than 800,000 views. At that time, I felt elated and thought that the cowherd was going to become famous. He had a tall frame and a very pure smile. However, his family was not well-off and thus he had never stepped one foot out of the mountains. The loyal followers on Kuaishou cared about him deeply and often asked about his situation in the comments. Some of them also sent clothes and shoes, while someone even sent a smartphone.

After achieving my first Trending video, my follower count increased to 2,000. Having established a solid follower base, my subsequent videos occasionally made it on to the Trending page and garnered 300,000 to 400,000 views, while my follower count continued to gradually increase. Back then, many people could not understand how a first secretary could have enough time to film short videos every day, and some of them even reported me for neglecting my proper duties.

I feel that the work of poverty alleviation requires not only practical implementation but also innovative thinking—it is through innovation that results can be easily achieved. Kuaishou is simply a medium for finding a robust model of development for the village, which is the most important thing.

When my follower count increased to more than 10,000 at the start of 2017, I began trying out livestreaming. At first, nobody watched my livestreams, but as time went by, my livestream channel accumulated 20 to 30 sticky followers.

Xiaojin County consists of 88 impoverished villages, and including the non-impoverished villages, more than 100 first secretaries have been delegated to the county to carry out the work of poverty alleviation. In total, there are nearly 1,000 first secretaries of poverty alleviation in Aba Prefecture, and I believe that there are also many first secretaries of poverty alleviation who are devoted to their work in various parts of China. What every one of us lacks is simply a channel for being seen by the outside world.

Finding a Market for Cured Meat on Kuaishou

In Ganjiagou Village, every household would rear one or two black pigs that would be made into cured meat and eaten at the end of the year. Whenever I saw that a villager has made some tasty, cured meat, I would conduct a livestream to sell it. At that time, the transaction and shipment methods for cured meat were very primitive. During the livestream, interested buyers would point out the pieces of cured meat that they wanted, after which I would paste a sticker with their names on the respective pieces of meat. They would then add me on WeChat and send me their Kuaishou account names and addresses. Subsequently, I would go to the county seat to pack and ship the cured meat. At times, to dispel the buyers' misgivings, I would collect payment only after the goods had been delivered. In this way, I sold several hundred kilograms of cured meat.

In 2017, despite selling a considerable amount of cured meat, the quality of the meat produced by the farmers was inconsistent. Some buyers returned their purchases, claiming that the meat was too high in fat. As they lived in various parts of China, we had to pay high shipping fees and thus lost a lot of money. Later on, my wife and I discussed producing our own cured meat so as to keep an eye on quality control. On October 3, 2018, we relocated from the county seat to Mazu Mountain Village, where we found a residence on the mountaintop.

Why did we relocate to Mazu? One day while I was working in Ganjiagou Village, I happened to see a sky full of adjoining crimson clouds on the mountaintop and felt that they were extremely beautiful. The mountaintop was spacious and scarcely populated, and thus the smoking of cured meat could be done without affecting other people. Following a discussion with my wife, I rented a stone house on the mountaintop and made the preparations for smoking cured meat. During the day, the stones would absorb the heat from the sun, while at night, the heat would be released. This keeps the interior of the house at a constant temperature round the clock, which is beneficial to the smoking and preservation of cured meat.

We would procure fresh black pork from the farmers. Whenever someone in the village was slaughtering pigs, they would ask us to go over. Within a span of two months, we procured 5,000 kilograms of fresh black pork in the village, paying the farmers fully in cash. If we did not have enough money, we would take loans to ensure that we could pay the farmers each time we collected the pork. Each pig produced at least 50 kilograms of meat, which we would procure for several thousand yuan. Since basically every household in the village reared one or two black pigs, they were able to earn a substantial amount of additional income.

The 5,000 kilograms of fresh meat was eventually smoked into 3,000 kilograms of cured meat. In order to sell the cured meat, we changed the name of our Kuaishou account to "Making Cured Meat Fly." Back then, when we heard that the African swine fever had broken out in some parts of China, I was worried that nobody would eat pork for the time being and did not know what to do. Furthermore, our account only had 25,000 followers when we made the move to the mountaintop and, thus, we did not have that many buyers. Hence, we spent all of December brooding over how to sell the cured meat.

Unexpectedly, things quickly took a favorable turn. In January 2019, one of our short videos made it on to Kuaishou's Trending page. It showed the scene of my family having a meal around a table on the mountaintop, with a sea of clouds forming the backdrop. As the viewers on Kuaishou really enjoyed seeing such snippets of the cloud-filled, paradise-like mountain life, our total video views rapidly increased from 1 million to 5 million while our follower count soared to 60,000. Subsequently, we uploaded a few more short videos that also made it on to the Trending page, causing our follower count to rise to somewhere between 200,000 and 300,000.

As a result, more and more people watched our livestreams and bought our cured meat. During the winter, my wife and I could be found packing cured meat at 3 a.m. while it was snowing outside. In this way, we sold out the cured meat within a week.

At that time, our loyal followers generally bought 10 to 15 kilograms of meat per purchase. A buyer from Enshi, Hubei Province, came from a family that did not eat fresh meat and only ate cured meat all year round. After finding my video on Kuaishou's Trending page, he placed a first order for five kilograms of meat. The day after receiving the goods, he placed a second order for 20,000-yuan worth of cured meat, as his family had enjoyed its taste.

Why do so many people like our cured meat? That is because we choose the best parts of the pork and are very fastidious about the process of smoking the meat. For example, we choose only the pork belly and pork butt cuts. Before it can be smoked, procured fresh meat must be aged and removed of blood, then pounded together with red wine, baijiu, white sugar, salt, and Sichuan pepper. The next day, the meat is hung until the alcohol and water have evaporated. It is only then that the meat can be smoked using a special Tibetan incense and grape skin. After a full day of smoking, the meat is air-dried in the stone house for a month, when it is then fit for consumption.

Expanding the Variety of Agricultural Products and Achieving Product Standardization

As our follower count kept increasing, our products gradually diversified due to the different demands of different consumers. For agricultural products, in addition to cured meat, we also promote Xiaojin apples, Xiaojin matsutake, yak meat, red wine, wild dried mushrooms, and Xiaojin pepper. Aside from agricultural products, we also help enterprises from Xiaojin County, such as a sea buckthorn beverage factory and Jinshan Rose Production Base, to sell their goods.

However, products such as apples and mushrooms are highly seasonal and run out of stock very quickly. To have things to sell in our Yellow Cart throughout the year, we looked around Xiaojin County for more good products. At the same time, the villagers would offer us their products on their own initiative.

What we want to do is keep an eye on product quality and distinguish what is good from what is bad. For example, all mushrooms look very similar, but feel different to the touch; the bad ones might become moldy if they are stored one day too long. Apples are likewise; even those that look good might contain worms or a rotten core, and thus they must be inspected carefully.

Among our agricultural products, it is the Xiaojin apples that we sell the most. They are mostly grown by the farmers who reside on the lower half of the mountain, and they are fairly difficult to find. The lower half of the mountain experiences a large temperature difference between day and night; it gets plenty of sunlight in the day, and thus the apples grown there taste better. However, as demand for them increased, I no longer had sufficient time to choose the apples I wanted; often, I would accept all the apples offered to me by the villagers. At the same time, apples need to be backed up by a strong aftersales system and are low in profitability, causing more work than my wife and I could possibly handle.

Nowadays, we collaborate with an agent who looks for sources of goods among the various households in Xiaojin County and carries out quality control on our behalf. He helps us choose the apples and also pack and ship a portion of the goods. If we want to ship the goods ourselves, we must procure them from the agent before we can pack and sell them. Over the past two years, we have sold 7,500 kilograms of apples.

On Kuaishou, we have been selling free-range honey for three years. From the 50th kilogram of honey to the 450th kilogram of honey that we sold, all of the reviews that we received were positive.

We first discovered free-range honey in the home of one of the farmers. He lives at the junction of a virgin forest and a grassland, where he owns a bee garden and a flower garden 3,500 meters above sea level. Although his gardens provide excellent resources, he only produces 10 buckets of honey every year. It was only after I helped him sell the honey via livestreaming that he dared to increase the scale of production. For the following two years, he produced 50-odd buckets and 130-odd buckets—equivalent to 450 kilograms of honey— respectively.

Later on, we also collaborated with two other beekeeping villagers. To ensure the quality of the honey, we signed an agreement with them stipulating that the bees must not be fed white sugar, and that the honey could only be harvested once a year. When we receive the honey, we examine its viscosity and measure the amount of active enzymes and use a few other primitive methods to evaluate its quality.

It was also through trial and error that I gained experience in standardizing agricultural products. During the pandemic, I attended the third phase of "Kuaishou Happy Village Entrepreneurship Academy." When attending Kuaishou's e-commerce training course online, the most useful lesson I gained was regarding the brand-building of agricultural products.

The purpose of brand-building is to enable a product to be sold in supermarkets and circulated in big markets. It is very difficult for people living in remote mountainous areas to carry out brandification of agricultural byproducts; we must register a trademark, own our own factories, obtain a food production license, and standardize the product packaging, all of which require large capital investments and very long time spans. Although we already have awareness of brand protection and have registered food and cultural tourism trademarks for "Carefree Paradise," we still have a long way to go in brand-building.

To this end, we have begun to collaborate with manufacturers that have the necessary qualifications for production. For example, we have engaged a local yak meat factory to handle the yak meat that we sell. They process the meat obtained from the farmers, and we then sell it on our livestream channel.

Jinshan Rose Production Base is likewise. They have the production lines and research strength necessary for producing products such as rose tea, rose jam, rose hydrosol, rose facial masks, and rose cream. Hence, they are able to impel the farmers around them to expand the scale of rose cultivation. In August 2020, we began helping them sell their goods. Within two months, we sold 30,000-yuan worth of goods, which was not a bad initial result.

In 2020, we piloted a pig ownership program. Previously, many netizens had commented that they wanted to buy ownership of the black pigs reared in the mountains because these pigs were a fine breed. When fed purely with grains and allowed to grow for at least eight months, they produce pork that is relatively more succulent and fibrous. Since there was such a demand among our loyal followers, I served as the middleman between them and the local folk and bridged the cities and the village, helping the farmers increase their income.

After more than 100 followers signed up to buy ownership of the black pigs, I picked out 10 of them for a trial run. They had to pay an ownership fee in advance, covering the costs of pig-breeding and daily management. At the end of the year, they would also have to pay for the costs of foster care and delivery. Every farming household in the mountains used to rear one or two black pigs for their own consumption, but they now reared an additional one or two black pigs.

This is akin to a channel of "futures trading," whereby trade is brought forward via Kuaishou. Every week, I would film short videos or conduct livestreams to provide updates on the growth of the pigs, enabling netizens to see which households the pigs were reared in, what the environment was like, and what the pigs were fed. As time went on, the netizens developed a sense of participation in the process of pig-rearing, which is a form of emotional sustenance.

Until this day, many netizens are still asking me via private messages whether there is a quota for pig ownership. Many people also want to buy ownership of chickens, but we have not started on this yet, mainly because of our limited energy. If possible, we may develop models for buying ownership of fruit trees, chickens, and sheep in the future.

Such ownership models have a very positive effect on poverty alleviation. They are no longer confined solely to goods promotion, which requires the livestreamers to have capabilities in background operations and livestreaming in order to sell the in-stock agricultural products. The most important thing about such ownership models is that the farmers earn an income in advance and can guarantee early-stage investments. Furthermore, be it for planting fruit trees or breeding black pigs, the farmers do not have to worry about finding a market and thus do not have to use insecticides or fattening feeds. Hence, "ecosystem greening" is truly realized.

Aside from Kuaishou followers, our clients also include enterprises. In May 2020, with Kuaishou Poverty Alleviation serving as a go-between, the deputy head of Xiaojin County and I had a voice chat with the boss of Jiujiuya on a livestream channel. We subsequently signed a procurement order for 5-million-yuan worth of Sichuan pepper online. Prior to this, Jiujiuya procured Sichuan pepper from Xiaojin County via a middleman company. This time, it was as if Jiujiuya had signed a strategic framework agreement with Xiaojin County and directly placed orders for the Sichuan pepper produced by the farmers there.

Making a Bunch of New Friends on Kuaishou

I have become acquainted with people from all over China via Kuaishou. Some of them are top livestreamers on Kuaishou, while some are loyal followers on the platform. I have learned many techniques of filming and editing short videos and many ways of promoting goods on-stream from those livestreamers. The netizens who come from various trades and professions are also very passionate; while interacting with me, they give me new ideas regarding life or my work in poverty alleviation.

In 2016, I followed a Kuaishou livestreamer to learn how to get on the Trending page. He was repeating the Long March on foot. As Mount Jiajin of Xiaojin County was the first snow mountain that the Red Army passed through on the Long March, I guessed that he would definitely pass through Xiaojin County, as well.

When I saw that he had reached Menggu Bridge, I went to look for him and brought him to Ganjiagou Village. We gradually built up a friendship. He taught me how to film videos: when to pause, how to add music, and how to choose a thumbnail. It was only then that I realized there were so many skills needed to produce short videos.

Later on, I was thrilled to discover that I had been followed by He Yu, who was a livestreamer who had several hundred thousand followers. Through my short videos on poverty alleviation, he had found out about a woman from a poor family in the mountains—she had mobility problems and could not get hot meals. He sent me a private message and donated 200 yuan, hoping to buy a microwave for her. I later became friends with him and learned a lot from him.

Later on, I got to know other livestreamers on Kuaishou in succession. Many of them would also visit "Carefree Paradise" for a few days occasionally. For example, when livestreamer "Brother Wan in the Netherlands" visited, he offered me new perspectives and showed me that I could increase the number of product categories that I promoted onstream.

Short Video Training: Repaying the Mountains with Skills

Although there are many resources in the mountains, we are only able to sell a limited quantity of them via livestreams. Take matsutake for example— every year, thousands of people dig for matsutake in the mountains behind Mazu Village from July to September. The mountains' annual output of matsutake is as high as 200 tons, which is worth nearly 50 million yuan. Nevertheless, I have only been able to sell approximately 500 kilograms of matsutake via my livestream channel, which is a mere drop in the bucket.

The traditional sales method is to sell the agricultural products to stall owners or middlemen in the county seat, earning money little by little this way. With the rise of livestream e-commerce, however, agricultural products can be directly sold to consumers all over China. For the farming households, this is akin to broadening their sources of income and increasing their sales channels.

As an early entrant into livestream e-commerce, I lead the villagers by example and show them that specialty products can be sold on Kuaishou.

Many of them have since followed my example. When I am out working in the fields, I also recommend Kuaishou to the people there.

At least 200 households from the villages in Meixing Town, Xiaojin County—including Ganjiagou Village, Dashuigou Village, and Mulan Village—have listened to me talking about short videos and livestreams. I hope that more villagers can change their mindsets that Kuaishou is only for people with more knowledge and culture than themselves. They, too, are able to create accounts and promote goods via livestreaming.

After they have registered accounts on Kuaishou, I teach them how to film videos. I have realized that, just like writing an essay, uploading a Kuaishou video requires five major elements: time, location, characters, plot, and outcome. I encourage everyone to be daring about facing the camera; just by standing in front of the camera, they have created a character, and they must then establish trust. The filmed content must also be consistent; it is meaningless to film a wedding video one day and a cooking video the next day.

For example, if they want to sell apples, they should upload lifestyle videos related to apples, film the growth process of apples, or link Kuaishou short videos to their specialty products. When they are just starting out, I tell them to persist in filming videos even if they only have 1,000 followers—as long as 100 of these followers are from outside the mountains, they would be able to sell their products. These 100 followers are not to be underestimated—it would be amazing enough if each of them bought a crate of apples—furthermore, they can influence their colleagues and friends to do the same. Perhaps by the next year, these apple sellers will sell out of their own apples and begin selling those from their relatives.

In 2020, together with a Kuaishou employee, I organized a short video training course in Mulan Village, with 20 to 30 participants. Today, some of them are already selling their goods on Kuaishou. For example,

Kuaishou livestreamer "Apple Sister" used to sell her family's apples to peddlers, but she now sells them on Kuaishou and uploads short videos persistently. She often calls me on the phone to exchange experiences in filming short videos.

When I have the time, I want to visit every village in Xiaojin County to organize similar courses. I hope that e-commerce can develop throughout the entire county, with the villagers transforming from viewers into livestreamers.

By connecting short videos and livestreams with rural life, the villagers will be able to sell their agricultural products.

Revitalizing the Local Economy with Tourism

At "Carefree Paradise," we did not think about opening our own guest house at first. All our ideas emerged slowly but surely over time. Our earliest tourists were a couple from Xilingol, Inner Mongolia. They arrived on the third day of the Lunar New Year in 2019. Subsequently, we began to think about whether, aside from selling the specialty products of the mountains, we could bring in our loyal followers on Kuaishou as tourists and drive the development of the local tourism industry.

In March 2019, I officially changed the name of my Kuaishou account to "Carefree Paradise."

Every day, I would receive many private messages from our loyal followers about coming to visit, but we were unable to accommodate them and thus had to reject all their requests. However, when a few followers came to visit us without prior notice, we had no choice but to bring them to stay in the farmers' homes on the mountaintop, and we even pitched a few tents for them. As of October 2020, more than 1,000 tourists have visited "Carefree Paradise." There are also a number of returning visitors—some of them have visited us five times. In April 2020, a couple from Chengdu decided to build an eight-room guest house here after they had inspected the place. The construction work began in May and was completed by the end of June, when the guest house was put into operation with an initial investment of more than 300,000 yuan. This provided us with preliminary accommodation capabilities. On National

Day that year, we received more than 200 visitors in total. Within just three months, we made more than 50,000 yuan in revenue. We have since signed a 20-year right-to-use contract with the couple; I believe that our revenue for the following year can reach 300,000 yuan.

The supporting facilities for tourism services here still must be improved, albeit the capital construction costs are very high. The government has also invested a lot of money here. When I visited Mazu Village in 2018, the road that led from the foot to the top of the mountain had already been built at a cost of at least 10 million yuan. As there was no Internet on the mountaintop, I made a request in October for the government to install network cables. In the future, we will probably need more government support to widen the roads here, to increase the safety of water consumption, and to build sewage facilities.

Conception of a Kuaishou Village

Mazu Village is a decrepit and deserted mountain village that nobody would visit in the past. Most of the native villagers have also moved elsewhere. Nowadays, however, more and more tourists are visiting the village, and it even became very crowded at one point in time. Why did such a change occur? The reason is none other than Kuaishou; it has enabled people outside the mountains to see the beautiful scenery of this place.

Nowadays, I think about how to build a "Kuaishou Village" even in my sleep. I want to build a Kuaishou Village because I am highly grateful to Kuaishou. It was on Kuaishou that my "Carefree Paradise" account achieved growth, and furthermore, it was the Kuaishou official team that first discovered us—they provided us with not only traffic but also many media resources, thereby "magnifying" this remote mountain village of ours.

At "Carefree Paradise," adjoining snowy mountains can be seen in the winter, while seas of clouds and the rising and setting of the sun can be seen in the summer. The resources in the vicinity are also excellent; every point can be strung together to create a model of tourism and sightseeing.

Let's take a three-day visit for example. On the first day, the visitors would stay in a stargazing dome made of glass, experience a cloud-high restaurant and yoga studio, taste the local red wine, and enjoy an "infinity pool." On the second day, they would experience mountain motorbiking in a grassland behind the mountains and one night of camping. On the third day, they would ride a bike to Tianyan Ranch and stay a night there. Thereafter, they could either descend the mountain to stay in a small snowy mountain cabin or climb a snowy mountain first. In the future, we will launch a small sightseeing train from Dujiangyan to Xiaojin County, with three sides of this train entirely made of glass—I am certain that it will attract more tourists.

In my conception of a Kuaishou Village, we will integrate Kuaishou elements such as the overall structure of the rooms, roads, signs, and houses, as well as soft interior designs. At present, several Kuaishou livestreamers want to buy ownership and invest in guest house rooms as a way of repaying their followers. For example, if a livestreamer buys ownership of several rooms, we would help them build the rooms. They would then introduce the guest houses here to their followers, who would thus visit us and stay in those rooms. In this way, the capital and follower resources provided by the livestreamer would be kept here.

TIP

The Results of Kuaishou Poverty Alleviation

From June 2019 to June 2020, 25.7 million people in China earned an income via the Kuaishou platform. Among them, 6.64 million people came from impoverished regions, where one in four people is an active Kuaishou user. Kuaishou users from national-level impoverished counties have uploaded more than 2.9 billion videos that record snippets of their lives; these videos have garnered more than 95 billion likes and more than 1.65 trillion views (from April 23, 2019, to April 23, 2020).

> *Zhang Fei is a Kuaishou-certified "Happy Village Leader." As of August 2020, this project has undergone three phases, provided coverage in 20 provinces or autonomous regions and 51 counties, cities, or districts, trained 36 rural enterprises or cooperatives, unearthed and trained 68 rural entrepreneurs, provided more than 200 local jobs, and helped more than 3,000 impoverished households increase their income. The total annual output value of the Happy Village Leaders in the real estate industry is 20 million yuan, while the development of this industry has impacted millions of people.*

THE AGE OF ATTENTION, ATTENTION POVERTY, AND INFORMATION FLOW EMPOWERMENT OF POVERTY REDUCTION

—YAN YILONG
Associate Professor at the School of Public Policy & Management, Tsinghua University, and Associate Dean of Institute for Contemporary China Studies, Tsinghua University

Key Points

- In the age of attention, content-based e-commerce has created the "infinite malls" sales model and changed the logic of business and poverty reduction. Problems of attention poverty have become prominent problems that have to be solved in the age of attention. By helping farmers seize the opportunities in the age of attention through information flow empowerment, we can give impetus to endogenous poverty reduction.

Since the coronavirus pandemic broke out in 2020, livestream promotions have become an intense social phenomenon, and they are currently creating one sales miracle after another. On the tenth of May that year, Dong Mingzhu promoted goods on Kuaishou Live for three hours and generated 310 million yuan in sales. When a United Nations official appeared on a Chinese livestream channel and promoted Rwanda coffee, 1.5 tons of coffee beans were sold out within a second—this was equivalent to the total sales volume of Rwanda Farmers Coffee Company over the past year. Taobao's figures have shown that, from September 22 to October 21, 2020, top Taobao livestreamer "Weiya" generated 146.4 billion yuan[1] in sales over 26 livestream sessions, surpassing the total retail sales of consumer goods in Ningxia, Tibet, and Qinghai for the entire year. These days, government officials, entrepreneurs, television presenters, and public figures are beginning to promote goods via livestreams. Livestream sales have not only become mainstream but also entered the strategic vision of China. Livestream promotions have become an important strategic tool for increasing domestic demand and stimulating the market. The General Office of the State Council has published a document encouraging brick-and-mortar businesses to come up with new business models such as "cloud shopping" through livestream e-commerce and social marketing. The Ministry of Human Resources and Social Security has also listed Internet marketing as a new profession. These changes were not brought about by the pandemic. Rather, they happened because we have entered an age of attention and the attention economy has been thriving in recent years—the pandemic merely compelled them to break out explosively.[2]

In 2019, we studied a few Internet giants and gained a deep understanding of the huge changes in the logic of the times that have given rise to the current trends. We have entered an age of attention that has not

1 *The writing of this text has drawn inspiration from research conducted on Kuaishou, Alibaba, and Bytedance, and also from the discussions of He Huafeng and Li Zhao of Kuaishou Research Institute, Chen Tao of Alibaba, and others. The author sincerely expresses gratitude to them and takes sole responsibility for the opinions in this article. The original text can be found in* Beijing Cultural Review. *The author has authorized Kuaishou Research Institute to edit and publish this article.*
2 https://www.taosj.com/taobao-live/index/#/influencers/?id=69226163&page=1& *sortType=desc ending&sortField=date.*

only changed the logic of business but also the logic behind poverty issues. Attention has become a precious resource, information has become a provider of productivity, and followership has become a creator of value. Through the empowerment offered by information flows, attention poverty can be eliminated, thereby giving impetus to the alleviation of poverty among the poor.

Since the 18th National Congress of the Communist Party of China, the state has proposed a strategy of targeted poverty alleviation and made the battle against poverty one of the three major battles that must be won in order to secure a decisive victory in building a moderately prosperous society. From 2012 to 2019, the number of people in China living in poverty fell from 98.99 million to 5.51 million, while the poverty incidence rate fell from 10.2 percent to 0.6 percent. In 2020, China became the first developing country to achieve the lofty goal of eradicating absolute poverty—an outstanding feat in the history of mankind's development. The empowerment of poverty reduction via information flows has enabled farmers to master "new tools" in the age of the mobile Internet; they are able to possess cutting-edge tools of production in the age of attention and thereby achieve endogenous poverty alleviation.

I. The Rise of the Age of Attention and Content-based E-commerce

1. Attention Resources Have Become Precious and Scarce

As early as 1971, Herbert Simon had already noted that in an information-rich world, the only scarce resource is attention. We live in an age of information explosion; according to a United Nations report, the global Internet protocol traffic in 2017 was 45,000 gigabytes per second, a 450-fold increase from the traffic per day in 1992 (100 gigabytes). Meanwhile, global data continues to increase at a rate of 40 percent per year. Corresponding to this is the scarcity of people's time and attention, causing attention to become one of the most precious resources in the world. This sort of scarcity is brought about by the infinite supply of information and the finiteness of attention resources.

The finiteness of attention resources manifests firstly in the finiteness of an individual's effective time. Aside from sleep and other periods of lethargy, an individual spends their 24 hours in a day paying attention to specific matters. This period of time can be called an individual's effective attention time, which can be multiplied by the population of a country to give the total domestic effective attention time. The total attention resources of a society are finite; aside from productive labor, they are also allocated to non-productive labor such as reading and social activities as well as various forms of consumption. The Internet has become a main space for the allocation of an individual's attention resources. The China Netcasting Services Association estimated that, in 2018, netizens spent an average of 5.69 hours surfing the Internet on their phones every day. This was an increase of one hour from the previous year, and one-third of this increase could be attributed to the time spent watching short videos.

Secondly, attention has a finite degree of vitality. An individual's attention cannot possibly maintain constant vitality; the expenditure of attention is essentially the expenditure of an individual's life. Aside from the expenditure of time, there is also the expenditure of energy, stamina, and so on. Like a flashlight that is focused on an object of interest, attention is the focus of an individual's thoughts, and it requires the expenditure of energy.

Thirdly, attention has a finite span. Attention is akin to the bandwidth by which we receive and process external information. When such a finite bandwidth faces an infinite supply of information, we would have to carry out information filtering.

In correspondence to the finiteness of attention resources, an information explosion causes attention resources to become scarce in society. In that case, how does an individual allocate their finite attention resources? There are two research paradigms in psychology with regard to attentionism: intent and interest. Psychologist Daniel Kahneman divided mental activities into two systems. System 1 is an autonomous system that does not require conscious effort, whereas System 2 requires the placing of attention on effortful cerebral activities. The activity of System 1 is akin to interest, while the activity of System 2 is akin to intent.

Intent is the active search for objects of interest by attention according to the inner desires of an individual, whereas interest is the focus of attention caused by external stimuli—this sort of stimuli is able to attract attention because it corresponds to an individual's inner obsessions. This implies that it is possible to arouse a certain obsession in an individual and produce stickiness between them and the obsession by manipulating external stimuli, thereby attracting attention resources.

As offline attention resources are dispersed, it is very difficult for them to form a scale effect. Instead, given that the people of China spend an average of 5.69 hours online every day, online attention resources are tremendous in scale and wide in reach. Furthermore, they can be gathered within a very small amount of time. The Internet has become one of the main channels for allocating attention resources, while information platforms on the Internet have become the biggest centers for allocating attention resources. In the Internet age, effective allocation of attention resources can be carried out via the distribution of information flows; controlling the information flows is equivalent to controlling the allocation of attention resources. As one of the biggest social platforms in China today, WeChat has attracted a large amount of attention resources by means of picture-and-text articles and social media. With the advent of the age of video, Kuaishou and other short video applications have become the main platforms for allocating attention resources. As the CEO of Kuaishou, Su Hua, has clearly stated, Kuaishou must allocate attention so that more people can receive attention.

In an age where attention is scarce, information platforms on the Internet must master the laws of attention allocation if they are to become centers of attention allocation. Firstly, they must provide a mechanism for filtering information to help users find meaningful information among the enormous trove of information. Search engines such as Baidu provide a tool for people to find information; WeChat carries out information filtering via social networking and features such as "Moments," "Group Chats," "Official Accounts," and "Wow;" while Toutiao uses AI-driven accurate pushes to enable individuals to access information that they are interested in, causing intent and interest to be matched more accurately and realizing the third generation of information filtering. Secondly, they must provide agile information and help netizens obtain the maximum amount of meaningful information within the least amount of time. When information is short yet condensed, it would be easy to browse through and easy for netizens to retrieve. The popularity of Weibo and short videos can be attributed to this reason. Thirdly, they must provide emotive information that can resonate with the audience and thereby elicit behaviors such as follows, likes, and reposts. Short videos are more attractive than picture-and-text information to users precisely because they are better able to stimulate the senses of users. Fourthly, they must guide users toward certain behaviors via subconscious cues. On various information platforms, unread information is marked with red numbers, red dots, and so on. At the same time, clickbait and eye-catching cues transmitted via text, video, and other forms of content are actually trying to induce users to click on them subconsciously.

The age of attention manifests not only in the scarcity of attention resources but also in the tremendous value of attention resources. Firstly, humans are naturally inclined to seek attention and appreciation and to prove their own worth by means of the interest they receive from others. Interest is in itself a form of value judgment paid toward the object of interest. Humans are the measure of value for everything; they can assess the value of and give meaning to other people and things. Regardless of how well artificial intelligence develops, it cannot surpass mankind in this regard. Secondly, interest is the precursor of other human behaviors; interest arouses appreciation, which subsequently produces emotional and psychological connections and gives rise to activities such as interaction and trade. Lastly, the value of attention resources could not be monetized as directly and quickly as it can today. The mobile Internet has provided a convenient channel for the monetization of attention resources. In particular, the convenience of payment has enabled the direct monetization of followers' appreciation (for a livestreamer) by means of tips, virtual gifts, online shopping, and so on.

2. The Rise of Content-based E-commerce

An important phenomenon in the age of attention is the change in the logic of commercial consumption. The fight for attention has become the precursor and main battlefield of business competition. The logic of consumption in the Internet age is shifting from "product is king" and "brand is king" to "attention is king." China's economy entered a buyer's market in the 1990s, and it has further entered an age of abundant supply today. In an age of product scarcity where what one has is what others do not have, product is king, and there is a market as long as there is supply. In an age where supply is relatively abundant, buyers compare different products, and thus brand is king; quality, brand, and extended services become the main considerations of consumers. In an age where supply is high in abundance, attention would be king; with so many products of similar quality to choose from, it would be very difficult to distinguish product quality by means of brands. These days, the importance of brand loyalty is diminishing, whereas the pursuit of new products and the consumption of products that are interesting, story-rich, and culture-rich are becoming a trend. This is because certain consumption scenarios and consumption caused by social interaction and interest have become new tipping points.

We can sum up the important reasons that content-based e-commerce is able to achieve such explosive results as the theory of "infinite malls." By moving shopping malls on to the Internet, traditional e-commerce has effectively built a supermall on the Internet. Customers develop a purchasing need before visiting a website to carry out search and selection. This is akin to upgrading an offline shopping mall into a commercial complex and thereby creating a new business model. Content-based e-commerce has effectively built a super "commerce-entertainment complex" on the Internet.

Content-based e-commerce is able to form "infinite malls" because it can gather a tremendous amount of attention resources, which are allocated before product resources are allocated. The Internet celebrity economy is essentially an attention economy, while content-based e-commerce is a product of the age of attention. In the virtual world, consumption and social interaction are intermingled. Compared to traditional picture-and-text information, the videos and audios of content-based e-commerce have lower barriers to entry and richer emotional content, thereby strengthening the entertainment and social features of Internet information and forming stronger emotional stickiness and connections between the providers and recipients of information. Not only can livestreamers obtain "private domain traffic" from their followers, but they also attract interest by guiding traffic from public domains; this gives prominence to their importance and the high value of their followers. For example, an ordinary e-commerce livestreamer on Kuaishou with 100,000 followers can make an annual gross income of more than 600,000 yuan.[3]

If it is said that traditional e-commerce has infinitized the number of shelves of goods and thereby brought about a long tail effect in sales, then content-based e-commerce has infinitized the number of shopping malls and thereby brought about an explosive effect in sales. Livestream channels have unlimited capacity for attracting everyone's attention—a single livestream channel can attract tens of millions of viewers, while some of the top livestreamers on the Internet can draw more than 100 million concurrent viewers. This is akin to the entire population of a big country being gathered in the same virtual shopping mall within a short period of time, bringing about an explosive effect in sales. As long as a certain proportion of them make purchases, a huge sales figure would be created very quickly. These top livestreamers serve as "super salespersons" in this infinite mall; like traditional salespersons, they also have to promote products, the difference being that they face hundreds of millions of customers at the same time instead of individual customers. Meanwhile, their 30-million-odd sticky followers are akin to returning customers. This is why they are able to produce monthly sales results that surpass the annual sales results of several provinces.

The festive promotional events of offline shopping malls can produce a pile-on effect in sales. This has also been applied to the Singles' Day events in e-commerce; because they are targeted at the entire market of China, the promotional effect is greatly magnified. When combined with content-based e-commerce, the power of this sort of promotional effect would be further demonstrated.

---

3 *China Netcasting Services Association. China Netcasting Development Research Report 2019 [Electronic Bulletin Board Online], http://www.xinhuanet.com/video/ sjxw/2019-05/30/ c_1210147518.htmm, 2019-5.*

Offline shopping malls provide credit to make the sale of goods possible, while traditional e-commerce enables people to do business with others from faraway places by means of user reviews, payment intermediaries, and suchlike. On the other hand, content-based e-commerce closes the distance between sellers and consumers who are far apart by means of online shopping malls, causing the buyers to, in a way, become familiar with the sellers and thereby providing new paths to credit.

A more important point about content-based e-commerce is that it has changed the market structure. Offline shopping malls are regional in nature; they serve the people who reside in their vicinity. Traditional e-commerce has caused the whole of China to form a unified market, while content-based e-commerce has further changed the market structure. Due to the relatively high stickiness of the 1-billion-odd monthly active users of content-based e-commerce, they serve as a potential market that has been pre-formed. Traditional businesses have very high operational costs precisely because they have many intermediaries and middlemen who earn a profit margin. Although the emergence of traditional e-commerce has greatly reduced the number of intermediaries, there remains a segment for e-commerce marketing. Meanwhile, content-based e-commerce has an even lower barrier to entry, enabling producers to serve as marketers themselves. A concept advocated by Kuaishou is "livestreaming + good source goods." The emergence of content- based e-commerce has further reduced the number of intermediaries—for example, Dong Mingzhu's promotion of goods is essentially a manufacturer directly facing the consumers, who thus purchase goods directly from the manufacturer. On the one hand, this offers a guarantee of credibility, and on the other hand, this brings down the prices and turns the livestream channel into a large site of direct sales.[4]

----

4 *The relevant figures are taken from the presentation conducted by He Haoxun, commercial director at Kuaishou Content Creation Center, in Conference Room 404, Tower W, Kuaishou HQ, on November 1, 2019.*

II. Attention Poverty

The age of attention is also changing the logic of poverty. As human society develops, humans' understanding of poverty is also changing. At first, we understood poverty to be about low incomes, which thereon causes a shortage of the means of production. Later, we became aware of the issue of capability poverty. Amartya Sen, a winner of the Nobel Prize in economics, believes that poverty should be conceptually defined as a lack of capabilities rather than a low level of income; poverty has to be measured according to one's capabilities. In 2000, the World Development Report published by the World Bank believed that poverty does not only refer to material deficiency (as measured using suitable concepts of income and consumption) but also includes low levels of education and health. Poverty also encompasses risks and one's vulnerability when faced with risks, as well as one's inability to express one's needs and lack of influence. The United Nations Development Program has designed the Multidimensional Poverty Index (MPI), which measures poverty based on the three aspects of education, health, and standard of living. This expands the concept of poverty from income poverty to human poverty. Humans' understanding of poverty has become multi-dimensional; it has expanded from the initial income poverty to human development poverty, knowledge poverty, ecosystem poverty, psychological poverty, and so on.

Poverty can be regarded from different dimensions as a deficiency of living or developmental resources, as a lack of ability to obtain resources, or as a high degree of vulnerability. As a precious and scarce resource, attention or the lack of it has become an important dimension of poverty in the age of attention. Society's allocation of attention resources is very unequal—generally speaking, the closer one is to being a social elite, the more attention resources one attracts. This includes the attention paid toward oneself and that paid toward one's possessions. On the one hand, this is because society naturally attaches greater importance to successful people. On the other hand, the limited page space of traditional media and specific communication agendas and needs have produced a spotlight effect upon a small group of elites, causing most people in society to not be afforded media attention. During the course of social information production, they serve as the invisible majority.

The state of attention resources on the Internet can be measured in four dimensions. The first dimension is the degree of exposure. The state of exposure of individuals, products, and brands on the Internet includes news reports, social media accounts, and read counts. The degree of exposure is near-zero for many poor people who do not have any public social media accounts. Conversely, a large portion of the attention resources on social media are concentrated on the top accounts, whereas the read counts and click rates of most accounts are very low. The second dimension is reputation. The state of the recognition attained by individuals, products, and brands on the Internet includes likes, positive reports, and reviews. Degree of exposure is not equivalent to reputation; many high-exposure incidents are negative in public opinion. At the same time, there are many cases of people who are very low in exposure yet very high in reputation, such as the recipients of high-level honors and unsung heroes who have done amazing things yet prefer to remain anonymous. The third dimension is the degree of loyalty. This refers to the continuity of attention, including one's follower count and follower stability. The fourth is the degree of monetization. This refers to one's ability to convert attention resources into income and wealth. There are many celebrities who have a lot of attention resources but are inferior to the top livestreamers and Internet celebrities in terms of their ability to monetize traffic. This has prompted many celebrities to become livestreamers as well. Although the phenomenon of Internet celebrities has been present since the birth of the Internet, the grassroots Internet celebrities of the past—such as Sister Furong, Sister Feng, and Brother Sharp—either were a flash in the pan or monetized attention offline. They were not like today's Internet celebrities, who are able to derive huge earnings from the attention that they get.

Attention poverty refers to a deficiency of attention resources and a lack of ability to obtain attention resources. The most direct manifestation of attention poverty is a form of social exclusion. This is because a lack of attention prevents the value of an individual's labor and products from getting full recognition and also prevents the meaning of life from being fully reflected. A deficiency of attention resources causes an individual to lack the precious resources for obtaining wealth in the age of attention. Another manifestation of attention poverty is a lack of ability to obtain attention resources. The attention poverty of rural dwellers also includes their lack of proficiency in the use of "new farming tools" to attract attention resources. Many of them have no idea how to use the Internet to promote their products and are unclear about the methods of planning, sales, and publicity for an Internet business, and are thus unable to find a market for their products.

Attention-poor groups cannot be equated with the impoverished population. There are many people who have a lot of other resources and do not require societal attention; they are an attention-deficient group but are not impoverished people. At the same time, this age has given rise to a large batch of grassroots Internet celebrities who possess a lot of attention resources and thereby have the opportunity to obtain wealth. For example, there is a vagrant called Shen Wei in Shanghai. Due to his ability to speak confidently and passionately about well-substantiated topics, he became a highly followed Internet celebrity almost as soon as he uploaded his short videos. Later, he became a contracted livestreamer with a six-figure monthly income. These grassroots Internet celebrities do not have economic and social resources in the traditional sense, yet their social status has skyrocketed because of the attention they received.

III. Information Flow Empowerment of Poverty Reduction

With the emergence of new information platforms in the age of attention, the methods of allocating attention resources in society have changed, creating a new model of poverty reduction—that is, the use of information flow allocation to solve the problems of attention poverty among the impoverished people. It has enabled these people to obtain attention and convert the obtained attention resources into value, thereby escaping poverty and acquiring wealth.

1. Ubiquitous Empowerment

The emergence of new information platforms has changed the means of information transmission from centralized to decentralized. To a certain extent, this has also propelled the flattening of the distribution of attention resources, breaking the monopoly of traditional elite groups on attention resources in society.

Firstly, it has made communication tools accessible to everyone. As Kuaishou has pointed out, short video software is a kind of "inclusive technology" that has changed the means of allocating attention throughout society. Traditional means of information transmission are monopolized in the hands of the media. The emergence of the Internet has enabled everyone to express their opinions online, while the emergence of short video platforms in the age of the mobile Internet has further lowered the barriers to entry for promoting oneself online—production of picture-and-text information is no longer required, but instead, one simply needs to know how to livestream and film videos. It used to be keyboards that were ubiquitous, but that has since changed to microphones and later to livestream channels and short video platforms.[5]

At the same time, due to their wide reach, accurate pushes and related technologies enable accurate connection of information producers and information consumers to be made. This has caused "niche" and "long-tail" information—which found it very difficult to capture attention at first—to receive a certain degree of attention. All videos and official accounts would garner a certain number of clicks and reads, making it possible for everyone to be seen and heard.[6]

Nevertheless, we must remain vigilant; the emergence of new information platforms would not naturally promote a more equal distribution of attention. In the absence of intervention, new inequalities might form. The top livestreamers, the most popular videos and articles, and the like might draw excessive attention from society, preventing a large amount of high-quality content from receiving its due attention from society.

---

5 *Kuaishou Research Institute. The Power of Being Seen—What Is Kuaishou [M]. Beijing: CITIC Press Group, 2020.*

6 *Kuaishou Research Institute. The Power of Being Seen—What Is Kuaishou [M]. Beijing: CITIC Press Group, 2020.*

2. New Market Spaces and Communities

New information platforms have connected hundreds of millions of people, changed the traditional market structure and modes of communication, and created new market spaces and communities, thereby providing the marginalized and impoverished population in the traditional market structure with new opportunities for development.

As of June 30, 2020, Kuaishou's app and applets for China drew 302 million daily active users on average. This shows that short video platforms have become a potential market with hundreds of millions of users—simply by drawing their attention, it would become possible to convert them into customers.

Most of the impoverished population live in remote regions, where the economic distance serves as a hindrance to escaping poverty and acquiring wealth. However, with the introduction of information platforms, even large distances have become null. This has changed their originally marginalized standing in the market, which manifested not only as geographical marginalization but also as marginalization in the traditional market structure. The impoverished population is situated at the tail end of the production chain, in which products are either only sold in regional markets with a very small reach or exploited at every level by middlemen. New information platforms have created a new type of market space that Kuaishou calls a new "product–livestream–end consumer" market structure. This has enabled the impoverished population to face a broad market directly and brought them from the edge of the market to its center. For example, Haitou Town of Lianyungang, Jiangsu Province, is a fishing town that originally had to sell its seafood via a seafood market, and thus its fishermen earned very small profit margins. However, adhering to the idea of eating only the freshest, Kuang Lixiang produced livestream content about fishing and eating seafood on Kuaishou and other platforms. In this way, he transformed from a fisherman into a livestreamer with 2 million followers and a sales volume per livestream of more than 1,000 orders. At the same time, he has spurred the entire town to bring its sale of seafood on to livestreaming platforms. In 2018, with 16.5 billion clicks, Haitou Town became the town with the most video views on Kuaishou. In 2019, the entire town's sales of seafood on e-commerce exceeded 5 billion yuan.

The formation of new market spaces is accompanied by the formation of new communities. Traditional interpersonal relations gradually establish connections in real life via work or life—such a method is very high in costs and limited in search range. The creation of accurate push technologies has effectively enabled individuals to carry out search and matching among the hundreds of millions of users on an entire platform—this has brought about new relations and links and also created new communities. For example, while conducting research on Kuaishou, we came to know about Chen Libao, the performer of the famous suona piece "A Hundred Birds Paying Homage to the Phoenix." He became an active user of Kuaishou largely because Kuaishou provides a new type of community for suona enthusiasts. At first, these enthusiasts were scattered throughout China and thus connecting with one another was very difficult. Furthermore, "temple performers" like Chen had to spend a lot of time visiting different places to collect folk songs in order to listen to those "voices that had been buried in the corner." Nowadays, by understanding its users' needs and carrying out accurate pushes, Kuaishou is able to recommend short videos of folk suona performers from all parts of China to Chen, thus forming a community for this niche group of people. Chen has begun selling online courses, enabling folk performers to learn from such a famous performer as himself, while also enabling him to draw inspiration from them. Social exclusion is one of the reasons for the poverty of the impoverished population; their social relations provide little help toward solving their poverty-related problems. However, new communities have provided them with a window for broadening their horizons, enabling them to learn how to escape poverty and acquire wealth.[7]

---

7 *Taken from the presentation conducted by Chen Libao in Conference Room 404, Tower W, Kuaishou HQ, on November 1, 2019.*

3. Content Production and "Design" Building

The rise of content-based e-commerce implies the complete mediafication of the producers; they are no longer merely the producers of products but also the producers of information. By producing information content, they have attracted the attention of consumers and promoted sales of their products. Be it for attracting new followers or preventing the loss of followers, it is necessary to have enduring capabilities for content production. That information platforms are able to garner a lot of attention is inextricable from their possession of many producers of high-quality content.

In an age of abundant information and information overload, all transmitted information must have its own highlights and traffic if it is to attract attention and subsequently set off large-scale transmission. After undergoing theme planning and information packaging, the same sceneries and products become information with explosiveness and transmissibility.

This is a process of building Internet personas, scenery designs, and object designs. In the age of attention, what people actually consume are not just the products and services themselves, but more so the designs behind these products and services. People have personas, sceneries have scenery designs, goods have goods designs, and villages have village designs. Such designs are the feelings, stories, vibes, cultures, and others conveyed by products and services.

To attract a lot of attention, villages can also form new geographical identifiers by creating "village designs." Yugouliang Village of Zhangjiakou, Hebei Province, is remote in location and lacking in resources. As the villagers live in poverty, most of the young people have gone elsewhere to work. Lu Wenzhen, secretary of the village's Party branch, has led the elderly villagers to practice yoga and created a set of yoga exercises that is suitable for farm life. He has uploaded short videos of the villagers working out on to Kuaishou and other platforms, attracting many views due to the seemingly paradoxical sight of it all. As a result, Yugouliang Village has become famous online for its yoga practice, promoting rural tourism and sales of its specialty agricultural products such as quinoa and potatoes, and thereby escaping poverty.[8]

After these designs have been confirmed, they still have to be communicated more directly and at more levels to users via videos, pictures, and text if they are to improve the understanding of netizens and stimulate purchases.

4. The Allocation of Information Flows

The direction of information flows determines the channels for the allocation of attention resources. Information platforms can empower the impoverished population by means of information distribution. This is a whole-chain process of empowering information marketing, information transmission, and information value conversion.

At the same time, AI information technologies have made possible the accurate pushing and matching of information, enabling information to find people and vice versa, and also enabling information producers and information consumers to find each other. This has brought about the accurate linking of information suppliers and demanders, greatly increasing the efficiency of information transmission and helping the products of impoverished regions and people be understood by more potential customers.

IV. The Age of Attention and Post-2020 Poverty Reduction

After China ended absolute poverty in 2020, it was decided that poverty reduction would no longer be invested in with the strength of the entire nation. Instead, sustainable rural poverty alleviation would be assimilated into the country's rural revitalization strategy. Information flow empowerment, which can give poverty eradication an endogenous motive force, is set to become an important part of the post-2020 strategy for poverty reduction.

---

8 *Taken from the presentation conducted by Lu Wenzhen, secretary of Yugouliang Village, in Conference Room 404, Tower W, Kuaishou HQ, on November 1, 2019.*

In the age of attention, information has become a leading force of production, and attention has become the most precious resource of all. It is necessary to seize the opportunities in the attention economy and make use of information flow empowerment to inject new momentum into the post-2020 poverty reduction and rural rejuvenation plan.

At the national level, there must be a systematic design for encouraging local governments, villagers, Internet platforms, enterprises, content producers, and Internet marketers to join forces in building a whole-chain rural attention economy ecosystem, creating a rural attention plateau, and giving further impetus to rural poverty eradication and wealth acquisition. In other words, we must build a rural attention economy rejuvenation mechanism that is guided by the government, supported by platform enterprises, and widely participated in by society, with farmers serving as its subjects.

We must step up the construction of attention economy infrastructure for rural rejuvenation, strengthen investment in information infrastructure and the supporting facilities of peripheral industries, help impoverished regions build circulation service outlets, increase their comprehensive logistical service capabilities in segments such as warehousing, packaging, processing, and transportation, lower their product costs, and increase their market competitiveness.

We must push forward rural attention rejuvenation projects, systematically unearth and design rural industrial brands, and establish rural brand design and operations teams made up of rural cadres and noteworthy locals. We need large-scale marketing teams made up of top content creators, Internet experts, and others, as well as production teams made up of external capital, village clusters, and villagers. We must build a whole-chain rural attention economy ecosystem, using new media to increase the intensity of publicizing and promoting the agricultural products of impoverished regions. We will establish more popular online products that live up to their reputation, give impetus to total rural poverty eradication and wealth acquisition, and train a large group of new farmers that are proficient in tools of information transmission. By turning mobile phones into a new farming tool, we will enable traditional farmers to become new farmers. They will become Internet experts who are proficient in information tools, or Internet celebrities who are able to drive rural poverty eradication and wealth acquisition. They will be influencers who are able to publicize villages, farmers, and agricultural products.

APPENDIX

I. Overview of Short Video and Livestream Development in China

1. Overview of the Scale of Short Videos and Livestreams

China has the most users of short videos in the world. In 2019, approximately 80 percent of short video platform users in the world were from China.

China's short video platforms had a total of 495.7 million daily active users on average in 2019. This number is expected to grow to 899.9 million in 2025.

The average amount of time per day spent on short video platforms by each daily active user is expected to grow from 67 minutes in 2019 to 110.2 minutes in 2021.

China has the most users of livestreams in the world. In 2019, approximately 50 percent of short video platform users in the world were from China.

China's livestreaming platforms had a total of 213.4 million daily active users on average in 2019. This number is expected to grow to 512.8 million in 2025. The average amount of time per day spent on livestreaming platforms by each daily active user is expected to grow from 33.2 minutes in 2019 to 51.9 minutes in 2025.

Data Source: iResearch Consulting Group

2. Overview of the Scale of Livestream E-commerce

The total trade value of livestream e-commerce in China is expected to grow from 416.8 billion yuan in 2019 to 6.5172 trillion yuan in 2025, at a compound annual growth rate of 57.7 percent.

The total trade value of livestream e-commerce made up 4.2 percent of China's retail e-commerce market in 2019. This number is expected to grow to 23.9 percent in 2025.

Data Source: iResearch Consulting Group

3. Figures Related to Kuaishou Livestream E-commerce

In the first nine months of 2020 ending on September 30, Kuaishou's app and applets for China had 305 million daily active users on average and 769 million monthly active users on average.

In the first nine months of 2020 ending on September 30, Kuaishou E-commerce had a GMV of 204.1 billion yuan. According to iResearch Consulting Group, this makes Kuaishou the world's second-largest livestream e-commerce platform.

Kuaishou E-commerce had a GMV of 96.60 million yuan in 2018, 59.6 billion yuan in 2019, and 332.6 billion yuan in the first 11 months of 2020.

Data Source: Kuaishou Prospectus (January 2021)

As of May 2020, Kuaishou E-commerce's number of daily active users exceeded 100 million. At the same time, more than 1 million Kuaishou accounts had potential business behaviors.

Data Source: Kuaishou (May 2020)

II Annals of Livestream E-commerce

On April 20, 2020, General Secretary Xi Jinping visited a livestreaming counter in Jinmi Village, Xiaoling Town, Zhashui County, and complimented the local specialty Zhashui wood ear while on an inspection tour to Shaanxi Province. He emphasized that e-commerce can not only help people escape poverty but also boost rural revitalization efforts, and is thus well worth doing.

2020

January–November: Kuaishou E-commerce achieved a GMV of 332.6 billion yuan.

August: Kuaishou E-commerce announced that its order volume for that month exceeded 500 million.

June 22: 25.7 million Kuaishou users earned an income on Kuaishou within the past year. Among them, 6.64 million users came from impoverished regions.

May 20: Dong Mingzhu, chairman of the Gree Group, conducted a livestream promotion on Kuaishou and generated a turnover of 310 million yuan in three hours.

May: Kuaishou E-commerce's number of daily active users exceeded 100 million. At the same time, more than 1 million Kuaishou accounts had potential business behaviors.

April 12: Kuaishou held a charity livestreaming event together with CCTV News. Sixty-one million yuan worth of products from Hubei Province were sold, setting a new record among Hubei's charity livestreaming events.

2019

In 2019, Kuaishou E-commerce achieved a full-year GMV of 59.6 billion yuan.

December: Kuaishou Live's number of daily active users exceeded 100 million. The number of daily active users of Kuaishou's gaming livestreams reached 51 million, while the number of daily active users of gaming short videos reached 77 million.

During a Singles' Day event called "Kuaishou Sales King," Kuaishou livestreamer Xin Youzhi generated more than 400 million yuan in livestream sales.

2018

November 11: Taobao livestream Weiya livestreamed for two hours and generated more than 267 million yuan in sales. In total, her livestream channel generated more than 300 million yuan in sales for the entire day. November 6: Kuaishou livestreamer Brother Sanda sold more than 160-million-yuan worth of goods in one day.

June: Kuaishou officially launched the Kuaishou Store feature.

2017

October 10: In one livestream session, Taobao livestreamer Weiya helped generate 70 million yuan in sales for a store.

2016

May: Taobao Live was officially launched.
April: Kuaishou launched its livestreaming feature.

GLOSSARY*

A

1. AI (Artificial Intelligence): Used to simulate, extend, and expand human intelligence.

2. A-grade goods: For jadeite, A-grade goods refer to natural jadeite that has not undergone any chemical treatment.

3. AR (Augmented Reality): Refers to a technology that enables an on-screen virtual world to combine and interact with a real-world scenario by accurately calculating the position and angle of a camera image and utilizing image analysis technology.

B

4. BA (Beauty Adviser), turning of beauty advisors into Internet celebrities: Mainly targeted at the new retail application scenarios of the cosmetics industry. Refers to the conversion of beauty advisors into the traffic inlets of a brand, helping the brand carry out publicity and "grass-planting."

5. White brands: Refers to the unbranded products of several manufacturers.

6. Plain pieces of clothing: Sample pieces of clothing that are made using greige and are unpatterned.

---

*(Glossary compiled by research assistants Cai Yuhui and Tian Jiahui of Kuaishou Research Institute)

7. Batch flow: A production method whereby different parts of a piece of clothing are circulated in batches among many production workers until the product is completed.

8. Standard products: Refers to products with uniform market standards— such as clear specifications, model numbers, and material quality—and small price discrepancies. An example is mobile phone screen protectors.

9. B-end: Refers to the business or enterprise end.

10. B-grade goods: For jadeite, B-grade goods refer to natural but inferior quality jadeite that is acid-washed, waxed, and then processed.

11. B2C (Business to Consumer): An e-commerce model whereby enterprises cut out the middlemen and directly provide consumers with a new shopping environment via the Internet. For example, online stores enable consumers to shop online.

12. Glassy-type: Refers to jadeite that is highly transparent and uncontaminated.

C

13. C2M (Consumer to Manufacturer): A new business model in industrial e-commerce whereby consumers directly connect with factories via a platform. The factories accept personalized orders from the consumers and subsequently carry out design, procurement, production, and shipping in accordance with the consumers' demands.

14. C2 Internet celebrity 2M: A business model whereby Internet celebrity livestreamers serve as the middlemen and provide timely feedback on consumers' demands to the manufacturers.

15. C store: Generally refers to a Taobao C store. Refers to all individually-owned stores and market stores that are not Tmall stores.

16. C end: Refers to the consumer and user end.

17. Vertical-category: Vertical-category livestreamers refers to livestreamers who focus on a particular category, such as clothing, food, home appliances, or jade stones.

18. CPA (Cost Per Action): A model for calculating advertising rates. Actions (such as the consumers' order volume) are used as indicators for calculating rates, and there are no limitations on the ad delivery volume.

19. CPM (Cost Per Mille): Refers to the cost of displaying ads to 1,000 people.

20. CPS (Cost Per Sales): Refers to the use of the actual quantity of products sold to calculate the advertising fees.

21. CS (Cosmetic Store) channel: Refers to a point-of-sales network system for daily chemical products, as made up of cosmetic stores, daily chemical stores, and boutique systems. For example, Watson's, Sephora, and other large offline channels.

D

22. Stall: Usually refers to a store that engages in wholesale business in a wholesale market.

23. One-piece flow: Refers to a highly efficient management model whereby each production procedure is made consistent in terms of time expenditure by using reasonable production standards and processes to allocate an appropriate number of workers and equipment to each procedure, thereby shortening the production cycle, increasing product quality, and reducing transfers.

24. Big V: Refers to users who have obtained personal verification (verified users will have an icon that resembles a "V" behind their nicknames) and have many followers on platforms such as Sina, Tencent, and NetEase.

E

25. 80/20 rule (also called the "law of the vital few," the "Pareto principle," and other names): Refers to the idea that the most important portion among a group of things only makes up approximately 20 percent of the group. Although the other 80 percent form the majority, they are secondary in importance.

26. Second-tier (short for second-tier wholesale businesses): Refers to wholesale businesses that procure and resell goods from the direct clients (distributors or direct wholesale businesses) of a manufacturer.

27. ERP (Enterprise Resource Planning) system: Refers to a management platform that provides decision-making methods to the employees and decision-makers of an enterprise in the form of systematic management ideas.

F

28. Non-standard products: Refers to products that do not have uniform measurement standards and fixed export channels but have relatively personalized product characteristics and service forms. For example, women's clothing.

29. Service providers: Refers to businesses or agencies that provide various services (such as brand positioning, content production, and traffic management) to clients.

G

30. GIF (Graphics Interchange Format): Refers to a public format standard for image files.

31. Gongpan: A form of jadeite auction. Refers to the bidding process whereby raw jade materials are gathered and publicly displayed to buyers, who can then appraise and bid for the materials on their own.

32. Supply chain base: Refers to organizations that gather a large number of supply chains for livestreamers to choose their products from and that provide livestreamers with services in operations, aftersales, logistics, etc.

33. GMV (Gross Merchandise Volume): Refers to the total amount of sales made over a period of time.

34. Public domain traffic, also called platform traffic: Refers to traffic that does not belong to an individual but is instead collectively shared.

H

35. Alliance of Good Things: Refers to the alliance of brand product supply chains officially launched by Kuaishou E-commerce. Its goal is to lower the barriers for experts to enter e-commerce, and to provide more high- quality products to livestreamers and experts.

36. Siphon effect: Refers to the phenomenon of a particular region attracting all the resources from other regions and thereby making itself more attractive than everywhere else, thereafter perpetuating and consolidating this process.

I

37. IPO (Initial Public Offering): Refers to the first time that an enterprise puts its shares up for sale to the public.

38. IP (Intellectual Property): Refers to an individual's right of possession to a certain creation.

39. ISV (Independent Software Vendor): Refers to enterprises that specialize in software development, production, sales, and services. For example, Microsoft.

J

40. JIT (Just in Time): A production system whose basic idea is to "produce the necessary amount of a necessary product only when necessary." It seeks to have zero or minimum inventory.

K

41. KA (Key Account): Refers to important or major clients.

42. Pit output: The unit price of a displayed product multiplied by the sales volume. (Pit refers to a product's display position on an e-commerce platform or a livestream channel.)

43. K12 (Kindergarten through Twelfth Grade): A special term used in education. Short for pre-school education to high school education. Now commonly used to refer to basic education.

44. KOC (Key Opinion Customer): Refers to consumers who can influence their friends and followers to develop consumption behaviors. Less influential than KOLs.

45. KOL (Key Opinion Leader): Refers to people who possess a relatively large amount of accurate product information, and who are accepted or trusted enough by relevant groups of people to have a significant influence on their purchasing behaviors.

46. Quick response: Refers to a business's carrying out of production in rapid response to a demand made by a consumer.

47. Kuai brand: Refers to a brand that became popular on Kuaishou.

48. Purchaser: Refers to a person who travels around the world, has a grasp on fashion trends, and makes a large number of orders. China has had a long-term shortage of professional clothing purchasers. In this book, it mainly refers to procurement personnel who serve a livestream base.

M

49. MCN: A management agency that incubates and serves livestreamers. Its functions include video content design and traffic management.

50. Miaobang: During a livestream, users can quickly send a large number of gifts to the livestreamer, causing themselves to rank first in the gift rankings of the livestream channel. During or after

the livestream, the livestreamer will often get their followers to follow and increase the popularity of the top-ranked user.

51. Unpolished goods: Refers to jadeite that is only the polishing step away from becoming a finished product.

O

52. ODM (Original Design Manufacturer): In the clothing industry, this refers to a brand's commissioning of a factory to produce its products, with the factory taking charge of everything from design to production. The brand simply sticks its label on the products and takes charge of sales.

53. OEM (Original Equipment Manufacturer): In the clothing industry, this refers to a brand's placement of production orders to a factory, and then buying out the products at a low price and directly sticking its own brand trademark on them. The brand does the product design, whereas the factory is only in charge of manufacturing the goods and providing manpower and a site.

54. O2O (Online to Offline): Refers to the integration of offline business opportunities with the Internet, enabling the Internet to become a platform for offline transactions.

P

55. Scheduling: Also known as the arrangement of dates. For example, a livestreaming team would arrange the theme and product category of each upcoming livestream.

56. PC (Personal Computer): Includes desktops, laptops, tablets, and ultrabooks.

R

57. ROI: Return on investment.

S

58. SaaS (Software as a Service): Refers to the provision of software services over the Internet.

59. SC certification: A license certification for food production.

60. SKU (Stock Keeping Unit): In the clothing trade, a specific design of a pink S-sized shirt (design + color + size) counts as one SKU.

61. Private domain traffic: Refers to the relatively enclosed trust traffic produced after a business has established relations with its followers.

62. SOP (Standard Operating Procedure): Refers to a description of the standard operating steps and requirements for a particular task in a uniform format to be used to guide and standardize daily work.

63. S2B2C (S stands for large suppliers, B stands for channel businesses, and C stands for customers): Refers to a new e-commerce marketing model that brings suppliers together to empower channel businesses and co- serve customers.

U

64. Uploader: Refers to people who upload video and audio files on video websites, forums, and platforms.

V

65. VR: Virtual Reality.

X

66. Yellow Cart: Kuaishou E-commerce's tool for selling goods. It is a link for placing products on a livestream channel.

Y

67. Cloud warehouse: A digital and intelligent warehousing system, with a big data platform serving as the cloud end. The goods, materials, and relevant information of a warehouse are integrated and processed by means of connection with big data on the Internet and data analysis.

68. First-tier (short for first-tier wholesale businesses): Refers to distributors or wholesale businesses that procure goods directly from manufacturers.

Z

69. Account matrix: Refers to the use of a verified account as an operating subject and subsequently setting up or linking together multiple accounts, causing the accounts to attract traffic for one another and ultimately maximizing the marketing results by means of an account group.

70. Jadeite density: Normally speaking, the denser and more translucent a piece of jadeite, the higher its quality would be.

71. Walkstream: Has several meanings. It can refer to a model whereby a livestreamer conducts a livestream while shopping in a market. It can also refer to a model whereby a livestreamer does not have a fixed livestream studio and instead conducts livestreams at a special counter in a shopping mall or in a supply chain base.

www.ingramcontent.com/pod-product-compliance
Lightning Source LLC
Chambersburg PA
CBHW050238270326
41914CB00041BA/2037/J